"As early as 1962, John Habraken had discovered that mass housing was based on two incorrect principles: 1) all people want the same thing; and 2) professionals know what is good for them. The reality is that no two people have the same preferences, and their wishes and possibilities are constantly changing. Based on life-time experiences, John and Stephen Kendall discuss in this book the interaction between those people – in their homes, office, schools and healthcare centers – and the built environment and who should decide on it."

Frank Bijdendijk, *Former Managing Director of the Housing Association Het Oosten (later Stadgemoot), Amsterdam; Founder and President of the National Renovation Platform; Board of Inspiration, Re-Born – Circular Real Estate*

"This book offers a good opportunity for architects to quickly know what's happening in Open Building practice in different contexts all over the world. The book reflects the impact the Open Building approach can have on the relationship among architects, developers and occupants in the whole life of buildings. This reflection should inspire and encourage architects to rethink and practice in a more empathic and sustainable perspective."

Liu Peng, *Chief Architect, Senior Architect, First Grade, Beijing Institute of Architectural Design*

"This is an extremely useful book that is both theoretical and practical and both for the developed and the developing world. It opens discourses on wicked questions of top-down vs. bottom-up approaches, architecture as a product vs. process, architects' control over built form, and straddling the past and the future. A truly one-of-its-kind book."

Vishwanath Kashikar, *Assistant Professor of Architecture, Faculty of Architecture, CEPT University, Ahmedabad, India*

Open Building for Architects

Open Building is an internationally recognized approach to the design of buildings and building complexes with roots in the way the ordinary built environment grows and regenerates. The Open Building approach recognizes that both stability and change are realities to be managed in the contemporary built environment. Buildings – and the neighborhoods they occupy – are not static during the most stable times or during times of rapid social and technical change. They are living organisms that need constant adjustments to remain attractive, safe and valuable.

Using case studies of built projects from around the world, this book explains the Open Building approach and discusses important characteristics of everyday built environment that the Open Building approach designs for. It also presents a key method that can be used to put the approach into use. It addresses questions such as:

- How can we design large projects for inevitable change?
- How can we balance the demands of large projects for efficient implementation with the need for 'fine-grained' decision-making control?
- How can we separate design tasks, one task being the design of what should last a century, the other task being the design of more mutable units of occupancy?
- How can we identify and share architectural themes and, at the same time, make variations on them?
- How can we use the Open Building approach to steward the earth's scarce resources and contribute to a circular economy that benefits all people?

This book is an essential resource for practitioners, investors and developers, regulators, builders, product manufacturers and educators interested in why the Open Building approach matters and how to practice Open Building.

Stephen H. Kendall is Emeritus Professor of Architecture at Ball State University in the United States. He holds a professional degree in architecture from the University of Cincinnati, a post-professional degree in architecture and urban design from Washington University in St. Louis and a PhD from the Massachusetts Institute of Technology. In practice, he designed hospitals, schools and residential buildings and before that worked as a carpenter. In his academic career, he taught architectural design and urban design studios and courses in building technology and design theory in the US, Taiwan, Italy, Indonesia, South Africa, Japan and PR China. He is vice president of the Council on Open Building. He has written more than 45 papers and book chapters; is the co-author (with Jonathan Teicher) of *Residential Open Building* (Routledge, 2000), available in English, Japanese, Chinese and Korean; and has authored many technical reports and funded research projects, including "Healthcare Facilities Designed for Flexibility" for the US Department of Defense Health Agency. He has lectured widely to university and professional audiences around the world. His edited books include *Healthcare Architecture as Infrastructure: Open Building in Practice* (2019) and *Residential Architecture as Infrastructure: Open Building in Practice* (2022). With John R. Dale, FAIA, he co-edited *The Short Works of John Habraken: Ways of Seeing/Ways of Doing* (2023). All are part of the Open Building Series of books published by Routledge.

N. John Habraken is a Dutch architect and educator. He served as founding director of the SAR Foundation (1965–75) and founding chair of the Department of Architecture and Urban Design at Eindhoven Technical University (1967–75). He was Head of the Department of Architecture at the Massachusetts Institute of Technology (1975–81), and professor, where he became Professor Emeritus after his retirement in 1989. He has lectured around the world to academic and professional audiences. Habraken is the recipient of many awards worldwide, notably including the BNA Kubus award (Dutch Society of Architects) and honorary membership in the Architecture Institute of Japan. He is the author of more than 62 published essays, book chapters, research reports and articles and numerous books (many translated into other languages) including *Supports: An Alternative to Mass Housing; Variations: The Systematic Design of Supports; The Structure of the Ordinary: Form and Control in the Built Environment; The Appearance of the Form: Four Essays on the Position Designing Takes between People and Things; Palladio's Children – Seven Essays on Everyday Environment and the Architect;* and *Conversations with Form: A Workbook for Students of Architecture* (with Teicher and Mignucci).

Open Building Series

The Routledge Open Building Series is a library of titles addressing the Open Building approach to design theory and methods, architecture and urban design with an international perspective. These titles augment a growing literature in sustainability and resilience in the built environment by focusing on the fourth dimension.

Open Building advocates separation of design tasks: the design of what is shared (the commons) and what will last from the design of what belongs to individual occupancies and is expected to change more quickly. This is both a social/political and a design skills issue. Urban design projects, office buildings, shopping centers and airport concourses are examples of separation of design tasks. The same should become the norm in multi-unit housing, healthcare and educational facilities and other project types making up our everyday world. The Open Building approach addresses how to establish the boundary between what is shared and what is decided independently; how to separate the distribution of utility lines between the two; how to evaluate a building's or urban design's capacity to accommodate a variety of interventions initially and over time; and what shared patterns, types and systems help designers cultivate coherent variety. More generally, Open Building helps design professionals work with change and to cooperate in the flowering of everyday environment.

This series provides answers to these questions, and more, and is designed to be the go-to resource for anyone seeking to understand and practice Open Building.

The Appearance of the Form
Seven Essays on the Position Designing Takes Between People and Things (Routledge Revivals)
N. John Habraken

Supports
An Alternative to Mass Housing (Routledge Revivals)
N. John Habraken

Healthcare Architecture as Infrastructure
Open Building in Practice
Edited by Stephen H. Kendall

Residential Architecture as Infrastructure
Open Building in Practice
Edited by Stephen H. Kendall

The Short Works of John Habraken
Ways of Seeing/Ways of Doing
Edited By Stephen H. Kendall and John R. Dale

Open Building for Architects
Professional Knowledge for an Architecture of Everyday Environment
Stephen H. Kendall and N. John Habraken

For more information about this series, please visit: www.routledge.com/Open-Building/book-series/OB

Open Building for Architects

Professional Knowledge for an Architecture of Everyday Environment

Stephen H. Kendall and N. John Habraken

LONDON AND NEW YORK

Designed cover image: Getty Images

First published 2024
by Routledge
4 Park Square, Milton Park, Abingdon, Oxon OX14 4RN

and by Routledge
605 Third Avenue, New York, NY 10158

Routledge is an imprint of the Taylor & Francis Group, an informa business

© 2024 Stephen H. Kendall and N. John Habraken

The right of Stephen H. Kendall and N. John Habraken to be identified as authors of this work has been asserted in accordance with sections 77 and 78 of the Copyright, Designs and Patents Act 1988.

All rights reserved. No part of this book may be reprinted or reproduced or utilised in any form or by any electronic, mechanical, or other means, now known or hereafter invented, including photocopying and recording, or in any information storage or retrieval system, without permission in writing from the publishers.

Trademark notice: Product or corporate names may be trademarks or registered trademarks, and are used only for identification and explanation without intent to infringe.

British Library Cataloguing-in-Publication Data
A catalogue record for this book is available from the British Library

Library of Congress Cataloging-in-Publication Data
Names: Kendall, Stephen H., author. | Habraken, N. J., author.
Title: Open building for architects : professional knowledge for an architecture of everyday environment / Stephen H. Kendall and N. John Habraken.
Description: Abingdon, Oxon : Routledge, 2024. | Series: Routledge open building | Includes bibliographical references and index.
Identifiers: LCCN 2023034061 (print) | LCCN 2023034062 (ebook) | ISBN 9781032152141 (hardback) | ISBN 9781032152165 (paperback) | ISBN 9781003243076 (ebook)
Subjects: LCSH: Architectural design—Methodology. | Buildings—Utilization.
Classification: LCC NA2750 .K47 2024 (print) | LCC NA2750 (ebook) | DDC 729—dc23/eng/20230912
LC record available at https://lccn.loc.gov/2023034061
LC ebook record available at https://lccn.loc.gov/2023034062

ISBN: 978-1-032-15214-1 (hbk)
ISBN: 978-1-032-15216-5 (pbk)
ISBN: 978-1-003-24307-6 (ebk)

DOI: 10.4324/9781003243076

Typeset in Syntax
by Apex CoVantage, LLC

Contents

Acknowledgments   *xi*

Preface   *xiii*

Introduction   **1**

    Focus on Practice   *1*

    Separating Design Tasks   *1*

    Separating Design Tasks Requires Cooperation   *2*

    What We Mean by Everyday Built Environment   *3*

    The Open Building Approach Started with a Focus on Large Housing Projects   *4*

    The Open Building Approach has Broader Applications than Housing   *4*

    Improving Our Skills   *5*

    Who We Hope Will Read this Book   *5*

    The Structure of the Book   *6*

Built Projects that Exemplify the Open Building Approach   **9**

    Background   *9*

    What Open Building Designs For   *9*

    Examples of the Open Building Approach in Practice   *9*

    Urban or Campus Design   *10*

        Sydhavnen/Sluseholmen: Copenhagen Harbor, Copenhagen, Denmark   *10*

        Westpolder Bolwerk: Berkel en Rodenrijs, the Netherlands   *19*

        Katwijk Inner Harbor Project: Katwijk, the Netherlands   *25*

        Master Plan for the Inselspital Hospital Campus: Bern, Switzerland   *29*

    Residential   *37*

        Molenvliet: Papendrecht, the Netherlands   *37*

        NEXT21: Osaka, Japan   *43*

        Plus-Home: Arabianranta, Helsinki, Finland   *51*

        TILA: Helsinki, Finland   *56*

        TOPUP: Amsterdam, the Netherlands   *62*

    Healthcare   *69*

        INO Intensive Care Facility: Inselspital, Bern, Switzerland   *69*

        Sammy Ofer Heart Building: Tel Aviv, Israel   *78*

        Oregon Health Center: Portland, Oregon, USA   *84*

    Education   *96*

        Shenzhen University Engineering School: Shenzhen, PR China   *96*

        Santa Monica High School Discovery Building: Los Angeles, California, USA   *102*

CONTENTS

The Open Building Approach Explained   **109**

    The Origins of the Approach   *109*
    The Prototypical Urban Problem, Not Limited to Housing   *109*
    Basic Terminology   *111*
    The Problem of Evaluation   *112*
    The Problem of Coordination   *112*
    Using the Approach: Operations, Communication and Evaluation   *113*
    Designing a Base Building   *114*

Five Characteristics of Everyday Built Environment that Open Building Designs For   **115**

    Introduction   *115*
    An Explanatory Note   *115*
    Separating Design Tasks: Deciding What Is Shared and What Is Decided Independently   *116*
        Separation of Design Tasks in Urban Design or Campus Planning   *117*
        Separation of Design Tasks Has Been Commonplace in Office Buildings and Shopping Centers   *118*
        Separation of Design Tasks Is Becoming Familiar in Healthcare Facilities   *119*
        Multifamily and Attached Housing Continues to Ignore Separation of Design Tasks   *120*
    Thematic Design: Sharing Themes and Making Variations   *121*
        Enabling Coherence with Variety   *121*
        A Natural Phenomenon   *122*
        Patterns   *123*
        Systems, Variants and Structure   *124*
        Designing with Themes   *125*
    The Importance of Territory   *126*
        Understanding Territory Helps Us with the Distribution of Control   *126*
        Control of Space   *127*
    The Inherent Hierarchy in Built Environment   *128*
        Levels   *128*
        The Levels Model Helps in Several Important Ways   *129*
        Historical Examples of the Use of Levels   *129*
        Levels and Change   *130*
        Relating to a Higher Level   *131*
        Relating to a Lower Level   *131*
        Relations on the Same Level   *132*
        The Disappearance of Levels   *133*
        Levels and Our Modernist Legacy   *134*
        The Emergence of an Infill Level   *134*

    Balancing Permanence and Change   *135*
        Technical Strategies for Handling Change   *136*
        Change and Large Projects   *137*
        The Importance of Studies of Change in the Built Environment   *137*

Capacity Analysis – A Key Tool of the Open Building Approach   140

    Introduction   *140*
    What Is Capacity Analysis?   *140*
    Capacity Analysis as Part of a Design Process   *141*
    A Methodological Problem   *142*
    Evaluating Possible Uses   *143*
    How Capacity Links Form to Function   *144*
    The Use of Zones and Margins   *145*
    Zones and Margins as Part of Capacity Analysis   *146*
    Zones and Margins in Urban Design   *146*
    Using Zones and Margins in Housing Design   *146*
        Sectors   *148*
        Basic Variants   *148*
    Grids as Design Tools for Buildings and Urban Tissues   *149*
        Kinds of Grids   *150*
        Grids in Urban Design   *151*
        Summary of the Use of Grids in Designing   *153*

A Detailed Study of Capacity Analysis in Adaptive Reuse – Office to Residential   154

    The Challenge of Conversion of Office Buildings to Residential Use   *154*
    Getting the Design Constraints Right   *154*
    Studying MEP Constraints is a First Step for Capacity Analysis   *155*
    DWV Systems in an Open Building Design Strategy   *157*
    Description of Fixtures   *157*
        Toilets   *158*
    Organizing Piping 'Traffic' Inside Infill Partitions   *159*
    Capacity Analysis Study of the Kales Building   *160*
    An Open Building Alternative to Conversion   *161*
    Vertical MEP Pipe Shaft Positioning Study   *162*
    A Design Process for Conversion Using Capacity Analysis   *164*
        Step 1 – Initial Floor Plan Study Process   *164*
        Step 2 – Placing Demising Walls to Create Basic Unit Sizes and Margins   *165*

    Step 3 – Developing an Individual Dwelling Unit *165*
    Step 4 – Placing Rooms Inside the Unit *166*
    Step 5 – Locate the MEP Stacks *167*
Using the Constraints *169*
Organizing Drainage Piping in a Bathroom in Three Variants *182*
Conclusions *183*

How a Residential Infill Industry Will Change the Culture of Building   **184**

    Introduction *184*
    An Outdated Residential Industry Culture *184*
    One Developer's Perspective *185*
    How Infill Companies Would Work *187*
    A Question of Business Structure and Culture *188*
    Developments Toward an Infill Industry in PR China *189*
        Governmental Initiatives *189*
        Heneng *190*
        An Example of a Heneng Installation *191*
        Problems with Heneng and Recent Developments *193*
        V3 System Development *193*
        Photographs of the V3 Industrialized Infill System *194*
        Redefining Base Building and Infill Contents *196*
    What We Have Learned *197*
    Open Building and Government *198*
    What We Should Be Arguing For *199*

Postscript 1: Toward a New Research Agenda   **201**

Postscript 2: Tools of The Trade   **202**

    The Quality of the Commons   202

    APPENDICES   *206*
    Appendix One: A Brief Overview of the International Open Building Movement   *206*
    Appendix Two: Sources of Information of the Open Building Approach, Thematic Design and a Glossary of Terms   *210*
    Glossary of Key Terms   *213*
    Index   *216*

Acknowledgments

We would like to acknowledge the friendship and support of John Dale, FAIA, co-founder with Stephen H. Kendall of the Council on Open Building, for his careful reading of early drafts of the book. We also want to express our appreciation to all those colleagues around the world who, over many years, have shared their experiences and insights about the everyday built environment and how it can flourish. Finally, we want to acknowledge Bas de Bruin for his support in communication between the two authors across time and space in the work leading up to the completion of the manuscript.

We also want to thank those architects, clients and companies who helped us assemble the case studies at the beginning of the book. They are listed here:

URBAN OR CAMPUS DESIGN
- Sydhavnen/Sluseholmen Copenhagen Harbor (Sjoerd Soeters)
- Westpolder Bolwerk, Berkel en Rodenrijs, the Netherlands (Henk and Robbert Reijenga)
- Katwijk Inner Harbour Project, Katwijk, the Netherlands (Hans van Olphen)
- Master plan for the Inselspital Hospital Campus, Bern, Switzerland (HENN Architects and Steve Weissbaum, Inselspital Office of Campus Planning)

RESIDENTIAL
- Molenvliet, Papendrecht, the Netherlands (Frans van der Wer)
- NEXT21, Osaka, Japan (NEXT 21 Design Team (Midori Kamo, Shinichi Chikazumi and Osaka Gas)
- Arabianranta, Helsinki, Finland (Esko Kahri and Petri Viita (Open Arch) and Tokomon
- TILA, Helsinki, Finland (Pia Ilonen – ILO architects Ltd.)
- TOPUP, Amsterdam, the Netherlands (Tom Frantzen et. al Architecten)

HEALTHCARE
- Inselspital Hospital, INO Intensive Care Facility, Bern, Switzerland (Giorgio Macchi, former Chief Architect, Canton Bern Office of Properties and Buildings)
- Sammy Ofer Heart Building, Tel Aviv, Israel (Nirit Pilosof, PhD, Head of Research in Healthcare Transformation, Sheba Medical Center)
- Oregon Health Center, Portland, Oregon, USA (Karl Sonnenberg (retired), ZGF Architects)

EDUCATION
- Shenzhen University Engineering School, China (Jia Beisi, Partner, BE Architects)
- Santa Monica High School Discovery Building, Los Angeles, California (John Dale, FAIA + MRY Architects)

"I am sure that the power of vested interests is vastly exaggerated compared to the gradual encroachment of ideas."
— Robert Heilbroner, 1953. The Worldly Philosophers. Simon and Shuster, New York

Preface

We decided to write this book on the encouragement of Francesca Ford, senior publisher and our editor at Routledge. Her earlier recommendation to launch the Routledge Open Building Series suggested the need for a primer on the subject. None of the other books published in the series so far did the job. This primer would be neither a coffee-table book, a theoretical manifesto nor a detailed textbook. Instead, it would open with fourteen built projects at various scales from around the world and across project types, discuss what the Open Building approach designs for, and present a key method that can be used to put the approach into use. It would close with a return to one of the major propositions put forward in the book that launched the approach in 1962 – the development of a residential Infill industry. Finally, the book would reflect on the urgent necessity of a new research agenda and how the concept of architects sharing themes can re-enliven architectural education.

We hope that this book adds substance to important questions that continue to occupy practitioners, investors in real estate developments, regulators, builders and product manufacturers as well as educators, such as:

- How can we design large projects for inevitable change, both during design and long term?
- How can we balance the demands of large projects for efficient implementation with the equally important need for 'fine-grained' decision-making?
- How can we learn to separate design tasks, one task being the design of what should last a century, the other task being the design of the more mutable parts of buildings and neighborhoods?
- How can architects and urban designers, while separating design tasks, learn to share architectural themes and, at the same time, make variations on them?
- How can we avoid making a choice between tradition and innovation or between mindless conformity and exhausting self-expression?
- How can we do our work in recognition of our responsibilities to steward the earth's scarce resources and to contribute to a circular economy that benefits all people?

Answers to these questions will strongly influence our practices, investments and teaching, and the quality of everyday built environment in the years to come. We hope this book will be a contribution on that journey.

Introduction

FOCUS ON PRACTICE

This book is written for architects, urban designers, interior architects and our engineering colleagues. It's also addressed to clients and investors who make projects happen, the builders who construct what we design and product manufacturers and packagers/bundlers whose products and product/services we specify.

The Open Building approach aims to make our buildings and urban fabric last for a very long time. It also assures a capacity for change in large projects – that is, the opportunity for fine-grained agency or control. This is very important when projects increase in size and complexity, and when the overwhelming tendency is to centralize decision-making in the name of risk-reduction and efficiency. This granular capacity for change in turn adds near- and long-term value in ways we explain. In a historic perspective, this goal can be seen as a return to age-old qualities that largely got lost in the movement toward centralized control in modern times, across all kinds of political economies, in both the public and private sectors. This centralization has resulted in excessive rigidity of our physical environment. The recognition of these historic roots and their contemporary relevance calls for a fundamental shift in attitudes, priorities and skills.

It's important to say right up front that the approach this book discusses is not an end in itself. Rather, it's a means to sustain and invigorate our building stock and our communities, allowing them to grow in value over the course of time while also embracing the forces of change present in contemporary societies. The approach is most effective when it is consciously applied in support of several characteristics of thriving everyday built environment which we discuss later in the book.

We focus on practice and the importance of developing and using methodical ways of working. We show built projects and discuss new knowledge and changed attitudes toward what we do and methodical skills commensurate with new realities. We hope that educators as well as their students will also be interested, because the future of our professions lies in the coming generations of young practitioners attuned to new approaches needed to face pressing challenges and often confusing times.

The Open Building approach is rooted in the understanding that everyday built environment is a living, autonomous organism. What this means is that built environment exists on its own – it doesn't depend on design professionals or any other class of experts. Rather, we all depend on it as a source of knowledge and inspiration and, for many of us, for our livelihoods as practicing professionals, developers and builders. In other words, everyday built environment exists independent of the many professions and everyday citizens who work hard every day to steward its continuous transformations. We can help bring new buildings and neighborhoods into existence and help renew them and sustain them. But we can't invent or control a given built environment in its entirety. No one can. Recognizing this limitation is the basic attitude we need to adopt if we are to practice Open Building.

The approach we are talking about does not consist of formulas or recipes or prescribed performance rules. It is not a style. We are talking about changing the rules of the game of making and transforming built environment in keeping with our times. When the new rules of the game are deeply shared, we will assuredly find many ingenious and imaginative 'plays' in the game of cultivating everyday built environment.

SEPARATING DESIGN TASKS

The Open Building approach calls for separating design tasks. This means making a judicious separation in large projects between what belongs to 'the commons' and will last for generations and what is the responsibility of individuals or small social units, and that changes every generation or sometimes much faster. To be effective, this separation needs to recognize the importance of 'territory,' and must therefore be congruent with the local societies' understanding of the freedoms and responsibilities of those operating in their own 'territories.' The clarity of this separation is called for, because, not surprisingly, no single party can or does design everything. Cooperation is of fundamental importance. Finding a balance between what can be decided on individually in the context of collective decisions is one of society's challenges. The manifestation of this balance in the built environment is what the Open Building approach aims to support.

One thing is clear. The design of what is short-lived must not determine what should last 100 years. In a social sense, this

INTRODUCTION

means that individual or small-group freedom and responsibility must be exercised in respect to the commons, or what is shared.

There are many pragmatic reasons to separate design tasks. One is to provide decision flexibility by assuring that decisions about aspects that change (for example, independent units of occupancy and their service systems) do not dominate decisions about aspects of projects expected to have a very long life (the shared architectural infrastructure). Still another reason is to enable work at various levels of intervention – by those engaged in the separate design tasks – to proceed simultaneously, or in sequence, thus speeding the work.

Perhaps most importantly, the Open Building approach of separating design tasks as we discuss it in the book is a key tool with which the building industry can slow the depletion of our scarce natural resources. By building solidly for 100 years while preparing for fine-grained change, we can contribute to the urgent necessity of fighting climate change and to achieving a circular economy.

This separation – and cooperation – can be achieved while recognizing the innate hierarchical structure of built environment. This structure has been familiar for some time in distinctions made within the design professions: we have urban planners, urban designers, architects, interior architects, furniture and equipment designers and so on. Each level of decision-making 'sets the stage' – never neutral, always 'giving form' – for the work of others operating on the next lower level, whether they are professionals or nonprofessionals. This separation and this hierarchy are the essence of built environment as a living organism, alive and sustained and yet continuing to evolve while retaining coherence. This principle can be applied to many kinds of projects, as already noted.

Separating design tasks also reveals opportunities for working out new interfaces – technical, legal and spatial – between actors and the territories and building elements they temporarily control.

We hope to show that this way of working is necessary for stewarding the quality and resilience of everyday built environment. We hope that readers will see that it can be inspiring. We also hope to demonstrate that it is completely congruent with the way infrastructure systems of all kinds are designed, built, incrementally updated and managed for long-term viability. In this sense, we can say that the Open Building approach is an extension of the way infrastructure design is handled – such as transport and utility systems – into all aspects of the design of the built environment.

SEPARATING DESIGN TASKS REQUIRES COOPERATION

The separation of design tasks is a technical issue, since we are dealing with the design of buildings, building complexes and neighborhoods. The approach involves core decisions design professionals make about built form, technical systems and spaces.

But separation of design tasks also involves work in the social sphere: cooperation. The tool of cooperation is method. Methods are no more or less than generally accepted ways of working. A good method allows each of us to do our own work with a minimum of fuss and time-consuming negotiation. Method comes into play wherever we have to work together but want and need to maintain individual responsibility.

Methods don't dictate results but facilitate interaction among designers, leaving judgment to individuals, allowing each to experiment and explore. In architectural or engineering design, as in music, methods foster coordination, thereby also stimulating improvisation. In music, we play together because we accept scales, tonalities, harmony and notation. Given an accepted theme, each can even improvise as part of a larger evolving whole. Methods must not be mistaken for formulae, which are ultimately sterile. Momentarily, we may separate the methodical from the expressive, but they are never completely isolated and should not remain apart for long.

Achieving good relations while separating design tasks between designers working on different levels (for example, urban design, architecture, interior architecture) demands skill. In the same way, designers need skills while working with others on the same level – for example, in the design of adjacent units of occupancy in a building or adjacent buildings in an urban tissue or campus design.

In fact, in designing, we relate in three directions at the same time:

INTRODUCTION

- We must honor and explore the limitations offered by a higher-level design,
- We must be stimulating and generous to lower-level design that is subject to what we did, and
- We must be able to share architectural values (themes) with other designers working at the same level.

In all of these situations, we need to be familiar with the separation and distribution of design tasks and seek ways of cooperation to get the work done effectively.

When we master the skills to practice Open Building successfully and learn to thrive with new and evolving methods, we can help cultivate varied yet coherent built environment at all levels. We can help buildings and communities live and incrementally change for centuries, long after our time with them has passed. This depends on changed attitudes and on a deepened understanding of *thematic design* – the knowledge of and skill at manipulating shared patterns and systems to make variations on them. We discuss all of this in this book, in various levels of detail and with many examples.

WHAT WE MEAN BY EVERYDAY BUILT ENVIRONMENT

What do we mean when we talk about 'everyday built environment?' We think of this as the wholeness and continuity of buildings and spaces where we work, live, play, learn and move about – the ordinary fabric against which we recognize what is truly special. We all know that not every building or space can be special. It's a contradiction in terms to think so, although powerful incentives exist to push us to try for this. We call built environment an autonomous organism because, as with the natural world, it follows its own laws. It can live and die, grow and decay. Its many parts – neighborhoods, buildings, parts of building and spaces – can change over time and have their own lives as well. Built environment is, of course, subject to human agency or control as well as the forces of nature. Those actors, including many kinds of professionals as well as its inhabitants, are part of the organism. In that sense, built environment is a socio-physical fabric.

Some design professionals already practice in an Open Building way and don't necessarily use that term. That's perfectly fine and important to recognize. However, we think there's a problem when those 'doing' Open Building, realizing it or not, choose to use very different terms to explain what they do and how they work. That's because, with the resulting lack of common terminology and accounting, we as design professionals can't contribute as effectively as we could to build our shared knowledge base and tool kit – essential foundations of any profession – while we each seek competitive advantage. The challenges now facing the built environment demand more than the ad-hoc, 'Tower of Babel' approach that focuses on self-expression, inventing private and trendy terms and languages, and making 'unique' designs, tendencies that still dominate the design professions, the public perception of architects and the education of architects. The many forces affecting the well-being of our built environment require a more systematic, broadly strategic approach based on a common language and shared understanding of the laws that govern the production and transformation of our built environment.

Just imagine if doctors all had different names for human organs, their interactions, diseases and their symptoms and healing methods, or if farmers described their work in entirely individualized ways. Imagine if these professions refused to build on the work of their predecessors. So a growing knowledge base is critical. Yet as Donald Schön has taught us, there is an artistry at work in all professions, a way of working that goes beyond a knowledge base. Architecture is not unique in that respect.

While reading this book, we ask you to think about the Open Building approach the way farmers work – planting seeds, tilling and fertilizing the soil, erecting fences, pulling up weeds, pruning early growth. Such an attitude about the everyday environment doesn't come naturally today. Professionals involved in the production of the built 'field' may never have thought much about it in this way. Our professions work hard enough already. To be asked to change attitudes to help make everyday environment flourish and to plan it for change is a large challenge that goes far beyond our design professionals. Yet this may be one of the most important things societies – and our design professions – must consider and apply ourselves to, with all the imagination and tools at our disposal. We hope readers agree that the health and sustainability of our built environment depends on it.

INTRODUCTION

THE OPEN BUILDING APPROACH STARTED WITH A FOCUS ON LARGE HOUSING PROJECTS

Open Building – initially called Supports and Detachable Units – started as a radically new approach to the design of large housing projects. The approach aimed to give architects a renewed role in a process in which architects were limited to stacking up largely predetermined floor plans and wrapping them with a façade. The goal was to overcome the rigidity and uniformity of 'mass housing' then being built in Europe and in many parts of the world. The remedy had to do with a new pattern of decision-making – the reintroduction of residents into a decisive decision-making role in their immediate environment. Implementing this new decision-making process would require a radical change in the way architects and their clients worked and a new distribution of power. The question posed for architects was simple: how could we design large residential buildings when the floor plans were not known and would change later?

The solution was a design method separating design tasks, already referred to; a redistribution of control and a new way to harness industry. In contrast, today, throughout the world, multi-family housing projects or other large projects – with only a few exceptions – are organized as single, unified design jobs. As a result, they largely ignore the full power of industrial processes, the increased individualization of users and the urgent need to steward the earth's natural resources.

Ironically, large or even middle-sized residential real estate projects remain outliers up to now in Open Building implementation. These projects today typically follow a purely professional organizational process that centralizes decision-making. But even very expensive for-sale condominium projects, as we show later, are severely entangled and rigid, making full autonomy of individual dwelling units impossible. This conventional process allows little room for occupants to have more than trivial decision-making agency and offers no decision-making flexibility to investors or developers. This entanglement also thwarts the capacity of these real estate assets to adapt, one unit of occupancy at a time, to new technical and energy performance standards, market conditions and lifestyle preferences. This rigidity also runs against the urgent necessity of addressing lack of equity and housing affordability.

The paucity of examples of residential Open Building in the United States is perhaps the most surprising and difficult to explain, given the culture's stress on individual freedom and responsibility. Yet similar questions arise in many countries: "Why are households in large residential projects denied – or do not demand – the freedom and responsibility for their homes that is assumed in suburban sprawl?" "Why do developers not demand the decision flexibility in large residential projects that comes much more easily in single-family detached developments and, for that matter, in office and retail real estate investments?"

THE OPEN BUILDING APPROACH HAS BROADER APPLICATIONS THAN HOUSING

Today we see the separation of design tasks as a broader, more general practice. In office building design and in shopping malls, airport concourses and some other large multitenant projects, individual occupants or user groups need – and get – a collective architectural infrastructure within which to make autonomous design decisions and investments within their own territories. In fact, what we consider everyday environment is, to a large extent with the exception of housing, the result of projects where a distinction or separation is made between the collective environment and individual, fine-grained interventions.

The separation of design tasks in housing has been the subject of lengthy discussions and countless reports, books and academic papers over the years. Sometimes, this essential principle has been called flexibility, adaptability, participation or other similar terms. We don't intend to discuss the history or theory of the idea very much. We do, however, discuss the Open Building approach as such, introduce one key method, and provide a brief history of the Open Building movement in Appendix One and an abbreviated selection of key writings in English in Appendix Two.

In what follows, we will consider how urban design and architectural design practice can, along with our consultants, serve clients and add value to large real estate projects by explicitly and methodically planning them for change.

INTRODUCTION

We won't limit our discussion to housing, although since it remains the project type that occupies most of our urban areas and remains the most significant outlier, we will focus on residential architecture and the challenges of multifamily housing.

We know from the experience of practitioners around the world that separating design tasks along with cooperation among the parties involved can be done successfully and with excellent results while meeting client and investor expectations. That's why the first part of the book shows some of many such cases.

IMPROVING OUR SKILLS

Finally, we're writing this book because we believe that to improve our practices, it's often necessary to step back and rethink. It's also necessary to make what is implicit explicit in learning new skills. That is to say:

We can usefully spend time formulating the Open Building approach and stating clearly what it takes to practice this way. That is, we can benefit from being methodical. A new shared language may then emerge, along with new methods of notation or practices or ways of working. Afterwards, as with much learning, the new skills we develop may well go into 'background' or 'default' mode. Readers will therefore notice the emphasis on explicit methods and notation rather than ad-hoc 'one-off' approaches. This may be off-putting, but we know from experience that working with explicit methods and notation helps – at least as we begin learning how to play a new game. When new teams come together to solve new problems, having such methods adds real value.

We see the development of explicit tools happening in the urgent drive toward 'net zero' building, for example. An entirely new lexicon has come into use that, for many, is now taken for granted but still faces headwinds. The same thing is needed in the case of the Open Building approach.

Since computational tools of all kinds have come into our repertoire to aid designing, we especially need to explore how these powerful tools can be tuned to the Open Building approach. But to use computers and artificial intelligence successfully, we need to be able to explain very clearly what practicing Open Building entails in a methodical way. If we fail to learn to do this, we can't ask experts in the development of computational tools to help us and avoid having those powerful tools getting in the driver's seat. Technique for its own sake cannot be our goal.

Some may argue that the business of improving our skills is an academic exercise, that busy professionals, who are hammered constantly by the many pressures of obtaining jobs and getting projects done, have little time for this. Others may say that doing this methodical work will blunt creativity and imagination and that everyone has their own way of working anyway. Others may say that design practice hasn't really changed much for many decades or generations, so what is the fuss all about?

Some might say that designing for change is too difficult because it is too complex and that, in some fundamental way, change in the built environment is random and inexplicable. But we don't think so. We believe that those are bogus and limiting arguments. If our professions are to remain vibrant and relevant, we will need a broader view that can't retreat behind those arguments. There is an orderliness in the way that built environment comes into being and transforms. There are universal principles at work if we look hard enough in a detached way.

WHO WE HOPE WILL READ THIS BOOK

In addition to designers of all kinds, those who we hope will consider what we have to say includes many kinds of professionals involved in shaping everyday built environment. It includes investors. In addition, we hope what we offer will be of value to those working in the public sector as well as those working in private-sector organizations and companies and citizens in voluntary associations and those acting alone to steward the inevitable transformations of the built environment. We also hope that product manufacturers, product bundlers and building contractors will find this book useful if not inspiring as a basis for introducing new product/services and opening new markets.

All of these, individuals and groups, want to take control of that small part of the whole over which they have temporary responsibility. In doing so, each seeks to enlarge their sphere of control, to improve what they control for their purposes and,

INTRODUCTION

finally, to conserve their resources. In that play of forces, we hope that all these agents – more now than ever – recognize and give value to the importance of 'the commons' – that is, what is shared. This is an urgent necessity, whether we work at the level of neighborhoods, buildings or products/systems. Adopting the attitude of nurturing 'the commons' is, after all, the only way we can fight the onslaught of climate change.

Open Building's most important contribution is, in short, a new vision of practice that asks for a shift in attitudes. We know from personal experience and from communication with practitioners and clients around the world over many decades that this shift can be very difficult to make. This is why we're writing this book – to help those who are open to changing their minds. We hope what we've written contributes to a continuing dialogue, in many voices. In doing so, we acknowledge historical cases, research studies as well as exemplary built projects. We're sure readers can think of other cases.

This is not a journey of nostalgia or wishful thinking. We believe, instead, that what we discuss is a much-needed addition to a growing literature and set of design tools focused on sustainability and resilience.

We believe that any approach to sustainability and resilience must be expanded to include the imperative of designing for change: not one-off changes but continual change. This new imperative is of equal importance to the imperative of designing fire-proof buildings, buildings that can withstand earthquakes and buildings and neighborhoods that perform at net-zero energy consumption.

We are audacious enough to hope that the Open Building approach becomes normative in the production and transformation of everyday environment. We also hope that it can find its place in already-packed curricula in the education of the next generation of architects and engineers.

THE STRUCTURE OF THE BOOK

Because built work is probably the most powerful way of explaining this rather complex, multifaceted subject, we begin the book by showing 14 realized projects. We've selected cases from around the world out of many hundreds that we know about, at various scales and use types, that exemplify the Open Building approach in one way or another. Some are decades old, while more are recent at the time of writing. As noted, we do not include examples of office buildings or retail facilities because they are so commonplace.

We then give an outline of basic principles and 'operations' of the Open Building approach, with its origins in the design of large multifamily residential projects. We sketch its relevance for other kinds of projects too.

Because the Open Building approach is not an end in itself, we explain why we engage in the practice to begin with. This requires discussion of five interrelated characteristics that we believe are at the core of everyday environments that are sustainable and that we are instinctively attracted to. These characteristics are embedded in the projects discussed at the beginning of the book. We draw on lessons from everyday and historic built environments generally familiar to most readers, in which these characteristics are most evident. We invite readers to conjure up in their minds' eyes other buildings and places where these characteristics are manifest.

To help readers understand that specific skills or methods can be applied in practicing Open Building, we discuss one of them in depth: CAPACITY ANALYSIS. In doing so, we introduce three concepts and their respective notations – zones, margins and grids – and explain how they can be used.

To bring this general discussion of capacity into more practical terms, we give a case study of capacity analysis in the conversion of an office building to housing. We include this rather detailed study not because we want readers to think it is the only way to go but because it gives a sense of the sort of issues that need to be considered when doing capacity analysis – including the design of constraints.

This detailed study of a conversion project had real relevance at the time of writing this book. The COVID pandemic (2019–2021), along with other societal changes in the nature of work, has produced a massive surplus of office space in center and edge cities around the world. This is not entirely new, but the sheer magnitude perhaps is. The economic and social vitality of cities is under stress. Added to the complexity of the issue is the fact that – according to some studies – only a relatively small percentage of empty office buildings lend themselves directly to conversion to housing, at least using conventional thinking and methods. We think that the Open Building approach – and, by extension, the concept of an Infill industry – has some advantages to offer.

Next, we return to the roots of the worldwide Open Building approach and explain how a residential Infill industry would work in broad terms. We explain why the development of an Infill industry to serve the fine-grained transformation of buildings of all kinds is important. We discuss the headwinds such a development faces. We also offer our view of the role of government in this development. As an illustration, we discuss developments toward an Infill industry in PR China, and the headwinds it faces.

We conclude with two Postscripts.

The first Postscript suggests the urgency of a new research agenda, in which we should be able to frame pertinent research questions in a compelling way, based on Open Building principles.

The second Postscript focuses on *The Quality of the Commons* by way of the introduction and conclusion to a set of ten short essays that one of us (John Habraken) wrote summarizing a lecture he gave at the Department of Architecture at the Massachusetts Institute of Architecture in 1996 called 'Tools of the Trade.' These words are addressed to colleagues in the academy where both of us spent many years.

Finally, we offer two Appendices:

- **Appendix One** offers a brief overview of the worldwide Open Building movement.
- **Appendix Two** offers a list of further reading on Open Building in the English language.

Built Projects that Exemplify the Open Building Approach

BACKGROUND

We begin by showing 14 realized projects from hundreds on record around the world. All exemplify the Open Building approach in one way or another. They are of various scales and use types: urban design, housing, healthcare and educational facilities. Several were realized decades before we began writing this book, an indication of the timespan during which the approach has been in use, starting with experimental projects and becoming more and more 'mainstream.' Many of the projects are discussed in the words of the architects or urban designers responsible for them.

We decided not to show cases of office buildings and shopping centers, the most obvious examples of the approach. We also do not include mixed-use projects. Those kinds of projects are so ordinary and familiar that we don't think discussion of them is needed here. That said, we do refer to these use-types later in the book to show how and why many aspects of the Open Building approach came into existence in those sectors.

WHAT OPEN BUILDING DESIGNS FOR

We want to reiterate that the Open Building approach is not an end in itself. Rather, it's a way of working that recognizes the importance of interrelated characteristics of enduring everyday built environment, characteristics that are the raison d'etre of using the approach in the first place. We discuss these interrelated characteristics in more depth later in the book. In short, they are:

- Separated design tasks
- Thematic design
- The importance of territory
- The inherent hierarchy in built environment
- Balancing permanence and change

We selected the following built cases out of the many hundreds on record because they are some of the clearest examples. They represent these characteristics in one way or another – some represent many of them, some less than all of them. All are of high quality. This selection enables us to show how all are characterized by separation of design tasks. All show the use of themes and variations. All demonstrate the use of 'levels of intervention.' All are cognizant of territorial boundaries as legal constraints as well as means of architectural expression. The balancing of permanence and change is evident in most of the cases.

It's also important for readers to recognize the architectural diversity of these cases, and that the implementation of the projects has occurred in quite different social, economic, political and technical circumstances. After all, Open Building is not a style, a technology or a formula. It's a way of seeing how everyday built environment comes alive and sustains itself and a way of working as well.

We hope readers will refer to these examples as you proceed through the book, because they are perhaps the best way to explain this approach to practice.

EXAMPLES OF THE OPEN BUILDING APPROACH IN PRACTICE

Urban or campus design
- Sydhavnen/Sluseholmen – Copenhagen, Denmark
- Westpolder Bolwerk, Berkel en Rodenrijs, the Netherlands
- Katwijk Inner Harbor, Katwijk, the Netherlands
- Inselspital Campus Master Plan, Bern, Switzerland

Residential
- Molenvliet, Papendrecht, the Netherlands
- NEXT21, Osaka, Japan
- PlusHome – Arabianranta, Helsinki, Finland
- TILA, Helsinki, Finland
- TOPUP, Amsterdam, the Netherlands

Healthcare
- INO Intensive Care Facility, Inselspital, Bern, Switzerland
- Sammy Ofer Heart Building, Tel Aviv, Israel
- Oregon Health Center, Portland Oregon, USA

Education
- Shenzhen University Engineering School, Shenzhen, PR China
- Santa Monica High School Discovery Building, Santa Monica, California, USA

URBAN OR CAMPUS DESIGN
Sydhavnen/Sluseholmen
Copenhagen Harbor, Copenhagen, Denmark

Figure 1 View along a canal (*Credit*: Soeters Van Eldonk Ponec)

Project Data

Client:	Municipality of Copenhagen
Planning & Urban Design:	Soeters Van Eldonk Ponec architecten (Sjoerd Soeters)
Building Architects:	Arkitema
	C.F. Møller
	C. Stenberg + C. Holgaard
	Cubo
	Dissing+Weitling
	Force 4
	Format Arkitekter
	Gröning Arkitekter
	Hvidt & Mølgård
	Juul & Frost Arkitekter
	Kasper Danielsen Arkitekter
	KHR Arkitekter
	Kim Utzon Arkitekter
	Ladegård Arkitekter
	Marie Kaarøe
	ONV
	Oscar Breyen Groning
	Perlt & Black Arkitekter
	Schmidt, Hammer & Lassen
	Soeters Van Eldonk architecten
	Tage Lyneborg
	Thora Arkitekter
	Vandkunsten
	Vilhelm Lauritzen Arkitekter
Construction Company:	Various
Implementation:	The design and execution process extended from 2000 until 2009.
Dwellings:	1310
Support type:	Various
Infill provision:	Various companies
Website:	https://pphp.nl/project/sluseholmen/

SYDHAVNEN/SLUSEHOLMEN

Figure 2 Situation before the redevelopment (public source)

BACKGROUND

Sydhavnen is the southern harbor district of Copenhagen, located south of the historic city. With Java Island in Amsterdam as a successful precedent, Sjoerd Soeters was asked by the Municipality of Copenhagen to make a plan for the transformation of Sydhavnen into a residential area. This plan consists entirely of city blocks, situated so as to be oriented toward the water on all sides. In order to achieve this, kilometers of canal were added to the area. The size of the blocks in Sydhavnen is based on the dimensions of the large city blocks in the center of Copenhagen. The twists and curves of the canals create constantly changing spatial effects and sight lines.

Sluseholmen was the first application of the Sydhavnen plan. The island is characterized by a panoramic view of the surrounding water and a more intimate inner side. The inner area is formed by a curved main canal and several short lateral canals. Each city block is a single structure that contains a variety of dwelling types. The façades of the blocks were worked out by different Danish architects, supervised by Sjoerd Soeters. Architectural guidelines were set for materials, colors, spatial effects and building height to ensure that each city block remained coherent and fitted in with the greater ensemble.

THE SITE

The south harbor of Copenhagen, Sydhavnen, is situated south of the city center. The south harbor area is a set of peninsulas along the main water streaming through Copenhagen in a south-southwest direction, each of the peninsulas separated by a side canal with minor branches or a bigger surface of water, each with three different-sized docks. As the harbor activities have been moved out farther north to a new and bigger port, the south harbor became redundant.

THE HOUSING PROGRAM

With the prospect of the opening of the Øresund Bridge from Copenhagen to Sweden in 2000, modern big high-tech companies set up their head offices in the harbor areas and on the waterfront of the city of Copenhagen, thus attracting young, highly educated professionals. However, the housing possibilities in the old city, mainly small two-room apartments in social housing projects, didn't answer the demands of these young urban professionals. There was an urgent need for the kind of housing that would satisfy them and that would keep them from seeking settlement in the suburban districts farther away.

By transforming the southern harbor with its long waterline into a residential area, the city could offer an alternative.

A primitive illustration therefore was drawn up, showing that the plan was aiming at a house on the waterside with a small jetty and a boat (*havne bolig*) instead of the traditional house surrounded by a hedged garden (*have bolig*) – blue instead of green.

THE SYDHAVNEN MASTER PLAN

A concise plan for the four elements of the south harbor was designed in a few months. The importance of the water was enhanced by the addition of an enormous length of new canals in an attempt to give all dwellings a water orientation. Following the ideas of French-influenced 18th-century city planning in Copenhagen, big perimeter blocks dominated the plan, reserving space for first, second and third 'backhouses' and creating interior courtyards the size of small parks. The second peninsula, Teglholmen, posed specific problems of how to deal with the existing office building and shed of the ship engine factory and how to weave in the green crossing area for bicycles and pedestrians that the local planners had foreseen within a pattern of canals and waterfronts (Figure 3).

SHRINKING PUBLIC SPACE

The problem of most newly planned city extensions is that although they may be beautifully designed, they are completely dead. The purist and abstract beauty of design, unity in color and in volumetric composition may play a very big part in this feeling of deadliness, but this is not the whole story. Big blocks generate big in-between spaces that are mostly occupied by cars, driving by or parked on the spot. Even when most of the cars are stored in underground garages or under buildings, the open spaces feel uncomfortable. People see each other at great distance, the frequency of meeting one another is very limited and the new city feels anonymous. Part of this is caused by the extensive unbuilt ground surfaces in modern city planning; the other cause is the low population density. Even in traditional cities, their built volume kept as they are, the number of people per hectare has decreased with a factor of at least 10. In 19th-century Amsterdam it was common for a family with eight children to live in a two-room flat, whereas today, a four-room apartment is likely to be used by two people. So while the streets of the old city quarters used to be full of human interaction, nowadays, they are usually empty.

Figure 3 Sydhavnen's overall master plan (*Credit*: Soeters Van Eldonk Ponec)

For these reasons, we tried to reduce the public area as much as possible. A limited public surface is the best condition for people to meet each other more frequently, for safer dwelling environments, for more commercial activities nearby, for more pedestrian and bicycle movements, for more effective public transport, etc.: dense and happy cities are the best and maybe the only answer to most of the environmental problems that we face.

Figure 4 Aerial view of the entire redevelopment showing the blocks (*Credit*: public source-internet)

SLUSEHOLMEN

Attempting in the next phase of development to maximally shrink the public area, it was decided to eliminate most streets in the Sluseholmen plan. By doing that, perimeter blocks would seem to rise up out of the water as much as possible. The main canal was laid out in a slow curve so that at the beginning of a walk on the quay, the end of it is not yet visible. This principle of 'serial vision' (ala Gordon Cullen's *Townscape*) is applied here to create an area in which visitors and users can wander and be constantly surprised, experiencing the intimate quality of provisionary closed spaces. The concave stretch of buildings facing south is dominant and this sunny image is longest in view, while the convex shady row of buildings facing north is seen shortened in perspective. Because the summer season is short, Scandinavians love to have a walk in the sun. That is why the promenade quay is only stretched out as compacted public area at the north side of the main canal section.

Due to the reduction of public surface area, most of the housing in the perimeter blocks is entered by way of the interior courtyards. Because of this, these courtyards become communal urban spaces, shared gardens where people who live around them can meet one another, have their children play safely, have barbecue parties and so on.

As a reference, Java Island in Amsterdam consists of long peripheral rows of 27-m wide 'houses' (buildings) with rows of canal houses perpendicular to them and palazzos of uniform dimensions as well. In Sluseholmen, most blocks are not rectangular, and they form an intricate fabric of apartments, stairways, elevators, galleries for access, etc. It therefore seemed impossible to commission separately designed 'houses' of standard dimensions as was done on Java Island. For Sluseholmen, so-called block architects were commissioned to sort out the best way to organize an entire block with its public access to the courtyard and, from there, its varied entryways to different apartments and maisonettes, to the parking under the courtyard, to storage units, bicycle parking, and so on.

THE URBAN BLOCKS

SEPARATING DESIGN TASKS

Different architects' offices were commissioned to design the floor plans of the blocks: Architema was the most important, working for the major client/developer. Gröning architects were introduced by and worked for a second developer. These block plans were discussed with city officials, developers, and ultimately the supervising architect, Sjoerd Soeters (Figure 4). The building structures were organized in such a way that the load-bearing concrete walls were used as separation between the apartments. Within the contours of each apartment, different layouts were and will be possible, but crossing the load-bearing walls is not

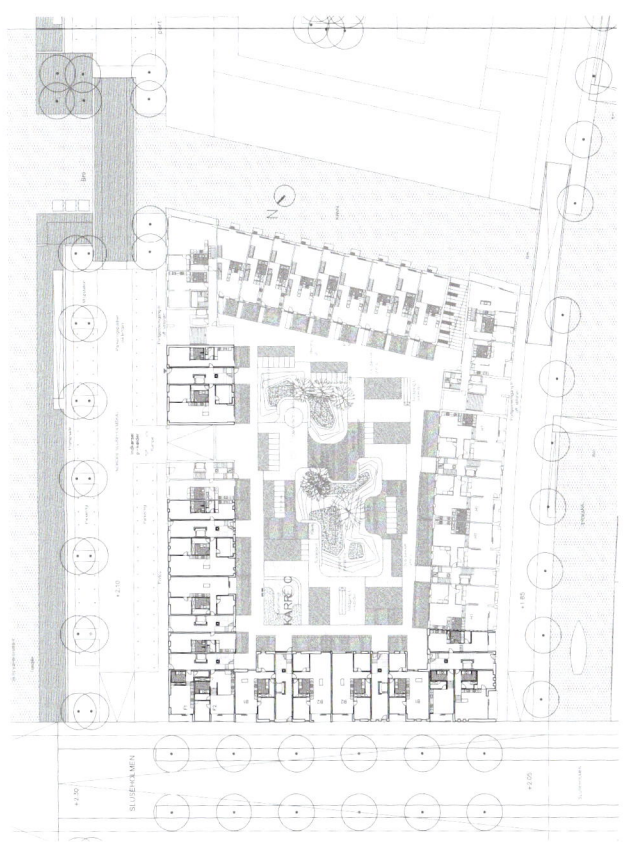

Figure 5 Block plan (*Credit*: Soeters Van Eldonk Ponec)

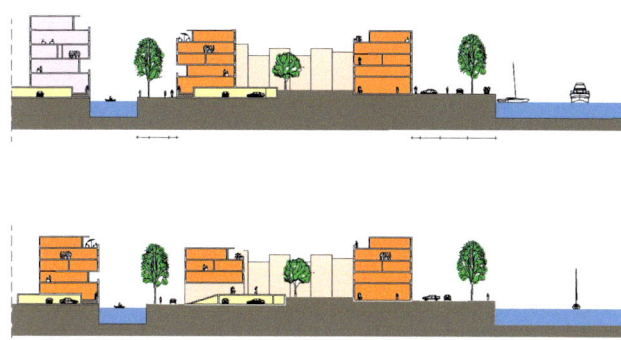

Figure 6 Prescribed cross sections through Block 2 (*Credit*: Soeters Van Eldonk Ponec)

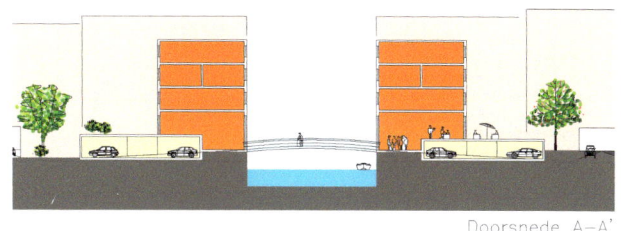
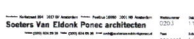

Figure 7 Prescribed cross section through a canal (*Credit*: Soeters Van Eldonk Ponec)

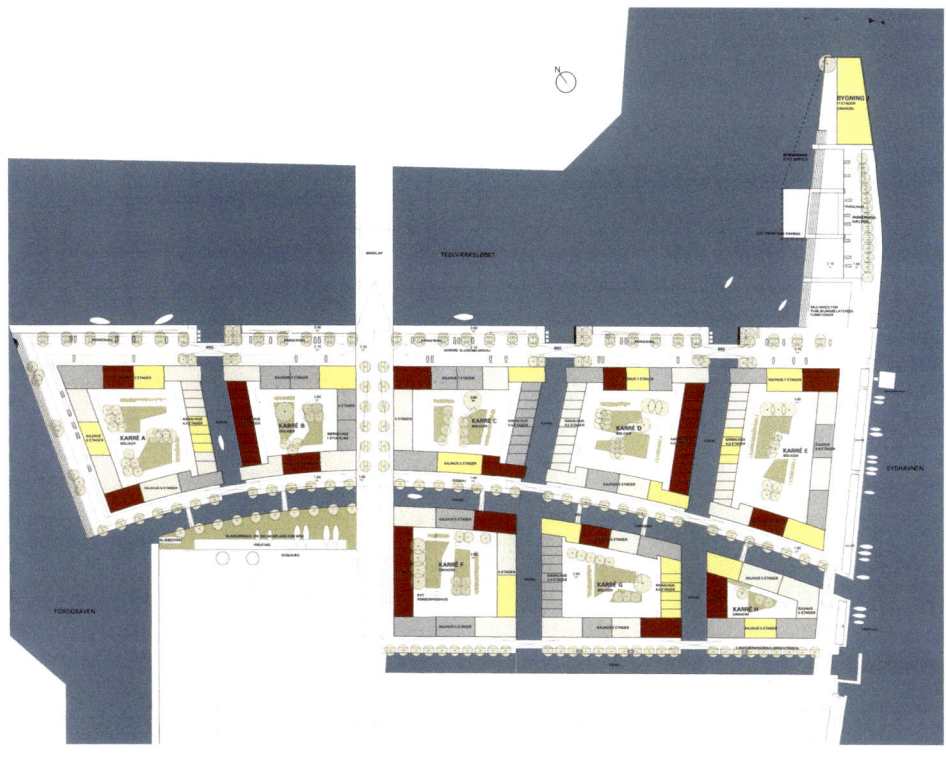

Figure 8 Sluseholmen master plan, showing different parts of each block designed by different architects (shown by different colors) (*Credit*: Soeters Van Eldonk Ponec)

Figure 9 Mock-up model of three blocks (*Credit*: Soeters Van Eldonk Ponec)

foreseen in the buildings. The contractors who built the project had a contract for the Base Buildings as well as for the outfitting of bathrooms and kitchens.

In the urban plan, the exterior size of the blocks was established, and so were the sections of the buildings in relation to the street and the level of the interior courtyards. Learning from Java Island, we positioned the inner courtyard level at a half-floor level above street level to get a more or less neutral ground balance. Doing that meant also that the ground floor apartments had a 'piano nobile' position (in US terms, the 'second floor') with more privacy, as they were lifted a half floor above street level with better views on the quays and the water. Also learning from Java, it meant that the level of the corners on the blocks next to the bridges were equal with the level of the bridges and could be used for commercial functions. Floor-to-floor heights were according to Danish standards, and so were building techniques (prefab concrete) and installation specifications, all according to what was 'normal' at that time. The territories of the two developers were in whole blocks. Opposite the most eastern canal, the difference between two developers and their respective architects is visible in the architecture.

The (Base) Building designs were completed first. Then the order of the different façade parts was established by the supervising architect (see discussion on the separation of design tasks for the façades). The separation between apartments per floor and the position of balconies is an important item in the designation of the separation line between two different façade parts. The façade architects first brought together their preliminary sketches on paper, glued together in the right order, to discuss the quality of the composition with the supervisor and fellow architects (Figure 9). Adolf Loos once stated that a city is built of simple houses (buildings) standing next to each other, very similar to their neighbors but still recognizable as individuals. "*Architectur isst für die Grabdenkmaler und die Palässte.*" In that sense, we didn't want extreme architecture and asked architects to tone down their too-loud architectural language. I remember Hugh Newell Jacobsen, an American architect, explaining that "a building should not shout at the neighbors." As an exception, the supervisor's office designed the floor plans and the façades of two complete blocks.

The technical drawings for building permits were made by Arkitema Architects and Groning Arkitekter. They brought together the different façade proposals and their detailing in these drawings. The city made a contract with me (Soeters) for the design process of the urban plan. Also, during the whole process of supervising the process, all fees of the supervising architect were paid by the city. In that way, they were representing the city in steering and evaluating the contributions of the architects who worked for the different developers. Support from the side of city officials consisted of two planners, who helped the team to understand the bureaucratic problems and upcoming attacks ahead.

According to the supervising architect:

"*The process was efficient. Having a supervising architect with a strong mandate means that a lot of bureaucratic red tape can be cut. Direct interaction took place between developers, architects and the supervisor, all intensely involved in the design process: proposal, critique, new proposals, etc. This is a very efficient way to work because the circle of professionals involved is small. Being in such a process, you have to earn your right of decision making all the time by being efficient in asking the right questions and helping the architects to find the proper solutions. The developers experienced in the activities within the supervising*

Figure 10 View into one of the internal canals (*Credit*: Soeters Van Eldonk Ponec)

Figure 11 View inside one of the canals (*Credit*: Soeters Van Eldonk Ponec)

team the advantage of avoiding the necessity of going to all the departments in town hall to collect agreement and permits. A few local planners helped to smooth conflicts with the city architect, who didn't understand the project."

"For the design of façades, a very primitive set of architectural guidelines was drawn up in a cartoon fashion and some thirty highly modern and mostly famous Danish architects were invited to design 'only' the façades of the pseudo parcels into which the blocks were divided. The architects were not amused, not to say that they felt flatly insulted. But they nevertheless took up work and came together to discuss the paper and cardboard models (Figure 9) that showed the progress of designs of every block. The sometimes strong debates nevertheless resulted in blocks that were very satisfactory to the whole team of city representatives, developers and the supervising architect."

ARCHITECTURAL GUIDELINES FOR SLUSEHOLMEN

Main Structure
The main structure of the building blocks (island blocks) is surrounded by canals and harbor basins. The buildings on the individual islands must appear homogeneous in size and rhythm in order to maintain continuity. Every 'house' (apartment building) in the block has its own plan, organization and architectural expression. The individual dwellings along the cross canals are smaller and so have a smaller individual (vertical) expression.

Height
There is variation of height between the individual buildings. North, East, West quay: A variation of 5 to 7 floors with an average of 6 1/2. South quay: a variation of 4 to 5 floors with an average of 4 1/2. Canal buildings: a variation of 3 to 4 1/2 floors with an average of 3 1/2. Note: The difference in height from to another can be one floor.

Elevations
The vertical arrangement in the façade is important for the proportion of the façade. The façades are individual faces of the buildings to the public space. The balconies are a part of the architectural façades; no balconies project into the public space. The annexes and balconies project out from the façade to a maximum of 30 cm to 40 cm (12–16 inches). The gates in the block have to be a part of the building. The façades should end with a designed trim – a finished 'cornice' – in a modern way. This subtle element can also be used to articulate the height differences. The windows in each façade are set back with a specific depth per house or building. The variation of windows from house to house or building to building are made to avoid continuous horizontal lines in the façade.

Materialization and Colors
The materials of the façades of the buildings should prevent deterioration but instead should age in a nice manner by using materials such as brick, copper, zinc and wood. Glass only in openings, not as a main mass: materials used in the Danish tradition and seen in Copenhagen. A color palette had to be worked out. This palette maintained the harmony of the area; each area has a specific color palette.

Roof Landscape
The roof can be penthouses and/or roof gardens. The installations on the roof are preferably not higher than the height of the designed cornice. Individual pipes are grouped and hidden in chimney enclosures.

Corner Buildings
The corners of the different urban blocks are designed according to the situation with different solutions for different situations with the possibility to place public functions there. Therefore, the fronts of the buildings are more open. The transition of the corner

building at the cross canals, where the lower meets the higher building, are designed individually. The solutions relate to the scale of the smaller cross-canal buildings.

Public Space
A proposal had to be worked out for the hierarchy of the different places in the public space including functions, activities, etc.

Bridges
The bridges are an important part of the public space. Through their heights, the quay is divided into different areas, which enriches the experience of the public space. The bridges would be as high as possible, with a maximum slope of 1:20, according to the rules for people with disabilities.

Parking and Courtyards
The basic idea is that the main part of the courtyard should be a green area with incidental hard pavement. A minimum of two-thirds of the whole area should be green and grass, one-third hard pavement. Each courtyard differs. Guidelines for the specific landscape in the inner courtyards of the blocks was worked out. The exact guidelines for parking based on these ideas followed.

Functions
The ground floors of the buildings following the height level of the Sluseholmen have to be filled with public or work functions. All of the ground floors of the blocks on both sides of the southern entrance to Sluseholmen are designated to have commercial, cultural and educational functions where the ground floor is level with the street. Public functions may also be created on the ground floor of the corner buildings. It is very important that the kindergarten is integrated in one of the building blocks near the main entrance of the area.

Procedure
Every architect had to agree on the guidelines and be willing to design a project based on these guidelines.

CONCLUSIONS

According to Sjoerd Soeters, the supervising architect, "Sluseholmen has received various architecture and planning awards since its completion in 2009. Inhabitants send fan-mail. It seems to have become a place that people are proud of and love to live in."

Westpolder Bolwerk

Berkel en Rodenrijs, the Netherlands

Figure 1 A view of the residential neighborhood. This is an example of a street within the 1,500-home residential extension of Berkel en Rodenrijs

Project Data

Location:	Lansingerland, the Netherlands
Client:	Berkel Rodenrijs
Design period:	Design was done from 2002 until 2014
Construction:	Execution started in 2005 and was still ongoing in 2022
Supervising architect:	Henk Reijenga, Urban Design and Architectural Coordination *www.henkreijenga.nl*
Architects:	Van Manen Architects – Noordwijk
	Henk Reijenga – Voorburg
	PBV Architects – Wassenaar
	Schippers Architects – The Hague
	RPHS Architecten
Photography:	Photography Robbert H. Reijenga
Drawings:	Office of Henk Reijenga

WESTPOLDER BOLWERK

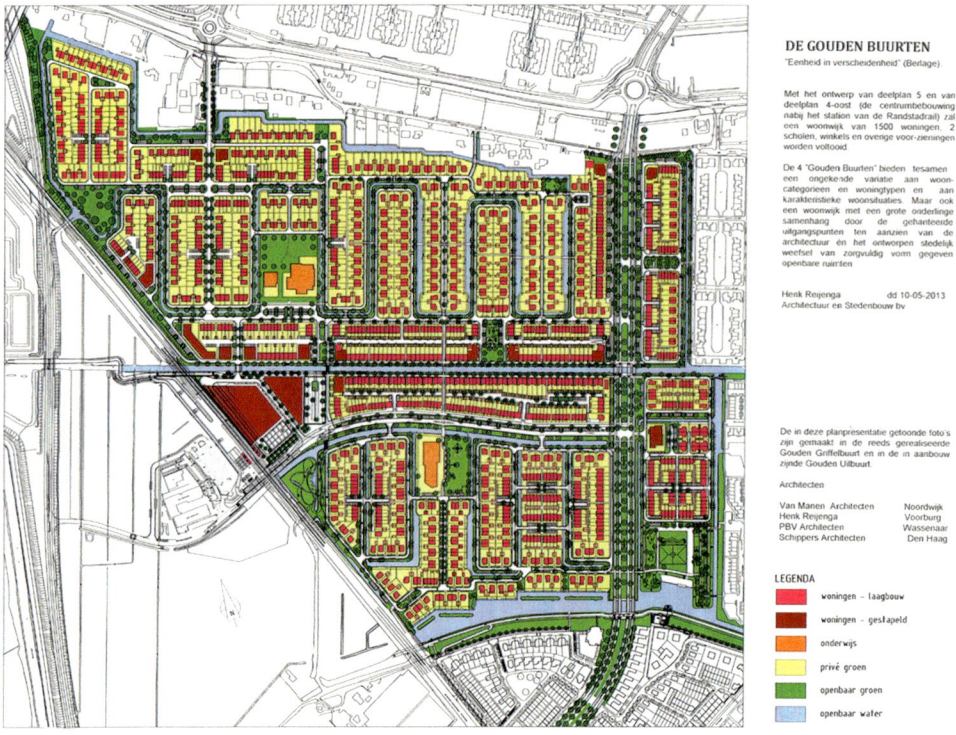

Figure 2 The overall development area 'Unity in Diversity' (Berlage)

BACKGROUND

The township of Berkel Rodenrijs is part of a larger municipality called Lansingerland in the Netherlands. It is now the location of a large urban development named Westpolder Bolwerk.

The plan discussed here is part of that development. It offers an urban environment with 1,500 dwelling units and two primary schools. The part of it already executed at time of writing comprises more than a thousand inhabited dwelling units, while the last phase was in the preparatory stage.

The office of Henk Reijenga was asked to realize a 'village-like' environment within a growing middle-sized town. 'Village-like' means small scale, identifiable as a particular location, making people feel secure and showing coherent variety.

The architectural environment in response to that task is the result of a new way of distribution of architectural design responsibilities in a spirit of well-organized cooperation in the design team. No two houses of the 1,000 units are exactly the same, but the variety is entirely coherent.

The urban design was also developed in a team spirit. In addition to the client/developer and the urban designer, various other professionals were included who were specialized in infrastructure like roads, water, cabling and piping (drainage and supply), etc., landscape architecture and traffic planning. Consultation among these specialists took place in the design phase every two or three weeks. They also met during the execution of the plan, corresponding to the reality that an urban design is never finished. A representative of the municipality Lansingerland chaired these meetings and reports to the town hall.

THE OVERALL DEVELOPMENT AREA

With the design of subplan 5 and of subplan 4-East (the center buildings near the Randstadrail station), a residential area was planned with 1,500 homes, two schools, shops and other facilities.

The four 'Golden Neighborhoods' (Figure 2) together offered an unprecedented variety of house types and characteristic living situations, thanks to the principles used with regard to architectural quality and to an urban fabric of carefully shaped public spaces. It has become a residential area that demonstrates a remarkable coherence among the various architects each responsible for a part of the whole.

ARCHITECTS

Van Manen Architects – Noordwijk
Henk Reijenga – Voorburg
PBV Architects – Wassenaar
Schippers Architects – The Hague

LEGEND

Low-rise housing
Clustered housing
Education
Private green space
Public parks
Public water courses

- **Planka Street**/example distribution of design tasks (Figure 3)

Figure 3 Planka Street district

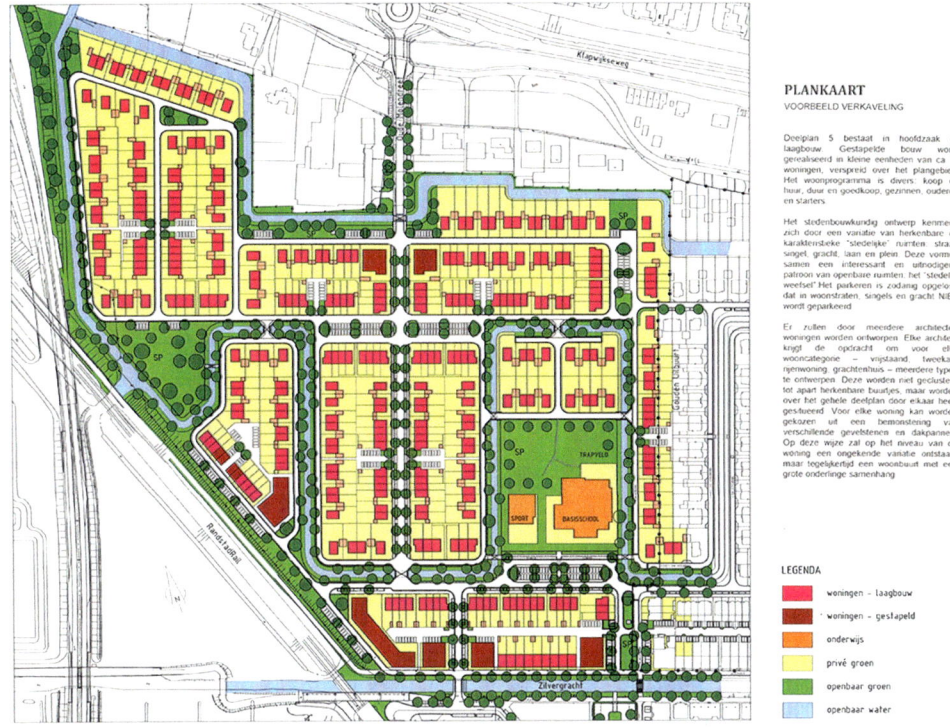

Subplan 5 mainly consists of low-rise housing. Clustered construction is done in small units of approximately 12 residences throughout the plan area. The housing program is diverse: buy and rent, expensive and low-cost, families, the elderly and starter households. The urban design shows a variety of recognizable and characteristic urban spaces: streets, small water channels, canals, avenues and squares. Together, these make an interesting and inviting pattern of public spaces: the 'urban fabric.' Parking is not allowed in residential streets or along canals or small water channels.

"Houses were designed by a variety of architects. Each architect was asked to design several examples for each given residential category, such as detached, two-under-one roof, terraced houses, canal houses and several other types. One architects' designs were not kept together to make a homogeneous neighborhood designed by a single architect. Instead, their designs are distributed across the entire project area by the supervising architect."

A choice of variously colored bricks and roof tiles was available to choose from for each individual house. In this way, at the level of the individual house, an unprecedented variety is possible, but at the same time, residential areas can be identified by selecting a shared building typology, while single homes remain different from one another.

Windows and doors in façades had to be in wood with the same off-white color, while the window and door details were standardized. But their size and the design of their subdivisions could be decided by each architect. This made the work of the builders predictable and efficient while variety in house design remained assured.

KEY

- Housing – low-rise
- Houses – stacked
- Education
- Private green
- Public parks
- Public water

BERKEL STREET/THE GOLDEN NEIGHBORHOODS (FIGURE 4)

The assumptions guiding the design of this area and its houses were:

- Village-style buildings
- Small scale
- Encouraging inhabitant identity/recognition of one's own place

All to be achieved by offering a wide variety in the architecture of houses within a coherent unity of the whole urban scene.

The variation takes place on three levels:

1. The public spaces (urban design level)
2. The collective use of the shared building types (Base Building design level)
3. The buyer options (at the Infill level)

Distribution of homes per architect
Red   RPHS Architecten
Yellow   Schippers
Blue   V. Manen

The starting point was a reasonable mixture of the various price categories; all categories would be found in the 300 house types. Clustered construction is located in characteristic places along Stationssingel and Oudelandselaan.

- **Berkel Street**/The housing program

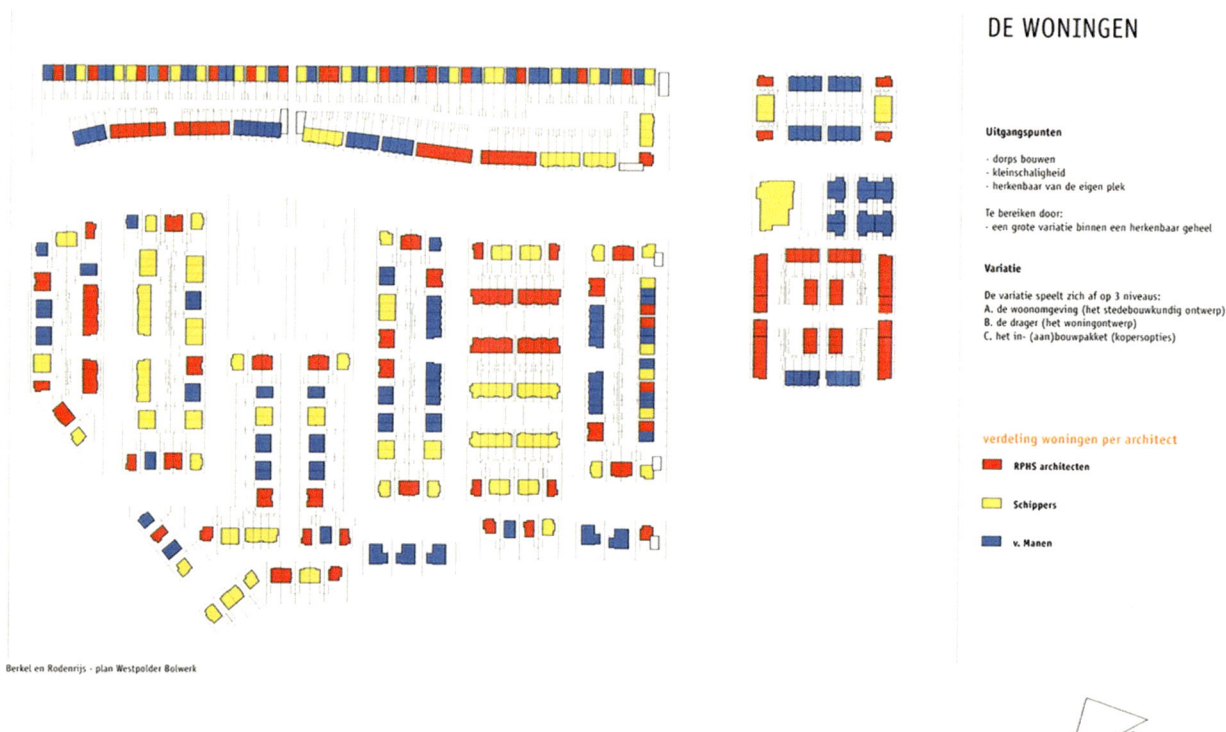

Figure 4 Berkel Street. The houses designed by three different architecture offices

The Residential Program	
Red: Social Rent	**20%**
Terraced houses	56
Clustered houses	24
Apartments	19
Total 99 houses	
Blue: Midmarket Rent	**10.5%**
Terraced houses	40
End units	4
Canal houses	8
Total 52 houses	
Light blue: Expensive type 1 owner-occupied homes	**25%**
Terraced houses	103
Patio houses	12
Canal houses	10
Total 125 houses	
Yellow: Expensive type 2 owner-occupied homes	**44.5%**
End houses	20
Canal houses	56
Duplex houses	92
Detached houses	48
Detached 'reed' houses	5
Total 221 houses	
Total homes	**497**

WESTPOLDER BOLWERK

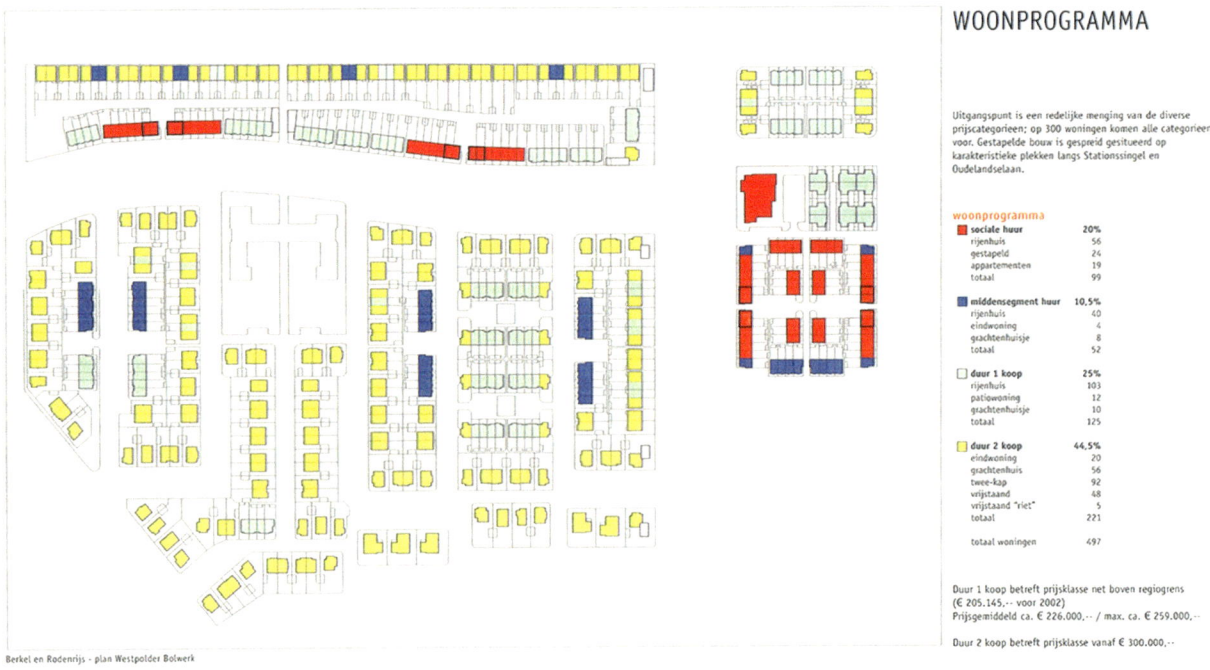

Figure 5 The housing program

Figure 6 An aerial view of part of the development

Figure 7 One row of houses by different architects sharing many thematic elements

Figure 8 A small square within the development

Figure 9 Single-family detached houses along a small canal. No two buildings are exactly alike

Expensive type 1 owner-occupied houses are in the price range just above the regional median price: (€205,145 for 2002); average price approximately €226,000/max. approx. €259,000. Expensive type owner occupied houses are in the price range from €300,000.

Katwijk Inner Harbor Project

Katwijk, the Netherlands

Figure 1 The new development at the head of the canal. This view shows the variety of architectural schemes shown in Figure 4 (*Photo credit*: Google Earth)

Project Data
Location: Katwijk, the Netherlands
Client: Building Contractors Consortium Katwijk (ACK)/Rabo Vastgoed, Utrecht
Chronology: Period of design through completion of construction: 1995–2005
Floor space: 400 apartments, 5,000 m² of retail and commercial space, two parking garages (600 spaces)

KATWIJK INNER HARBOR PROJECT

Four parties working together in the project:

- The investor: RABO Vastgoed (owned by RABO Bank Utrecht)
- Contractors Consortium Katwijk" (ACK)
- Five architects and Hans van Olphen as supervisor
- Bouwstart: provided the final drawings, thus forming the link between the designers and the contractors

Five collaborating architecture offices:
Jan Poolen (www.zeep.eu)
Theo Verburg (www.theoverburg.nl)
Cees Brandjes (www.brandjesvanbaalen.nl)
Bert Tjhie (www.tekton-architecten.nl)
Gerben van Manen (www.van-manen.com)
Urban design supervisor: Hans van Olphen Architects Partners, Amsterdam
Awards: Nomination Incentive Intensive Land Use STIR

BACKGROUND

In the old harbor of Katwijk, local fishing company facilities have made room for 400 new apartment units and shops. The requirements of the development, dubbed Princehaven, stated that it needed to become a place that Katwijk citizens could identify with. The residents of Katwijk did not want to experience any separation between themselves and the adjacent village of Port Prince. This has been considered in the design and architecture of the development. The investor, RABO Vastgoed, worked closely with local developers and the municipality to negotiate a land development scheme that was amenable to all parties. The apartment blocks are focused around the harbor and provide residents of the upper floors views of the town of Katwijk. Large arcades provide residents with a desirable level of protection from inclement weather while maintaining a sense of community. The new neighborhood functions as a 6-meter- (20") high 'bowl' that frames the town, whereas portions of the development experience direct access from the street level with the older fishing cottages. The architecture of the apartments is sensitive to the vernacular style and scale of the existing fishing cottages.

Throughout Princehaven, physical connections have been established in the form of stairways, lifts and roads, providing residents with easy accessibility to the town. The inner courtyards of the development include playgrounds, green space, air movement and pedestrian circulation, thereby giving a sense of intimacy between the blocks. The new development has become a critical component of the success of the town.

NOTE FROM HANS VAN OLPHEN, SUPERVISING ARCHITECT

"I was one of three architects invited to propose a scheme for the renovation of the inner harbor area of the town of Katwijk in the Netherlands, an area close to the town center. The municipality of Katwijk was the initiator, working in close cooperation with three local building companies (ACK) and a national bank as investor. They asked for an integrated plan for a large number of residential units combined with facilities like retail space and other commercial space and sufficient parking.

My plan was unanimously preferred after one meeting because it combined two important aspects.

1. The proposal offered a vision of the expected kind of environment without defining the exact final result. It allowed various ways of execution by other architects. This satisfied an important request from the municipality.
2. The proposal defined the envelope for built volumes while differentiating capacity for residential units, parking and commercial functions. This made calculation of the costs for execution possible before the actual partial designs were done.
3. The harbor area is situated at a lower elevation than the surrounding streets of the town. Because of the limited daylight, the lower levels behind the arcade contain the parking facilities (underground) as well as shops serving the whole neighborhood, opening onto the arcade.

My task was to design an Urban Plan in the sense of a Master Plan. Five architects participated in the project and accepted the rules of the Master Plan. My task was to protect the total as a whole. That was the reason I designed the 200-meter-long arcade to bring unity to the project despite the differences in architecture. Architects are generally individualistic, but in this project, they had to follow my organizing concept. The variation the architects realized was not in the ultimate façade or structure but in the living possibilities: for example, in the design of floor plans.

I was asked to work out the Master Plan within which were defined building heights, the parking garage and other infrastructural elements like stairways and elevators that, in turn, could be translated into rules and constraints within which architects had to work. After approval of the Master Plan, I was given the task of supervision of the designs done by the yet-to-be-invited architects.

Together with the municipality and its partners, I organized an excursion to several coastal towns in the north of France, to show that a general building height of seven floors need not result in the massive uniformity that the municipal representatives worried about as long as the buildings were designed by a variety of architects working on a variety of locations while sharing architectural themes. In Le Havre, Honfleur, Rouen, and other towns, we could see how narrow parcels make height of buildings a relative concept. This, after all, is also typical for the buildings along the Amsterdam canals. The excursion also helped to strengthen social contacts, which made for a stimulating experience in spite of the different interests of the participants.

The architects to design the buildings were selected by the various client development parties. I could help steer it as well. The invited architects had to accept the detailed constraints of the Master Plan. The actual process towards the final design approval included workshops chaired by me. I completed the preliminary design for the arcade before the workshop with the architects had begun. The design of the arcade did not change after discussions and my explanations.

At that time, this offered an entirely new concept for the participating architects. The designs were discussed every two weeks with all architects present, a process which stimulated all participants. Architects could do proposals for the façades of their buildings, etc. But staircases, lifts and other more structural elements were collectively decided. The beginning was somewhat difficult; the limitations set by the Master Plan and its rules were seen as a handicap. Gradually, this was forgotten, particularly when it appeared that good architecture usually had its own rules and limitations that were often self-imposed. The architects found their way to design their own façades, window frames, balconies, etc., something that I stimulated (see Figures 1–5). Variation should be possible within my master plan; otherwise, my plan was not good. Eventually, everybody subscribed to the final result.

One office (Bouwstart) was selected to make the entire set of building construction drawings after the definite design was finished by all the architects. Bouwstart finalized the project for the contractors, controlled the costs and managed the project execution. Parts of the arcade were built together with the adjacent residential buildings. The Contractors' Combination Katwijk appointed one of its members as the responsible contractor to build the whole project, including the parts on the opposite sides of the harbor.

The contracts with the architects included all ownership rights and are comparable to other normal jobs. Professional fees are paid by RABO bank. Bouwstart and the architects worked

Figure 2 The new development along the canal with the unifying arcade within and behind which different developers and their architects realized their own residential and commercial schemes (*Photo credit*: Hans van Olphen)

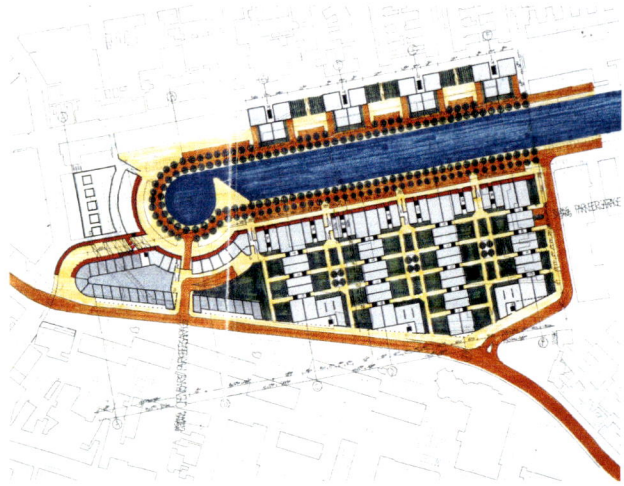

Figure 3 The concept drawing of the site (*Drawing credit*: Hans van Olphen)

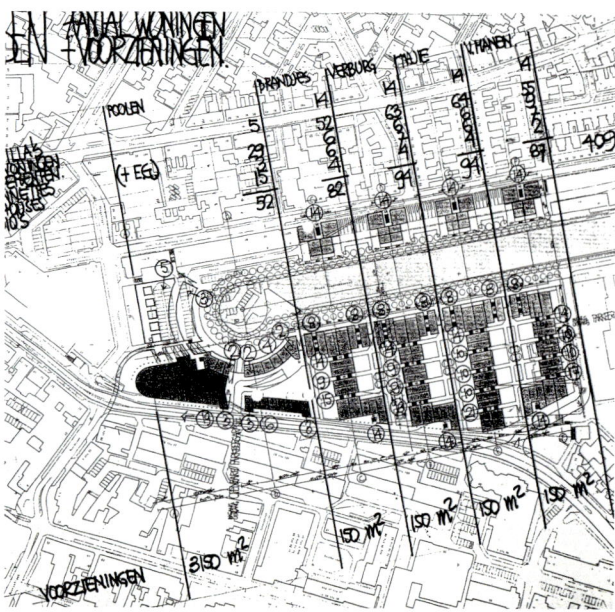

Figure 4 Division of responsibilities among the various architects. Each architect's 'territory' extended across the water to include both sides of the harbor (*Drawing credit*: Hans van Olphen)

Figure 5 A view along the colonnade (*Photo credit*: Hans van Olphen)

Figure 6 A view looking up the stairs from the colonnade to the housing over the parking (*Photo credit*: Hans van Olphen)

together, as is usual in our profession, without any exceptional guidance.

Using the Open Building principle of separation of design tasks and sharing thematic elements, and the ensuing workshops, were a great experience in the Katwijk project. This way of cooperation points individual efforts to the quality of the whole and away from the individual identification of each architect. The project as a whole is central. It seems to me a real achievement that a residential project combined with shops, offices and hidden parking has become an environment of which no one knows exactly anymore who did what exactly."

The supervising architect predetermined the location of elevator shafts that allow residents to reach their dwelling units directly from the underground garage. This makes these shafts part of the higher-level framework and an extension of public circulation around which the actual buildings, designed by different architects working for different developers, were designed. Apartment buildings behind the continuous urban wall interact intimately with this public circulation.

More than 25 years after the project was realized, the area remains very popular thanks to the collective efforts of all participants.

Master Plan for the Inselspital Hospital Campus

Bern, Switzerland

Image 1: Master plan model with spatial frames and example of possible building bulk and massing (*Credit*: HENN Architects)

Project Data
Location: Bern, Switzerland
Client: Canton Bern Office for Real Estate and Public Buildings
User: Inselspital University Hospital
Campus building footprint: Current floor area: 280,000 m² (3,013,900 sq. ft.); growth to 600,000 m² (6,458,300 sq. ft.)
Urban designer: HENN Architects, Berlin
Implementation period: 2010 to 2060
Users: Around 44,000 inpatients per year; 6,400 employees, in addition to 900 students

"The masterplan is valid indefinitely, but is not finite." (Giorgio Macchi, chief architect of the Office for Real Estate and Public Buildings, Canton Bern, 2011)

BACKGROUND

Founded in 1354, the hospital has moved several times and was located in its current site in 1867. Several master plans were initiated, the latest in 1956. Then, the accident and emergency and surgical center 'INO' was built and completed in 2012 to act as a new center of gravity for the Inselspital site.

At that time, new facilities were built largely without consideration of the site structure as a whole, which led to a certain fragmentation of functions. Existing process-related and organizational restrictions made adjustments to the changing functional requirements of the new buildings impossible. As a result of this geographical and functional fragmentation, organizational processes became inefficient and insufficient for the qualitative requirements of a modern university hospital in both medical and operational terms. Due to this, the national and international position of the Inselspital was threatened. Significant drivers of success, such as interdisciplinary cooperation, impromptu exchange of knowledge and a high degree of interconnection appeared impossible to realize within the existing infrastructure.

Figure 2 The Inselspital campus, with the INO at the very center of the campus (the large building with many skylights) (*Credit*: Google Earth)

In 2010, an international urban planning competition was held to design a 'Masterplan 2060' of the Inselspital. HENN Architects won the competition. HENN'S master plan created a strategic planning tool to steer development of the site. Acting as a rulebook guiding all future development activities, the master plan enables rapid planning decisions. It allows for various forms of functional organization while additionally leaving space for flexible operational decisions. In addition, it supports sustainable values for urban planning and facilitates with high-density building on the site.

Single construction projects were to be facilitated step by step without impacting the ongoing hospital functions. Strengthening the local identity as a healthcare campus and its positive characteristics was required. Generally, the requirement of ecological, economic and social sustainability was set. However, the biggest challenge of the competition was the requirement to develop a planning tool that remained meaningful and usable for the next generation.

Based on all these requirements, the competition master plan proposed three key ideas:

TOPOGRAPHY

The bulk and massing increases in density toward the center of the site and thus elevates the existing topography. As a result, the massing increases its significance in its external appearance within the urban context. Towards the site periphery, the building volumes and heights reduce to facilitate a connection to the scale of the neighboring buildings and urban fabric.

FORMING URBAN QUARTERS

The urban structure of the master plan derives from the idea to form small urban quarters within the site. Listed buildings form the center of each quarter, each arranged on a new urban square.

KNEADING DOUGH

The required floor area per building plot serves as the so-called dough, which can be 'kneaded' freely within the limits of a volumetric frame. Hence, various volumetric forms can emerge within a set three-dimensional boundary. This idea ensures the freedom

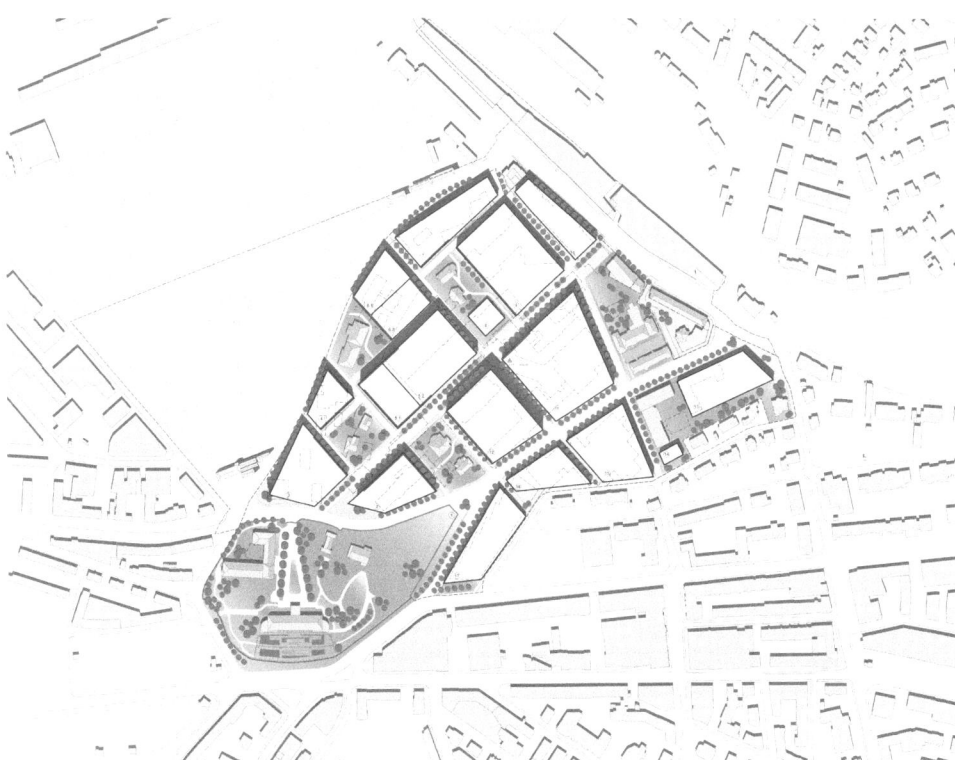

Figure 3 Masterplan 2060 showing the small 'urban quarters' each with a listed building at the center of each (*Credit*: HENN Architects)

to newly interpret and realize future functional, economic and architectural demands.

MASTER PLAN

HENN was asked to continue developing the Masterplan 2060 up to a stage at which it could be transferred into a legally binding document. The three key ideas – topography, urban quarters and kneading dough – continued to build the foundation of the Masterplan 2060.

During a time span of two generations, the master plan not only has to fulfill social, economic and ecological requirements through urban planning, it also has to hold up to unforeseeable future requirements of a medical campus. Hence, the master plan cannot be a rigid planning document that will lose its relevance over the course of time due to changing requirements. On the contrary, this master plan is to be a strategic spatial planning tool: It defines a frame for structured urban development but does not prescribe function or architecture of single building projects. This way, an open-scenario structure emerges in which varying organizational and functional concepts can be realized on each plot, e.g., the arrangement of medical centers or, alternatively, the arrangement of functional centers.

All central plots have dimensions designed to accommodate various kinds of clinical functions. A largely orthogonal grid supports flexibility and neutrality of use. Moreover, the plots were arranged to maintain existing buildings such as the newly built INO so that they remain fully operational and functionally integrated within the master plan until they finish their life cycle.

The Inselspital master plan intends for the site to form a permeable, integral part of the urban fabric and to serve as an attractive public space. Simultaneously, the Inselspital has to exude the positive air of a healthcare campus, not just a place to cure sickness. This places high demands on external spaces with regard to atmospheric quality, wayfinding and spatial permeability. Nevertheless, it has to be possible to connect buildings in a way to facilitate easy transport of people and goods. Currently, the Inselspital site offers diversified spatial experiences ranging between busy hospital life at its core and nearly bucolic landscape gardens on the so-called Englaenderhubel toward the western end of the site. The master plan, therefore, intends to not only strengthen these characteristics but also to create a connection between these contrasting elements.

Master Plan Objectives

The master plan's legal document consists of a graphic plan of the site and a written rulebook. The graphic plan defines the urban structure, i.e., future plots, listed buildings, landscaping, etc. and quantifies floor area requirements and volumetric limits. Additionally, the rulebook describes in a qualitative manner the overriding objectives and key ideas including tangible rules.

The question remained: How to leave a planning document for the next generation, describing ideas in an easily retraceable way, thus eliminating the need for the author to be present for explanations? The rulebook tries to develop a framework that shows how ideas derive from objectives and how these ideas then generate rules. This framework, establishing overarching abstract objectives which further define the finer details within the master plan, has proved to be highly effective in the development process.

In detail, the rulebook defines five primary objectives. These objectives originated from requirements during the competition.

Identity
The Inselspital site should be strengthened in its uniqueness and identity. Preserving and integrating listed historical buildings plays a central role.

Structure
The aim is to create an urban quarter with the character of a healthcare campus. This puts a focus on the quality of external space and landscaping. Hierarchies in the new part of urban fabric should be clearly legible and thus enhance orientation and wayfinding on the site and within buildings.

Capacity
This means keeping development perspectives open on the long run. Various forms of functional organization should be possible as and when required. A further consideration is to facilitate change of use and temporary usability of buildings, which requires floor layouts to be functionally neutral to a high degree (this complies with the System Separation mandate for all public buildings in the Canton Bern – see the case of the INO following).

Economic Efficiency
A prerequisite of all planning activity is to make built space economically efficient to use. Part of this objective, therefore, is to extend the life cycle of buildings in a sense of sustainability. It should also be possible to offer spaces for external businesses with medicine-related purposes, e.g., med-tech startups emerging from research departments.

Availability of Building Plots
At any time, there should be a free plot of land available for new buildings in the sense of 'crop rotation' in order to start new building projects easily and quickly, depending on the situation and demands at any point in time.

Key Ideas
Based on these five objectives, seven key ideas were formulated. Subsequently, these key ideas became the basis for a set of rules. The three key ideas at the heart of the competition design were amended and extended so that the rulebook now defines seven key ideas:

1. Forming Urban Quarters
Like the competition design, the Masterplan 2060 aims to create urban quarters on the site. A single or group of listed historical buildings defines the center of each new quarter. The building is located centrally on a new urban square or pocket park. This square or park is defined at its boundaries through new building fronts. Pedestrian routes and visual connections connect single quarters with each other. This supports orientation and wayfinding but also strengthens the cultural and historical identity of the Inselspital site.

2. Open Space
A central axis connects the new urban squares and makes it possible to experience a series of varying ambient atmospheres from the busy Murtenstrasse high street through to the Englaenderhubel-landscape garden. This again supports and enhances the local identity of the Inselspital site. The appearance and quality of the open space significantly influences the perceived amenity of the whole site and, as such, plays a leading role for the whole master plan.

3. Density
The density of mass increases toward the center of the site. Along the site boundaries, the massing adjusts to match its context and to ensure a seamless connection with the overall urban fabric.

4. Kneading Dough
As opposed to the usual approach, the Inselspital master plan neither defines nor locates buildings on plots. A given total floor

area per plot can be freely formed within a certain volumetric limit, depending on the functional and architectural requirements of each building. This allows each building to individually adapt to future requirements determined at the time of its development and realization.

5. Interconnection
Neighboring plots on the site should be well connected with each other in order to ensure maximum capacity as well as functional variability. Through linking elements or passages above and below ground, functional areas can be connected and extended horizontally between separate buildings.

6. Disentanglement
The aim is to separate motorized and pedestrian traffic as well as transport of patients and transport of goods across the site and within buildings. Introducing priorities and hierarchies for traffic and transport aims to improve the experience of wayfinding, especially for patients, visitors and all other users.

7. Crop Rotation
The principle of 'crop rotation' intends to offer empty plots for fast but nevertheless sustainable development while keeping all existing hospital processes intact and operational. This requires available empty plots, so-called fallow land, for the next step of development. As soon as a construction project is planned for an existing fallow plot, a new empty plot must be located. In case a plot is too large for the intended building, it can be divided into subplots with the prerequisite to achieve the required floor area once all subplots have been built.

Rules
In the third and final step, rules were derived from the defined key ideas. These can be found at a lower position in the framework, becoming rather precise urban planning requirements.

Green Spaces and Routes
As the bulk and massing of future buildings is unknown, it is essential that all greenery serves the wayfinding on the site.

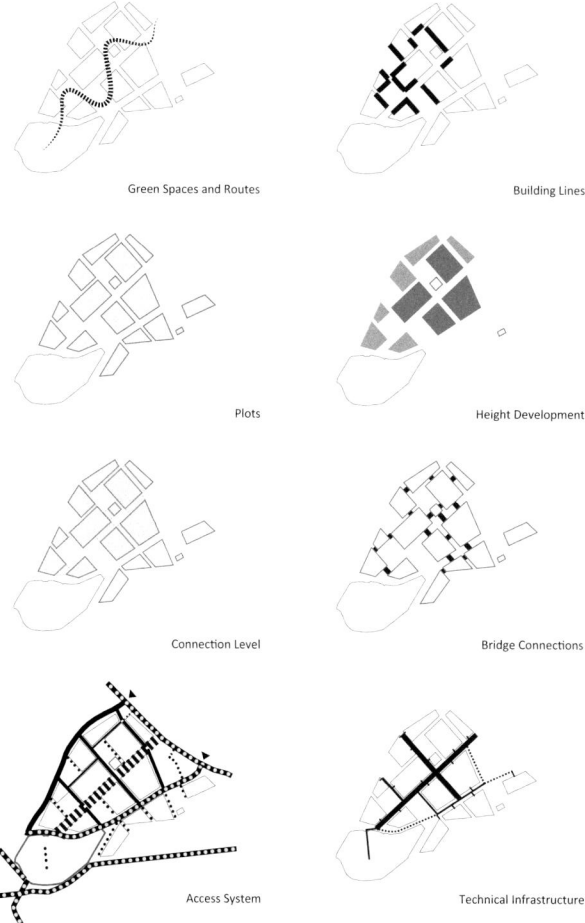

Figure 4 Eight implementation rules (*Credit*: HENN Architects)

Therefore, all Primary and Secondary routes in the master plan are lined by alley trees and linear parks. All linear greenery is interrupted where the route meets an adjacent square in order to open up the views toward the square. This also helps to interconnect and weave routes into squares.

Building Lines
According to the master plan, each urban quarter has a square at its center. However, only certain building proportions

provide the right structure to generate the sense of an urban square. Even if form and location of new buildings on plots surrounding the square are still unknown, it has to be ensured that the volume of adjacent buildings helps to form this square. Therefore, building lines were introduced to define the requirement for closed building fronts on boundary lines surrounding each square. To avoid towering buildings that suffocate a square by their sheer vertical dimension, the requirement for a closed perimeter only applies to the plinth of each building. The building mass above should be set back from the plinth. The height of the plinth is not set in absolute terms. Instead, the height of the plinth of each building adjacent to a square is defined to range between a minimum and a maximum relative to a set level for each square. There are two variables on each building plot: (1) ground floor location relative to topography and (2) free choice of floor-to-floor dimension. Because the highest point of the site is 35 m (115") above the lowest point, the possible number of stories for each building plinth can vary. The objective is to achieve a consistent edge line of building plinths around each square.

Plots
By their set dimensions, plots define the space where new buildings can be constructed on the site. Buildings can be shaped according to project requirements within the extent of a volumetric spatial frame (Figure 1). In order to determine the shape and appearance of the buildings, a separate competition is to be held for each plot. The Plot rule is amended by the Building Line rule around squares, requirements of total floor area per plot and maximum possible height requirements.

Height Development
One of the three competition ideas, Topography, can be found here. By increasing the density and thus building height towards the center of the site, which is already located on a hill, a superelevation of the topography is achieved. This has significant impact on the physical appearance of the site within the urban context of Bern. Today, the inpatient tower is the Inselspital's landmark, as it can be seen from most points in the city and its surroundings. As soon as it will be replaced, new high buildings at the core of the site will take over this role.

Connection Level
Setting a fixed reference level for all plots enables the horizontal connection of new buildings at the core of the site. This rule only refers to one floor per plot so that ceiling heights above and below the connection level remain unaffected. Therefore, functional and organizational connections across and between buildings become possible.

Bridge Connections
A connection between buildings or plots is possible via bridges. This adds an efficient system of internal routes to the already-existing transport tunnels below ground. By this means, patients no longer need to be transferred through unwelcoming logistics tunnels but can be moved above ground. In addition, internal visitor routes can now be offered between buildings. The rulebook requires these bridges to be designed and proportioned in a way that leaves the buildings legible as autonomous architectural elements.

Access System
The main aim of the traffic and infrastructure concept is to disentangle traffic flows by prioritizing routes and developing a concept of route hierarchies. In the future, all motorized traffic, especially emergency ambulance traffic and logistics traffic, is to access the site directly from both main roads around the site and one historical main road that crosses through the campus. All further internal routes are reserved for pedestrian and bicycle traffic. A new main pedestrian 'street' from East to West will become an important feature of the campus.

Technical Infrastructure
The aim of this concept is to simplify the infrastructure network on the site by introducing two Primary data and infrastructure tunnels below ground. In order to guarantee maximum flexibility for the plots, all technical infrastructures including the two main tunnels are to be run parallel to plots beneath the roads.

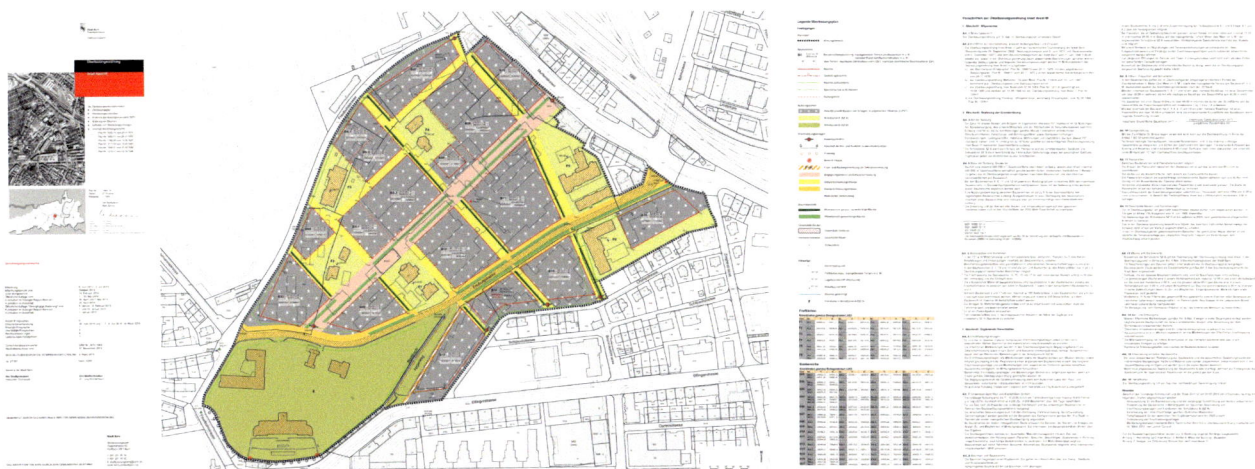

Figure 5 Zoning Plan. Source: Stadtplanungsamt Bern (*Source*: Bern City Council Planning Department)

Through all these objectives, key ideas and rules, the rulebook tries to detail the intent of the master plan. Qualitative descriptions have been chosen over quantitative prescriptions (exceptions being the total floor area per plot and maximum height per plot) in order to give the master plan 'space to breathe' in the future.

Spatial/Organizational/Sustainable Master Plan
While HENN developed the master plan that refers to all things urban and architectural, a team of operational specialists developed a master plan that mainly refers to organizational functions. Both of these master plans were then additionally amended by a third element, the master plan for ecology and sustainability. While the spatial masterplan provides a stable urban planning tool to ensure structured spatial development through the next decades, the organizational masterplan depicts current and acute requirements of a complex hospital organization within a highly dynamic context. The idea to build a master plan out of three components (spatial, organizational and sustainability) emerged during the process of shaping the spatial master plan. Both the organizational and sustainability master plans were then mainly developed by the client (i.e., the Inselspital).

To start the organizational masterplan, an intense quantitative analysis of medical data had to be undertaken. The aim was to visualize patient routes in order to determine the functional dependencies and physical proximity between clinical departments.

The Inselspital's mission statement puts the patient as the central focus. Therefore, an executive decision was made to make the patient process the key driver for future functional structures. The new core idea is interdisciplinary collaboration. This means that in the future, clinical departments cannot constitute spatially independent centers for specialists. Thus, a new organizational form had to be found for the Inselspital.

In the next step of the modelling process, the existing organizational structure was dissolved and replaced by a new model of 'gravitation.' The model simulated how closely different units approach each other when patient movements between them amplify the attraction. The result was a clear but not exactly surprising picture. The A&E, radiology and diagnostics units and operating rooms are medical core functions, which are strongly connected with most other disciplines. Consequently, these core functions need to be centrally located.

In 2012 the newly opened Accident, Emergency and Surgery Center INO with radiology and laboratory medicine houses these core functions. There was now a new requirement recognized for three medical centers: three other medical centers, i.e., the Comprehensive Cancer, Comprehensive Neuroscience and Comprehensive Cardiovascular Center should be sited in immediate adjacency of the INO. This pragmatic proposal, which reflects the day-to-day necessities of clinical process, found fast and broad approval among the hospital management. Thus, the first steps to develop the Inselspital site were set.

The Inselspital took its first steps toward a structured development immediately after the approval of the zoning plan in March 2015.

The realization of the Inselspital masterplan has been proceeding steadily. At this writing, at least four plots have been built or are nearing completion. Two further plots have also been subject to architectural competitions in 2020. On two core plots, the Organ and Tumor Center and the Swiss Comprehensive Cardiovascular Center, are being built. A new Center for Translational Research will form the face toward the city center on a plot close to the main entry route to the Inselspital site.

The zoning plan requires an architectural competition for each plot and the open space of the Inselspital site. The

MASTER PLAN FOR THE INSELSPITAL HOSPITAL CAMPUS

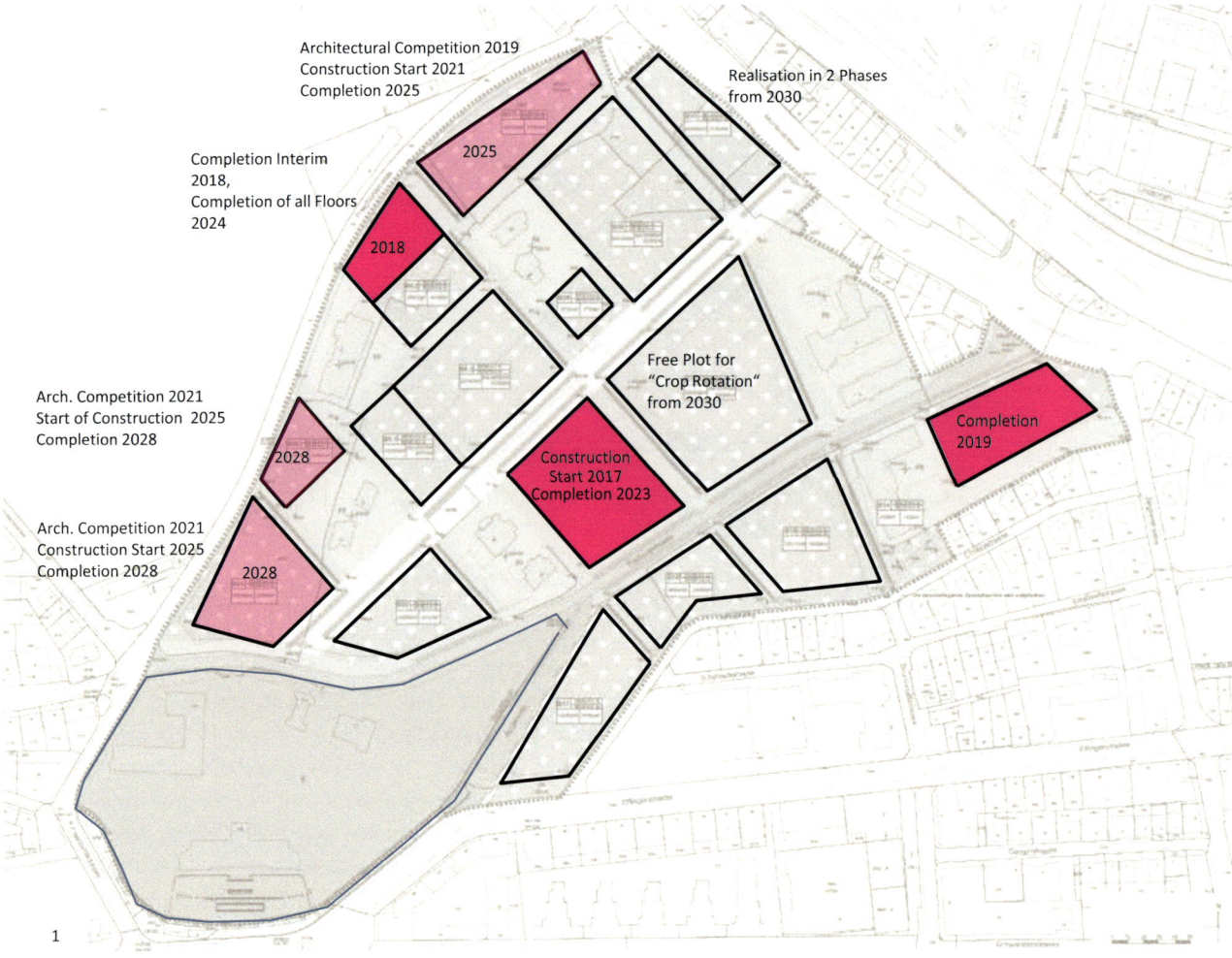

Figure 6 Implementation sequence following the master plan (*Credit*: HENN Architects)

architectural master plan has been complemented by an 'exterior master plan,' providing guidance on the structure of hard and soft landscaping.

Three project competitions have already taken place (as of 2021), with additional competitions planned in the near and distant future. Each of these project competitions will deal with a variety of architectural and organizational requirements for a huge, technically complex building project. Each of these competitions will see new participants and new jury members, selecting a winner based on different criteria. So not only context but also the actors will vary from project to project. Due to this variability, the question arises, "How will it be possible to keep in mind the bigger picture, i.e., the qualitative aspirations of the master plan?"

An advisory board was formed to steer the implementation of the master plan, deciding which plot will be built next and which function/user it needs to be built for. The advisory board consists of the heads of Inselgruppe, Bern city planning authorities, city council, Bern University, etc. That is the group of persons responsible for all high-level decisions regarding the Inselspital area. Even contrasting interests have to be brought to the table and discussed until they are resolved, which is a great democratic tool. Gunter Henn is part of the board in a consulting capacity.

As before in the Inselspital's long history, the site will continue to evolve and develop. Part of this process is to continue 'curating' the master plan in the long term.

RESIDENTIAL
Molenvliet
Papendrecht, the Netherlands

Figure 1 Aerial view of the Molenvliet project with its red-tile roofs in 2022 (*Source*: Google Earth)

Project Data

Location:	Papendrecht, the Netherlands
Architect:	Frans van der Werf, KOKON Architects
Construction:	Support: 1976; Infill: 1977 (renovations at intervals since that time)
Owner:	Housing Association 'Papendrecht'
Dwellings:	124 rental dwellings; 4 office spaces
Support construction:	Roos Bouw, Rotterdam: Concrete tunnel-formed concrete cast in place, with openings in slabs for shared vertical mechanical systems and internal stairs; kit-of-parts façade prefabricated off-site
Infill provision:	Nijhuis Infill System, Rijssen, completed by conventional Dutch interior construction
Unless noted, all photo and drawing credits:	Frans van der Werf

MOLENVLIET

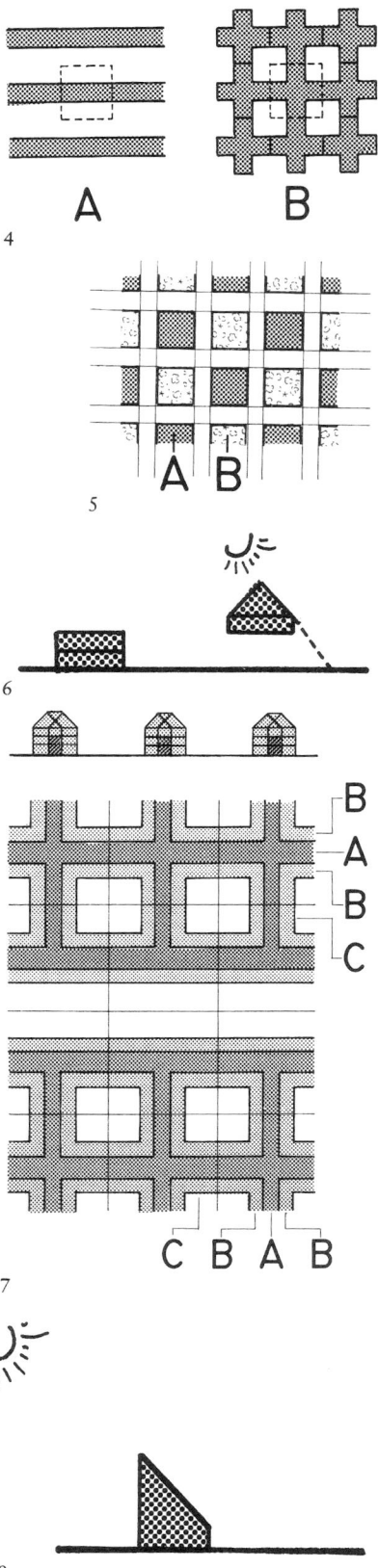

BACKGROUND

The winner of a competition for 2,800 dwellings at 30 dwelling units/hectare, this project won on the combined merits of its urban design, architecture and participatory decision-making process. It is organized on four environmental levels: the overall urban plan, the tissue or urban design plan, the Support and the Infill.

URBAN TISSUE

The principle of the *urban tissue* is a 'matrix,' as indicated in the diagram below (Figures 2, 3 and 4). Within that pattern, open-space 'courtyards' are alternately A type (entry courtyards) and B type (garden courtyards). The drawing shows a section view of the tissue, which also indicates the basic pattern of the *Support* (Base Building) vis-à-vis solar access.

The diagram also indicates the idea of 'zones' within the tissue diagram: Zone A is consistently built; Zone B is either built or open space. The B zone is therefore essentially an indication of the position and dimension of variations – a kind of capacity at the urban tissue level – evident in what was actually built. Zone C is consistently unbuilt/open space.

THE SUPPORT

The project's 123 realized dwellings surround courtyards in two- to four-story blocks featuring steeply pitched red-tile roofs. Most units are entered via several 'entry' courtyards, with backyards or rooftop terraces that open onto adjacent 'backyard' courts. All courts are closed to vehicular traffic (Figure 1).

The Support (Figures 6, 7) consists of a highly uniform cast-in-place concrete framework, with bearing walls all running in the same direction. Regularly spaced openings are provided in the slabs for vertical mechanical chases and stairs within individual units. To allow for variation and changeability in unit designs, placement of Support elements was determined by a series of capacity studies. Tunnel forms – reusable steel forms put in place and moved by cranes – were used in constructing the Support. The concrete walls between bays of the building are regularly spaced, with regular 'block-outs' making construction fast and efficient while still allowing a wide variety of unit sizes and

Figure 2 Use of Alexander's Pattern Language in developing the urban tissue concept

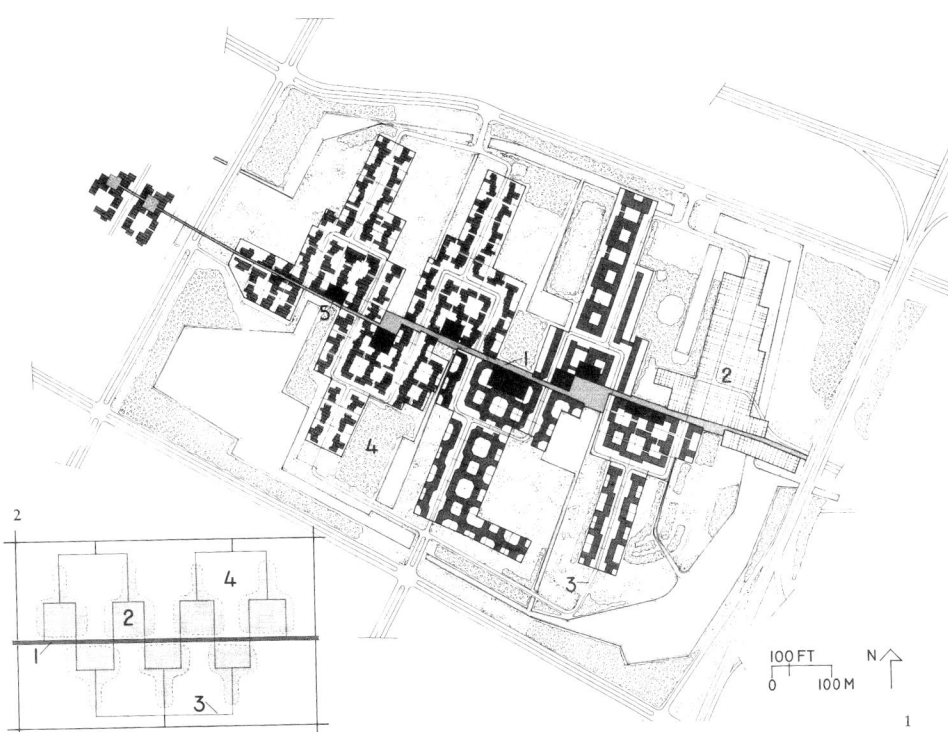

Figure 3 The principles of the urban tissue as it might be applied over a larger area of the town. The realized part of the master plan is to the upper left

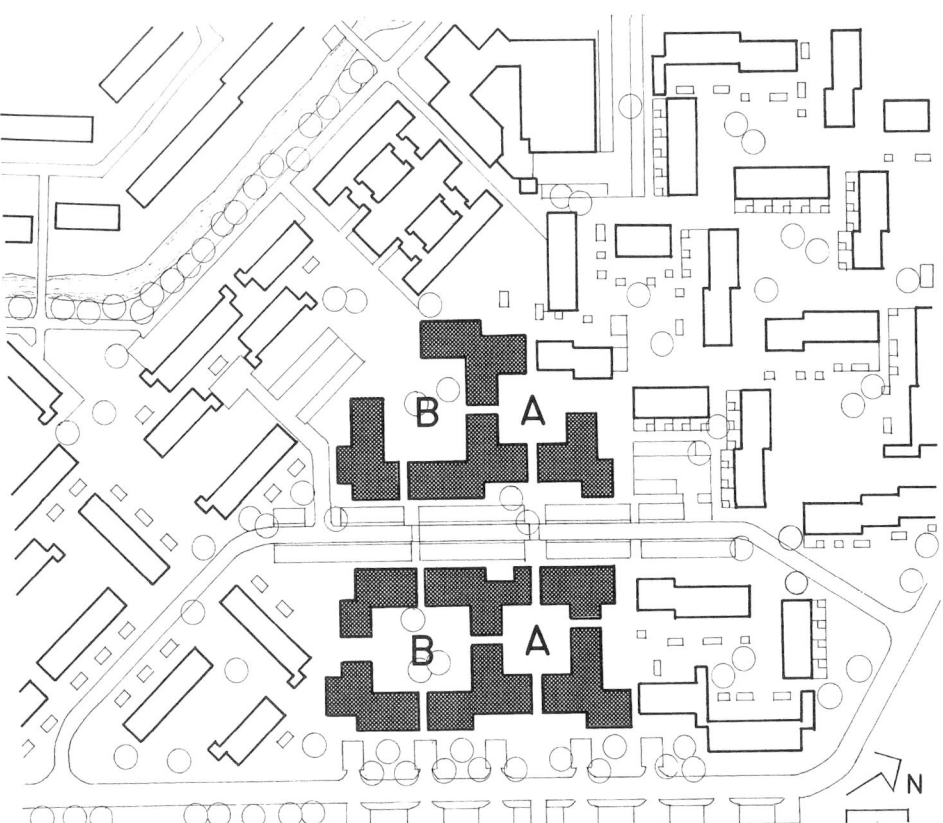

Figure 4 The principle of the urban tissue realized in the Support: a continuous building, 2 to 4 stories high, with alternating entry and garden courtyards and the central parking street

MOLENVLIET

Figure 5 An aerial view of the project, clearly showing the alternating courtyards and the parking street (Courtesy Frans van der Werf)

Figure 6 The Support construction

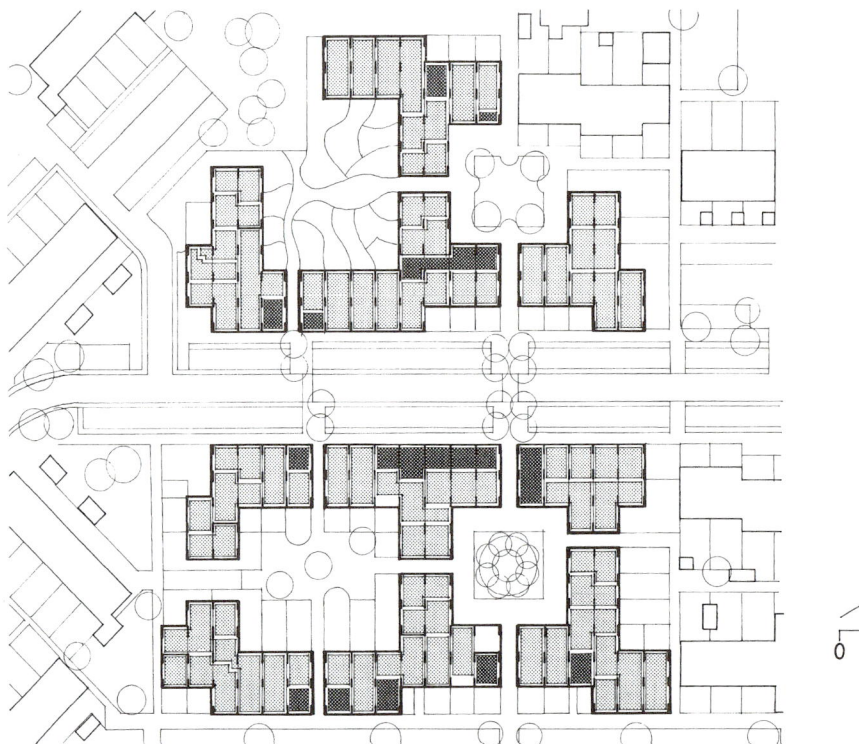

Figure 7 The Support, showing that the structure runs in one direction, within which dwellings of varying sizes can be made. Nonresidential functions are indicated in the dark tone, including shops and offices, generally on the ground level

configurations. A prefabricated wooden façade framework – an updated version of the typical medieval Dutch canal house façade comprised of a series of joined wooden frames – was installed as part of the Support (Figure 9).

Infill for each unit was determined after arranging units of required floor area, or 'parceling out' or subdivision of the support (Figure 8). This process, like the subsequent fitting out, involved user participation. Each household met individually on several occasions with the architect, progressing from rough sketches to final drawings. Once they had been signed by the occupants, these drawings were translated into construction documents. The Infill of each unit included interior walls, doors, trim and finishes; bathroom cabinets and equipment; kitchen cabinets and fixtures; electrical and mechanical equipment for the unit; closets; as well as the selection, configuration and color of window and doors inserted into the support façade framework.

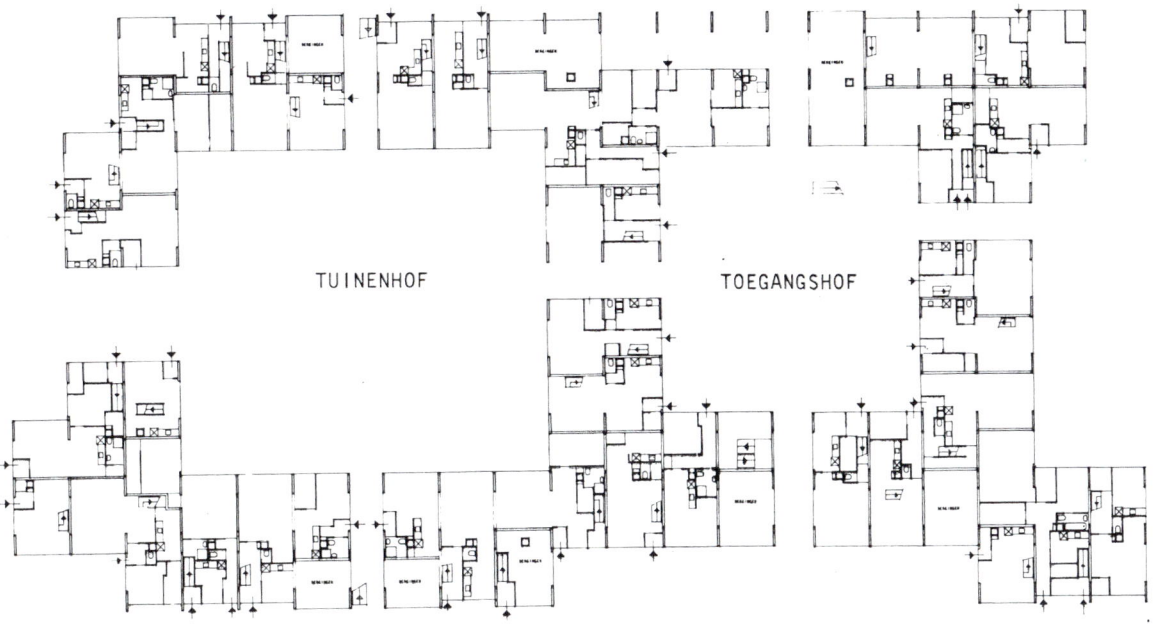

Figure 8 Ground-floor layout of dwellings showing the variation in unit sizes and layouts

Figure 9 A view of one of the entry courtyards in 2002. Façades are prefabricated wooden frames with panels (color and placement) selected by dwellers from a catalog specified by the architect. All courtyards (both entry and 'backyard') are connected by pedestrian passages, as seen here, at ground level and above

Figure 10 A resident's living room (Photo by Stephen Kendall)

FAÇADE

Large, subdivided window frames were part of a fixed design, but within each frame, tenants could select a variety of components and decide which parts should be transparent and which not, and where movable parts like doors and windows would go. Moreover, for each dwelling unit, two colors could be chosen, from a total of six, to paint the various façade parts. This way of working gave identity to the individual units by color and design and served their functional requirements. At the same time, it assured an overall harmonious architectural result. It was also technically simple and inexpensive (Figure 9).

The project incorporates many traditional elements of Dutch urban housing – pitched roofs, wooden windows, doors opening onto courtyards and some mixed use: the project incorporates doctor's offices, small shops and commercial offices, even a motorcycle parts shop. This project demonstrated that even in multifamily housing, the variation characterizing households can be expressed easily and beneficially on the exterior of the building. In this case, inhabitants worked with designers to determine window frame color and arrangement to complement the custom interior layout of each unit.

PERSONALIZATION OVER TIME

Interiors and rooftop gardens reflect the personal preferences of residents (Figure 10, 11).

Figure 11 A private rooftop garden (Photo by Stephen Kendall)

NEXT21
Osaka, Japan

Figure 1 NEXT21 in its urban context (*Photo credit*: Osaka Gas)

Project Data

Location:	Osaka, Japan
Planning/Design:	Osaka Gas and NEXT21 Planning Team (Utida, Tatsumi, Fukao, Takada, Chikazumi, Takama, Endo, Sendo)
Building Architect:	Yositika Utida, Shu-koh-Sha Architecture and Urban Design Studio
Construction:	Obayashi Corporation
Initial construction:	1994 (continuous ongoing renovations/transformations since)
Design system planning:	Kazuo Tatsumi, Mitsuo Takada
Dwelling design rules:	Mitsuo Takada, Osaka Gas, KBI Architects and Design Office
Modular coordination:	Seiichi Fukao
Owner:	Osaka Gas Company
Dwellings:	18 (some have been combined and divided over time)
Support (skeleton):	Reinforced concrete + Façade System (the façade has been reconfigured over time corresponding to changes in unit designs)
Infill provision:	Various companies

BACKGROUND

Within the context of Open Building, the NEXT21 project introduced a number of innovations, some of which still have not been equaled by later initiatives.

Professor Yositika Utida, the leader of the team of architects invited by Osaka Gas to design NEXT21, once described the project as 'three-dimensional urban design." This concept is indeed a logical result of the separation of Base Building (Support) and Infill (S/I). This large building is no longer a building but becomes part of an 'urban tissue.' Just like a city is extended by the design of streets and squares complete with trees and sidewalks and the utility lines underground, NEXT21 provides public space of bridges, elevators, stairs and corridors/pathways connecting a public garden on the ground floor with another one on the roof. The public circulation in three dimensions from the street level to roof garden connects individual dwellings to the urban street network, and just as in urban design, these individual dwellings can be built, changed, removed and replaced like buildings along a street.

Although the NEXT21 project fills no more than half a block, it is easy to imagine its concept applied on a larger scale, accommodating a very large number of individual dwellings in a three-dimensional urban fabric. The transformation of the large building into a neighborhood, offering internal public spaces that give access to dwellings that can be shaped individually, is perhaps the greatest potential of the Open Building approach. NEXT21 shows how this can lead to a new architecture and urbanism that is different from just 'flexible buildings.'

PROFESSIONAL COOPERATION ON TWO LEVELS

A design team in collaboration with architect Shinichi Chikazumi guided the entire project. Thirteen different architects were initially invited to design the 18 individual houses contained within the NEXT21 framework. This was a logical step once this vision of a three-dimensional urban fabric had been adopted.

In all Open Building projects, design decisions are made on several levels: the lower level of the interior fit-out (Infill) is to accommodate the user, while the higher level contains all that the users have in common: the load-bearing structure, the main utility systems and the public spaces.

To have separate architects do the lower-level design is consistent with conventional practice in urbanism, office and shopping center construction. The traditional urban designer expects other architects to do the buildings along the streets and squares she proposes. In the case of office buildings and shopping centers, large areas of empty floor space are made available, and leaseholders are expected to hire their own architect to design interior layout and finishes. The same can work in residential Open Building as well as other kinds of buildings shown in this part of the book.

In the case of NEXT21, only a few of the dwellings were designed in direct response to the demands of the inhabitants. In most cases, Osaka Gas submitted 'user scenarios' as 'guidance documents' for the architects to follow. This was done to obtain a wide range of different lifestyles that could demonstrate the buildings' capacity to accommodate a variety of dwelling solutions. It also secured a broad base for ongoing research. Having the individual dwellings designed by different architects could stimulate variety even more. At the same time, this way of separating and delegating design responsibility suggested a new model of professional cooperation among designers to better serve an emerging, consumer-oriented real estate market.

DIMENSIONAL AND POSITIONAL COORDINATION GRIDS

Organizing all the different players and all of the piping and cabling infrastructure without conflict, in combination with the deployment of internal partitioning and the equipment of bathrooms and kitchens, posed a very difficult methodological problem. The NEXT21 design team confronted this problem in a sophisticated way. By doing so, they have expanded our knowledge about the use of coordinating grids and zoning. Based on the careful studies of Professor Seiichi Fukao, in close cooperation with Shinichi Chikazumi of Shu-koh-sha Design Studio, coordinating grids on several levels, closely interrelated, organize the design of all the subsystems. This methodological aspect of the NEXT21 project should be studied carefully.

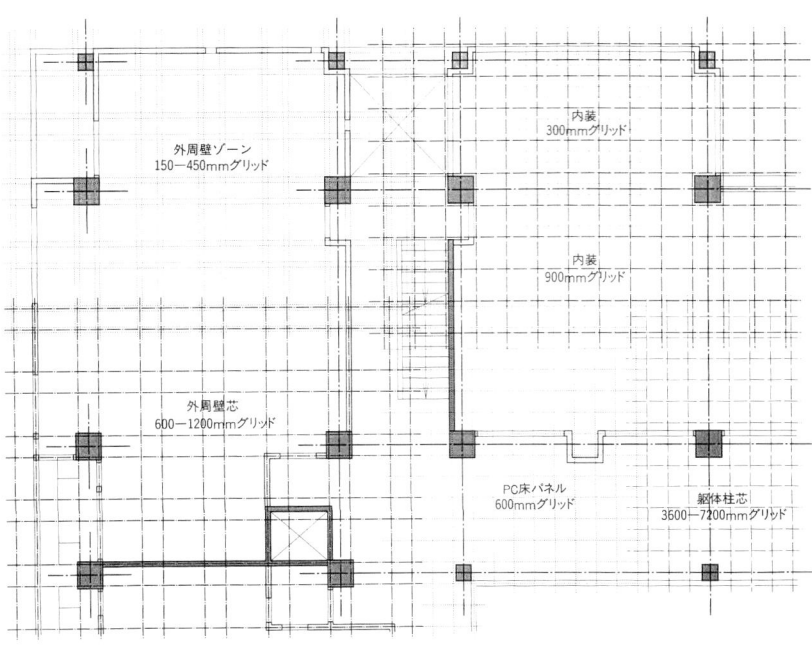

Figure 2 Dimensional coordinating grids used to manage the separated design tasks (*Credit*: SHU-KOH-SHA)

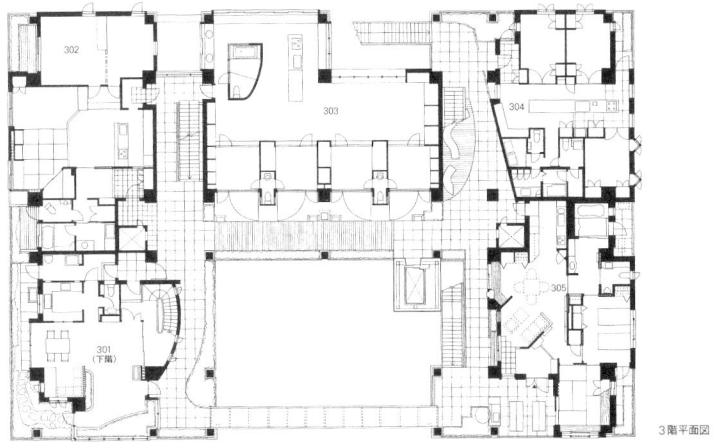

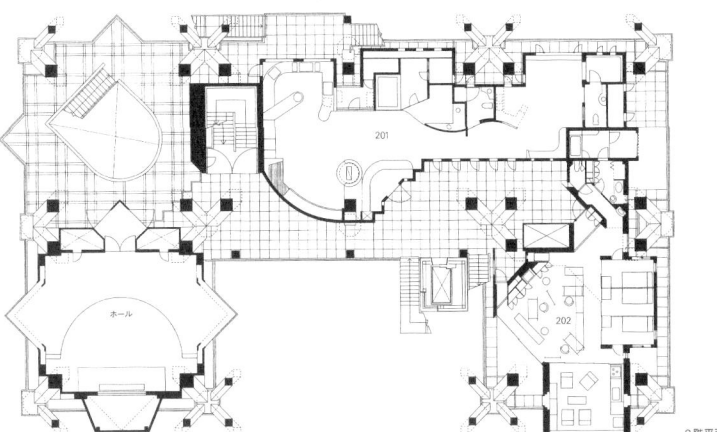

Figure 3 Two floor plans showing wide variety of dwelling layouts, each designed by a different architect and utilizing the coordinating grids (*Credit*: Osaka Gas Company)

PRIVATE GARDENS

Another innovation consistent with the idea of a 'three-dimensional urban structure' was to provide individual units with their own exterior green space distinct from the common gardens on the ground level and on the roof of the building. Several of the units had small outside spaces for plantings as part of the private residential territory. Of course, the size and number of such little 'gardens' depended on the individual unit designs (which could change over time). But the addition of green outside spaces was encouraged as part of the overall experiment, and the high space available for ducts under the floors made it easier to grow plants.

THE FAÇADE SYSTEM

A façade system was designed specifically for the NEXT21 lower-level design. Using the system, each architect could design a façade reflecting the interior layout of individual dwellings. Keeping in mind future changes, the façade system was designed in such a way that it could be taken apart and installed again 'from the inside,' without need for exterior scaffolding.

Figure 4 Private gardens and the public rooftop garden. The façade system, designed by one team, is used differently by each architect responsible for each individual dwelling. Some changes to dwelling unit plans called for adding outdoor garden space; some required eliminating or moving outdoor terraces (*Photo credit*: Osaka Gas)

In the Open Building experience, the role of the façade has been a difficult but important issue. A range of solutions has been considered over time. Proposals have been made that each unit should be entirely free to publicly express – on the exterior – its own interior as well as its owner's personal stylistic preference. Le Corbusier's famous Algiers proposal already suggested this possibility more than 70 years ago, and among the ill-fated Operation Breakthrough ideas for innovative housing solutions in the early 1970s in the US was a proposal for a minimal load-bearing framework containing a variety of house designs.

At the other end of the spectrum are the many OB projects that limit themselves to interior variety behind a fixed façade designed for the entire building.

Making façade parts demountable and replaceable requires sophisticated detailing. If, moreover, the façade's position must be flexible as well, parts of the floor and ceiling that first were interior may become exterior or the other way around, posing a number of difficult technical problems. For practical reasons alone, a strong case can be made for a fixed façade design behind which interior variety is possible.

In many countries in history, façades always sought to express individual dwellings within a given typology, resulting in a rich and thematic variety along an entire street wall. In contrast, the Parisian boulevards show how uniform and monumental façades can shape urban space without expressing interior variety. The same can be observed around the Bloomsbury squares in London and the public spaces of St. Petersburg. Different cultures seem to have different preferences in different times. The question whether the façade – or parts of it – should follow higher-level design or lower-level design is not just technical but has important cultural aspects.

The NEXT21 project offered a new possibility: its façade system is part of the higher-level concept intended for overall application. But the actual use of the system is part of the lower-level design. This combines lower-level variety and change over time with higher-level harmony on an urban scale. Here, too, NEXT21 set a most interesting new precedent.

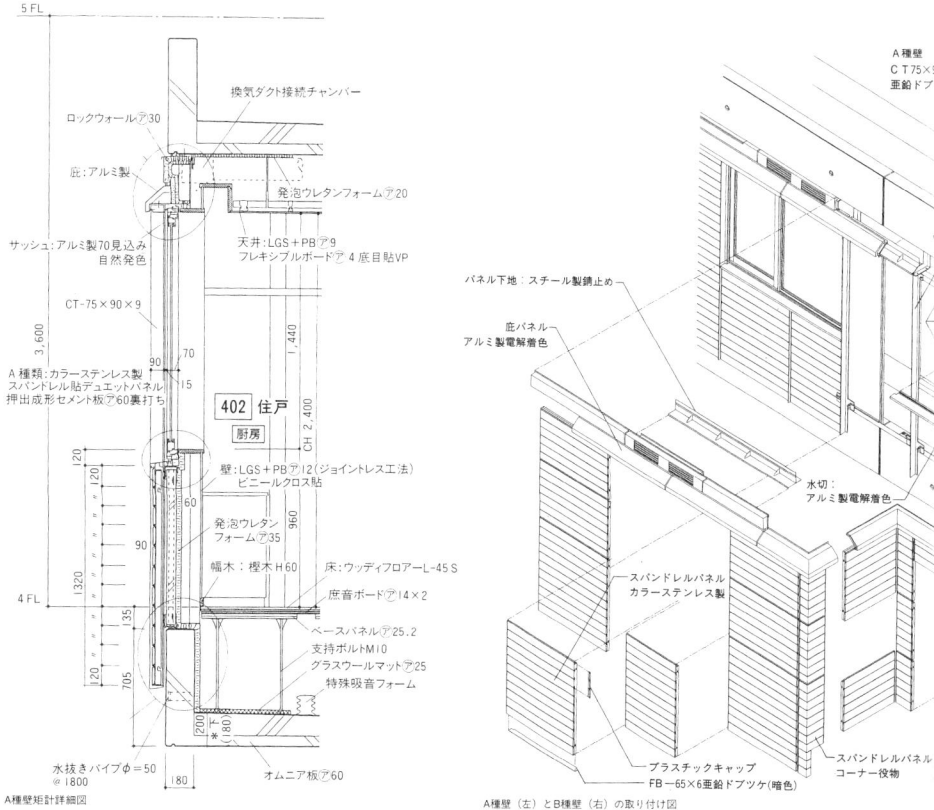

Figure 5 The NEXT21 façade system (Copyright: SHU-KOH-SHA)

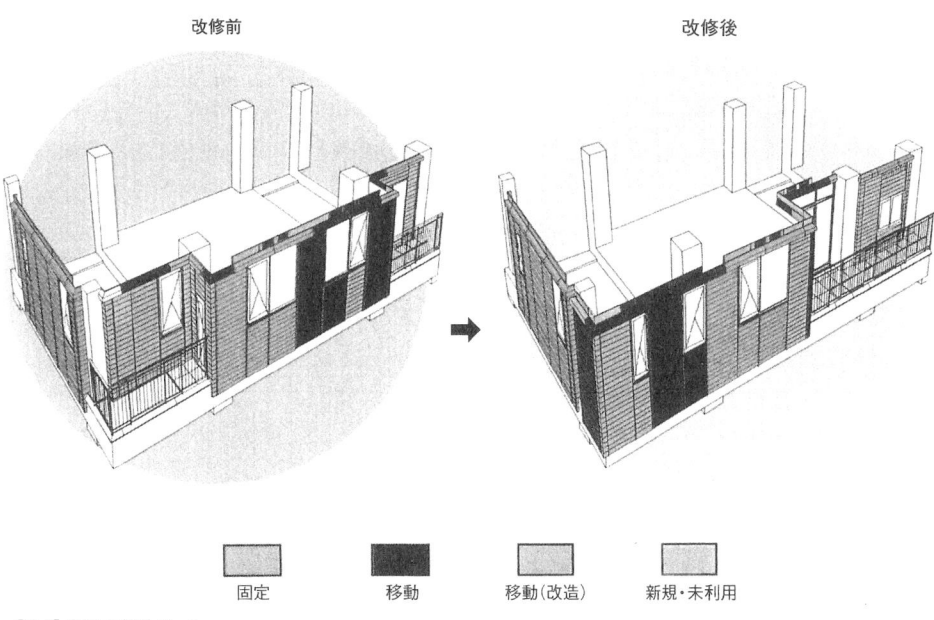

Figure 6 Complete change of a dwelling unit floor plan and the associated change in its façade, showing that some elements are rearranged, some are introduced from a storage of façade elements and some are put into storage for future use (*Credit*: Shu-Ko-Sha)

CHANGING DWELLING UNIT INTERIORS

Over the years, many of the original dwelling units have changed, part of the experiment with adjusting Infill to changing lifestyles of a variety of household sizes and preferences. During those changes, the interior Infill elements are stripped out, leaving only the skeleton and the insulated façade, as shown in Figure 7.

One such change is pictured in Figure 8, in which Unit 404 changed within the boundaries of the original space.

Figure 7 A view of one dwelling space after its Infill was removed, in readiness for a new Infill (*Photo credit*: Osaka Gas)

Another dwelling (Unit 304) also underwent changes, as shown in the following Figures 9 and 10.

AN OPEN BUILDING RESEARCH LABORATORY

In the years after its initial completion in 1994, the NEXT21 project has served as a laboratory for a large number of experiments. This was consistent with Osaka Gas's solid reputation for innovative research in building technology and environmental control systems in buildings. There is no precedent in the Open Building experience of a similar long-term commitment to research by a single company, and here again, the NEXT21 project sets an example.

As already noted, not all research projects done in the NEXT21 context are specific Open Building issues. Development of new heating/cooling sources and waste management systems are stand-alone subjects. But the distribution of utility lines, including cabling, ducts and piping of all kinds to each unit, is very much an Open Building issue. For future 'three-dimensional urban frameworks' to serve future generations, service lines must coincide with public spaces in the frameworks to allow their renewal, maintenance or replacement as new technology develops. Moreover, the testing of a 'computerized energy-providing service,' for instance, could be done because users actually participated in it, contributing valuable feedback information.

Many other parts of the extensive research agenda have direct bearing on the Open Building approach. All were related to the redesign and change of dwelling units, a process that led to a reexamination of many issues.

There are, of course, the experiments dealing with the technical issues of changeable or flexible Infill and also the displacement of parts of the façade system as examples of new product development and evaluation.

There are also the lifestyle-oriented social studies in which the small-scale interaction between user and equipment and space is considered. And there are also design-oriented research items on the agenda, like the scenario-based technique of housing planning and also the study of the capacity of a given floor plan in which an entire range of possible use scenarios could be accommodated by shifting the position of the kitchen unit combined with a few minor alterations of doors and partitions.

It is important to note that for all of these experiments and studies, the NEXT21 infrastructure was available and remains in continual use. Similar research issues have been conducted in the past, but because no real-life experimental environment was available, they necessarily had to be done in a more abstract manner. The availability of a real-life adaptable environment offered a new and very different context for study and experiment, the potential of which we have yet to fully understand.

If we look at the NEXT21 project as a permanent environment for experimentation, we begin to appreciate its almost total 'openness' as compared to most other Open Building projects. To successfully realize an Open Building project in real life within the budgets normally available and for the sake of users with average needs and preferences, the question as to what can be fixed for all the inhabitants and what must be adaptable for the individual is crucial. We have learned that 'maximum' flexibility is not only impractical but also undesirable. What is fixed and common has real meaning, and the balance with what is adaptable and individual must be studied each time with great care. The answer to that question will be different from project to project, depending

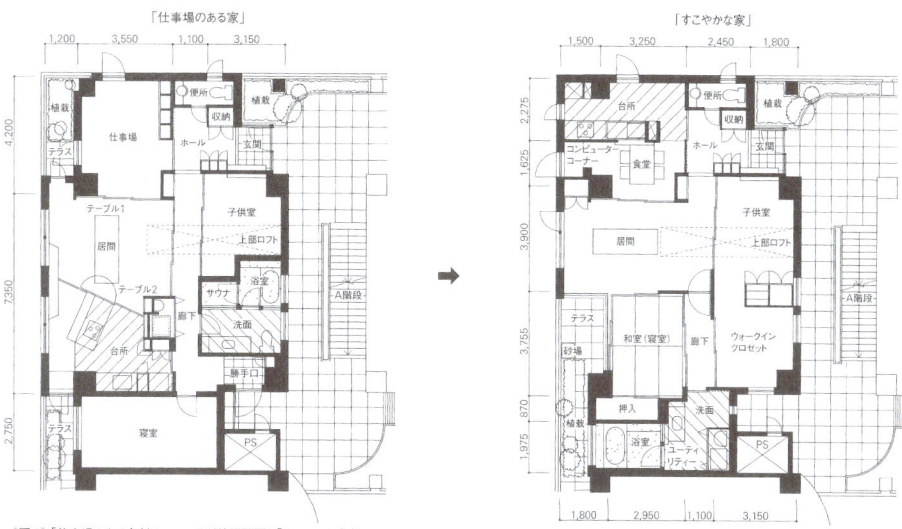

Figure 8 Drawing showing how one dwelling unit (404) was changed within the same space (*Credit*: Osaka Gas)

Figure 9 Unit 304 before renovation (*Credit*: Osaka Gas)

Figure 10 Unit 304 after renovation (*Credit*: Osaka Gas)

on the agents involved and the culture we try to serve. The question must remain on the table until enough experience has been gained. Only when Open Building has become a general and normal approach will we understand more fully how that balance can work well and will we be able to make predictions. And even then, we can safely assume, there will be more than one answer.

For an Open Building project to serve as a laboratory, as in the case with NEXT21, an extremely 'open' technical solution is the right answer; experiments can be done without pre-determined constraints. The NEXT21 environment is indeed a large systemic composition within which the balance between truly collective and permanent on the one hand and truly individual and adaptable on the other hand can be experimented with.

THE PRESENT AND FUTURE CONTEXT FOR NEXT21

The completion of NEXT21 in 1994 implied a long-term commitment by Osaka Gas Company toward Open Building experimentation. That commitment continues. This too was a precedent. Many earlier projects of an experimental character had been the result of extraordinary efforts by architects, clients and government agencies, but so far, they had been one-at-a-time events. It is in the nature of the building industry to experiment on an ad-hoc basis just as the entire industry operates on a project-by-project basis.

Ad-hoc experimentation allows the demonstration of the separation of two levels of design control. NEXT21 did this in a rigorous and convincing way. But the development of new and more flexible subsystems is another matter. This cannot be done as easily on an ad-hoc basis, and here, NEXT21 could do something entirely new. It offered a stable context for installation and comparison of new subsystems that might become available over

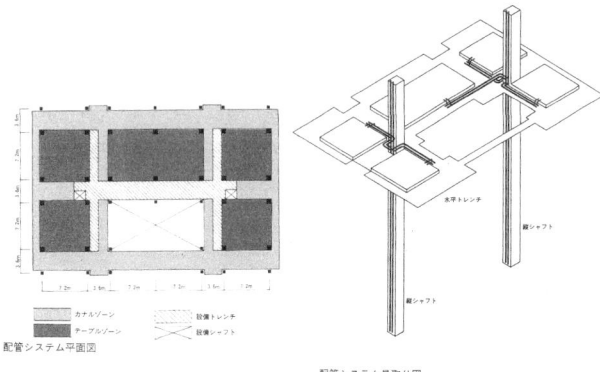

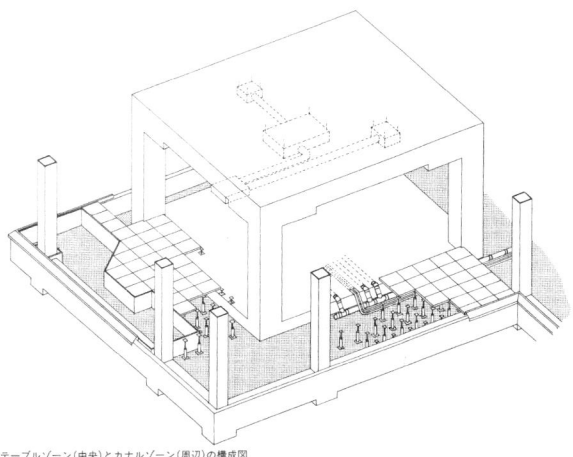

Figure 11 a, b, c: (a) Plan of a typical level showing (in dark gray) the 'tables' for dwellings surrounded by common spaces for horizontal MEP distribution; (b) diagram showing the deployment of vertical MEP systems; (c) diagram of one 'cell' showing the hollow floor under the common spaces in which Base Building MEP is placed, and internal to the dwellings, under the raised floor and dropped ceiling (*Credit*: Osaka Gas)

time. The desire for easier installation and better service already had moved the market in the direction of the Open Building approach. For instance, in the last quarter century, we have witnessed the introduction of flexible and 'home-run' water lines, snap-together drainage piping with push-fit joints, smaller and more efficient hot water units capable of heating a single dwelling and small enough to fit in a closet, new space-cooling systems, electric cabling by means of click-together connections, easier-to-be-installed partition systems, 0-slope gray water drainage systems and many other improvements.

As the Open Building approach makes progress, it becomes increasingly desirable for new products and sub-systems to be tested in an Open Building context. Here, the example of the Osaka Gas Company may lead to emulation. We may eventually witness the emergence of similar experimental sites where new subsystems can be demonstrated and tested in a context of real-life inhabitation and management. Such permanent experimental sites might be run either by the manufacturing industry consortia harnessing pre-competitive R&D agreements, government bodies or public/private organizations.

A NOTE FROM SHINICHI CHIKAZUMI, ONE OF THE ARCHITECTS OF NEXT21

"Why did the SI concept rapidly lose momentum in Japan? This is a question I ask myself.

I continue to experiment with the remodeling of NEXT21 with the exact same passion as before, having remodeled 11 units in 18 years from 1994 to 2022. I am currently planning to remodel one unit for 2025. Osaka Gas has not lost any of its ambition, and the SI concept still attracts more than 1,000 visitors during the open-house period each year.

Everyone says that NEXT21 is exceptional. No other company can compete with it. Osaka Gas continues to spend a lot of money to maintain the number-one position. I believe it is possible to keep the NEXT21 concept and turn it into a commercially viable approach. However, the reason why no Japanese developers are willing to ask me to do so is because Japanese developers have no challenging spirit to break out of their old framework. They have a safe business and make enough profit by selling buildings and the land as a set as they always have.

In Japan, the business of building new detached houses in large quantities is still successful. People are jumping into the new houses and leaving the houses they have lived in unoccupied. Millions of vacant houses have already been created. I do not believe that a business and an industry as distorted as this can continue much longer." (Shinichi Chikazumi, President, Shu-Ko-Sha Architecture an Urban Design Studio, April 2023)

Plus-Home

Arabianranta, Helsinki, Finland

Figure 1 Garden side of the project, showing large sliding screens on each south-facing balcony that can be used for privacy (*Photo credit*: Petri Viita, ArkOpen Ltd.)

ARABIANRANTA
Project Data

Project location:	Kaj Frankinkatu, Helsinki, Finland
Chronological information:	Completed in 2005
Project design team:	Architects Esko Kahri and Petri Viita (Kahri and Co.), Petri Viita, Juhani Väisänen and PlusHome Ltd. project team authors; Esko Enkovaara and Timo Taiponen (formerly Tocoman)
Number of dwelling units:	77
Project site and building area:	Site area: 3,900 m^2/floor area 6,600 m^2
Project client:	Private developer SATO
Structure type:	Steel frame, hollow core slabs + 'upside-down floor system'
Installation utilities:	Horizontal piping installation and piping layout per dwelling is installed in a 'wet zone' in an 'upside-down floor system,' with adaptable electric distribution system in all partition walls
Infill system/approach:	Clear separation of Infill and Support. The information system was developed to coordinate inhabitants, designers, client and developers.

BACKGROUND

In 2002, the second of several technology competitions was organized by the city of Helsinki. The winning PlusHome proposal was developed by architect Esko Kahri (Kahri and Co.) and Tocoman data-cost office with SATO as developer. On that basis, Kahri and Tocoman founded the PlusHome company and, together with SATO, started a working relationship with a focus on customer orientation and implementation of Open Building principles.

The pilot project is located in the neighborhood of Arabianranta. This new housing area along the seashore was developed starting in 2000. It is located about 5 km (3 miles) from the city center.

PlusHome consists of three decision levels: a building structure and envelope that allows variations of apartment sizes, different layout options within given apartment sizes and a selection of surface materials and fixtures that inhabitants can choose from. The PlusHome concept enables a high degree of dwelling unit variability through technical solutions.

This project consists of one six- and one five-story-high building with, at time of sale, 77 for-sale dwellings ranging in size between 39 and 125 m^2 (420–1,345 ft.^{2}). There is a 84 m^2 (904 ft.^{2}) commercial space on the street level, as well as seven street-level workshop spaces for artisans, four of which are connected directly to the dwellings above by internal stairs.

THE BASE BUILDING

The structural frame differs from traditional building methods in Finland. Here, the load-bearing walls are the longitudinal outer walls instead of the inner cross-walls dividing the apartment units. This allows a higher degree of longitudinal variation of unit sizes within the Support. The outer walls are made of steel frames on which the precast concrete floor slabs bear. Most of the slabs are hollow-core concrete slabs with a 10 m (32.8") span, which is popular in Finland. In the 'zones' where wet spaces (bathrooms and kitchens) are considered likely, a special floor design is used in order to allow plumbing to be accessible from the top – i.e., from the spaces served. It uses steel beams with regular holes for horizontal piping, a concrete 'bottom' slab providing fire and

Figure 2 Detail of the sliding privacy screens on large, south-facing balconies (*Photo credit*: Petri Viita, ArkOpen Ltd.)

acoustical separation and a removable top concrete slab. The hollow-core slabs, steel-frame outside walls, vertical piping in staircases and horizontal zones make the basic structure renewable over time. An accessible hollow profile at the top of interior non–load-bearing metal-stud/gypsum board walls allows free placements of electrical and low-voltage wires, which run down inside the walls to switches and plugs, allowing easy change or addition of terminations later. The exterior load-bearing steel frames allowed for off-site fabrication in large elements, as well as an almost unlimited option of window placements. Walls between apartments are not load-bearing; they are of light construction with double plasterboards on steel studs providing standard acoustical isolation. The façades are redbrick or clad with thermal plastering; some parts use profiled metal plates. Large balconies for each dwelling, running across the south façade of the building, have shading elements on rollers to allow occupants to freely

PLUS-HOME

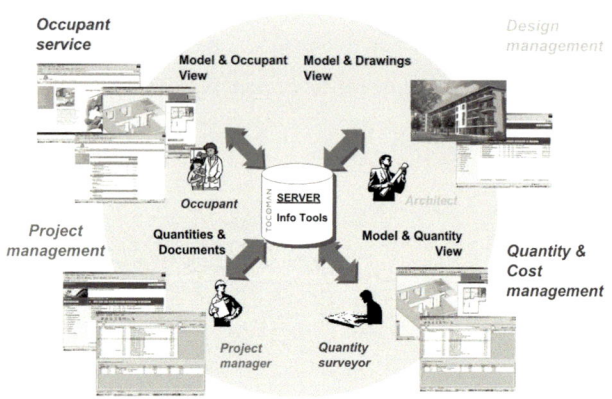

Figure 3 A diagram of the information system developed by IT and data consulting company Tocoman (*Credit*: Tocoman)

position them as desired. One innovation was the steel building frame (which received an award from the Finnish Steel Industry Association).

INFORMATION/DATA MANAGEMENT SYSTEM

The other main innovation was the information system developed by IT and data consulting company Tocoman, which ensured good management of the added complexity for the project.

The data management system allowed the architect to work on the model, with real-time project quantity and cost information and an online internet platform for inhabitants' use. Residents could choose between alternative floor plans, which were presented in the premarketing stage via internet. A wide selection of floor plans was offered, both different apartment sizes and variations within the same size. This stage was open till about 6 months after the construction started. The building would fill up following the sequence of inhabitants' choices. All the floors became individualized. After that, inhabitants had another 3 months to choose surface materials and fixtures while seeing an instant cost estimation of their choices. The buyers could see the change in the total price of their apartment directly after making their choices and could also go back and revise before finally accepting the order. After selections, quantity information was

Figure 4 Drawing showing how, within a simple Base Building structure, a large variety of dwelling unit sizes and layouts could be offered (*Credit*: ArkOpen Ltd.)

automatically collected and delivered to the contractors. This system allowed smooth implementation on a rather large scale.

CAPACITY FOR DWELLING VARIATION

The design of the project, supported by the PlusHome data management system, enabled residents to choose from a wide selection of unit sizes and layouts, as shown in Figures 4 and 5.

THE FLOOR SYSTEM FOR ACCESS TO HORIZONTAL DISTRIBUTION OF PIPING

INTERIOR VIEWS OF DWELLING UNITS

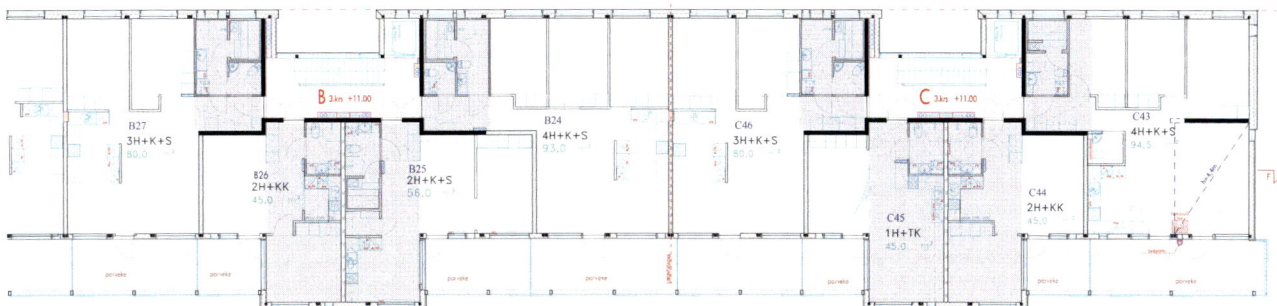

Figure 5 Drawing of part of one floor, showing the variety of dwelling unit sizes and layouts. Of particular interest is the variety of positions of bathrooms and kitchens, made possible by the Kvantti-zone floor system (toned area, also Figures 6 and 7). Also shown (in black) are the concrete shear walls around the elevator/stairs as well as the steel-frame columns at the building's façade (*Credit*: ArkOpen Ltd.)

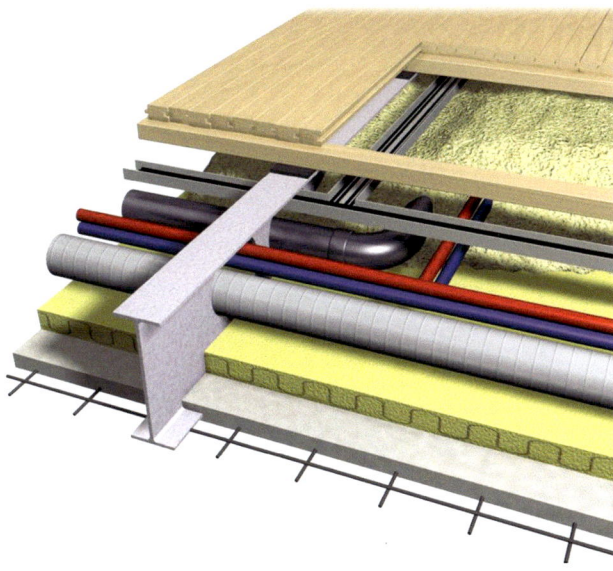

Figure 6 A drawing of the Kvantti-slab floor system, making piping for bathrooms and kitchens accessible from the top, in a zone near the fire stair and elevator cores (*Credit*: ArkOpen Ltd.)

Figure 7 The two-part Kvantti-zone floor system under construction. The 'upside-down' floor – also shown in Figure 6 – was only used in the zones where bathrooms and kitchens were expected to be placed. The rest of the floor structure used conventional hollow-core precast concrete slabs spanning the entire width of the building and resting on the steel façade (*Photo credit*: Petri Viita, ArkOpen Ltd.)

Figure 8 Photo of the interior of one of the dwelling units (*Photo credit*: Petri Viita, ArkOpen Ltd.)

Figure 9 Photo of the interior of one of the two-floor 'mezzanine' dwelling units at the top of the building (*Photo credit*: Petri Viita, ArkOpen Ltd.)

TILA
Helsinki, Finland

Figure 1 View of TILA from the south

Project Data
Location: Helsinki, Finland
Building architect: Pia Ilonen, TALLI Architects, Helsinki (now ILO Architects Ltd)
Developer: Sato Development
Construction: Support: 1.5 years from 2007–2008. Infill: from 2008 on, requiring from 1 month to 1 year depending on each occupant's decisions
Owner: Housing company (Asunto Oy°© the shareholders and inhabitants)
Dwellings: 39 'loft' dwellings
Support: Concrete structure; access balconies of steel
Infill provision: Various DIY and professionally installed Infill
Image credits: ILO architects have all the rights for the images and photos. The exterior photos are by KUVIO; interior photos are by Stefan Bremer.

BACKGROUND

The TILA housing block, comprising 39 loft apartments, is a pilot project for neo-loft apartments in the Arabianranta neighborhood of Helsinki. The apartments face southward through a fully glazed façade and with a balcony running the whole width of each dwelling. The dimensions and structure of the apartments allow for the occupants to build an upper--floor mezzanine or gallery. The neo- loft concept is based on the concept that within the available building frame, the resident determines and builds the required subdivision of spaces. The dwellings are occupiable at the moment of purchase (they have bathrooms) but become completely habitable with the installation of kitchen equipment. The residents can build individual rooms or expand their dwellings with gallery--type spaces, because the height of the main space is 5 meters (16.4"). The basic loft unit of the TILA housing block is 102 m² (1,098 sq. ft.), including two bathrooms (Figure 5).

The Base Building is carefully prepared. The bearing concrete structure of the floors allow for the occupants to build an upper-floor gallery. The dimensions of the unit are such that it makes possible a lot of layout variations (capacity). The technical connections for the kitchen, which are located on the main room side of the bathroom modules, allow for different kitchen layouts, especially in the bigger 102 m² unit, which has two bathrooms installed as part of the Base Building. Because it was obvious that people are not so good in knowing all the regulations, the architect made a booklet of instructions for how to manage the process.

DEVELOPMENT/OCCUPANCY PROCESS

The development-occupancy process was as follows: Base Building: normal time 1.5 years from 2007–2008. Building (Infill) from 2008 on: from 1 month to 1 year depending on what each occupant did. In case someone bought a 50 m² space with a ready-made gallery floor, they could just install the kitchen and start living. In case of bigger units and bigger families with rooms, it took longer.

Figure 2 The empty 'raw space' with the layout of the dwelling marked on the floor

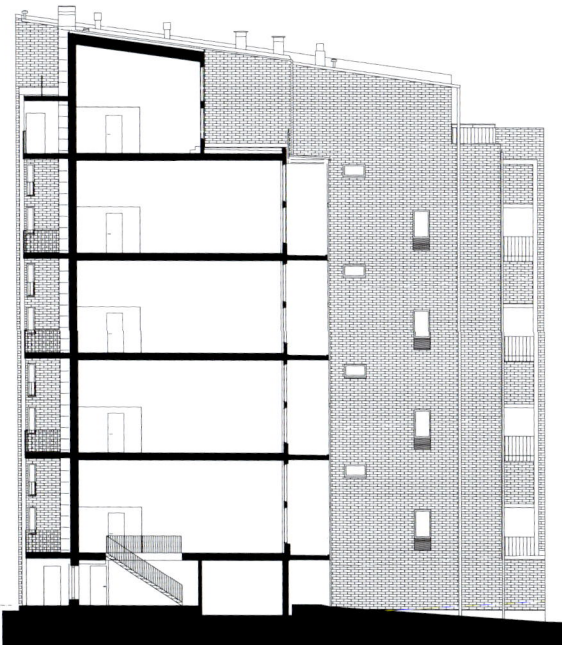

Figure 3a The building cross section

TILA

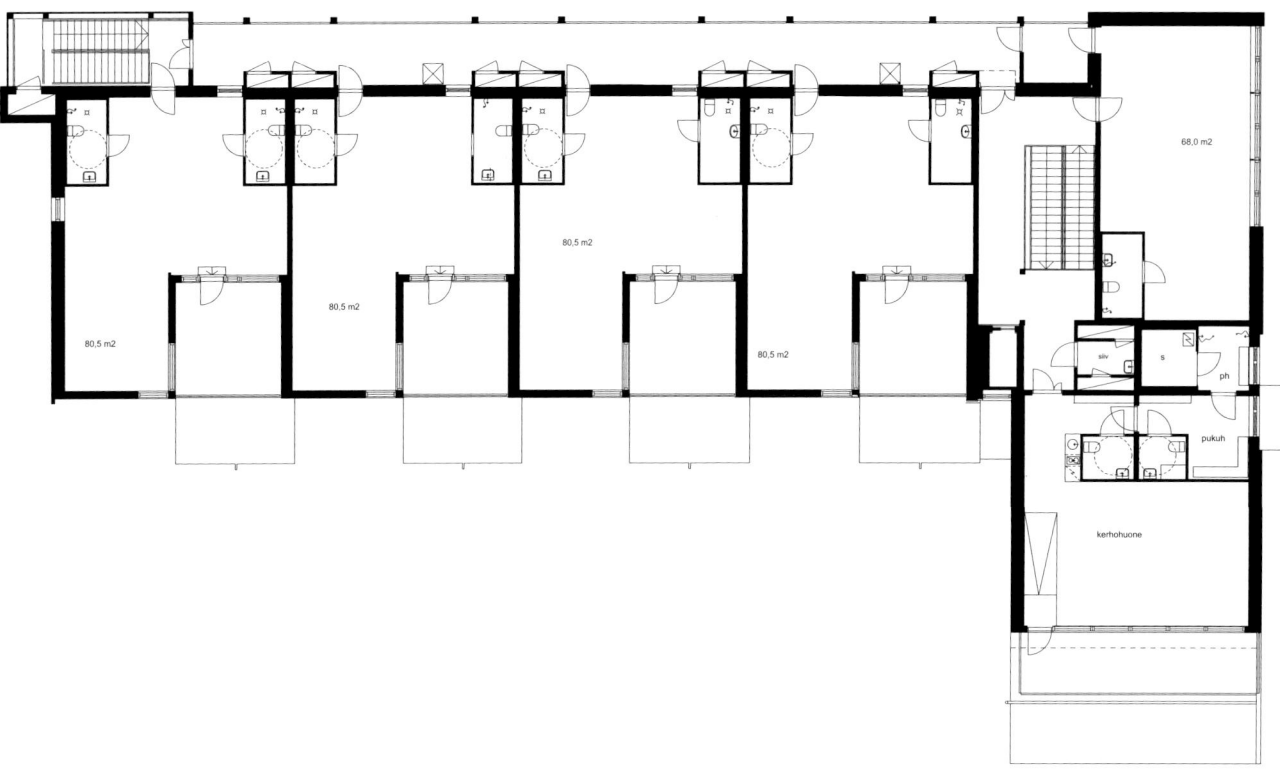

Figure 3b Fifth-floor Base Building

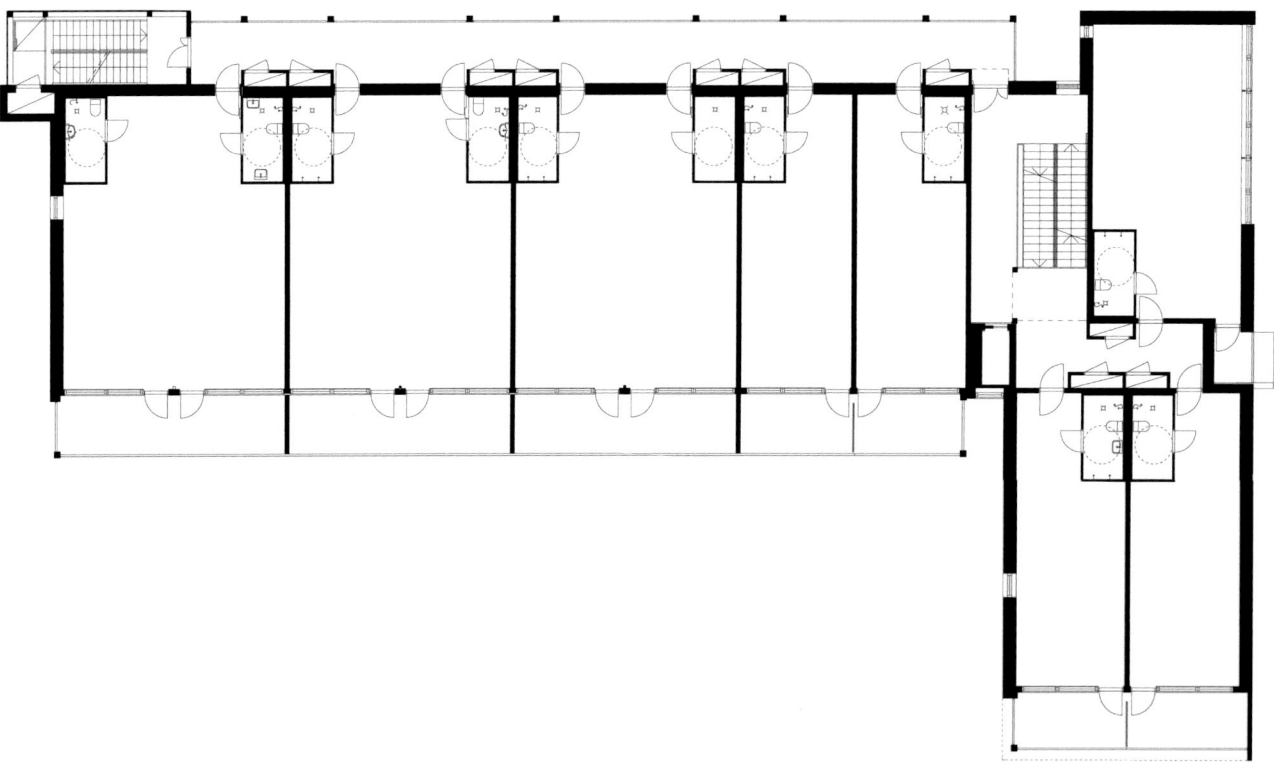

Figure 3c Second-floor Base Building

TILA

Figure 4 a, b (4a) Upper drawing – third floor, finished; (4b) lower drawing – the mezzanine of the third floor, finished (Infill is shown in red)

REGULATORY REVIEW PROCESS

The city building official inspected the whole building as usual before the 'moment of purchase,' that is, before the Sato developer with their constructors finished their job. That was also the end of the architects' role in the project. Every apartment was then 'habitable,' a big one-room apartment. The question of what is habitable was very important to discuss with officials and lawyers in the early stage of the concept-design.

Figure 5 The bathroom module in place during construction of the Base Building

For them, the fact that there was the so-called wet space with water isolations on the floor and walls ready-made (i.e., the bathroom) was sufficient. As for kitchens, it was enough to show the outlets for electricity, drainage and water supply and ventilation for the kitchens, which are located on the main room side of the bathroom module (which allows for different kitchen layouts – and are of course left for the occupants to build themselves).

As for inspectors, after the developer leaves the building, the housing company, i.e., the shareholders, inhabitants, own the building. It is up to inhabitants what you do and when you do it, and which designers and contractors/building companies you use if you are not building yourself. The situation is very much the same when you buy an old apartment and start renovating it. In all housing companies, the company has to take care that if the 'shareholders' make changes, they have to contact the board of the housing company.

When you are constructing bearing structures (like the gallery floor in TILA), you have to follow the building regulations and have all the required building permissions from the city building inspections department for that.

In principle, you could just take your mattress and espresso machine and start loft living . . .

INDIVIDUALIZATION

In fact, the inhabitants have built individual rooms and gallery-type spaces as expected. During the concept stage, the architect was afraid that if everybody started heavy construction at the same time, it would be a mess. To avoid that, they gave the possibility to have the gallery floor structure – with stairs and railings – ready-made during the Base Building construction period, before the moment of purchase. There were different layouts to choose from. In TILA, there were 26 apartment owners who selected this, and 13 lofts were without it. There was not an unbearable mess during the building period, because the occupants could create quite a good communal spirit among the habitants, helping each other and such (Figure 6a–f).

Figure 6 a, b, c, d, e, f: Some of the dwellings' interiors

TOPUP
Amsterdam, the Netherlands

Figure 1 TOPUP (center) in its urban context in the Buiksloterham district (Patch 22, also by Frantzen et al.) is to its immediate left, and Blackjack, another Open Building project is to its left)

Project Data

Project location:	Buiksloterham, Fonteinkruidstraat, Amsterdam
Chronological information:	Start of project 2016; completion of the Base Building and façade 2020
Project design team:	FRANTZEN et al. architecten, project architects Tom Frantzen, Karel van Eijken, contributor VNDP Amsterdam/Enschede
Number of dwelling units:	14 apartments, 14 living–working apartments, 3 commercial spaces
Ratio of parking spaces per dwelling unit:	49 parking spaces in a separate building
Project site/building area:	Site area: 4,844 m² + 1,346 m² parking garage; lettable floor area: 3,981 m² + 49 parking spaces
Project client:	Lemniskade projecten (project developer), Tom Frantzen and Claus Oussoren
New construction	
Structure type:	Concrete vertical core, timber laminated columns and beams, precast concrete floor elements; façade: timber frame construction with double façade, with indoor balcony on southwest and northwest façades
Installation utilities:	Central city heating, water and electricity per dwelling with main connection and meters in central corridor on each floor, distributed via vertical shafts in the central core; thin raised floors for horizontal distribution
Infill system/approach:	Clear separation of Infill and Support. Partition walls with fully insulated metal stud construction with double sheeting. The homeowners design and build their own Infill (with or without an architect and contractor).
Image credits	All drawings: FRANTZEN et al/Lemniskade. All photos: Isabel Nabuurs

BACKGROUND

In 2016, Tom Frantzen and his development partner Claus Oussoren developed the plot adjacent to PATCH22 (Figure 1). The site was occupied by an abandoned industrial warehouse with round concrete structures to house huge cable reels. To use as much of the existing structure as possible, Frantzen designed a structural concept based upon the one in PATCH22, planned it on top of the existing foundation and called the new building TOPUP.

LEGAL/REGULATORY CONSTRAINTS

The architect–developer opted for the division of the available floorspace into the maximum number of 14 legal units per floor to give the prospective buyers the opportunity to create a maximum of 6 custom-made dwellings per floor. Compared to PATCH22, where the floors are indeed divided into the maximum number of legal units possible, this time, the municipality was less flexible in approving the number of legal units and the variation in uses. It wanted more control over the permitted uses in new projects. The municipality prescribed a combination of working and living, with the bigger offices and retail functions on the ground floor.

On the upper floors, the municipality limited the number of legal units to the actual number of apartments: six per floor on floors 2–6, five on floor 7 and four on floor 8. The smallest legal units on floors 2 to 7 had to be dedicated workspaces. Moreover, because of the high land price, the dwellings on the lower floors proved hard to sell for a competitive price, pushing the margins of the project to an uncomfortable level. Even with an award-winning, successfully used proof of concept next door (PATCH22), this project shows that for each deviation from the 'conventional,' both developer and architect need to be prepared for a long process to be able to accomplish their (short and long-term) goals with Open Building. Nevertheless, TOPUP offers at least as much capacity, and is as sustainable and energy efficient as PATCH22, offering its residents freedom to design their own Infill.

TECHNICAL APPROACH

TOPUP used the CD20 system (lightweight precast concrete structural floors) in combination with a laminated timber column structure and timber frame construction for the façades of the Base Building. The strategy for the Base Building utility installations was copied in part from the PATCH22 project: using the vertical core of the building for distribution to the different dwellings, this time placing the required meter boxes on each floor in the 'public' corridor. In PATCH22, specific installations were routed inside a hollow floor structure (SlimLine floor system), which proved to be somewhat of a legal 'gray zone' for future adaptations. In TOPUP, the horizontal utility installations are installed between the massive concrete precast floor slabs (part of the Base Building) and a thin raised floor (part of Infill) to make a clearer legal division between dwelling units on adjacent floors. The height of the thin raised floor (24 cm or 9.5') was set by the slope of the black-water drainage pipes running from toilets placed at expected distances to the vertical pipe shafts in the buildings' core. The raised floor is composed of standard building materials available in the market (see Figures 3, 4 and 5). Timber framing was used for the Infill walls of most of the dwellings, each dwelling being individually designed by its owner and/or their architect.

CAPACITY FOR A RANGE OF DWELLING UNIT LAYOUTS

As noted, the architect–developer opted for the division of the available floorspace into the maximum number of 14 legal units

Figure 2 A view of the interior at the completion of the Base Building construction: precast concrete planks for the floors; prefabricated concrete core (to the right) and laminated-timber columns

Figure 3 View of the building core, showing connections to Base Building MEP systems. Infill MEP will be installed under the raised floor and in the ceiling

Figure 4 The Infill floor installation

per floor to give the prospective buyers the opportunity to create a maximum of 6 custom-made dwellings per floor (Figure 6).

CLASSIFICATION OF TOPUP AS AN OPEN BUILDING

The Dutch Open Building community (www.openbuilding.co) has developed a rating system on which various projects can be

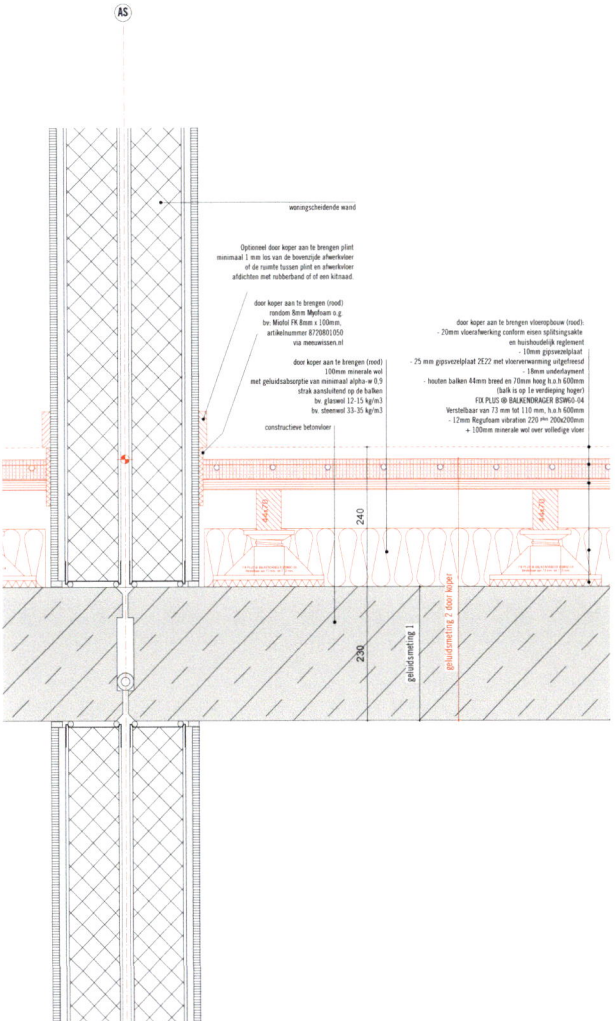

Figure 5 A detail of the raised floor at a 'party wall' separating dwelling units. The precast concrete floor slabs are 23 cm (9.4') thick; the raised floor is 24 cm (9.5') thick, the thickness determined by the diameter and slope of black-water drainage piping from toilets placed at the maximum distance from the vertical pipe shaft in the building core

classified in terms of their ability to achieve maximum capacity for change. The following matrix (Figure 12) shows this rating system. For example:

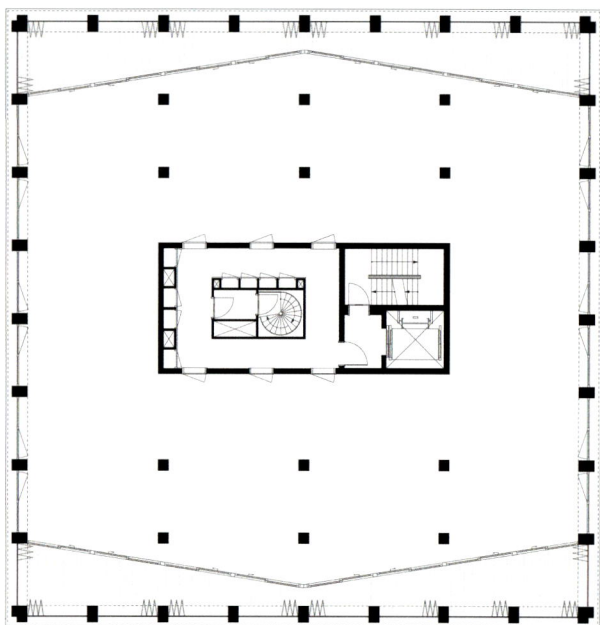

Figure 6 A typical 'empty' floor of the Base Building, with the central core containing all vertical MEP risers, utility meter cabinets and stairs and elevator. Balconies are evident on two sides of the building

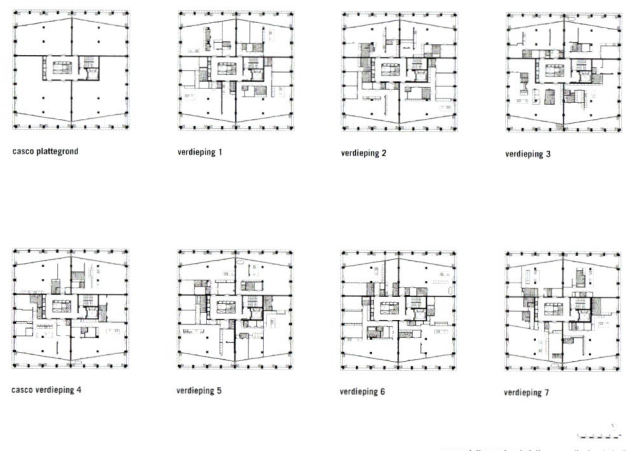

Figure 8 Variations in dwelling sizes and layouts on one floor. The figure on the upper left shows a floor divided into four units. The seven other figures show the variety of layouts actually realized on different floors

- If the division walls are the load-bearing structure and installations are fully integrated in this structure, the project will only be regarded as 'nonflexible/one-time flexible.'
- If the division walls are the load-bearing structure and installations are only partly integrated in this structure, the project can be regarded as 'slightly flexible.'
- If the division walls are the load-bearing structure and installations are only partly integrated (buried) in this structure, but the project has extra floor height and a façade that is adaptable in the future, so the project can be regarded as 'flexible.'

Finding a rating between very flexible and max-flexible is difficult. TOPUP scores on many aspects in the Max-flexible range, but it does not score on the more legal aspects in the Open Cities category.

Figure 7 Sketching in a dwelling unit at one of the sales workshops

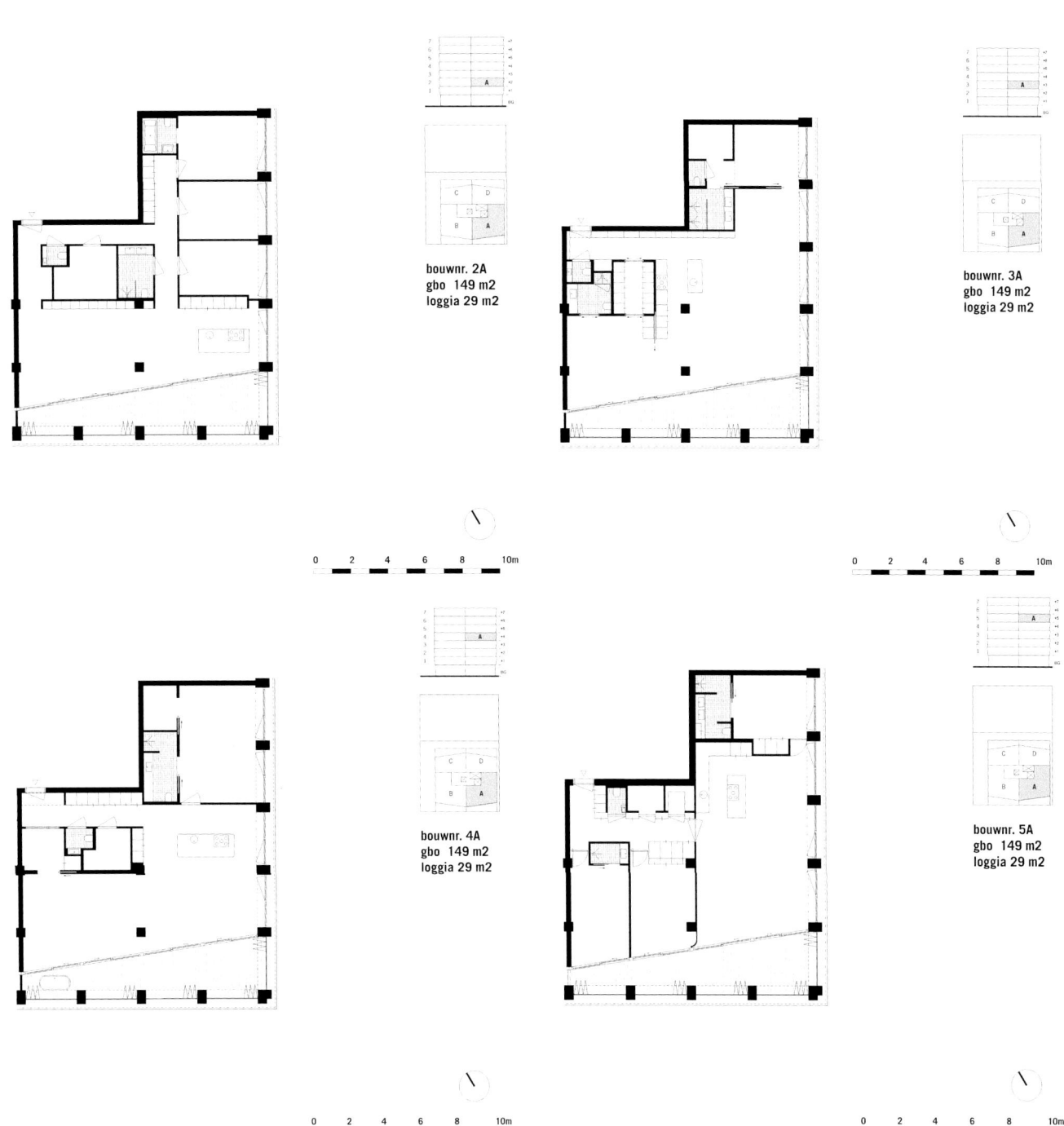

Figure 9 a, b, c, d: Details of four realized Infill layouts in the same unit size and configuration but on different floors

Figure 10 An interior view of one occupied dwelling, showing the CLT (cross-laminated timber) columns and wooden façade

Figure 11 Another interior view of a completed dwelling; ceilings are exposed in most cases but also can be lowered, for example, in bathrooms to conceal ventilation duct connections

	Open Cities >		Open Buildings >				Open Systems >			
	Free functional zoning (to allow programmatic transformation)	Number of apartment-rights > number of apartments (to allow reconfiguration of apartment sizes)	Extra Floor Height	Division walls coincide with load bearing structure	Division walls independent of load bearing structure	Façade independent from load bearing structure	Façade optimised for or adaptable to changing future use	Installations fully integrated in load bearing and apartment-dividing structure	Installations partly independent of load bearing and apartment-dividing structure	Installations fully independent of load bearing and apartment-dividing structure
Non-flexible / one time flexible				X				X		
Slightly flexible				X					X	
Flexible			X	X			X		X	
Very flexible	X		X		X	X	X		X	
Max-flexible	X	X	X		X	X	X			X

Figure 12 The rating chart showing TOPUP according to the most updated version of the classification system of the Dutch Open Building community. The blue fields mean TOPUP scored these aspects. The red x's show what aspects TOPUP explicitly did *not* score, making the project 'only' very flexible and not maximum flexible

HEALTHCARE
INO Intensive Care Facility
Inselspital, Bern, Switzerland

Figure 1 Phase One of the INO (*Photo credit*: Stephen Kendall)

INO INTENSIVE CARE FACILITY

Project Data

Location:	Bern, Switzerland
Architects:	Primary System: 4D PLUS General Planner (architect: Kamm+Kundig)
Secondary System:	Itten and Brechühl AG
Tertiary System:	HWP Planungsgesellschaft mbH
Client:	Office for Real Estate and Public Buildings of the Swiss Canton of Bern (OPB); Giorgio Macchi, Chief Architect and Director of the OPB Office (Retired)
Construction:	2007–2013
Building area:	51,000 m² (550,000 ft²) for flexible use
Primary System:	The framework is of concrete construction with a column grid of 8.4 × 8.4 m (27.5 × 27.5") using precast concrete columns, in-situ concrete slabs with 'knock-out' panels (without reinforcing) at the center of each column bay.
Secondary System:	Conventional construction for non–load-bearing walls; Secondary System 'floating' concrete slab separated from Primary System slab by a waterproof membrane

Figure 2 Mind-opening bottle crate – (a) crate (Primary System); (b) bottles (Secondary System; (c) liquid (Tertiary System) (*Credit*: Canton Bern Office of Properties and Buildings)

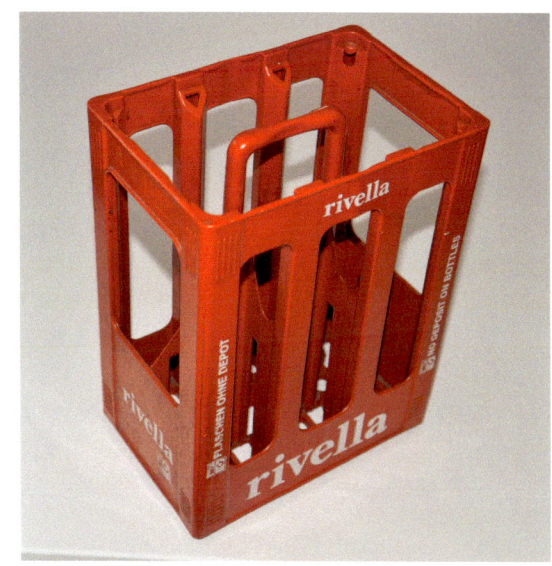

BACKGROUND

Giorgio Macchi, chief architect and director of the OPB office, told one of the authors in a private conversation:

"Instead of being refined over time, what was being built on the Inselspital Campus at a specific time, to a large extent, conflicts more and more with what ought to be. Dealing with change should become a fundamental aspect of how we perceive architecture, and consequently also how we conceive it. As long as time is not a guiding factor, the planning processes will be dominated by stress."

The INO offers insights into a strategy for overcoming this basic dilemma. The strategy is called *System Separation (SYS)*. The core principle of this strategy for designing buildings is this: fix few things, to keep flexibility, but fix them firmly, to achieve reliability. What emerges is high utility value. Buildings of high utility value remain useful over a very long time, are effectively renewable, convertible and developable, and generate a growing cultural identity. SYS fosters sustainability and facilitates change necessitated by technical life cycles or by life spans of use.

The Office for Real Estate and Public Buildings of the Swiss Canton of Bern (OPB) started developing the strategy in 1998. It has since become a binding guideline for all projects (more than 25 at the time of writing this book). The OPB's portfolio includes approximately 2,000 public buildings worth 5 billion Swiss francs ($5.6 billion) as well as annual investments of 150 million to 200 million Swiss francs ($170 million to $225 million).

SYS separates both requirement planning and building design into three levels, referring to long-, medium- and short-term perspectives. The managerial backbone concept of SYS is divide, allocate and delegate. Components and steps are well defined and manageable. The whole maintains complexity at a specific time as well as over time. Architecture – conceived and perceived in this way – emerges through its use.

Decision-makers generally dislike openness and particularly uncertainty. Their job is to eliminate openness and uncertainty by means of decisions. However, they are accessible to priorities and especially to hierarchies. The idea of SYS used the comparison with a bottle-crate to communicate the basis ideas of SYS to skeptical bureaucrats.

The crate stands for the long term, the bottles for the medium term and the drinks for the short term. Crate, bottles and drinks are a useful, reliable and proven product and procedure.

SYSTEM SEPARATION'S FIRST PROJECT

The INO project was launched in the mid-1990s. It was the first project guided by SYS. As part of the University Hospital of Bern, it had to fulfill high-tech requirements in a comprehensive academic medical center. INO mainly involved the intensive care units, emergencies, surgeries and laboratories. Substantial changes took place already during the planning and realization phases. The first intensive transformation while the building was in use concerned the laboratories.

The PS was the result of an international competition (typical for Swiss public projects) and was designed by architects without specific experience in hospital planning. Fittingly, the project was called Time-Space, showing that the authors had caught on to the essential idea of the architectural task that SYS imposed.

The subsequent competition for the SS was open exclusively to highly experienced hospital planners. The possibility to compare very different solutions for SSs within the same PS was a paradigm shift in decision-making. The team for the TS was selected based on its experience, as was the team for project management.

The three levels for building design are the Primary System (PS), the Secondary System (SS) and the Tertiary System (TS). The PS (Base Building) is oriented on the long term and concerns the building structure, including the façades and the site area's development availability. The SS (the Infill) is oriented on the medium term and concerns the internal nonstructural building construction, the technical installations and mechanical systems. The TS is oriented on the short term and concerns the building facilities, devices, equipment and furnishings. Designing and managing the planning and building procedure respecting this hierarchy of life spans means that replacement or modification of shorter-life elements does not affect or damage those of greater durability or longer use.

The PS has no structural complications, a minimum of structural barriers, high net loads, high floor heights and explicit spatial reserves for installations, and it strictly respects the partitioning or disentanglement of building components. There are no pipes or conduits in the PS. The precautions for site area availability, besides guaranteeing a general openness, are justified by the fact that all traffic and transport to and from a building has almost the same impact on the environment as the building's operation. The potential of well-connected areas must therefore be built up to the maximum, whether at the time of construction or in the future, even if current building regulations do not yet allow this. The robust PS therefore enables vertical and horizontal expansions.

The PS has a characteristic shape and comprises 51,000 m² (550,000 ft²) on very spacious floors for variable use. The framework is of concrete construction with a column grid of 8.4 × 8.4 m (27.5 × 27.5"). The lateral stabilizing structural elements are limited to four cross-shaped shear walls. Statically, each field or cell of the column grid allows for an opening of 3.6 × 3.6 m (11.8 × 11.8") to be cut out of the floor slab (Figures 3, 4 and 5). These 'knock-out fields' can be used on the level of the SS

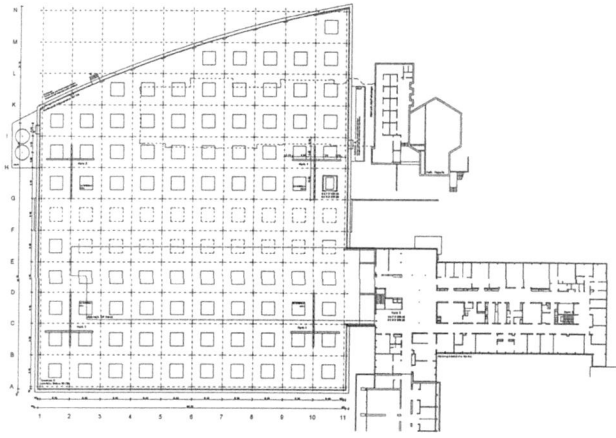

Figure 3 A typical floor of the INO, showing the connection to the adjacent existing building. The drawing also shows the regular 24-foot concrete cast-in-place structural grid (using precast concrete columns) with the square 'knock-out' opportunities in the center of each structural bay, where no steel reinforcing would prevent cutting out the slab with no danger of damaging the structural integrity of the whole (*Drawing credit*: Canton Bern Office of Properties and Buildings)

INO INTENSIVE CARE FACILITY

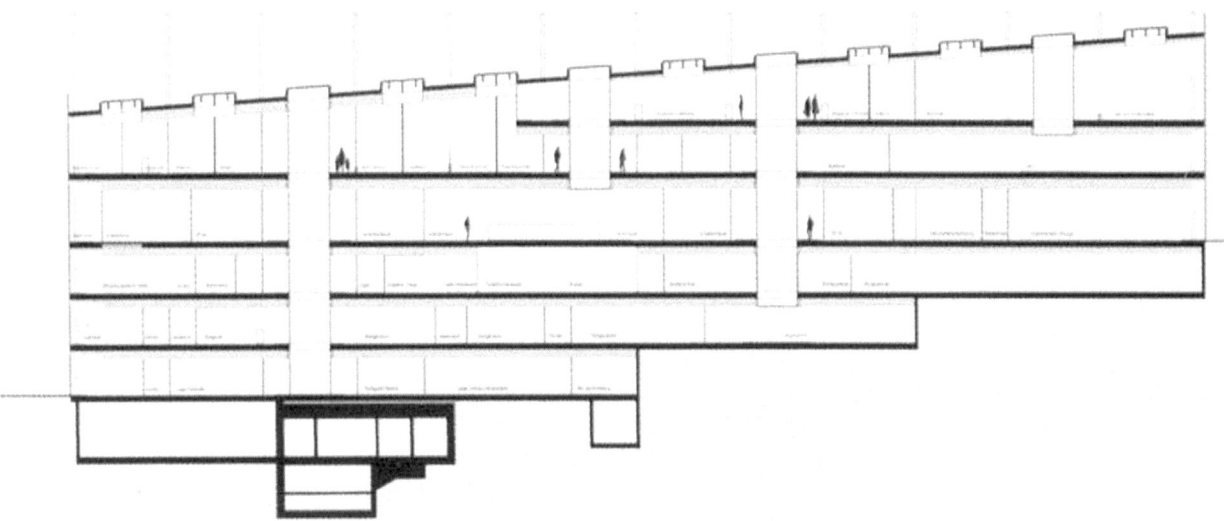

Figure 4 Cross section of the INO Primary System, showing how the light shafts can be inserted to introduce natural illumination deep into the building (*Drawing credit*: Canton Bern Office of Properties and Buildings)

Figure 5 Image of the top floor of the Primary System showing four drainage pipe sleeves at each column. Skylights are indicative of the 'punch-out' panels on all floors in the center of each structural bay for future light wells and other vertical services (*Photo credit*: Canton Bern Office of Properties and Buildings)

to enable daylight, visual contact, and vertical access during the planning as well as later on for transformations (Figure 4). All technical installations supplying a given floor are installed on that same floor, including drainage and other piping and air-handling ductwork. Each column-head has four block-outs (pipe sleeves) for vertical outlets for drainage pipes. The concrete floor structure is strictly free of installations, in line with the principle of the partition of building components.

PARTITIONING BUILDING SYSTEMS: A MANAGEMENT STRATEGY

Handling these system levels in a strategic way generates the three main principles of SYS: *the partition of building components* – limiting all entanglements on or across the three levels to a minimum; *flexibility* – above all ensured by the structural capacity and geometries of the PS and appropriate SSs; and *site area availability* – ensured by appropriate PSs in order to develop the building site densely over time.

Tasks and mandates have to be aligned with the principles of SYS from the very beginning. Planning in line with SYS is not just an additional planning criterion. It is a radical new way to do things.

Planners including architects, structural engineers, engineers for technical installations and experts for operation domains have to cooperate to optimize the whole. Because SYS differentiates the whole into long-, middle- and short-term perspectives, the organizational structure of the cooperation of the planners must be in compliance with this paradigm shift. The strategy of separation defines new starting positions for all parties involved and for all components to be built and installed.

CHANGES

During the planning for the Secondary System, the chief of surgery left for a position at another hospital. His team had worked out a surgery suite layout with the Secondary-System architects. When the new head of surgery was hired, he insisted on another

INO INTENSIVE CARE FACILITY

SPATIAL ORGANIZATION

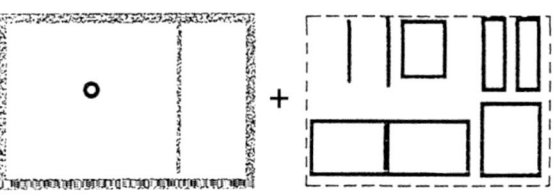

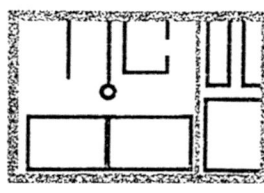

TECHNICAL SYSTEM ORGANIZATION

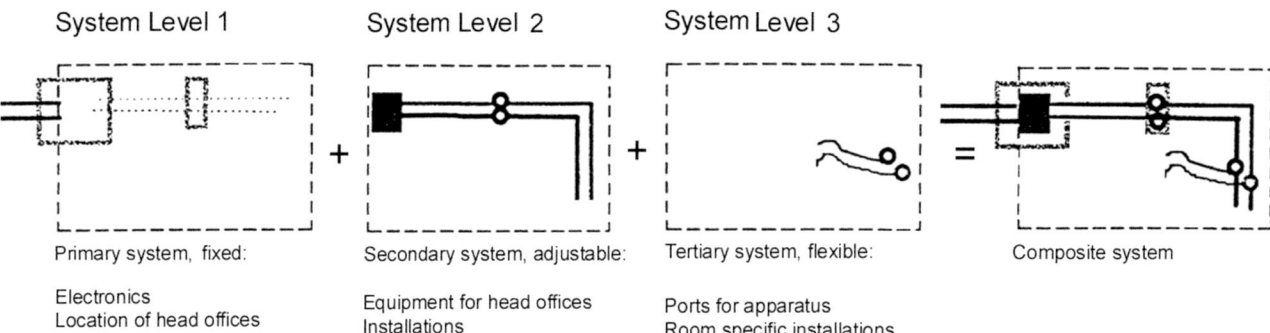

ORGANIZATION OF DESIGN ON LEVELS
INO HOSPITAL. BERN, SWITZERLAND

Figure 6 The spatial and technical organization per system level (*Drawing credit*: Canton Bern Office of Properties and Buildings)

layout of the surgery suite. The capacity of the Primary System was immediately evident because the new layout was quickly adopted and implemented.

After the building was in operation for several years, the medical laboratories needed to be reconfigured to accommodate new research equipment. This too was accommodated quickly with no disruption to other functions in the building. This was enabled in part due to the Secondary System's 'floating' concrete slab, which is separated from the Primary System slab by a waterproof membrane. Some conduits are in this floating slab.

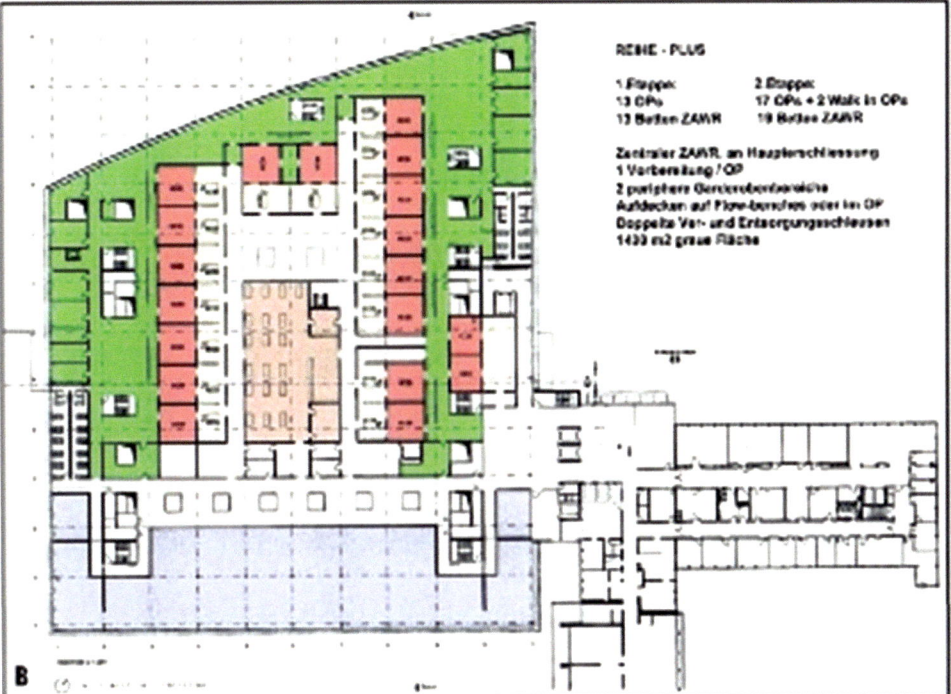

Figure 7 Surgery suite layout changes from A to B due to a change of head of surgery (*Credit*: Canton Office of Properties and Building)

Figure 8 Image of the Primary-System concrete slab and column, a pipe sleeve used for drainage piping and membrane separating the Primary-System slab from the secondary lightweight concrete slab (*Photo credit*: Stephen Kendall)

Figure 9 An image of one of the corridor spaces showing a light well in Phase I (*Photo credit*: Stephen Kendall)

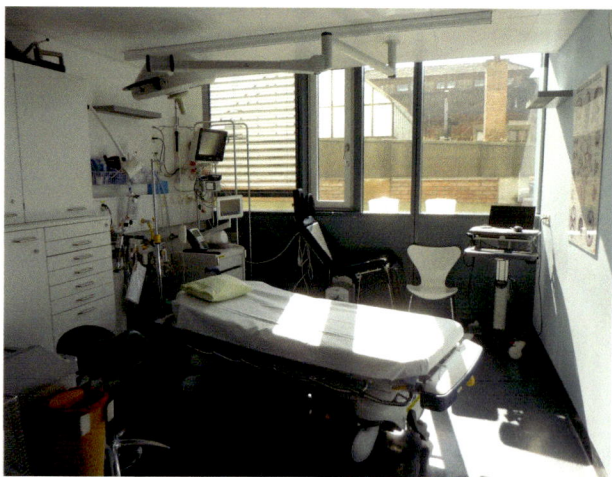

Figure 11 A typical exam room (*Photo credit*: John R. Dale)

PHASE TWO

After the INO had already been in operation for several years, the hospital decided to complete Phase II. This time, due to budgetary constraints, the original double-skin façade was dropped, but the same structural grid and pattern of skylights and light wells were maintained (Figure 12).

Figure 10 A view of one of the many light wells, looking into a laboratory (*Photo credit*: John R. Dale)

INO INTENSIVE CARE FACILITY

near Bern — Berne

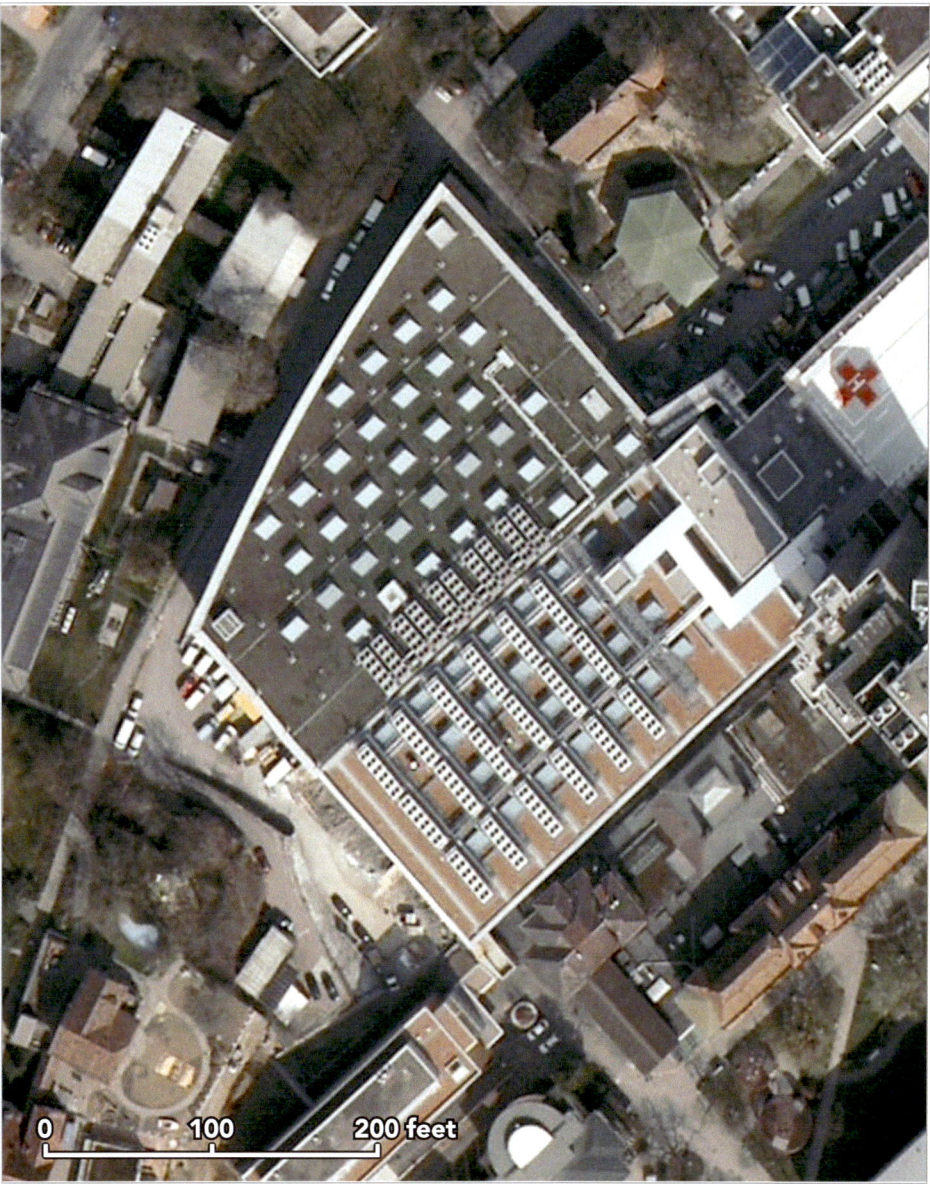

Figure 12 Aerial view showing Phase I (upper part) and Phase II (lower portion) (*Source*: Google Earth)

Sammy Ofer Heart Building
Tel Aviv, Israel

Figure 1 Sammy Ofer Heart Center (*Source*: Ranni Ziss Architects & Sharon Architects)

Project Data

Location:	Tel Aviv, Israel
Architects:	Ranni Ziss Architects and Sharon Architects
Client:	Tel Aviv Sourasky Medical Center in Israel
Building area:	70,000 m² (753,500 sq. ft.)
Design/Construction:	Design started in 2005. Primary System constructed in 2008–2011; Secondary and Tertiary Systems ongoing construction from 2008
Primary System:	Structural grid of 7.6 × 7.6 m (25 × 25"), central core of elevators and stairs, distributed MEP shafts and the building envelope
Secondary System:	Non–load-bearing walls and MEP systems
Tertiary System:	Ward equipment, including medical devices, digital tech, and furniture
Case study report:	Dr. Nirit Pilosof

INTRODUCTION

The case of the Sammy Ofer Heart Building at Tel Aviv Sourasky Medical Center demonstrates the contribution of the Open Building approach to the evolutionary process of a healthcare building over time. While most hospital facilities are tailor-made – designed for a highly detailed functional program – the design team of the Sammy Ofer Heart Building challenged this traditional practice and proposed a flexible design for unknown future functions (Pilosof, 2020; Sharon, 2012). To maximize the value of a private donation and expand the hospital capacity to evolve in the future, the hospital CEO decided to defer the decision on the uses of 7 of its 11 floors for later consideration. Accordingly, the need to design a Base Building as a 'container with capacity' that could accommodate unknown functional programs led to the implementation of system separation (Figures 3 and 4). Although the Open Building approach (Kendall, 2008) was not explicitly stated by anyone in the design process, its methods of system separation and distributed design management implicitly supported the construction of the project in phases, enabled the design of a variety of changing functional spaces and enhanced the management and coordination of the design process by different consultants, designers and contractors.

THE DESIGN PROCESS

The project was designed by Sharon Architects and Ranni Ziss Architects, a joint venture, and was developed starting in 2005 and constructed in 2008–2011. The building, located in the center of Tel Aviv, was designed as a monolithic cube clad in glass with prominent red recessed balconies. The building was designed to connect to an adjacent, historical Bauhaus hospital building through an atrium with iconic red recessed balconies (Figure 1). The 70-m- (230″) high building consists of 55,000 m^2 (592,000 sq. ft.) and includes 13 medical floors of 3,100 m^2 (33,300 sq. ft.) per floor and four underground parking floors designed with the possibility of conversion to an emergency 650-bed hospital. The 15,000-m^2 (161,400-sq.-ft.) underground 'sheltered' floors were designed in an innovative way to be resistant to chemical and biological warfare.

The main force behind the design and construction of the building was the generous donation of the Sammy Ofer family to the Tel Aviv Sourasky Medical Center in 2005. Since hospital development in Israel relies primarily on private funding, hospital directors attempt to maximize the potential of each donation. In the case of Tel Aviv Sourasky Medical Center, it was clear from the start that the hospital would construct the most extensive structure possible even by applying pressure on the municipality planning guideline limitations (Figure 3). This strategy led to the design of a Base Building with seven 'shell' floors for future completion and was even more evident in the last-minute decision to add two more shell floors to the building just before construction began. This change of the building's height required redesigning the buildings' Primary System, including the structure, MEP systems and façades and caused a delay of a few months in the design and construction process. In 2022, a decade after the building was opened, the hospital management decided to add three more floors to the top of the existing building to offer more space in the highly dense urban site (Figure 3).

The project was programmed and designed by the architects in collaboration with the hospital CEO, deputy director, head of cardiology units, head nurse and various internal and external consultants and project managers. Like most hospital facilities, the project was planned under tight budgetary, regulatory and environmental constraints. The design process, which began in 2005, reflected a variety of concepts. The realization of the project depended on finding a solution for an existing (but now obsolete) two-story outpatient building that had been constructed on the site in the 1960s for use as an emergency department. After much discussion, that building was demolished. Because the hospital management was undecided regarding its strategy and program, the design team developed a method of presenting and evaluating diverse design options for the new project.

The building, defined as a cardiac care center, was initially programmed to relocate all the hospital cardiac units, clinics, and surgery division onto three main floors and include an additional two floors for internal medicine units and outpatient clinics. Seven additional floors were also built but left empty for future programming and Infill. Accordingly, the new building was constructed in five main phases: (1) the underground emergency hospital, (2) core and envelope (Base Building) of floors 1–10 including a mechanical roof floor, (3) interior fit-out of floors 0–3, (4) interior fit-out of floors 4–6 and (5) interior fit-out of floors 7–10. The hospital plans to construct three additional floors on top of the existing building in 2023, adding 8,500 m^2 (91,500 sq. ft.) for diverse inpatient and outpatient units (Figure 3).

The design process from the beginning included capacity studies to analyze if the Primary System could accommodate the predicted development of the building in the future as defined by the hospital CEO and medical directors. The preliminary studies included schematic drawings of a typical floor with two inpatient medical units to illustrate the capacity for both: two identical mirrored units versus one major unit with more ICU rooms and a minor unit with semiprivate rooms (Figure 2). The client also required the architects to prepare a schematic design for the research lab and neurology units that were expected to be installed in the shell (empty) floors of the building. The Primary purpose of the capacity studies was to analyze if the Primary System (Base Building) would support future anticipated programs, the location of heavy equipment, possible connections to MEP infrastructures and efficient configuration of functions. Research on the evolutionary process of the building over 13 years revealed that the preliminary capacity analysis study drawings were retained and were later used to evaluate the potential of the building for future change and to analyze the interfaces between the different system levels (Pilosof, 2018). In this sense, these drawings became a communication tool between the initial design team and the following design teams, their importance unknown at the time of the initial design, to demonstrate the Open Building approach (which at that time had no formal name to the design team or client) and to explain the decision-making throughout the design.

 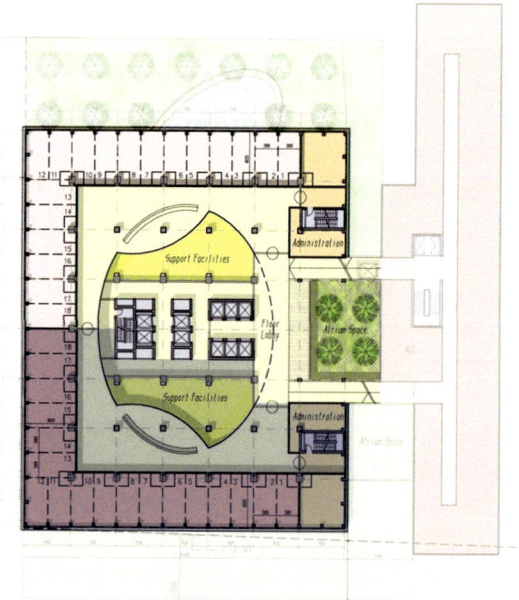

Figure 2 Preliminary study of schematic design options of a typical floor, 2005 (*Source*: Ranni Ziss Architects and Sharon Architects)

THE EVOLUTION OF THE BUILDING

The Sammy Ofer Heart Building, defined and designed as a cardiology center, has changed its functional program considerably. The cardiology division, in fact, occupies less than 30% of the building. The building now contains neurology, dermatology, internal medicine and oncology units in addition to research labs and outpatient clinics (Figures 3 and 4). The change of program can be explained by changing needs since cancer became the number-one cause of death and statistically surpassed cardiac diseases. The logic of centralizing the oncology units in one location to enhance the hospital efficiency and health services could only have been accomplished in the new building. The hospital management also decided to relocate other functions to the building since their previous locations required renovation or extension or received funds to reconstruct a specific medical unit. In some cases, the decision to relocate medical units to the new building

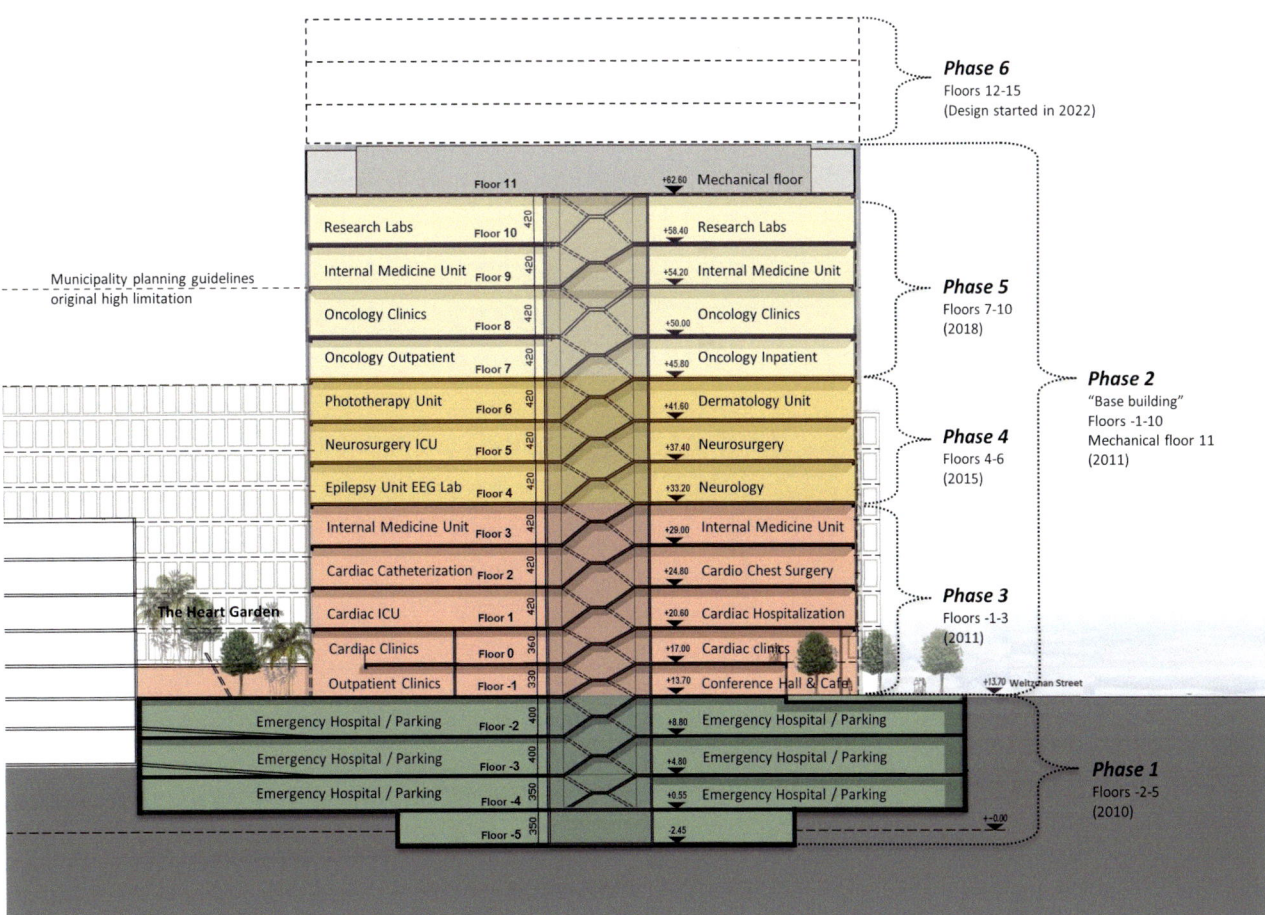

Figure 3 Section of the building illustrates the five phases of construction and the dynamic hospital program (*Source*: Ranni Ziss Architects & Sharon Architects and the author)

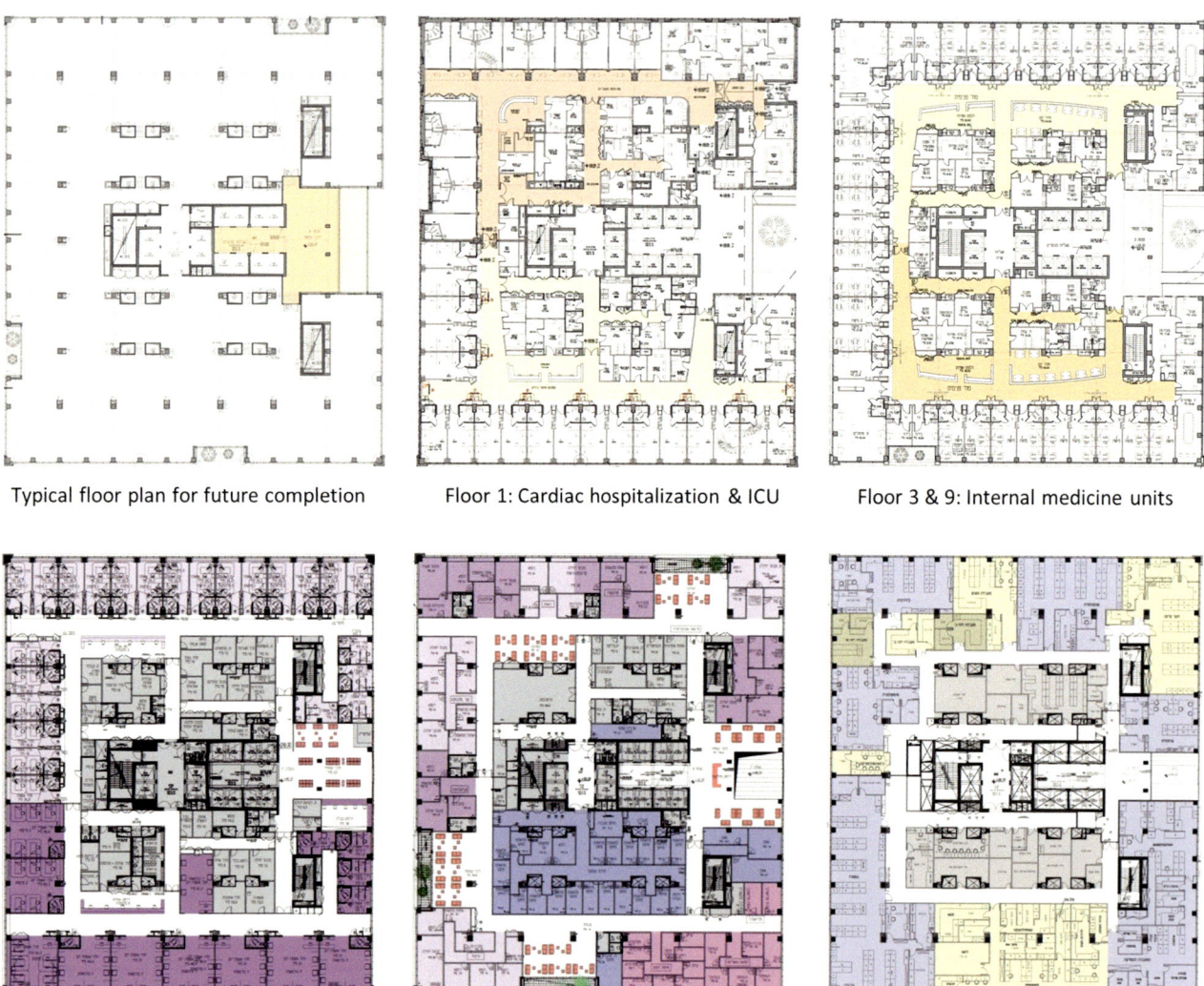

Figure 4 Architecture plans of the variety of medical programs on different floors (*Source*: Ranni Ziss Architects & Sharon Architects)

was the result of competition with other hospitals or a strategy to attract highly accomplished medical directors. Throughout the years, the hospital's dynamic development plan has been driven by forces of economics as well as internal and external organizational politics.

Most of the changes took place after the building was occupied. Although this process of deferred completion of Secondary and Tertiary Systems was planned in advance, it still created a challenge for both the construction and the operation of the running units. The phasing stages, divided by the buildings' floors, created a fit-out process from the bottom upward. This strategy might be efficient in order to avoid interruptions of the completion to the operating units, but it limits decision flexibility during the design process. In many cases, the considerations in the fit-out installation phases overruled the importance of locating some medical functions close to other units for process optimization. For example, the inpatient internal medicine units under construction on the ninth floor should have been located on the fourth floor above the existing internal medical units (on the third floor) to centralize the internal medicine division and enhance staff and equipment flows among the four units.

The separation of the building into system levels was also useful as a project management and budgeting tool in the design process. The long design process of 13 years, which was still running in 2018, involved many different professionals and decision-makers. Many of the project team members of the hospital were replaced, including the CEO of the hospital, heads of medical units and head nurses. Each change of personnel resulted in reconsideration of the design and requests for alternative design options. The design team included a collaboration of two architecture firms, the replacement of two project management firms and consultants who changed over time. The development of the project by phases, using system levels, allowed the architects to divide the workload between the two offices. Each office was responsible for designing specific floors' Secondary Systems, with minimal need for consultation and coordination. The design control was distributed between the two firms on each level (e.g., the Primary, Secondary and Tertiary System levels) to avoid unequal division between the two firms. The study also indicates that capacity study drawings that were developed at a preliminary stage were used as communication tools later, among design teams not even known initially, because they defined the anticipated interfaces between the system levels. The recent decision to add three floors to the top of the building demonstrates the capacity of the original design to grow even beyond its initial build-out. It highlights the unpredictability of future needs and the necessity to plan for change over time.

ACKNOWLEDGMENTS

This research was supported by the European Research Council grant (FP-7 ADG 340753) and by the Azrieli Foundation. I am grateful to the Tel Aviv Sourasky Medical Center management and staff and to Ranni Ziss Architects, Sharon Architects, CPM and M. Iuclea project managers for their collaboration.

READINGS

Pilosof, N.P. (2018). The Evolution of a Hospital Planned for Change. *Healthcare Architecture as Infrastructure* (editor Kendall, S.H.). Routledge, London, pp. 91–107.

Pilosof, N.P. (2020). Building for change: Comparative case study of hospital architecture. *HERD: Health Environments Research & Design Journal*. https://doi.org/10.1177/1937586720927026

Sharon, A. (2012). Flexible building design offers future-proofing. *IFHE Digest*, pp. 96–98.

Oregon Health Center
Portland, Oregon, USA

Figure 1 View of main entry from the south and across a public park

OREGON HEALTH CENTER

Project Data

Architects:	Zimmer Gunsul Frasca Architects, LLP (ZGF)
Client:	Oregon Health & Science University, Portland Oregon, USA (OHSU)
Building area:	39,292 m² (401,412 sq. ft.)
Primary System:	Structural system (steel) grid varies due to existing below-grade parking structure. Maximum bay size is 42'-9" × 28'-0" (13.03 m × 8.53 m) and smallest (at corners) is 20'-5" × 16'-6" (6.22 m × 5.03 m). To improve grid spacing, there are some transfers of columns to the parking levels via angled columns. Lateral seismic system is a moment frame. Two stair cores are off center and grouped with elevators (split between public and patient/staff), main mechanical/heating ventilation air condition, HVAC, shafts, stacked electrical and technology rooms. Smaller plumbing risers are adjacent to structural columns.
Floor-to-floor heights:	Generally, 15'-0"/4.57 m, increased at podium levels (16'/4.88 m), first floor (20'-10"/6.35 m) and the interstitial mechanical level (24'/7.32 m) Location of primary mechanical and electrical systems, those typically found in a central plant, are described later under 'System Organization.'
Secondary System:	Non–load-bearing interior walls and mechanical electrical plumbing, MEP, distribution
Tertiary System:	Medical equipment (movable and fixed), office equipment, computer technology, furnishings and art
Sustainability:	The project was certified as LEED Gold® by the US Green Building Council.
Project schedule:	Start of design: 2014
Groundbreaking:	2016
Opening:	2019

INTRODUCTION AND BACKGROUND

Oregon Health & Science University is a nationally prominent research university and Oregon's only public academic health center. It educates health professionals and scientists and provides leading-edge patient care, community service and biomedical research. In 1919, the University of Oregon Medical School (OHSU's predecessor) moved from downtown Portland to its present location on Marquam Hill in Southwest Portland. In 2003, OHSU begin developing a campus along the Willamette River connected to Marquam Hill with the Portland Aerial Tram. In 2006, OHSU opened its first new building on the South Waterfront campus, the Center for Health & Healing (CHH) including new ambulatory services, faculty clinics and underground parking below the building and a vacant block to the south. Since then, riverfront development has continued with new research, education (dental school) and outpatient facilities.

The site for this case study, Center for Health & Healing South (now called CHH-2), was on top of a three-level underground parking structure and across the street from the original CHH (now called CHH-1). The building's massing was set by City of Portland zoning regulations as follows: Levels 1–4 are a full city block (200' × 200'/61 m × 61 m) and upper floors are 200'/61 m in east–west direction and 115'/35 m in north–south direction.

The building program was varied and included:

- Surgery and interventional procedures suites
- Extended-stay outpatient rooms
- Clinics
  - Digestive health
  - Preoperative
  - Women's health
  - Multidigestive health
- Knight Cancer Institute
  - Clinics & diagnostic imaging
  - Infusion
  - Cancer trial clinics (research)
  - Research offices
- Clinical laboratory & outpatient blood draw
- Pharmacy
- Outpatient
- Compounding
- Shelled space (6% of floor area including entire sixth floor plus space on the fifth floor)
- Support services including sterile processing, food service, staff facilities and central plant/primary mechanical and electrical services for the three-building complex

A Primary design challenge was to accommodate these various programs (and potential future programs) in a multistory building with the uniformly positioned vertical elements (structure, circulation and mechanical risers).

The Center for Health & Healing 2 demonstrates the Open Building approach in a healthcare building, although the term 'Open Building' was not used in the design process. A Primary project goal was long-term ability of the building to accommodate both changes in the initial program's needs and to allow for future new programs.[1]

THE DESIGN PROCESS

Client goals were clearly stated at the outset:[2]

1. Incorporate future trends in design with capacity to accommodate varied and changing uses.
2. Drive value from each functional and operational component.
3. Maximize the use of products and labor from the state of Oregon to the extent possible.
4. Embrace and push lean design and construction principles.
5. Reap maximum value of a fully integrated team that inspires creativity, collaboration and innovation reflective of the ambitious nature of the client's facilities.

OHSU also was looking for a design team and individuals who are willing to bring innovation to project delivery.

OHSU desired an *integrated team* with a proven track record of working together. Therefore, architects, contractors and consulting engineers self-selected to form teams prior to proposal submission. The selected team consisted of Zimmer Gunsul Frasca Architects LLP, Hoffman Construction, Affiliated Engineers

Figure 2 Design events: using gameboards and tabletop exercises left and center and full-size mockup of physician/nurse/medical tech teamwork area

Inc. (mechanical and electrical) and KPFF Consulting Engineers (structural and civil) plus specialty consultants. The major team members had successfully worked together on several projects, including for OHSU.

As an extension of the integrated team, a design process was developed that had two unique aspects:

1. An integrated project delivery approach was developed by OHSU, ZGF and Hoffman. This involved the co-location of the owner, architect, engineers, general contractor and major subcontractor team members in a *co-location space* of more than 100 workstations, from early design through construction, in temporary facilities adjacent to the construction site. This facilitated rapid and deep analysis of design issues by all parties, including capacity to accommodate varied and changing uses. The co-location fostered communication among the owner, design consultants, general contractor and trade partners who were brought onto the project in the design phase.
2. Nine rounds of integrated design events (IDEs) were orchestrated to develop lean process improvements (LPI) of medical operations and building design. Nine IDEs involving hundreds of stakeholders resulted in clearly defined goals, operational improvements and a better understanding of budget, costs and schedule. Early events defined the current state of operations and then developed future state operations. In later events, participants walked through *full-scale mockups of entire clinical departments* in a 30,000 sf (2,800 sq. meters) warehouse to get a feel for "a day in the life" and fine tune details in individual rooms. A description of an IDE in early schematic design is described below under 'Space Planning Process/IDE Events.'

The result was a design that not only accommodated opening-day clinical processes but is adaptable to both incremental medical process improvements and major renovations. Another design goal was emphasis on a healing environment, patient experience and taking advantage of the excellent views. This helped drive floor plans that were more open and understandable, which in turn meant more adaptable to change.

DEVELOPMENT OF OPEN BUILDING CONCEPTS

As noted previously, the term 'Open Building' was not used. However, project goals and design processes had many parallels to 'the Open Building approach,' including capacity analysis and separation of Base Building and Infill.

CONCEPT PLANNING

The project team evaluated buildings with similar programs for lessons learned, starting with the existing and adjacent Center for Health & Healing 1. CHH-1 had identical floorplates and similar programs and had experienced some renovations since its design in the early 2000s. Strategies to accommodate varied and changing uses were developed within constraints (e.g., zoning code envelope, existing parking structure below and connection points via a pedestrian bridge and service tunnels to other OHSU buildings). A Primary strategy was the grouping of building system risers (HVAC, system piping, plumbing, electrical and technology), with fixed vertical circulation cores (stairs, public and private elevators). These fixed elements are located off-center on the building floor plate to maximize an open loft-like floor area in the center of the building, offering capacity to accommodate varied and changing uses. Other strategies considered window mullion spacing (~ 5 feet (1.5 m)), with alternating glazed and spandrel glass to accommodate a variety of room widths, all with daylighting and test fitting of a variety of planning modules for initial and potential programs.

SPACE PLANNING PROCESS/IDE EVENTS

The IDE events for each major program lasted up to three days and occurred from programming through design development phases. The key period for space planning coordination with the Base Building was in schematic design; therefore, a simple overview of an IDE in that period is provided (Figures 3, 4 and 5).

- IDE events were client focused for OHSU staff, not the design team, to develop multiple layouts for each program within the proposed Base Building floorplate. OHSU participants included physicians, nurses, support and supply staff and patient representatives. The design team was there to assist with problems

OREGON HEALTH CENTER

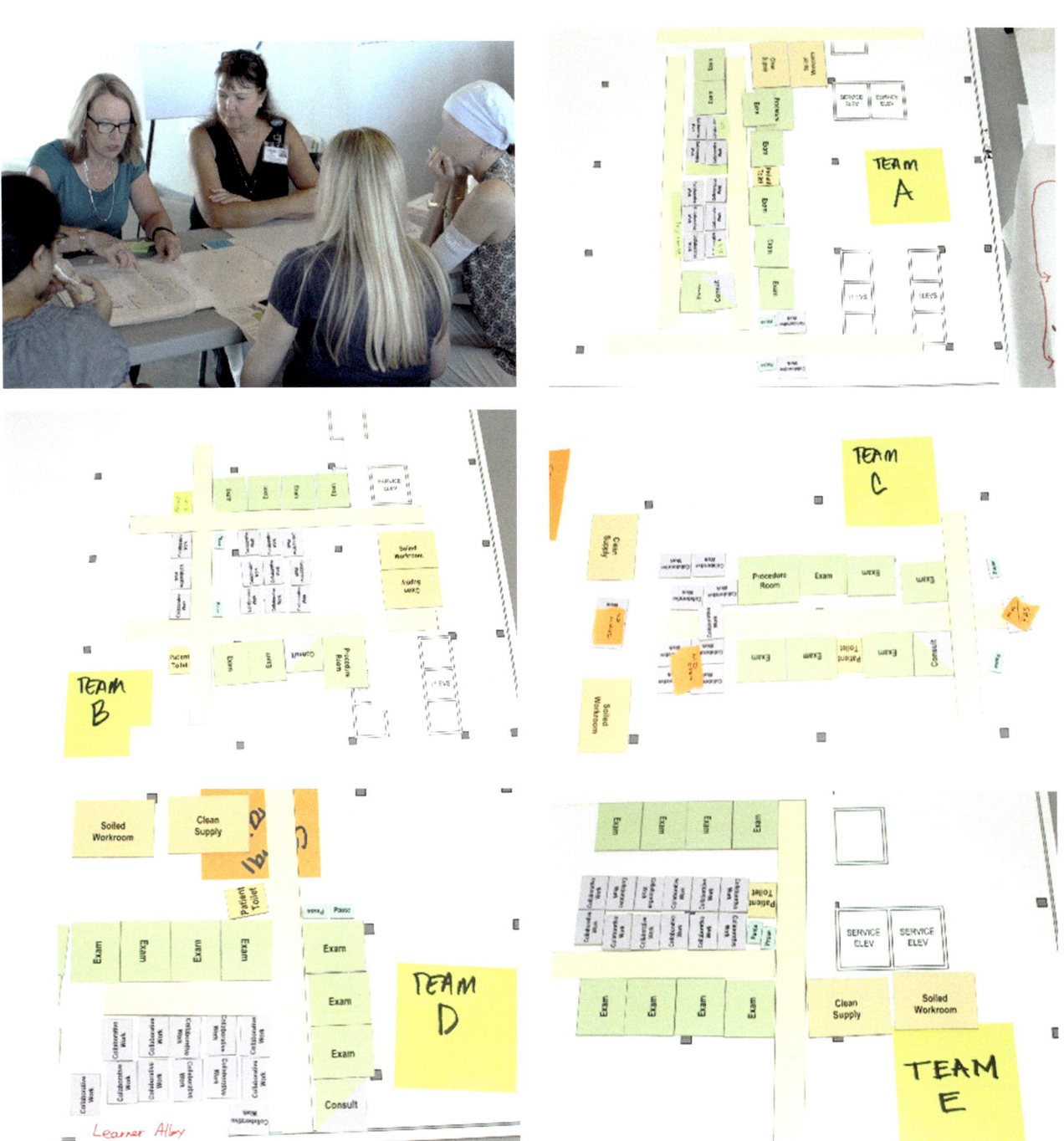

Figure 3 IDE event tabletop or gameboard uses cut-out program pieces to develop alternate designs of oncology clinic modules

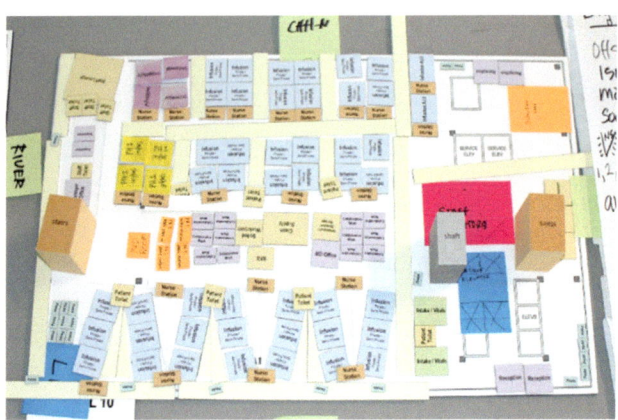

Figure 4 Example of a gameboard plan for an entire floor of oncology, showing relation to fixed Base Building elements

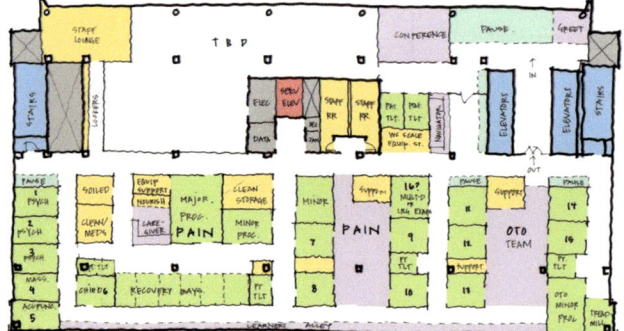

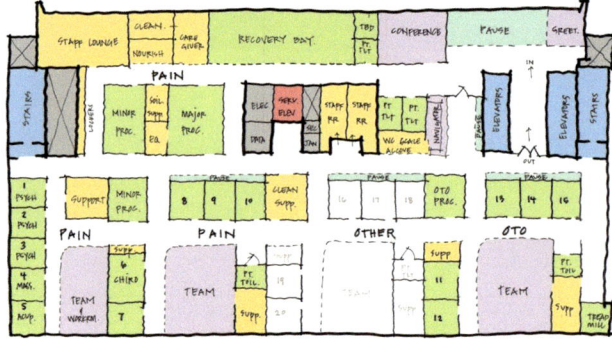

Figure 5 Example of comparative plan options for OTO voice/pain clinic developed by design team between IDE sessions is illustrative of informal capacity analysis depicting two of several plan options

and assure practicality including code compliance. These events, building on the 'future state' of operations developed in programming, were tightly scheduled with goals and outcomes for each session (two to four per day) with report-outs and discussion at the end of each session.
- For clinical groups, participants included all specialties so that a standard clinic layout could be developed to allow clinics to be shared. OHSU also wanted new clinic layouts that also could be placed in the existing CHH-1 building. Similarly, the two procedure floors, surgical and interventional, worked together to develop similar concepts on their respective floors.
- A typical IDE began with an overview of current project status and goals for the week. In early schematic design, each room in the space program was cut out in colored coded illustration board at 1/8"=1'-0"(~1:100) scale. Five-room program sets were provided for development of multiple layouts on the given Base Building plan by different teams for tabletop or 'gameboard' exercises. Options were compared to stated goals and data points, e.g., travel distances for patients and staff.
- Between IDE days (and events), the design team developed plans of the gameboard options for further development. The design team also studied whether modifications to the Base Building could or should be made that would improve layout and would coordinate those modifications between floors. At this point in the design process, these Base Building modifications might include adjusting the shape of a vertical mechanical shaft or changing access to an electrical room or stair to accommodate better clinical layouts.
- When the number of options was reduced to two or three, full-size models of the clinical floors were built out of cardboard so that staff could walk through their daily operations and compare the options.

This is a very simplified description of the IDE process, but it illustrates how multiple layouts and programs were developed and tested for fit within the proposed Base Building (which could be slightly modified), demonstrating its capacity to accommodate varied and changing uses.

MEP SYSTEM ORGANIZATION

Regarding MEP system organization, the project team worked together to evaluate dozens of system concepts with the goal of determining and implementing approaches that represented the best value to OHSU. Key considerations in these evaluations included:

- Design systems that minimize operating costs and represented responsible use of energy and other resources.
- Maximizing flexibility in the systems to accommodate a variety of program elements in the building and minimize the impact of future building modifications.
- Locate major equipment in areas that allowed for appropriate service access and minimized disruption to surrounding programs.
- Provide vertical distribution through the building that minimizes the number of large vertical MEP shafts on the floorplates yet provides appropriate horizontal access to these Base Building systems.
- Provide horizontal distribution on the floorplates that allows access to above-ceiling equipment and systems that require regular maintenance and allows for future system modifications both without undue disruption to surrounding areas.

The team co-location space and early involvement of major subcontractors was an important element in facilitating real-time and continuous intertrade concept development and coordination, allowing for the optimization of both design and construction and the MEP systems. The existing parking structure below and ground-floor program requirements coupled with a lack of adjacent land to satisfy MEP requirements necessitated central air conditioning plant functions be located higher in the building. The central plant also serves existing CHH-1 and the new Gary and Christine Rood Family Pavilion. Boilers, chillers and air handling units are located on an interstitial level at Floor 5 to directly serve downward to surgery and procedure suites (major air users), as well as the other adjacent buildings via below-grade connections, and upward to other floors. Emergency generators and cooling towers are located at the roof level. Besides the grouping of large risers noted earlier, smaller risers for plumbing were placed adjacent to structural columns to maximize floor plan flexibility, as opposed to risers in the middle of structural bays. Because CHH-2 provided central plant services to two other campus buildings, the vertical piping risers were larger than typical for a building of this size. Horizontal system runs were above suspended ceilings to serve respective floors' mechanical, electrical and technology needs. Exceptions were plumbing drains that served the floor above and occasional electrical/technology runs accessing floor outlets in the floor above. Raised floors were not seriously considered due to infection-control concerns about wet areas and body fluids getting into the below-floor space.

Specific strategies to provide capacity to accommodate varied and changing uses included:

- All systems generally provide 20% to 25% spare service capacity from source to distribution, e.g., spare electrical circuits.
- Horizontal 'zoning' of MEP systems pathways in the space above suspended ceiling
- Looping of piping (with shut-off valves), supply and exhaust ducts provided redundancy and ability to isolate sections for modifications.
- Plumbing location below floor slab and above suspended ceilings strived to avoid placement above sensitive areas (e.g., surgery and procedure suites) and above terminal HVAC units.
- Use of chilled beams in clinical and office areas provide space planning options (and energy savings).

To date, the systems have provided consistent and reliable support to the operation of the facilities. Since opening day, Portland has experienced record-high temperatures several times, and the building has performed well, as reported to project design engineers.

BASE BUILDING CONCEPTS

1. A wide variety of potential future changes were considered to test the Base Building's capacity to accommodate varied and

changing uses. A retrospective comparison to Open Building concepts follows, referring to the main principles of capacity analysis. Each area allows for several different layouts. The presence of many ambulatory programs in the building demonstrates provision for different layouts. Furthermore, for each program, the project team in IDE events was required to develop a number of functional layouts. For the few ambulatory programs not present, the project team experience determined if good layouts were possible and even hospital program layouts were tested. Some programs if considered in the future, e.g., magnetic resonance imaging (MRI) and audiology booths would require specific structural modifications as typical for such renovations. Radiation oncology would not be feasible due to extreme weight of radiation shielding.

2. It must be possible to change the floor area, either by additional construction (vertical or horizontal) or by changing the boundaries of the units of occupancy: Within CHH-2, there are programs that occupy full and partial floors. Program or suite boundaries and corridor locations can easily change as program space needs change. Horizontal expansion is not possible at the lower levels due to property lines and public rights-of-way, nor at upper levels where the building is at the maximum dimensions according to the existing zoning code. Future vertical expansion is not provided for, though one floor was added during design. The ever-tightening seismic requirements of the Pacific Coast have left many buildings planned for vertical expansion unable to do so without disruptive upgrade renovations. Therefore, building owners have generally declined to use this strategy.

3. Buildings should be adaptable to both residential and nonresidential functions, within reason: OHSU is a client with buildings more than 100 years old that are still in original use, and the university seldom demolishes buildings. Therefore, it is not anticipated that residential use would be sought. The presence of research offices demonstrates the building works well as general office use.

It should be noted that the project team did study potential conversion to other hospital uses at varying times in the design process (driven by reimbursement changes), but each time, such a potential conversion was not pursued due to programmatic-type issues, e.g., need for emergency department on first floor, which was not available due to other necessary ground-floor functions, fire life safety upgrades, increased seismic code requirements for hospitals as 'essential-use facilities' and impact on the project business case.

In conclusion, based on capacity to accommodate varied and changing uses of similar buildings and CHH-2's design and planning improvements, it is fully anticipated the building will serve OHSU's ambulatory needs for decades.

FINAL DESIGN
unit   clinic and pharmacy

SINCE COMPLETION
Since opening in 2019, post occupancy evaluation has occurred, with the caveat that COVID restrictions closed the facility down in early 2020, and utilization has been impacted since reopening later in that year. There has not been a need for renovations to the facility to test its ability to accommodate change. Early staff and patient feedback was positive, before COVID impacts. Patient satisfaction scores met or exceeded project goals.

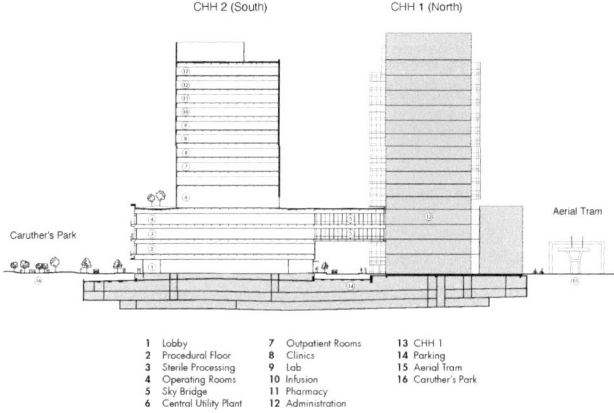

Figure 6 Cross section illustrating stacking of various program types (6 of 15 floor plans below). New CHH-2 on left and existing CHH-1 on right and existing parking below

Figure 7 Full block plan at Level 2, interventional

Figure 8 Level 4, surgery suite

ACKNOWLEDGMENTS

Project major team members:

- Owner: Oregon Health & Science University
- Architect and interiors: Zimmer Gunsul Frasca Architects, LLP
- General contractor: Hoffman Construction Company

Figure 9 Upper-level plan at Level 7 outpatient stay

Figure 10 Level 8 typical clinic unit

Figure 11 Level 11 Knight Cancer Institute infusion

Figure 12 Level 12 Knight Cancer Institute research

OREGON HEALTH CENTER

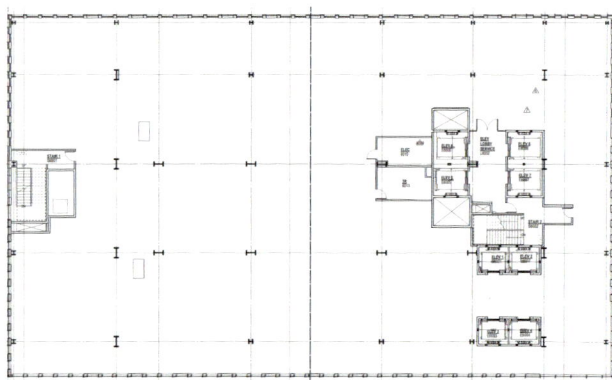

Figure 13 Upper floor level (typical) empty Base Building

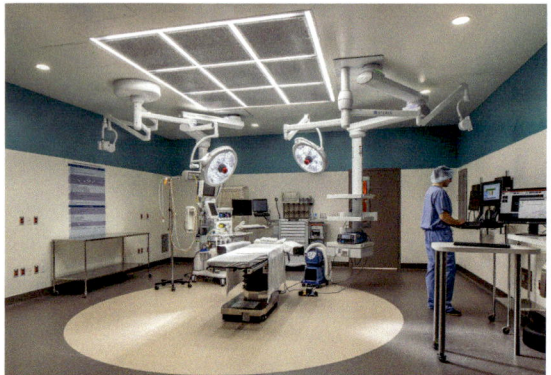 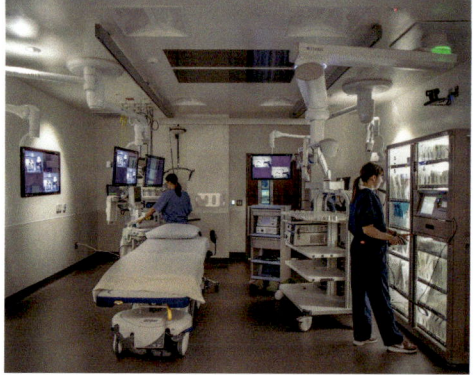

 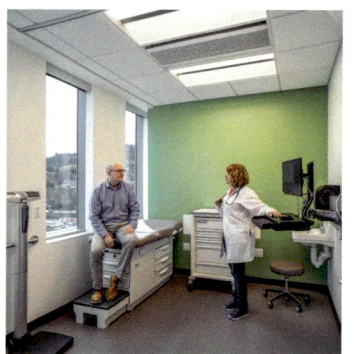

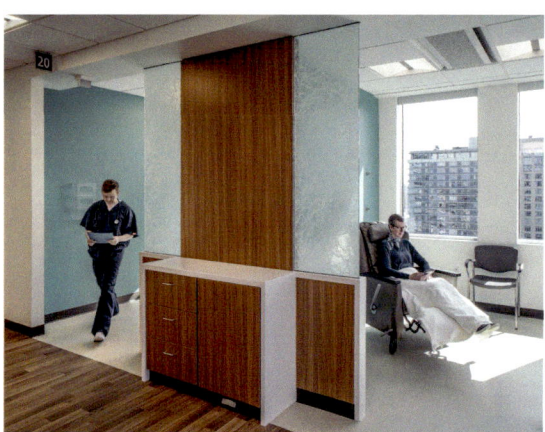 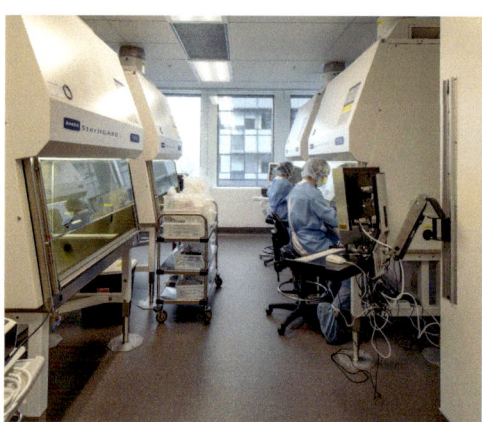

Figure 14 A variety of programs are accommodated within CHH-2. Top: surgery, interventional, extended-stay outpatient rooms. Bottom: clinics, infusion, pharmacy

OREGON HEALTH CENTER

Figure 15 CHH-2 viewed from north with skybridge to CHH-1 (at right)

- Structural and civil engineers: KPFF Consulting Engineers
- Mechanical and electrical engineers: Affiliated Engineers, Inc.
- Landscape architects: Place

Contributors: Karl Sonnenberg AIA ACHA, ZGF

Photography & Graphic Credits:

- Figure 1: Courtesy of ZGF Architects LLP; © Eckert & Eckert
- Figures 2–13: Courtesy of ZGF Architects LLP
- Figure 14: Courtesy of ZGF Architects LLP; © Eckert & Eckert
- Figure 15: Courtesy of ZGF Architects LLP; © Eckert & Eckert
- Figure 16: Courtesy of ZGF Architects LLP; © Bruce Damonte

NOTES

1 Designed and built simultaneously by the same team on the block to the east is the OHSU Gary and Christine Rood Family Pavilion, which includes guest rooms for out-of-town patients and families, parking, conference center and receiving docks for the three-building complex (CHH-1, CHH-2, and Rood Family Pavilion). The three buildings are connected by tunnels and/or skybridges. This document focuses on the CHH-2 building.

2 From the Oregon Health and Science University Request for Proposal Packet for Architectural/Design Professional Services for Center for Health & Healing-South August 2014.

EDUCATION
Shenzhen University Engineering School
Shenzhen, PR China

Figure 1 View of the project in the campus setting

Project Data

Location:	Shenzhen, China
Client:	South China University of Science and Technology, and Bureau Public Works of Shenzhen Municipality
Architect:	BE Architects – Hong Kong office
Design Phase:	January 2017 – January 2020
Completed:	August 2020

Gross built area: 115,000 m² (1,238,000 sq. ft.)

System	Lifetime (in Years)	Explanation
Infrastructure	200–1,000	All outdoor public infrastructure stand longer than buildings. A city's infrastructure may have a history of 1000 years. We have to be extremely careful about this when we design a building.
Load-bearing structure	100	The load-bearing structure, combined with staircase and elevators, related to all safety requirements, can stand more than 100 years without any change (unless an error has occurred in design).
Façade and service core	50–60	The façade and main interior MEP (mechanical, electrical and plumbing systems) should last 50 to 60 years. We do not frequently change façades in our culture because it is extremely expensive.
Functional layout	20	Interior partitions, utilities specific to each occupant territory.
Interior	10	Ceilings, lighting, cabinets, wall and floor finishes

BACKGROUND

The Engineering School, which is situated at the boundaries of the northwest campus, follows the overall concept structure of the campus – 'two-axis, three-corridor, and one-ring.' The massing emphasizes the boundary on the northwest. It has two U-shaped courtyards, which have openings toward the landscape on the east and south, hosting outdoor activities for the campus. The sloping roof, which is lower at the east/south and higher at the west/north, fully reflects the consideration of the terrain characteristic of the site.

The design of the Engineering School fully reflects the dignity, simplicity and economic features of the university architecture. Nine departments are found in the facility. Each of them intends to accommodate research laboratories, administrative spaces and offices for professors with assistants in a ratio based on their own preferences. However, a concrete program could not be provided at the design stage. On the technical aspects, the research laboratories are extremely different from one department to another. The project adopted a Base Building design (Figure 2) with capacity for variable departmental and laboratory sizes, efficient floor plans, sufficient service cores for research laboratories and capacity for various room layouts.

FAÇADE

In the Engineering School, the university – the user – addresses the identity in appearance and also focuses on views to the landscape from the windows of the building. The client – the construction department of the city – addresses the implementation of budget and safety. Considering that the budget was adjusted several times in the design process, approximately half of the meetings in the entire design process were about the façade. The façade was designed on the basis of the collective decision of the university. BEA architects provided technical services. A consistent character of neutrality is typically maintained to insure a large capacity for variable internal use and subdivisions.

CHANGE IN DEPARTMENTAL GROUPINGS AND CAPACITY FOR VARIABLE FLOOR PLANS

As with the newly planned university, the Engineering School is constantly changing in department composition, faculty

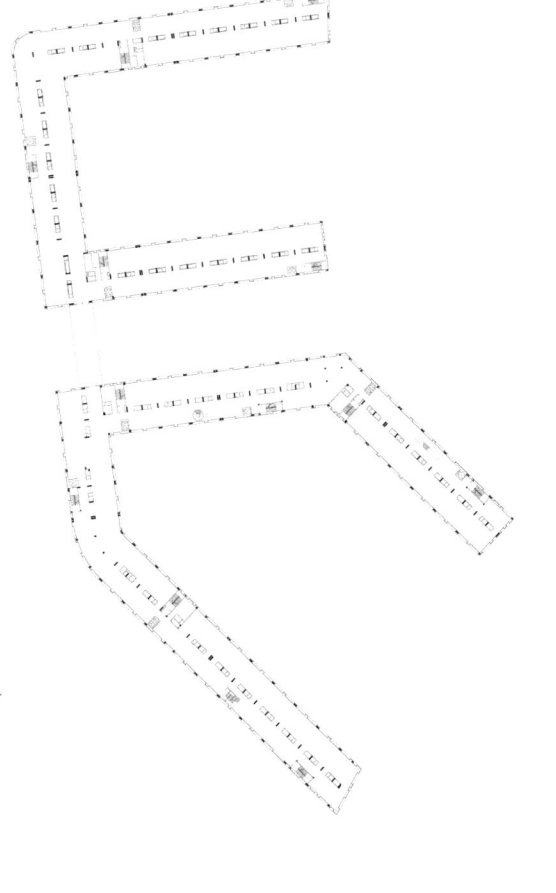

Figure 2 Typical Base Building floor

members, budget, leadership and requirements through the design and construction processes. These changes are ongoing (Figure 3a, b). However, the design and construction processes operated smoothly. In the design process, the constant changes in requests raised by departments were easily accommodated by separating the Base Building and the Infill (reflecting evolving departmental demands). Among the four projects under construction at approximately the same time on the campus, the urban layout, structure and general plan of the engineering

SHENZHEN UNIVERSITY ENGINEERING SCHOOL

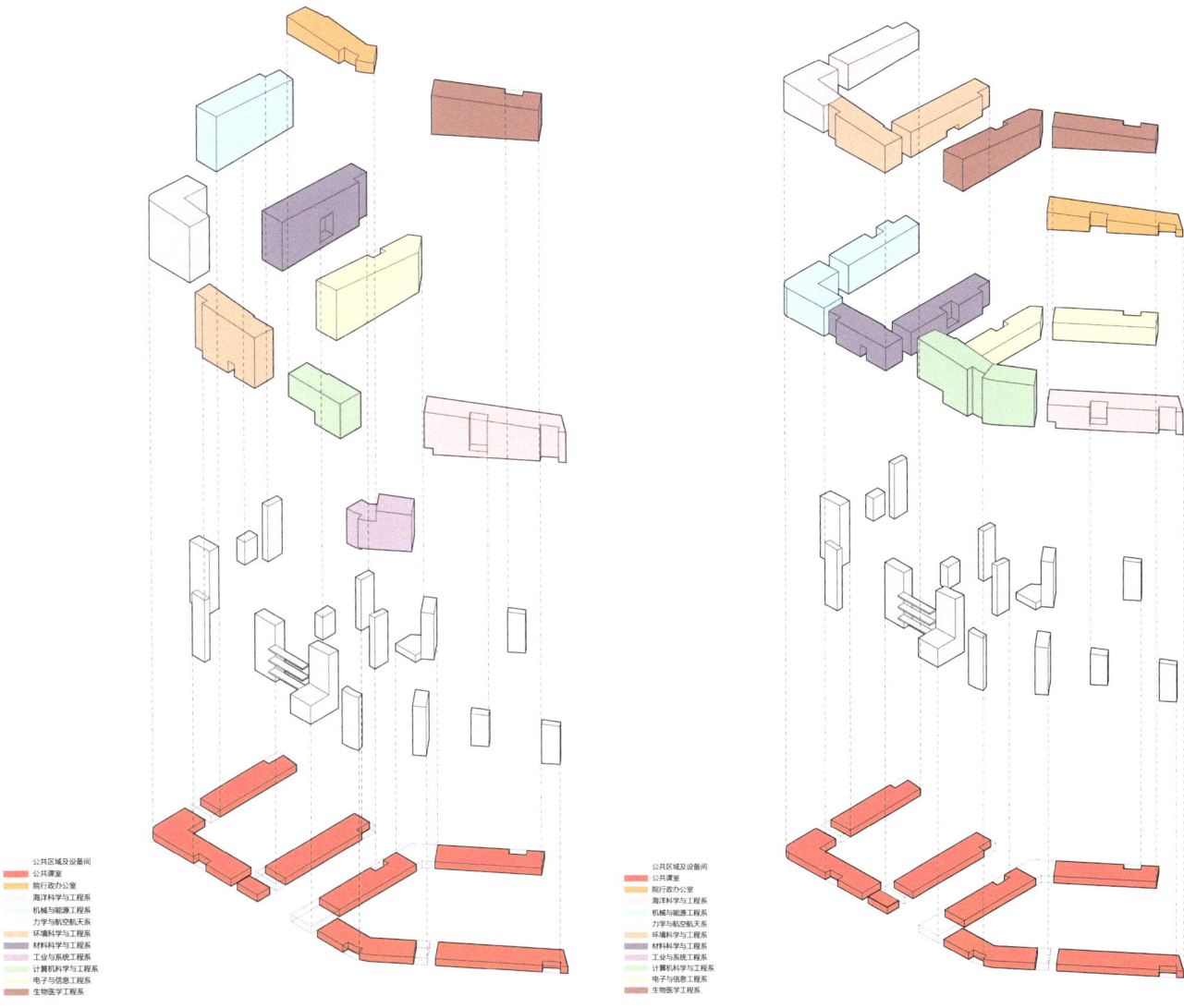

Figure 3a, b Engineering School: Changes of departmental locations from early proposal (a) to the final construction (b)

school remain largely unchanged. The final project will be exactly the same as the initial competition project submitted five years previously. This is possible because of the strategic layout of the BEA Project Book, where functional issues are independent of the Base Building (Figure 4). Through careful design of every functional requirement at the appropriate time (just before occupancy), the project fulfills highly diversified research laboratories of different departments and specialties and constant changes of the faculty and considers the quality of architectural space by the well-elaborated indoor and outdoor spaces and green architecture strategies.

INTERIOR DESIGN

The interior design was conducted with two local interior design firms in addition to BEA's design team. BEA's design covers the common areas of the school, the entrances, corridors, lounges, sanitary facilities, auditorium and faculty and administrative offices. A special consultant was in charge of the technical arrangements and the fittings of the laboratories in accordance with the specific requirements of departments (Figure 5).

Nine departments are currently located in the faculty. Each of them intends to accommodate research laboratories, administration spaces and offices for professors with assistants in a ratio based on their own preferences. However, as noted, a concrete program could not be provided at the design stage. On the technical aspects, the research laboratories are very different from one department to another. The project adopted a neutral Based Building system with an efficient floor plan, sufficient service cores for research laboratories and open design for various room layouts. A consistent character of neutrality is typically maintained to

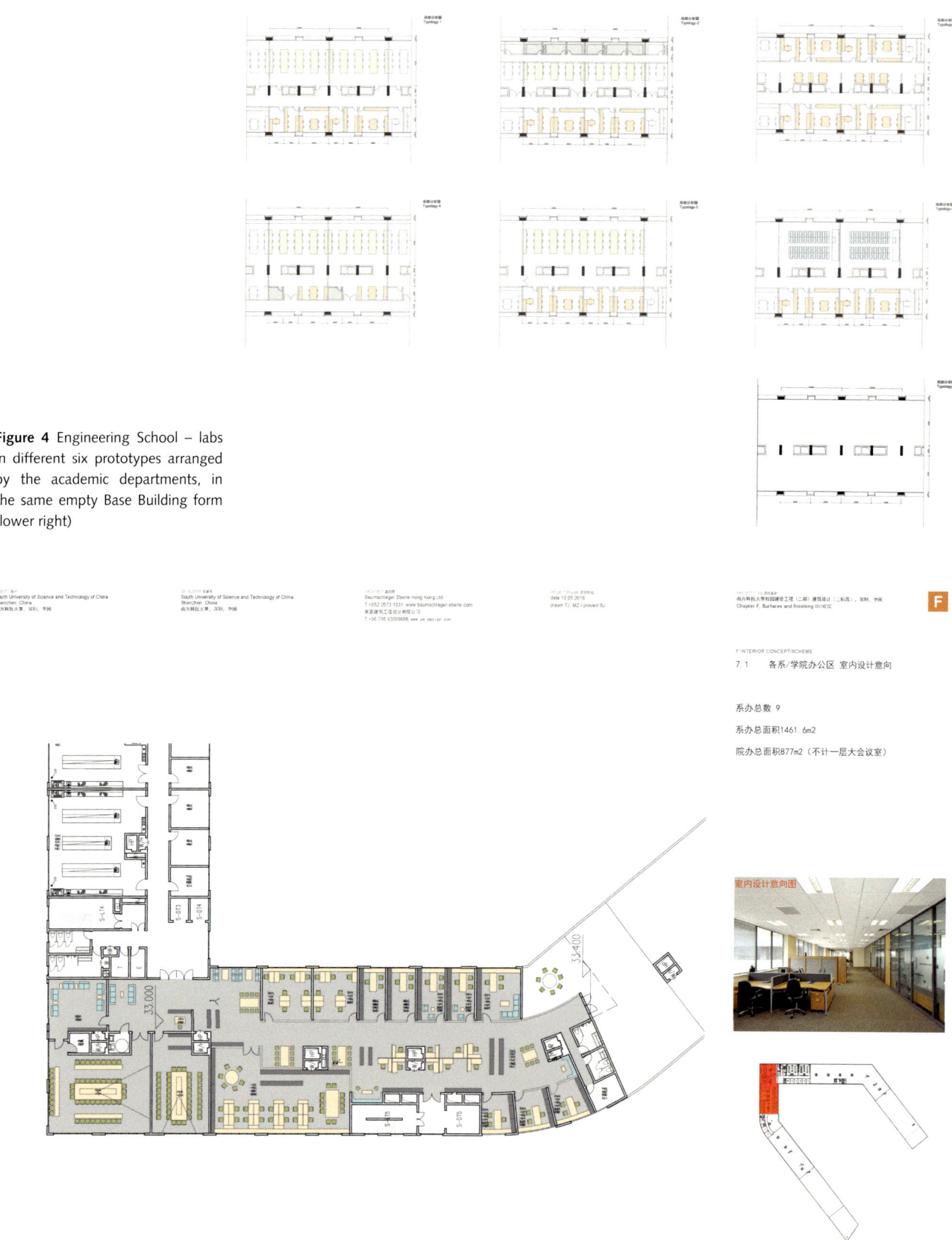

Figure 4 Engineering School – labs in different six prototypes arranged by the academic departments, in the same empty Base Building form (lower right)

Figure 5 Interior fit-out of part of one department

insure a large capacity for variable internal use and subdivisions (Figure 4).

SUMMARY

As a newly planned university, the Engineering School is constantly changing in department composition, faculty members, budget, leadership and requirements through the design and construction processes. These changes are ongoing. In the design process, the constant changes in requests raised by departments were accommodated. This is possible because of the strategic open floor plan, where functional issues are independent from structure and façade. Through careful design of every functional requirement at the appropriate time (just before occupancy), the project fulfills highly diversified research laboratories of different departments and specialties and constant changes of the faculties and considers the quality of architectural space by the well-elaborated indoor and outdoor spaces and green architecture strategies.

Santa Monica High School Discovery Building

Los Angeles, California, USA

Figure 1 Open courtyard entrance viewed from the southeast. Sustainability features include living wall, courtyard, operable windows and solar thermal and roof-top photovoltaic arrays

SANTA MONICA HIGH SCHOOL DISCOVERY BUILDING

Project Data

Architects:	HED (Architect of Record and Collaborating Design Architects; Principal in Charge: John Dale, FAIA); Moore, Rubel, Yudell Architects and Planners (Consulting Design Architects); James O'Connor Consulting Design Principal
Client:	Santa Monica-Malibu Unified School District, Santa Monica, California
General contractor:	McCarthy Building Companies, Inc.
Building area:	260,000 ft^2 (24,155 m^2)
Primary System:	• Prefabricated steel moment frame with a uniform structural grid. Typical bay size is 32' × 38' (2.97 m × 3.53 m). The structural grid extends into the two basement parking levels, where the structural system is concrete columns and flat slabs. The lateral seismic system relies on the steel moment frame with some concrete shear walls at the basement levels.
	• Three stair cores are positioned around the building's perimeter to maximize uninterrupted floor area. A fourth stair, combined with bleacher seating, cascades down through the central outdoor courtyard (see Figure 1).
	• The main mechanical/HVAC (heating, ventilation, air-conditioning) shafts and the stacked electrical and computer technology rooms are deliberately distributed to avoid large, fixed cores and maximize the capacity of the floor plates for reconfiguration.
	• Floor-to-floor heights: Generally, 14' (4.27 m), increased at ground level to 15' (4.57 m).
	• Most of the instructional spaces and 'commons' spaces are equipped with 21-inch raised floors, acting as plenums for supply air and also data and power cabling.
Secondary System:	Non–load-bearing interior walls and MEP (mechanical, electrical, data, plumbing) distribution
Tertiary System:	Educational audio-visual equipment, both movable and fixed; office equipment and mobile educational furnishings
Sustainability:	The project meets the equivalent of LEED certification following the guidelines of the US Green Building Council.
Project schedule:	Start of the design process: 2017
	Groundbreaking: 2019
	Opening: August 2021
Case study report and lead architect:	John R. Dale, FAIA, HED
Drawings:	By permission of HED
Photo credits"	Inessa Binenbaum

SANTA MONICA HIGH SCHOOL DISCOVERY BUILDING

BACKGROUND

When the design team was commissioned to develop a new multipurpose academic building for Santa Monica High School (Samohi), they were charged with designing a future-oriented facility that would provide a new direction for the redevelopment of the entire campus and respond to some key challenges facing the school district:

- The Samohi campus is over 100 years old; most of the buildings are outdated and inadequate for current needs, requiring drastic renovation or replacement;
- Campus land area is at a premium – the campus houses over 2,800 students on about 26 acres (10.5 ha);
- Typical classrooms are undersized, crowded and rigid, and supplementary meeting spaces are inadequate;
- Administrative offices are too few and too small;
- Inadequate, aging athletic and physical education facilities do not meet the needs of the student population;
- Inadequate parking puts pressure on limited land resources and the accessibility of facilities intended to be available to the general public;
- Congested pedestrian circulation networks lengthen walking time between classes in dispersed buildings.

In spite of the challenges faced by Santa Monica-Malibu Unified School District, it is blessed with a remarkably committed and supportive community that wants a progressive and well-equipped educational experience for its students. The key assets for the community are:

- A diverse, highly educated and committed community, administration, staff, faculty and students;
- Wide consensus around a progressive pedagogical approach now transforming education across the district;
- A central, prominent site in the heart of the city;
- Ongoing financial commitment on the part of the community for improving school facilities resulting from a highly effective series of local bond (fundraising) campaigns, the latest of which raised over half a billion dollars;
- The campus includes some memorable landmarks: the Greek Theater (an outdoor amphitheater) and Barnum Hall – a remarkable Art Deco auditorium and stage – that frequently serve the public as well as local school events.

THE CONCEPT FOR THE NEW BUILDING

The realization of an open, flexible 'loft' building enabling continuous change is at the heart of the design concept for the Discovery Building. The exterior of the building is intended to establish a permanent sense of place and last a century or more. It is characterized by generous bands of windows and undulating, white plaster walls that are a contemporary interpretation of the campus's Art Deco heritage. Grand, operable glass storefronts at ground level open the building up to surrounding terraces, courtyard and adjacent plaza. The learning environment is engaging, welcoming, comfortable and varied, allowing teachers and students alike to feel 'at home.'

In contrast to single and double-loaded corridor layouts common in California schools, the six-floor Discovery Building has relatively deep floor plates that allow the clustering of spaces and activities in a greater variety of sizes and formats, supporting different and evolving modes of learning. In addition to generous classrooms and science laboratories, there are a variety of 'breakout spaces' that form a series of 'commons' for project-based learning, small-group sessions, individual research and socializing. The program includes a computer graphics center, community meeting rooms, a medically 'fragile suite' for longer-term students with special needs and a large textbook distribution center. Two levels of underground parking at the base of this building have also been designed for change. With open column grids and flat slabs, these spaces can be converted to other uses in the future. Maximizing natural light and air has led to a healthy building with operable windows, trickle vents (that allow natural airflow to be filtered through a baffle system built into the window frames), folding glass walls and huge overhead doors that emphasize transparency, openness and the seamless integration of indoor and outdoor spaces, something that can be accomplished in the Southern California climate. The central courtyard, with its bleacher stairs and balconies,

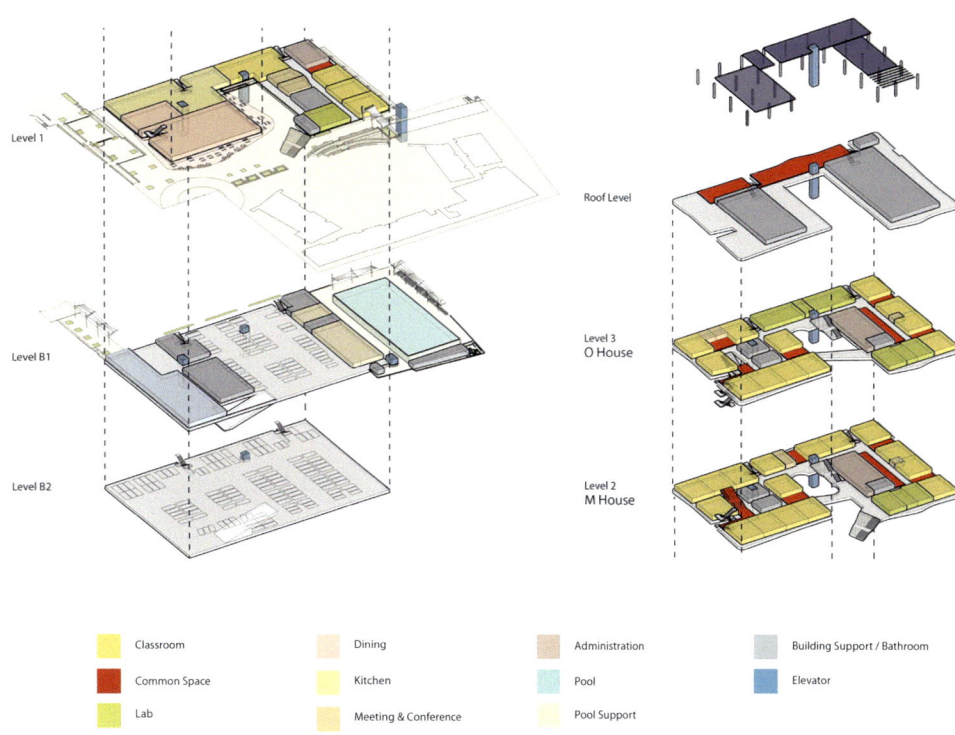

Figure 2 Drawings illustrating the highly varied program that the Base Building can accommodate

connects the new building to the adjacent Centennial Plaza and welcomes students in.

The design offers planned learning spaces, varied, interconnected spaces, inside and out, connected by external stairs and bleacher seating. Centrally located elevators and overhead bridges knit this complex together in a way that promotes chance meetings and casual socializing as well as a variety of teaching and performing opportunities. For example, the courtyard, with its open stairs and bridges, has already been the setting for a school choral concert; much more is planned.

APPLYING OPEN BUILDING PRINCIPLES

A typical school building is designed for a 50-year life cycle but is often obsolete long before it is replaced. Using Open Building principles, the design team designed an adaptable building that would accommodate frequent changes for at least 100 years, allowing teaching spaces to adapt incrementally and continuously to evolving pedagogy. The design clearly distinguishing between a fixed Base Building and an Infill system of nonstructural partitions. By introducing a raised floor system for horizontal distribution of conditioned air supply, power and data cabling, change is more manageable financially and technically. The building will maintain its utility and adaptive capacity for years to come.

The application of Open Building strategies led to the selection of two particularly important systems:

- A prefabricated steel moment frame (produced by ConXtech, Inc.)
- A raised floor system (by Tate, Inc.)

These components were chosen to achieve long-term resilience and adaptability. While these are premium systems, the additional costs of using them represented less than 1% of the total construction cost. They have already proven to be valuable assets, as changes have been made to the floor plans up until almost the conclusion of the construction phase of the project. In addition to these strategies, the modular rooftop mechanical system distributes conditioned air through a series of decentralized vertical shafts. The stair towers were pushed to the perimeter in order to maintain uninterrupted floor area capacity for change. At critical stages in the design of the project, the client and design team quickly came to consensus about what is essential to the future resilience of the building. The use of the steel moment frame structure means that there are no shear walls inside the building footprint (usually used in California's strict seismic design criteria), allowing spaces to be easily reconfigured without obstruction. Data, power and floor diffusers for air distribution can be easily repositioned within spaces employing the raised floor and can respond readily to incremental change, even if it is related to the needs and teaching preferences of a single instructor.

Open Building Components

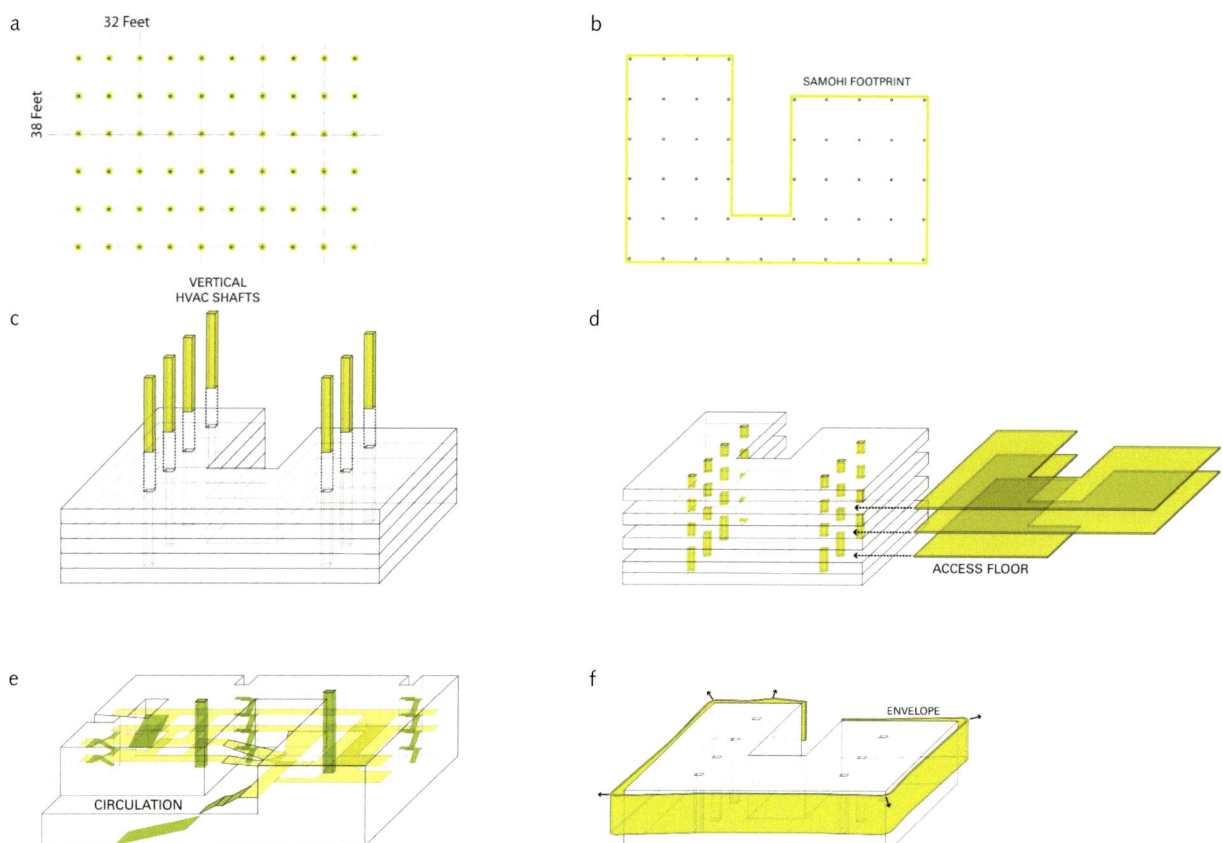

Figure 3 Open Building strategies for the Discovery Building. Clockwise from upper left corner: a: A 38' × 32' grid accommodates a typical plus/minus 1,200-sf classroom as well as other multiple uses. b: The building footprint is defined as two connected loft buildings with a courtyard preserving light, air, views. c: Modular rooftop mechanical units feed air supply from above through distributed shafts to minimize the size of fixed cores in the building. d: Access floor for power, data and air supply are provided in all potential learning spaces. e: Stairs and elevators are located at the perimeter of the building and in the courtyard to allow horizontal circulation to be reconfigured as internal spaces are reshaped over time. f: A distinct building envelope responds to the immediate historic Art Deco context and establishes a sense of place

SEPARATION OF DESIGN TASKS

To be sure that the design process was not dominated by the pressure of current needs only, Discovery was designed with the separation of design tasks in mind. HED developed the Base Building approach with MRY and then invited stakeholders to participate in design workshops to develop Infill options with oversight and approval from the facilities staff. Facilities staff initiated changes during the construction phase of the project, and HED provided the documentation to achieve these changes. Teachers individually then had a direct say before completion of the project to adjust power and technology based on how they wanted to lay out their classrooms. In this case, the raised floors facilitated these changes by the contractor. Presumably, in the future, the facilities staff will respond to faculty needs to adjust the floor plan. Will they document the changes in-house or seek architects to help with the changes? Probably the latter, but it will depend on the experience and expertise of the decision-makers at the time.

RESILIENCE AND SUSTAINABILITY

Sustainability strategies have been incorporated into this project. They ensure the building's resilience and reduction of its carbon footprint while establishing a distinctive presence on the campus. The building's orientation, massing and layout have, in turn, shaped these strategies. The courtyard, with its two-story living green wall, combines passive strategies that allow the building to breathe and achieve natural cooling. The courtyard also brings daylight deep into the building. At the same time, it creates a versatile social gathering space and extends the gathering space of the adjacent Centennial Plaza, providing supplemental program space in the most economical way possible. The rooftop

SANTA MONICA HIGH SCHOOL DISCOVERY BUILDING

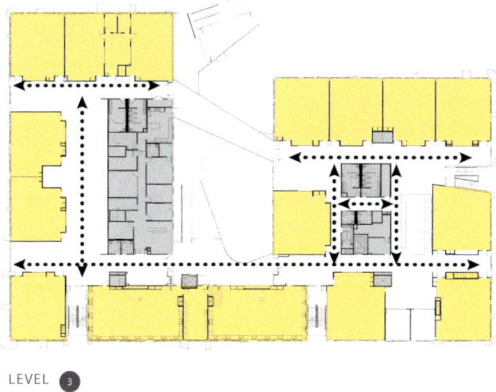
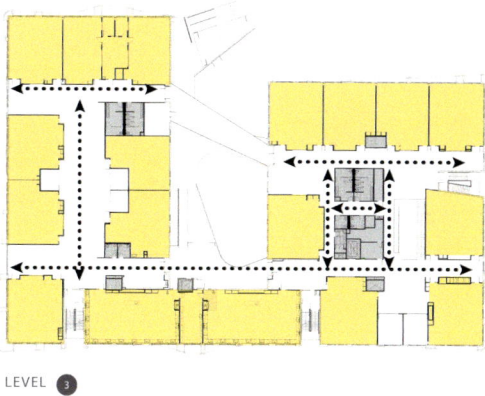
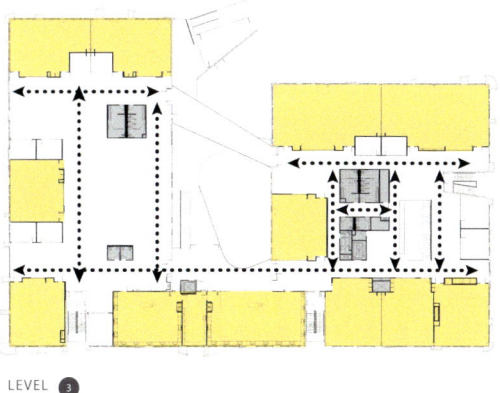

Open Building - Flexible Floor Plans

Figure 4 Capacity study illustrating potential variations on the configuration of classrooms, labs, seminar spaces and common areas on an upper floor of the building

Figure 5 Central cafeteria with large overhead doors connecting to outdoor dining terraces working comfortably within the prefabricated steel moment frame system

photovoltaic arrays, which offset power from the electrical grid by 34%, take the form of a highly visible canopy 15ft above the roof and provide economical shelter for the rooftops outdoor classroom. The visibility and clarity of its exposed systems becomes an important teaching tool. Similarly, the solar thermal array (which offsets 13% of heating demands of the large swimming pool that is part of the project) became a prominent cap to the living green wall and points to a more extensive array, which helps to reduce the heating load of the 50-meter swimming pool below. All of the outdoor spaces are accessible to students with physical disabilities, are well connected to adjacent indoor spaces and are readily available to all students and staff and are designed with the same palette of hardscape and plant materials.

UNANTICIPATED BENEFITS

From the time it was occupied, popularity as a new campus focal point has grown. It quickly became a home base for the

Figure 6 Typical flexible lab space with movable lab benches, raised floor with power, data and air supply and ceiling cloud providing easy access to perimeter return air ducts

Figure 7 Commons area learning spaces on a typical upper floor with glazed walls connecting to perimeter classrooms. All interior walls are non–load-bearing and easily reconfigured

Figure 8 The prefabricated moment frame allowed major floor penetrations such as this bleacher stair connecting second and third floors

Figure 9 The moment-frame structural grid extends to the rooftop outdoor classroom space and provides a framework for visible photovoltaic arrays

northeastern corner of the campus. Its courtyard extends from Centennial Plaza to expand outdoor venues for gathering, performances and socializing. The cafeteria, placed at the intersection of two major pedestrian routes, has expansive overhead doors and is open all during the day, thereby creating a seamless connection between well-populated indoor and outdoor spaces. The varied spaces defined within and outside the building to learn or just mingle informally quickly became well used and popular with students. To quote the high school's principal, "When they first walked into the new building, many said, 'Wow, this is like a college campus!'" and he adds that, at the end of the day, "We have to tell them, 'Hey, it's time to go home!'"

The Open Building Approach Explained

Since some readers may not know much about the Open Building approach and its origins, in what follows, we discuss the following topics.

- The Origins of the approach
- The prototypical urban problem, not limited to housing
- Basic terminology
- The problem of evaluation
- The problem of coordination
- Using the approach: operations, communication and evaluation
- Designing a support

THE ORIGINS OF THE APPROACH

The 'Supports' concept out of which the term Open Building emerged is based on the proposition that, in large housing projects, dwellings should not be understood as products that can be designed and produced like any other commodity. Instead, units of habitation should be understood as a result of *action*, a process in which decisions about each dwelling are made independently within a larger architectural infrastructure of communal services known as a 'Support' or Base Building. In its initial formulation, this 'commons' or architectural infrastructure would become a physical form when the philosophy was applied as an alternative to 'mass housing' in urban environments.

The fundamental principle of the Open Building approach is that large housing projects should be the result of action in two spheres and that these spheres of action require separation of design tasks.

While the original design methods for the design of 'Supports' focused on multifamily housing, the approach has shown its relevance for many kinds of buildings with multiple occupancies, and urban design projects as well, as the projects already discussed demonstrate.

The approach, as we know it today, has been adopted worldwide not as a defined goal but as a direction of developments in the design of everyday built environments. As already noted, the approach seeks to work with several interconnected characteristics of everyday built environment. It addresses professional design skills and ways of building. It is political, because it addresses distribution of decision-making power and challenges conventions in the regulatory environment and in project management and financing. It was never about style.

When the concept of 'Supports' was first introduced in the early 1960s, it was obvious by that time that it was not possible to think of housing only in terms of separate lots and individual houses. Larger structures containing large numbers of dwellings were being built everywhere by the thousands; they were monolithic, centrally controlled, rigid and turned out to be unsustainable, both in terms of their social fabric and management and physically. What the new approach sought to do was to provide the same opportunity for individual freedom and responsibility, investment and adaptation-per-unit-of-occupancy in higher-density situations that had been available for centuries in single-family low-density environments.

THE PROTOTYPICAL URBAN PROBLEM, NOT LIMITED TO HOUSING

The Open Building approach addresses the fact that if they are to retain value, large buildings outlive their original uses and their internal territorial boundaries and, just as often, their original floor plans and accompanying fixtures and utility systems. This fact, borne out in statistics and everyday experience of those involved in regulating, financing, design and construction work, as well as building managers and users, is the prototypical urban problem. To retain value, large buildings and neighborhoods adapt. This is not limited to housing.

This fact of life of a living building stock is why the Open Building approach separates the design of the long-lasting Support or Base Building from more mutable Infill. This is, in fact, the definition of a Support: any building intended to contain multiple occupancy units, each of which can be independently adapted to changing needs and preferences or changes in the market, building and energy standards, etc. These changes can and do occur during design and construction as well as over the long term. These changes must be possible not once but repeatedly as needed. This is the problem that has to be faced in any environment in which large numbers of people have to share a limited amount of space.

The basic proposition made in *Supports: An Alternative to Mass Housing* in 1962 was radical. The proposition was that the redirection of a country's housing efforts (public and/or private sector) toward the large-scale building of Supports and the industrial production of Infill systems (by many certified companies) could be justified on many grounds: social, industrial, economic and organizational. The Dutch Foundation for Architects Research (SAR) was charged, in 1964, with developing the methods architects would need to design Supports. Other experts in other fields would be needed to investigate financial, regulatory and other critical aspects of the concept.

From the beginning of their work, the SAR hoped that the design of Supports would help solve some of the problems traditionally associated with the design of mass housing. The design process in mass housing is based on the floor plans. Once the units (or unit types) are designed, they are repeated and arranged, woven together by structure and utility systems and wrapped in a façade, to create the larger building as an 'integrated' or unified whole and to be approved and built as such. In a situation in which costs must be minimized and standards and codes followed, while complex problems of space and utilities must be accommodated in a restricted area, the basic floor plan is always a compromise. It is the result of complex negotiations between architect, client, lender, builder, structural and mechanical engineers and other professionals. In fact, most of the design effort is directed toward finding a good-enough solution to justify continuous repetition of the floor plan(s).

This is reversed in the case of the design of a Support. The floor plans will not be predetermined; floor plans are not known at the initiation of the design process. The Support is designed to provide potential (*capacity*) to accommodate varying floor plans, initially and over time, in such a way that a change to one territory will not intrude on another territory or force change to the Support.

Such potential is not neutral. A well-designed Support offers inspiration and direction. At the same time, a Support must be capable of accommodating dwellings or other uses that meet the standards normally accepted in any particular society or market. The problems of limited resources, money and space are still present. Adaptability and variety must be available to those who finally occupy the support building. Maximum choice – with associated responsibilities – is a goal, without requiring technical or architectural expertise or excessive effort or cost. The range of choice offered to the Infill level corresponds to the view society in that locale holds as to the freedom and responsibility of individual occupants.

The use of this approach has its advantages, but its introduction in practice have been slow to happen. Because it stresses coordination and communication in the design process, it is of little use for an individual working in isolation to apply it. Its utility, therefore, is inevitably related to the organization of design as a decision-making process, as already noted. It is useful if those involved really want to separate design tasks and yet coordinate and communicate. This, of course, is not always the case. The desire to coordinate and communicate usually becomes apparent only when individual efforts start to yield diminishing returns.

Faced with complex problems, we tend to try to simplify them. This is a fruitful strategy when purely technical problems are involved, but if human social, economic and psychological needs are oversimplified, the result is a reduction of human life itself. This is what mass housing in the Netherlands taught the SAR team, and it is a lesson that must be learned elsewhere as well, either by example or by experience.

Simplification of the design problem led, in mass housing, to the elimination of the user/inhabitant in the decision-making process. The reintroduction of users created problems that needed solutions. To avoid oversimplification of the organizational and/or technical aspects of creating a decent living environment, new design methods were needed: means to coordinate and communicate during design and construction while respecting the need for continuous exercise of value judgments at all levels.

One way to simplify the problem and still create good housing solutions is to use large areas of land and extensive physical infrastructures to make that land accessible and useable for detached dwellings or buildings. This approach has resulted in the typical suburban sprawl that is evident around the world. The suburban example offers a solution that assumes a degree of user control and future adaptability in combination with a relatively simple design and planning process that everyone can understand. It is a process, moreover, that offers each participant – user, builder, regulator, developer or investor – a clear role and a certain balance between their interests.

The problem is inevitably complicated when complexity increases either due to a change in the balance of interests or when space is limited. The more people who have to share a given amount of space, the more complex the problems become. When this happens, individual dwellings must be clustered, and a much more intricate interweaving of spaces, systems and functions is needed. One way to arrive at a solution is to eliminate the individuality and independence of the dwellings – that is what mass housing does – in either public- or private-market housing. But this oversimplification also eliminates the user as an active, responsible participant with economic interests, and the balance of interests that, throughout history, has been vital for the process of creating an acceptable and regenerative human habitat is broken.

The Open Building approach, exemplified in projects shown earlier and many more besides, recognizes the importance of balancing interests in the typical urban situation, where higher density should not reduce but enhance the duality of private and public life and shared responsibility for its flourishing.

BASIC TERMINOLOGY

Three basic terms are worth reviewing.

Urban tissue is used to describe a level of intervention – and a separate design task – between the stage set by urban structure and planning (largely two-dimensional urban infrastructure and land use) and individual buildings or building complexes. It is the domain of urban designers, who set a 3-D stage of public space, basic building form and thematic qualities that lower-level interventions will follow. In this book, we do not spend very much time on this level of work except to show exemplary cases at the beginning of the book, several historical examples and the way in which grids can be helpful to urban designers. This subject deserves a new book in its own right.

A Support. A Support belongs, legally speaking, to the immovables. It is real property. It is for habitation and use of various kinds and is designed in such a way that within it, occupant spaces can be designed in which the layout and the equipment of each can be independently specified and can change over time without forcing the Support to change. In this way, a Support is an architectural infrastructure. It is not an empty or neutral structural skeleton. A Support is architecture. Designing a support is a separate design task.

Around the world, there are many words for Support, including Skeleton, Primary System and Base Building. We will use the term 'Base Building' instead of 'Support' from this point on in the book.

The Infill. Infill constitutes a set (or system) of elements belonging, legally speaking, to the movables. Infill is specified per unit of occupancy, in such a way that by means of those elements, the layout and the equipment of each occupancy within the Base Building can be independently decided and changed without forcing change to neighboring 'territories' or the Base Building. The design of Infill is a separate design task.

There are also many terms around the world for Infill, including Secondary System, tenant work and fit-out. We will use the term 'Infill' from this point on in the book. This is to be distinguished from 'filling-in' an empty parcel on a city block.

The concept of Base Building and Infill was introduced in the design process in order to translate the independence of each unit of occupancy and the separation of design tasks into material terms.

- **The Base Building contains all that does not fall within the competence of those parties controlling individual occupancies (e.g., dwellings) and about which they have no responsibility. It is 'the commons.'**

- The Infill contains all about which those controlling individual occupancies have competence and about which they therefore hold responsibility.

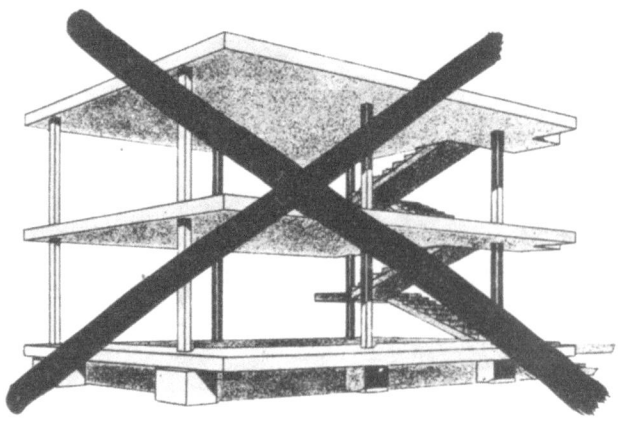

Figure 1 A support is not a skeleton (*Source*: from Habraken (1970))

We want to reiterate that the question of what belongs to the Base Building and what belongs to the Infill should be answered not only on technical grounds but on the opinion that society has of the role of the individual occupancy (family, office tenant, healthcare operating unit, etc.). That is, a judgment is needed on the amount of freedom and responsibility occupants can exercise within their territory. This is why we say – and explain in more detail later – that conforming to social structure is a key characteristic of everyday built environment that Open Building recognizes.

In each design process, large or small, *territorial boundaries* need to be clarified and division of responsibilities understood. Boundary setting and division of work will differ from region to region, country to country and project to project. In times of rapid change and with an increase in international practices, territorial boundaries and other aspects of design practice benefit from explicit specification and a common language. Territorial boundaries, it's important to emphasize, can have important architectural manifestations, such as gates of various kinds, 'margins' separating public and private space, division of façades and so on.

The separation between Base Building and Infill is different from the distinction between coarse building and finish building. That distinction is made entirely on technical grounds. Those terms refer to two phases of the production process. In contrast, a Base Building is a certain kind of architectural infrastructure; it can be a finished product within itself, but, again, it is not a raw structural skeleton (Figure 1). In the production/construction of a Base Building, a distinction can be made between a coarse building phase and a finishing building phase.

In the Open Building approach, therefore, every physical element and every space belongs either to the Base Building or to the Infill. Some kinds of elements, such as doors or pipes, can obviously appear in both: that is, we can and usually do have doors and pipes in both Base Building *and* Infill, but they will be different doors and pipes. Public corridors, fire stairs and elevators and the building façade (or parts of it) are typically part of the Base Building. The building façade can belong entirely to the Base Building, or some parts may belong to the Infill. The Infill does not necessarily have to be industrial products. Masonry walls can belong to the Infill if those walls can change independent of the Base Building and without impacting other occupant territories.

The cases at the beginning of the book show a range of interpretations of such distribution between Base Building and Infill.

THE PROBLEM OF EVALUATION

In conventional practice, the evaluation and regulatory approval of a building is heavily influenced if not determined by its floor plans. But in the case of the Open Building approach, it's not possible to evaluate the design of a building by examining the occupancy unit floor plans, since there are none. The Base Building has to be judged in a different way. This presents a *problem of evaluation*. The Base Building must be judged on its *capacity* to accommodate dwelling (or other occupancy) plans, which satisfy the individual requirements of different (and changing) users, throughout its life span. To solve this problem, a systematic way had to be found to evaluate Base Building designs by generating a series of representative possible floor plans and judging them by a set of general criteria. The method for this developed by the SAR (*SAR65*) provides tools to cope with the problem of evaluation. One of the central methods – *capacity analysis* – is discussed in detail later in the book.

THE PROBLEM OF COORDINATION

There is another important aspect to the design of Base Buildings and the Infill systems or products to be used in them. When a Base Building is designed – or even a system that lends itself to their construction – it is expected that Infill elements will be used that have been designed and produced independently. This is no different than the way that all manufactured products are made available in the market – from bricks to toilets and refrigerators. They are produced independent from the projects in which they will be used.

There will also be two production processes: one for the Base Building and one for the Infill. It is impossible to foresee the kinds of Infill elements or Infill packages that will eventually be used in a particular building. To enable these different processes to independently produce compatible systems or elements, the *problem of coordination* must be solved. This is the same problem that is addressed by industrywide interface standards in, for example, plumbing and electrical components manufactured by different companies but that are expected to fit together in a fully functioning building. Such interface standards push products into the category of commodity products and, with competition, enable providers to seek competitive advantage while lowering per-unit cost, knowing that specifiers have substitutes available to choose from.

Some like to call the relationship between Base Building and Infill '*loose fit*.' That is only accurate up to a point. Eventually, Infill material must meet Base Building material. If the two material 'systems' are independently produced and yet must go together in a project, meeting high quality and safety standards, reduced and quiet on-site work and offering solutions at a range of price points, 'fitting' dimensions need to be described and addressed. That is also what *SAR65* dealt with.

The method developed by the SAR provides the necessary principles and notation to arrive at such evaluation and coordination. But it is also clear that these are principles that require further development as the industry and society evolve and as AI and computational tools are brought to bear.

USING THE APPROACH: OPERATIONS, COMMUNICATION AND EVALUATION

We can explain briefly some of the ways the Open Building approach can be used. To do this, a few words must be said about the nature of the approach itself. As noted, in the design of large building projects – not limited to housing – the process of evaluation must test what is possible within a given architectural infrastructure – for example, the possible final floor plans – against what is generally desirable – that is, explicitly stated standards.

The same evaluation process is needed for building complexes, neighborhood and urban design as well as product design.

The Open Building approach basically offers a series of operations that give such comparisons, in increasingly complex situations. For example:

- Given the width of a building's structural bay, what meaningful combinations of spaces or functions can be accommodated?
- Conversely, given certain necessary relationships between functions, what bay width offers an optimum solution within certain technical and financial constraints?
- In what specific areas of a structure can certain desirable activities be located?
- Where should common installations (for example, piping of various kinds, wiring, ducts, etc.) be positioned to enable a suitable range of layout variations while respecting the territorial autonomy of each occupancy and meeting cost constraints?
- Where should fixed elements for fire egress and vertical circulation be placed?
- What façade design will be most satisfactory for the expected variety of interior layouts? Should some façade elements be Infill elements?

The result of each separate operation within the method is always what is called a series of *variations*. Variations are a number of possible solutions that give us the information we need to make decisions and proceed in the design process.

In order to make the resultant variations comparable with other variations that result from other operations, generating and notating them in a systematic way is very helpful. This means that the way we notate the variations and the way that the system of notation is arrived at must be formalized in order to avoid ambiguity and facilitate easy communication. Essentially, the operations that constitute the approach deal with the kinds of questions always raised in any design process:

- What consequences do certain decisions about physical form have in terms of possible uses and layouts?
- If we want to facilitate a range of uses and layouts, what forms can be found which will not only accommodate them but also inspire them?

When a single individual faces such questions, and the problem is not too complicated, an intuitive approach may suffice. No formal analysis or formal communication with other people is necessary. But if several participants are involved in the decision-making process, if the problem becomes more complex, if accountability is required, or if the norms and standards to be applied must be made more explicit and decisions made transparent, we need formal methods of analysis and notation.

Generally speaking, the need for a systematic approach becomes more apparent when:

1. Several participants, with different values, experience, interests and skills, are involved in the decision-making process;
2. Matters of quality must be made explicit in terms of standards and norms to be understood and agreed upon by the different participants;
3. Decisions must be made incrementally in such a way that each decision leaves open a number of options to be dealt with at a later stage;
4. Several participants need to be able to operate independently but simultaneously in a coordinated way;
5. And different participants need to be able to operate independently and sequentially in a coordinated way.

In other words, if the design process becomes a process of decision-making about physical forms in which different participants have to make coordinated decisions, formal communication conventions are very helpful if not absolutely necessary. This is crucial in order to record decisions and evaluate such decisions in terms of use, feasibility of implementation and cost. Without such conventions, communications can easily break down, and a structured process becomes very difficult to achieve.

DESIGNING A BASE BUILDING

The basic concept of a Base Building presupposes that at least two participants are making decisions independently and sequentially. First, there is the designer of the Base Building, who provides an architectural infrastructure in which, at a later date, a dwelling (or other use) will be designed and installed using an independent decision-making process.

The idea of a Base Building is quite different from an empty structural skeleton, as already noted. Many misunderstand this point. A Base Building is architecture. This is the reason that one of the defining drawings explaining the Open Building approach is the one shown earlier (Figure 1).

At least three participants are involved: the architect (or design team), the regulatory power and the client/investor. Active citizens' groups are also involved in many cases. All participants have to comply with clearly formulated norms and standards in such a way that these can be effectively applied to compare different series of possible uses of the Base Building. Finally, the design of a Base Building involves a number of technical experts: architect, structural engineer, builder and electrical, mechanical, sanitary, heating and ventilating engineers, etc. As in any other building, their various efforts have to be combined, but in this case, they all operate within familiar cost and space constraints while having to arrive at a Base Building solution that offers *capacity* (discussed in more detail later).

Thus, the problem of Base Building design forces the consideration of design as a *two-step* decision-making process in which the decisions result in physical built forms, while the criteria are based on technical and economic feasibility and adaptability in use. This problem led the SAR team to develop tools to aid in the solution of problems that can be recognized in many other design situations, totally unconnected with the problems of adaptable housing. Even the design of urban fabric must address these issues.

READINGS
Habraken, N.J. (1970). *3R's for Housing*. Scheltema & Holkema, Amsterdam.

Five Characteristics of Everyday Built Environment that Open Building Designs For

INTRODUCTION

We'd now like to step back from the specific operations of an Open Building approach to discuss five interrelated characteristics of everyday built environment, mentioned earlier, that the Open Building approach designs for. We discuss these characteristics – which may seem overly abstract on first reading – because we want to emphasize once again that the Open Building approach is not an end in itself. That's true of any method. By discussing these characteristics, we want to be clear that the approach goes well beyond such limited technical concepts such as 'flexibility,' 'adaptability,' 'disentanglement' and so on. It also goes well beyond style.

We hope readers will agree that these characteristics – or attributes – are evident everywhere that ordinary built environments flourish and sustain themselves over many generations. They are not the only such characteristics, but they are, in any case, what the Open Building approach designs for. To explain them in what follows, why they matter and how they interconnect, we draw on personal experiences studying and visiting diverse environments around the world that we believe many readers will also be familiar with. We also use examples from historical environments we hope are already familiar, and refer from time to time to the built projects shown earlier in the book.

- **Separating design tasks:** This may be the most important characteristic. It is most evident and effective in large building projects and in urban or campus design. This means that we separate the design of what is shared and thus long-lasting from what is tuned to individual or small-group requirements and thus likely to change at the pace of generations, or more quickly. In doing so, we conform to the local society's concept of the distinction between the 'commons' and the freedom and responsibility of individuals or small groups to control their own territories.
- **Thematic design:** Especially because design tasks tend to be or are separated in large interventions, sharing architectural themes such as patterns and systems and types is very important. Further, not only is this sharing important, but making variations on shared themes brings richness, complexity and coherence to our built environment.
- **The importance of territory:** Decision-making control – as with design tasks – is inevitably distributed to enable environments to sustain themselves. An understanding of territory is key to avoid conflict but, of equal importance, presents wonderful opportunities for new ideas in architectural form-making.
- **The inherent hierarchy in built environment:** Built environment is universally structured into 'levels of intervention.' This has found its counterpart in the way we organize our design professions (urban planning, urban design, architecture interior architecture and so on). Working with knowledge of these levels helps us manage complexity and change.
- **Balancing permanence and change:** Finally, since change is inevitable in any truly alive and sustainable built fabric, knowledge of the balance of permanence and change is a key to gaining insight into and working with the behavior of buildings and neighborhoods.

We hope readers will agree that together, these characteristics are very important to fully alive and regenerative buildings and urban fabric. They help make the places we want to live and work in have value and endure. Of equal importance, they need to be at the center of our creative energies as we cooperate with others and conduct our practices.

AN EXPLANATORY NOTE

Before explaining these characteristics, several notes about them are in order. First of all, as we said before, we need to dispel the myth that the Open Building approach can become a formula. We have heard many times that the operations of the approach could be turned into one or more algorithms. Algorithms may be useful. However, what we are discussing here is a new *game* with new game rules rather than some kind of fixed performance. In games, there are rules to be studied and followed, but players can be and are expected to use their imaginations and skill in making moves. This is true in soccer, chess and designing. But analogies can only go so far; designing is not a game of winners and losers but a process we undertake in which reaching agreement with others about what to build is the outcome.

Second, these five (of many) characteristics are frequently taken for granted as passé when they are considered at all or are ignored completely in our discussions among ourselves or with our clients. Or they are thought to be in opposition to 'good design.' We find this particularly true in the case of the idea of thematic design. Sharing themes and making variations on them in the design of buildings or urban complexes goes against attitudes that are so ingrained that only a major shift will be able to unlock the potential of sharing patterns, systems and types to make a lively and coherent built environment. This is particularly important when tasks are separated and control distributed, thus making cooperation ever more important. Themes and variations, as in music, need to become familiar to us in our practices.

We believe that these characteristics deserve serious consideration because of the widespread – and we believe misguided – belief among architects and clients that:

- Projects we design will not need to change if we do a good job in the first place;
- To achieve good results, full unified control of projects is needed, exercised across as many levels of the environmental hierarchy as possible;
- Architecture has the power to shape social structure and behavior rather than what is more often the case that social conventions shape what we do;
- Originality is paramount.

We think these beliefs produce a troubling disconnect between the actual forces at play in shaping contemporary built environment and how we discuss our work, conduct our practices and make investments. This disconnect renders us less able than we should be to contribute to the stewardship and resilience of the quality of everyday environment. These attitudes undermine needed cooperation in meeting the urgent challenge of climate change and achieving a fully circular economy.

At the same time, thankfully, we see colleagues, especially those in a younger generation of practitioners, who are working diligently to close that distance and overcome those obsolete attitudes, often under the radar and too seldom recognized and celebrated for their efforts.

Helping our professional culture overcome this distance and applauding those whose work recognizes these interconnected characteristics is why we have written this book. When these characteristics are familiar to readers, we hope to add to what is already understood and applied in practice. For those for whom they seem strange or contrarian, we hope you will read on with inquiring minds and trust that you may find something useful for your work.

SEPARATING DESIGN TASKS: DECIDING WHAT IS SHARED AND WHAT IS DECIDED INDEPENDENTLY

As discussed throughout the book, the Open Building approach is based on the separation of design tasks. When we talk about buildings, the first question to ask is this: what belongs to the more permanent architectural infrastructure or Base Building and what belongs to the Infill – that is, what can be expected to change every generation or sooner? This question can be answered not only on technical grounds but on the opinion that society has of the role of the individual occupancy (household, office tenant, healthcare operating unit, discrete building, etc.), i.e., on the amount of freedom we can exercise in shaping the territory we occupy. This is why we say that separating design tasks must *conform to social structure*. In each design, this division must be explicitly stated. There is no formula for this. Nor will one way of separating design tasks necessarily reflect social structure in another locale, another project type or country or another time.

There is no 'correct' answer about what physical elements belong to each of the several design tasks. For example, one question that is incessantly – and rightly – debated in multifamily residential design is whether bathrooms are part of the Base Building's design or, instead, are part of the Infill. It ought to be clear by now that such decisions about what belongs in the scope or responsibility of each of the separate tasks has very important design, technical, financial and legal consequences.

For a long time, perhaps since the advent of modernism and the hubris that accompanied it, professionals believed that their designs could and would shape lives and transform society. Many held this dream with the best of intentions. But to a greater extent than we may wish, things work the other way around. Society eventually puts its stamp on the built environment.

While we say that design tasks should be separated in large projects, we don't mean that this separation necessitates distribution of design tasks to multiple design offices, although that usually happens, especially over long periods of time. One design firm or even one designer responsible for everything in a project can and should learn the skills needed to manage separation of design tasks, too. The separation should therefore mirror the distinction of different life cycles of parts of sustainable environments.

Separation of Design Tasks in Urban Design or Campus Planning

Urban designers, working on large urban extensions, new towns or academic campuses or industrial parks have long understood that one party cannot and does not 'do it all.' This, of course, is in contrast to the speculative and evocative proposals such as Frank Lloyd Wright's Broadacre City.

Broadacre City represents an astonishing vision that specifically eschewed separation of design tasks. Wright personally designed everything from the placemats on the table, the dining room table and the buildings, the streets to the automobiles in the streets and the helicopters flying in the air, and everything in between. Tony Garnier's Cite Industrial was another vision of this sort, as were most of Le Corbusier's city planning projects. These and many other visionary built environments were never – or rarely – realized, for practical if not political reasons. However, the vision of unified design of large urban projects remains very strong.

But in general, the job of urban designers has always been to set the stage for individual architectural interventions, on territories controlled by diverse parties. Working with separation of design tasks is, for them and their clients, a matter of course. We know from history that it is quite normal that sizable territories are planned, functions distributed, public spaces defined and their 'build-out' accomplished over time by many different architects and other design professionals, working for different property owners. We have countless examples in historic urban areas in

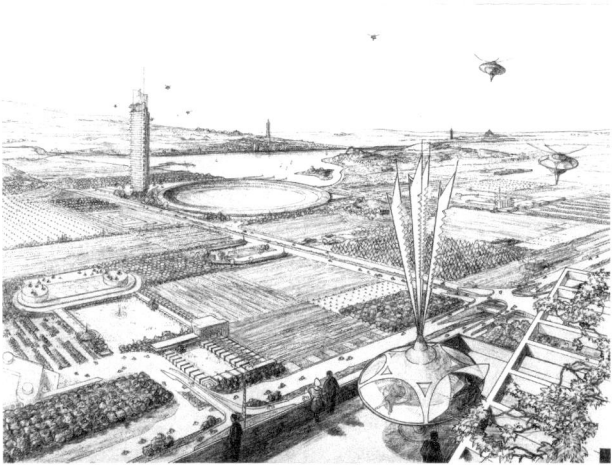

Figure 1 Broadacre City by Frank Lloyd Wright (*Credit*: Sdoutz, F. 2011)

which an initial build-out was undertaken to less than the full capacity of the available site, to be later added to incrementally by successive owners and occupants.

One result of ignoring separation of design tasks appears in many if not most contemporary suburban developments which entirely fill their allowed buildable 'footprints' or establish regulations built-in to the projects' rules that prohibit additions or exterior alterations, even within private territories. In these cases, the original designers and their clients do everything they can to control, from the top down, any possible changes, including changes in density.

Yet we also know of countless urban environments that gradually intensify in density over time, by subdividing territories, filling in empty space by adding built volume to meet new market demands and get higher utilization of expensive public infrastructure.

Sometimes, these urban design or campus design schemes involving separated design tasks have been and continue to be implemented with remarkably little controversy or explicit methodology. Conventions guide actions. In the best cases, the results can be sustained by their ability to change and adapt, part by part, over time. These are exemplary built fields that engage public and private interests and governance and that balance architectural variety as well as urban coherence, mentioned later when we discuss *thematic design*. Large sites are often developed with no explicit guidance for individual architects each doing a project, other than by the developer's individual selection of design firms, trusting them to do a good job by following accepted contemporary conventions and local building and zoning regulations. We know of too many such environments that are banal and well below the highest quality.

We also know of time-consuming but highly productive negotiations around large models where all parties can see the work of others and agree to adjust their own design under the leadership of a thoughtful and respected supervising architect. (See the

Figure 2 Sydhavnen/Sluseholmen Copenhagen Harbor renovation project. Planning & Urban Design: Soeters Van Eldonk Ponec architecten (Sjoerd Soeters). Working model that showed the progress of designs of every block (*Source*: Soeters Van Eldonk Ponec architecten (Sjoerd Soeters))

Sydhavnen/Sluseholmen case at the beginning of the book and what follows.)

Separation of Design Tasks Has Been Commonplace in Office Buildings and Shopping Centers

Commercial office architecture has experienced the separation of design tasks since the latter half of the 19th century. The advent of large high-rise buildings was, for example, enabled by the invention of steel construction, the elevator and the vented-trap toilet. This accompanied rapid urbanization and a boom in the formation of small private enterprises needing space for their offices but not wanting responsibility for entire buildings. Emerging technical and economic opportunities and evolving building regulations led to the separation of design tasks as a pragmatic response. Architectural texts discuss the new building type focused on the "warehouse-like building interiors with continuous, unbroken floor areas, waiting to be subdivided according to tenant requirements." (See Figure 3)

It's fair to say that no one paid particular attention to the benefits of separating design tasks – it 'came with the territory.' Of course, new problems emerged. Boundary frictions in contracts, learning to divide large floor areas into independent territories, management of a host of new subcontractors moving in and out of already-occupied buildings, new financing tools, new regulations, incorporating new technical products and their various suppliers and specialists, new heating, electrical and plumbing systems were all dealt with as circumstances arose. While this is now conventional practice, all problems arising from this practice have not been solved, as any facility manager will tell us. Of particular relevance to the Open Building approach is the continuing and problematic practice, discussed frequently in what follows, of running drainage piping from plumbing fixtures dispersed on one floor plate downward through the floor slabs into the ceiling of tenant spaces below. This, of course, violates the principle of territorial autonomy.

But something very important was happening during the evolution of office properties. A new *decision-making level* was emerging in the production and transformation of a building stock. We can say that this new level – and with it the natural separation of design tasks – became a powerful reality in office buildings. In the late 1950s, several large furniture companies, seeing a growing market for their products and opportunities to expand the definition of 'furnishings' in the office sector, began to market what came to be known as 'systems furniture' (Propst, 1968). These products accompanied changes in depreciation rates in the tax code, allowing an entire class of 'movable' products not attached to the building as real estate to be 'written off' in a much shorter time than the buildings in which they were installed. These new products/services included various kinds of raised floors for horizontal distribution of cabling and air-handling systems within the legal and fire boundaries of demised spaces, new partitioning and ceiling and lighting systems, quick-connect power and data cabling and so on.

Since then, the 'systems furniture' market has expanded to include more than a dozen multinational companies, with franchised subsidiaries and dedicated installation teams. A Secondary market for used systems furniture grew, as did many subsidiary product/systems and services. This period also saw the emergence of separate divisions within large design and general contracting offices specializing in 'tenant work' or 'fit-out.'

This was also the period during which the rapid rise of the interior design profession took place to take charge of this new

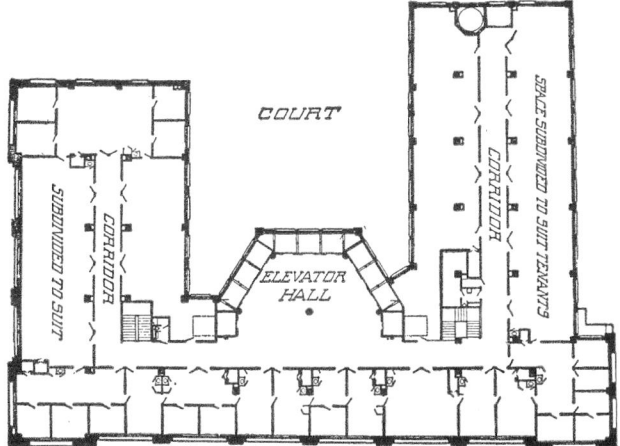

Figure 3 Holabird and Roche Marquette Building, Chicago, 1894. In most of these buildings, large portions of every floor were left without partitions so that they could be subdivided later to suit the tenants' changing requirements (*Source*: Gideon, 1963)

level of intervention. This new professional practice quickly came into conflict with the architecture profession's understanding of professional licensing and its professional 'sphere of control.' University degree programs in interior design and interior architecture had emerged. In North America, more than half the states in the US, Puerto Rico and the Canadian Provinces passed some form of interior design legislation. A certification examination (www.cidq.org) became the industry's recognized indicator of proficiency in interior design principles and a designer's commitment to that profession.

The inability and reluctance of the architecture profession to recognize and help clarify the emergence of this new 'level of intervention' was, of course, at the root of the conflict.

Over time, task separation took on a kind of normalcy in the real estate sector for office buildings. General contractors and subcontractors knew their roles, as did architects and interior architects, product manufacturers, building code officials and lenders. On a few occasions, a singularly powerful party tried to reconfigure these roles. One was an initiative by the large furniture company Steelcase, which, in partnership with a large real estate investment firm, embarked on an ambitious development called Workstage. In the late-1990s, it organized itself to provide a service to clients of a systematized Base Building of standard steel structural components organized on a 40" grid, a raised floor for horizontal distribution of cabling and conditioned air (provided by Tate, a large company specializing in this kind of product), and also provided all interior tenant work or fit-out using a patented (and astonishingly complex) 'closed' system called Pathways (which was subsequently withdrawn from the market). Each building using this system had an exterior skin designed by a separate architect to fit the particular features of each site. The approach was used for medical, office and educational facilities before closing down during a severe economic downturn. To our knowledge, this example has never been studied to draw lessons from it (ftp://ftp.steelcase.com/pub/158D/_pdfdocs/PathwaysTechWalls.pdf).

Governmental facilities in the United States such as office buildings also began to apply separation of design tasks as a practical measure, because the 'churn' of uses in these buildings, as in the commercial sector, is frequent and could not be managed without this strategy. There remains little current difference now between office buildings constructed for government agencies and offices in the private market. One initiative in particular pushed this development. In the 1970s, the U.S. General Services Administration (the arm of the US government responsible for procuring space for government agencies worldwide) made a concerted effort, in the GSA/PBS Building Systems Program, to adopt a two-step procurement process that distinguished the building's core and shell from the more systematized parts that go inside to form office spaces (Ventre, 1983). Again, this initiative has not been subjected to thorough longitudinal studies for lessons learned.

Separation of Design Tasks Is Becoming Familiar in Healthcare Facilities

Application of the principle of separating design tasks is increasingly evident internationally in healthcare facility construction, as discussed in the three projects presented at the beginning of the book and in previous work (e.g., Kendall, 2019).

More than any other building type, hospitals are functionally diverse and financially and technically complex. Changes in demographics, diseases and their treatment, equipment, doctors' practices and preferences, insurance programs and regulations are forcing the emergence of a shorter use-life Infill level, corresponding directly to healthcare functions that are the basis for the fiscal management and insurance reimbursements of most healthcare organizations.

This emergent Infill level is, in many instances, now undertaken by design teams and contractors other than the teams which designed the Base Buildings. This happens as a matter of course even if the initial project was not planned for change. It is also occurring when clients order 'shell spaces' to be constructed in the initial investment (when financing, interest rates, etc. are

Figure 4 AZ Groeninge Hospital, Belgium. The empty Base Building (*Photo credit*: Toon Grobet Architect: Baumschlager Eberle Architects)

supportive). Later, when the time comes to occupy these spaces, design firms other than the original firm often win the contracts to do the work.

Currently, it is not exceptional that a five- to seven-year period elapses between initiating the planning process for a large medical facility and start of operations. Much of that time is normally spent determining the specifics of the Infill and equipment in consultation with doctors, nurses, administrators and others, during which time progress on overall design is difficult, if not put on hold. The evidence is that departmental requirements (e.g., surgery, pediatrics, laboratories, emergency) and equipment specifics evolve during the design phase in any case, in part because heads of departments are transient and new leadership demands something different than their predecessors, but also because of innovation in products, competition, changes in reimbursement policies and so on.

To some extent, these projects are obsolete when they are first occupied. However, if a healthcare Base Building is conceived of (and financed and approved) as a design task by itself, using a well-organized capacity analysis (discussed later), construction can commence and functional layouts and equipment acquisition can be deferred without disturbing the construction schedule. There is already a partial distinction of this kind of separation of design tasks in the procurement of healthcare facilities for the United States Defense Health Agency called initial outfitting and transition (Military Standard 1691, 2016).

During 2019–2022, the ongoing COVID-19 pandemic shone a glaring light on the importance of medical facilities capable of rapid adaptation to new health services delivery demands. What is not clear is whether the separation of design tasks is explicitly or methodically employed in the initial design process within a single design firm doing a large healthcare project. We suspect methodical approaches are rare, making their improvement more difficult. This deserves much more study.

Multifamily and Attached Housing Continues to Ignore Separation of Design Tasks

Multifamily residential architecture remains an outlier in terms of separation of design tasks. This is in spite the fact that it makes up a much larger part of urban fabric – and aggregate real property investment – than any other building use. In many countries, in aggregate, more human and material resources are consumed in adjustments to this building stock than new residential construction to meet new requirements and market conditions in any given year.

As any building official, contractor, architect or occupant can explain, the work of adjusting residential buildings is too full of conflict, too expensive, too wasteful and takes too long. We believe that in large measure, these problems result from the fact that this project type follows an obsolete paradigm. Multifamily housing is conceived of, financed, designed, approved, built and managed as a single, unitary professional product.

It is interesting to note, however, that there were early experiments pointing in another direction. The advent of the high-rise buildings of 'the Chicago School' in the second half of the 19th century did see some apartment buildings constructed with removable partitions "so that a suite of five rooms could be thrown together into one" (Gideon, 1963). Yet this observation of change in Gideon and other writings of that time was not framed systemically and was never taken as something to study; no mention of design task separation or levels of intervention or independent units of occupancy is made. The same is generally true for most of the literature and reporting on 'flexible housing.'

Earlier in the book, we presented several exemplary cases from a growing number of multifamily projects in which design task separation was central. At the end of the book, we return to the roots of the Supports concept and discuss how the emergence of an Infill level and with it an Infill industry could reshape the culture of the residential building industry, enabling the separation of design tasks to begin to replace the unitary single design task model dominating the field so far.

THEMATIC DESIGN: SHARING THEMES AND MAKING VARIATIONS
Enabling Coherence with Variety

Once we take seriously the idea of separating design tasks, both in initial design but also over time, it is almost inescapable that we will have to recognize that sharing thematic qualities is the glue that helps assure coherent variation. We can share thematic qualities such as patterns (such as the margin or way of passing between public and private space or the design of façades on a street) and systems (both stylistic and technical) of various kinds. Sharing these themes, we can make variations on them. This is exciting and creative work. Doing so means that we can't keep insisting that our work must be wholly unique, special and invented anew each time.

Just to be clear: advocating that architects share themes does not argue for uniformity – stylistic or otherwise – which is an oft-heard criticism of such movements as New Urbanism. Nor does it sanction the opposite and recurrent propensity to design entirely without connection to context. Sometimes, thematic qualities are largely implicit or are conveyed informally. Sometimes, they must be methodically documented to assure that they are really understood. This begs the question of *how* these qualities are represented. Also, the number of thematic qualities is not fixed. But what we insist on is that the quality and longevity of everyday environment is only successful when we recognize the importance of shared thematic qualities – that is, what is held in common. If other characteristics we are discussing appear to focus on technique, this one focuses on matters of environmental coherence and quality. (See, for example, the Westpolder Bolwerk case shown earlier.)

We might assume that architects and other design professionals working on separated design tasks all understand quite well what we're saying. We may be told that colleagues understand intuitively how to design in a neighborly way, sharing some architectural qualities while differentiating their work by using variants on the shared themes or introducing new ones. But it's obvious when we look around that the skill at making variants is not well developed.

It's important to address sharing thematic qualities directly because it goes against the grain of much that we have been taught to value in our architectural education and that some part of the general public has come to expect. It goes against the grain of the widespread misunderstanding that architecture is an art form. Architectural education in general stresses individual self-expression, invention, breaking the rules and the production of unique projects.

We also recognize that the growth of historic preservation movements around the world and the adoption of style-based 'form-based codes' in the US are all, in part, a revolt against the ethos of hyper individuality in design. We need to say that we have absolutely no desire to thwart invention or self-expression, only to say that everything can't be unique.

Today, there are always explicit governmental regulations concerning use, height, bulk, setbacks and other stipulations such as ground-level/street-front transparency and use, energy and seismic codes, etc. In some cases, there are detailed stipulations requiring adherence to historic features of the context when an area has been declared a historic district. That said, the habit of being resistant to the regulatory environment is passed on from the academic training of architects, when students are encouraged quite frequently to 'break the rules.' When asked what a better set of 'rules of the game' might be, most students and practitioners will not be prepared to give a coherent response.

It's therefore important to study the way large sites are developed and evolve over many decades with a balance of both governmental regulations and largely implicit themes. In everyday environment, if we watch long enough, and in the best cases, new work picks up themes, patterns and systems 'baked in' to the conventions characteristic of the surrounding urban fabric. Variants on regulation-imposed themes or themes agreed to by architects and their clients may appear that introduce a new element or a new arrangement, at which point the social body in favor of the overall system can reject the new idea as an incidental occurrence or adopt it as an attractive innovation, thereby changing the structure of the underlying 'thematic system' somewhat. Thanks to their being socially embedded and adaptable, thematic

Figure 5 Amsterdam canal houses and stoops (*Photo credit*: John Habraken)

systems – either publicly mandated or privately adopted – can live a very long time, albeit always evolving. The balance between theme and variations is the most fascinating aspect of any built fabric.

A Natural Phenomenon

Everyday environments that we admire and love to visit – and live in – have always been highly thematic. We have no trouble recognizing Venetian Gothic palaces, Amsterdam canal houses (Figure 5), London's Georgian terraced houses, Kyoto's Machiya dwellings (Figure 9) or Philadelphia row houses as just a few examples of form families. More humble examples abound. Other built fabrics, on first sight, may seem chaotic and difficult to read – for example, any suburban commercial strip development – but on closer scrutiny, we always find thematic aspects even if we judge them to be banal or poorly handled. They are inseparable parts of the urban fabrics that were shaped with them.

In the past, biased Western observers thought traditional Middle Eastern urban environments were disorganized. In fact, they have a highly structured thematic complexity. Their coherence in variety came about in a largely informal manner. There are many other examples.

The famous 'Crescents' in 18th-century Bath, by father and son Wood, were originally designed as identical houses behind a common monumental façade. But since home ownership was dispersed, individual houses changed in time: expansions were made in 'the back' spaces, and interior spaces were altered. But the façades remained largely unaltered by common consent. The result, eventually, was similar to the Place Vendome distinction: variation behind an urban screen. Eventually, similar projects with unified façades came about in English domestic architecture. Most of them were built for speculation. Variations in the house plan might be made already when a house was sold before building started but otherwise would surely come later.

Boston's Back Bay is another example of a thematically coherent mixed-use environment. Stately row houses along straight streets exhibit a few important thematic qualities, with many variations (Figure 6a). Stretching along several blocks, a 'margin' is evident between the sidewalk and the building's façade. In

Figure 6a Boston's Back Bay showing the thematic variety that, over more than a century, has made this part of the city one of the most desirable places to live. Dominantly residential, large homes have often been subdivided into apartments for rent or sale or for professional offices. Ground-level commercial enterprises line some streets (*Source*: Open source)

that 'margin' are steps up to the main floor, raised 2 m or 6". about the public sidewalk. In that margin are steps leading to a lower level that is now sometimes a separate dwelling or rented flat, or was at one time a service entry (Figure 6b). That lower level opens out to a garden in the rear, sometimes accessed by an alley and garages for cars. This pattern is not unique; it can be found in London and Glasgow's 18th- and 19th-century urban fabrics.

Antonio Gaudi's famous apartment building, La Pedrera, in Barcelona is rightly considered unique (Figure 7). But it is also part of the famous 19th-century Barcelona fabric. Like most other buildings in that neighborhood, it has ground-floor spaces that are accessible from the street for shops, workplaces and offices, a formal carriage entrance that penetrates the building and leads

Figure 7 La Pedrera. Architect: Antonio Gaudi (*Photo credit*: Maria Laura Jofre)

Figure 6b The 'margin' separating the public sidewalk and the continuous row of stately houses in Boston's Back Bay (*Photo credit*: Paul Lukez)

Figure 8 Kyoto Machiya. In the historic fabric of Kyoto, we can see street after street of houses sharing the same architectural themes but each different (*Photo credit*: Stephen Kendall)

visitors to an open stairway which leads toward the main floor above and service courtyards that bring light into the back rooms of the apartments. Moreover, building height, floor heights and bay sizes are comparable with those of the other buildings in the neighborhood and thereby maintain a consistent architectural scale. In short, Gaudi's contribution fits into the urban fabric that it is part of as much as it stands out.

Throughout history, professional designers have always worked with familiar built environments, often cultivating/working with what they found in their context to design variations on existing themes. Or they have drawn lessons from them to make the few special buildings that, in their variation and exceptionalism, reinforced by contrast the thematic coherence of the place. It's wonderful to recognize that every culture has its own conventions, habits, ways of building and ways of working and using space. Recognizing this – and working with it – can quiet our anxieties that the world is becoming more and more homogeneous. Designers never invented built environments. But with modern times, we thought we could do that. We hope that readers understand why that belief can no longer hold.

In what follows, we briefly discuss two thematic qualities of many: *patterns* and *systems*.

Patterns

Not long after Christopher Alexander's *Pattern Language* came to our attention in the 1970s (Alexander, 1977), an architect friend talked about a job designing a neighborhood for a housing association. At the first work session, when the client team expected a first sketch plan, he showed images of all kinds of streets, building types, parking solutions and so on. He did so to start a conversation: "Is this the kind of streets you have in mind? Or is this a closer example? How about parking like this? How about front yards, and what about trees and sidewalks?"

He came to the next meeting with alternatives for street–house relations, parking solutions, playgrounds, house types, street profiles (setbacks) and landscaping. He made it clear that he was seeking to reach an understanding as to what the client and he would work on next.

Similar sessions were repeated in this way. The client team became restless, afraid that time was being wasted. Finally, they were shown a detailed plan for the neighborhood. Thanks to the preceding process, nothing in it was foreign to them. A meaningful, in-depth discussion could follow. Obviously, the client team did not accept everything proposed, but there was common ground, and therefore, no one was shy in suggesting changes, confident that they knew what they were talking about. The process turned out to be efficient and productive.

This example makes us think of the use of patterns in the way Alexander suggested. There are similarities, but there is an important difference. In the case described, the decision as to what patterns should be used was the outcome of a dialogue. The 'good' pattern was the pattern accepted by both architect and client, not something delivered as an a priori solution based on 'scientific' research, as Alexander seems to suggest.

Another colleague uses Alexander's patterns in a more formal manner. He used patterns when designing a teaching hospital. Asked to interview medical doctors and their staff to find out what their needs were, he wrote patterns and submitted them to the users for discussion and approval. He asked users to suggest patterns themselves. This provided a structured format for what otherwise might have been a discussion that was too open-ended or too technical a process for the users to be comfortable with. Sharing the principles of pattern formulation, both architect and user group could generate proposals and judge those put forward. Jointly accepted patterns became part of a 'program' or 'brief,' acquiring contractual status.

It seems that the power of patterns is exactly that people know them and agree to apply them and, by doing so, make the built environment a collective endeavor in which architects would benefit by participating. Without this conventional dimension, patterns are at risk of becoming catalogue items for architects to pick and choose from.

Seen this way, patterns are good instruments for coming to agreement on qualities in the environment. They are limited in scope, usually comprising a few parts in a certain spatial relationship, and therefore lend themselves to clear description and focused discussion. Patterns help to establish common ground with those who inhabit, pay for, and manage what we design. This provides much-needed help because, in today's pluriform world, we meet different environmental preferences from place to place and problem to problem. We need ways to find our bearings and connect to the social body we serve rather than coming with a set of predetermined patterns or solutions.

Systems, Variants and Structure

Systems occur where a number of parts, chosen from a predetermined set, are distributed following rules of selection and relation. All systems have thematic qualities. Although we make instances of our own within a system, the system itself is a collective property shared by a social body.

Systems can have a highly architectural content. Architects and builders in 17th-century Amsterdam, for instance, or 19th-century Bilbao, Spain, produced façades of strong and consistent kinship (Figures 5 and 9). Everyone uses the same set of parts – windows, doors, gables, bays – detailing them in a similar way and arranging them, according to shared rules, into instances of the same thematic system. While each façade has its individual identity, and designers of many are known, the system of which they are instances is a collective creation of great sophistication.

The façade system of NEXT21, a project shown at the beginning of the book, is a good example of this.

Figure 9 Bay windows in Bilbao, an example of the use of a pattern by different architects in great variety (*Photo credit*: Stephen Kendall)

These façades are systems with a high architectural content. The same is true of other examples like, for instance, the classicist system of architectural orders. Technical systems are more malleable – post-and-beam structures, for example, or load-bearing masonry walls combined with timber floors and roofs. These are systems within which we can build a wide variety of forms. They each allow a range of possible architectures. But nevertheless, they are not neutral and are able to inspire architectural articulation. Purely technical systems like those for plumbing or various utilities impose their constraints on form-making as well, but at a much larger distance from architectural form-making.

If the systems concept can be interpreted so widely as to range from the classical orders to plumbing, we need to appreciate that in all cases, there is a kind of social contract among those applying these systems. The purpose may vary from the aesthetic and symbolic to the purely practical, but the mechanism is the same: certain parties agree to work with certain parts in certain relations. They shape the parts accordingly and deploy them following relational rules. To operate in a system is to join a social body. To change a system is to convince others to change their mode of operation.

Because systems must live in a social body willing to sustain them, most successful examples have not been invented but were gradually developed within a society of actors. In that sense, systems have vernacular properties. What we normally call 'vernacular' systems – suggesting a lack of formal authorship or professionalism – are among the most resilient and durable. The story of Hassan Fathy's study and advocacy of the mud-brick vaulting systems of upper Egypt gives us a good example of how a technical system of strong architectural quality, in use for millennia, can die out, not for want of performance but because the social body sustaining it shifts its allegiance to other ways of building for largely social reasons.

All systems, even the very high-tech ones, develop, change and come alive through use. To learn about them, we should connect to the group that applies them. Books will only tell us what is no longer in discussion, what is conventional. The fully documented system may well be a dead system.

In premodern times, designers and builders, as well as their clients, operated within a limited and well-established range of systems. There were fixed ways to build and to design. Although we may be sure that over time, such systems changed like all living entities do, their change was incremental, and the systems endured. One could operate for a lifetime within the same systemics.

Today's world is astonishingly pluriform. The range of environmental systems has expanded dramatically, as noted before. At the high end, we have a large number of infrastructures for transportation and utilities that were unknown one or two generations ago. At the low end, we have an extension of these utilities – heating, ventilation, telephone, television, computing, electric power, gas, plumbing and so on – bringing conduits of all kinds, navigating the built environment to serve each nook and cranny of it. In the midrange where habitable space is made, we have steel, concrete, masonry, timber structures and a host of hybrid cases to work with.

Designing with Themes

The Open Building approach means cultivation of the five characteristics of everyday environment we've been discussing. This implies designing with themes and exploring variations on them. For many of us, this requires a change in attitude as well as development of particular skills. Many questions certainly arise. How are we to find a good balance between theme and variation, between what we share and what we do individually? How do themes come about in the first place? How to decide, for instance, on the consistent adoption of a building type or entryway pattern, or familiar issues like setback rules and height restrictions? Is it by top-down rules, collective ad-hoc agreements or implicit common understandings among designers? This balance can be studied and discussed and skills learned to artfully handle it.

Figure 10 A gate into a Hutong in Beijing (*Source*: Photo by Stephen Kendall)

Often a single higher-level design offers a shared context for many lower-level designs and, by doing so, sets thematic constraints for them that, to endure, are considered reasonable and representative. Urban design, for instance, makes a shared context for individual architectural designs, assuming they will follow certain architectural types or patterns. In a similar way, a Base Building design makes a shared context for individual units of occupancy of a certain kind. How do we know if a higher-level design offers the right context for lower-level design preferences? How do we inspire lower-level variety?

All of the cases presented at the beginning of the book show responses to these questions, demonstrating the wide variety of technical and architectural approaches that are possible.

All such questions have to do with relations among designers. These relations are relations of forms; forms sharing certain aspects, forms interpreting a given context, forms setting a context for others. In fact, all designing is intervention, and each intervention triggers response. Change of form is the language we share.

Nevertheless, we face a conundrum. For one thing, given the fierce search for competitive advantage among architecture firms, there is scant evidence today of a desire to build an evolving, renewable and shared architectural knowledge base consonant with the new realities of the built environment: sustainability, resilience and the need to plan our buildings and neighborhoods for longevity and, at the same time, incremental change.

THE IMPORTANCE OF TERRITORY

We know instinctively – and from practical experience – that when they are contested, territorial boundaries are the source of friction. But when boundaries are settled and respected, we can fruitfully do our work and distribute control in sensible ways. In one sense, this is already well understood in everyday practice – we always have 'contract boundaries,' defining the physical scope of a design project and of each consultant.

We can't emphasize enough the importance of understanding *territory* – and, with it, the control of space – as a key characteristic we need to understand for successful Open Building design. We instinctively understand what it means to control space. We know what it means to lock a door to keep others out, but we also understand that we are always free to leave the space we control. Otherwise, we are prisoners. We also instinctively understand that to enter a neighbor's territory, we move 'upward' in the environmental hierarchy into a shared or 'public' space, then knock on the neighbor's door and, on entering, move 'downward' in the environmental hierarchy into our neighbors' private territory. (This concept is fully explained in Habraken, 1998.)

The technical implications of territorial boundaries are very important to successful separation of design tasks and implementation of large projects of many kinds. We explain this further on. It is also clear that understanding such boundaries supports innovative technical and legal solutions such as new utility infrastructure systems, new façade systems and the emergence of an Infill industry – discussed later.

Understanding Territory Helps Us with the Distribution of Control

When we think about it, the question of 'who controls what and when' is related to territory and is therefore crucial when we design large projects. Control is, by definition, the exclusive

Figure 11 A living room in the Molenvliet project shown earlier (*Photo credit*: Stephen Kendall)

ability of a party to transform some part of an environment in their 'territory.'

Control is the central operational relationship between human beings and everything (space and material) that is the stuff of built environment. Control, to be clear, does not imply ownership; it does, however, imply the exclusive power of a party to change some physical part or limit access to a territory over some period of time. Control can be and often is delegated.

Territory and the distribution of control reveals itself most clearly when we observe change. In this sense, a study of control in the built environment is akin to how scientists understand the behavior of social and natural systems. In our considerations, we can never really know why control is exercised in one way or another or, for that matter, the 'meaning' of that exercise. Everyone, not only experts, exercises some control over built environment to make it come alive. It's the action that counts. We see this in people – individually or acting together – arranging books on a bookshelf, moving furniture around, tearing down or adding a wall to open or divide a space, enclosing a balcony, building a new building or opening up space for a park in an existing urban fabric.

For some strange reason, the word 'control,' or even 'power,' is seldom heard or used in professional design discourse. Yet centralizing or unifying control has been a dream of architects and clients for a very long time. We only have to think about Frank Lloyd Wright's or Le Corbusier's audacious plans, mentioned before. Unified control is now euphemistically called 'integration.' The argument is that integration will make the decision-making process more efficient and assure quality. What it really means is eliminating decision-makers. But there are consequences of cutting out parties from having a voice. Attempts at top-down unified control usually produce a governance and technical rigidity that can cause difficulties later. Cutting ordinary citizens off from having control of their immediate dwelling space in multifamily projects, for example, has caused many severe problems too well documented to have to repeat here.

A simple example may suffice to make the idea of territorial control palpable.

Consider a room in a retirement home, inhabited by an elderly lady. All of her furniture, as well as plants, pictures, photographs and other mementos of a long life, have been placed reflecting her preferences. She is free to rearrange the furnishings and her other things however she pleases. Her right to do so is fundamental and indisputable. These disparate objects share a common attribute: their placement relative to one another – the very fact that they are in the room at all – depends on the inhabitant's action – her control. She can move things around and determine their relative position. She can also discard things, give them to grandchildren or friends, or add others she receives. These parts within her dwelling space are under her control. She may or may not have similar control of the color of the walls, the curtains on the windows, and most certainly will not have control over the size of the bathroom or the selection and arrangement of its fixtures. She almost certainly has control of the temperature in the room.

The line between what the elderly lady can control and what is outside her control constitutes an essential question in the design of her environment.

Control of Space

Control of space can't just simply mean the possibility for transformation of space because, obviously, transforming space requires moving the material parts that make that space – that is, controlling form. But we know that controlling space is distinct from controlling form. Everyone understands that a complex form, for example, an office building, can harbor a variety of territorial claims of space in a given form, claims that can and do change as tenant spaces get bigger or shrink. From that, we can see that space – and territory – and material configurations (form) are inseparable.

Territorial control is the ability to close a space, to restrict entry – the ability to defend a space against unwanted intrusion. Nation-states exercise territorial control, and when it is violated,

Figure 12 A typical front door in a high-rise apartment building. This example is at the end of a corridor, giving a small opportunity for the resident to place personal possessions outside the door and in the 'public' space (*Photo credit*: Stephen Kendall)

the intrusion can cause war. On a more domestic scale, Oscar Newman wrote about 'defensible space' in his book of that title. He brought the concept of territory into discussions of public safety in housing environments in the 1970s (Newman, 1973). However, this work was forgotten and did not enter the general architectural discourse.

Space under control is territorial. Distinguishing territory is apparently a universally understood part of culture, yet it is manifested quite differently in different cultures. It is too often forgotten or ignored as a generator of form. Our generation doesn't think much about territory as something architectural. In history, territory was well understood. We used gates, front yards no matter how small (spatial margins, examples of which follow later) and formal elements of spatial hierarchy. We made space at the front door in apartment buildings to decorate and where a baby stroller could be parked safely. Perhaps starting in modernist times, signs of territory were eschewed in favor of uninterrupted flow of space. Now we too often handle territory by invisible electronic means devoid of architectural significance. We seem not to think of territory as inspiring. Ubiquitous glass façades of buildings of all kinds are one result of a lack of territorial understanding, as is the placement of front doors immediately on the property line on the sidewalk or apartment building corridor, lacking any margin for variation.

THE INHERENT HIERARCHY IN BUILT ENVIRONMENT
Levels

When we say that there is a hierarchical structure to the built environment, we need to mention again the concept of 'levels.' This concept is not really new. As we noted before, it is borne out in the names we have developed for different kinds of professionals, each responsible for a certain 'domain' or 'scope' of work. We are very familiar with the idea that urban designers 'operate on another level' than architects. This means, in this instance, that the built environment can be divided into two groups of things: those that are decided by urban designers and those that are the concern of architects.

When urban designers are doing their work, they look 'up' in the environmental hierarchy to see the stage set by urban planners. At the same time, they look 'down' in the hierarchy in setting the stage for those that design buildings that come and go on the urban design stage. Those designing buildings similarly look 'up' to understand the constraints and themes set out by the urban design, and 'down' in the hierarchy in setting the stage for the more mutable building parts, spaces and functions (the Infill); and so on.

We need designers to put themselves on these different levels to become familiar with how this environmental hierarchy works – both 'vertical' relations, as noted, and 'horizontal' relations, such as, for example, designers working at the same level as other architects, each designing part of a master-planned campus or a neighborhood (see, for example, the urban design projects shown at the beginning of the book). Recognizing these levels – in their formal, technical and territorial sense – makes clear that we need good skills and methods to help us to manage communication and to handle the complexity and the distribution of control effectively.

The use of levels is another way to explain the work of designers of any conventionally defined infrastructure system such as an electrical grid, public wastewater system or transit system. They, too, need good methods to design and manage these complex-adaptive physical/spatial systems. In such infrastructure systems, clear delineation of levels of intervention and effective interfaces enable substitution of higher-performing parts and

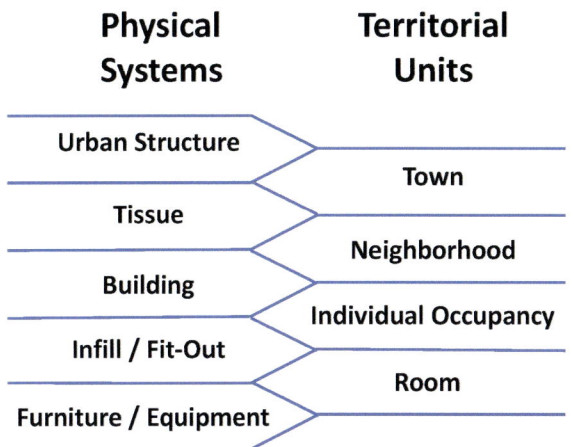

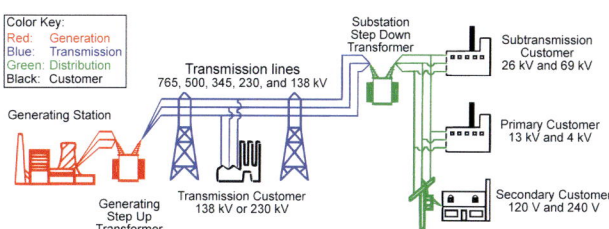

Figure 14 An electrical grid is an example of a utility infrastructure that operates on 'levels'; each of the elements (transmission, distribution and generation) can be and often is designed, financed and operated by a different party. www.ucsusa.org/clean-energy/how-electricity-grid-works (*Source*: www.ucsusa.org)

Figure 13 The concept of levels, showing both physical systems and territorial units and their relationships (*Source*: Habraken, 1998)

improved performance of the whole system. Most such infrastructure systems cross numerous territorial boundaries. And most operate by way of distributed control – that is, no single party finances, approves, constructs or manages the entirety of the system.

Sometimes, certain levels aren't in evidence. For example, traditional Japanese houses have no 'furniture' level. Sometimes, new levels are born, as with the emergence of an Infill level in the design, production and adaptation of large, complex buildings. We discuss this in several places in the book and how, in the industry producing multifamily residential projects, an Infill level is still missing.

The Levels Model Helps in Several Important Ways

The Levels concept allows us to choose the right process: we consider the different parties involved and can decide how responsibilities are best distributed. We also see how different projects can be structured differently with their own patterns of control distribution. As such it is a planning tool.

In the levels model, both professionals and nonprofessionals can have a place. The need to arrive at the most effective solution with the best possible use of resources will determine the control distribution. In some cases, users can do a better job; in others, professionals must do it. The most important point is that on each level, for each subsystem, the responsible parties can be clearly identified and roles documented to avoid misunderstandings.

As already noted, change over time can be related to levels. Change on a lower level is easier and can occur more frequently than change on a higher level.

To fit a project into the local urban context is always the responsibility of professional urban designers and architects. Their expertise should particularly be occupied with this question, leaving the lower-level decisions to those who live and work in the buildings, possibly, if not necessarily, hiring professionals to do the work. Several of the cases presented at the beginning of the book provide good examples, such as the TILA and TOPUP residential projects.

Uniformity can be efficient when one party has to do many things. To build a Base Building, for instance, repetition of the same bay, structural grid or mechanical shaft is most efficient. But when using levels, when spatial and physical systems operate on their own levels, different parties can use the same system simultaneously and work in parallel. Separation of the lower-level systems from the higher level allows for their change without disturbing the higher level. If that condition is fulfilled, adaptation to individual needs on the lower level is easy and efficient. In those instances, variety is not the purpose but the result. Molenvliet/Papendrecht, shown at the beginning of the book, is a good example.

The Base Building level can be designed to respond to local lifestyles, environmental conditions, work patterns and cultural values. This is what determines the quality of the everyday urban environment. This level can also use specific building types that people prefer. The still lower Infill level provides the evolving amenities that have become international preferences: good workspaces, good bathrooms and kitchens, more energy-efficient appliances, electricity and internet connectivity. Adaptation to higher standards is possible – and much easier – over time.

Historical Examples of the Use of Levels

Many of the cases shown at the beginning of the book are good examples of the use of levels.

One example from history helps explain levels. In 1699, Jules Hardouin Mansart, Superintendent of Buildings and Premier Architect to Louis le Grand, King of France, put his signature to the design for what we now know as the Place Vendome (Figure 15). His design included a monumental façade wall of exquisite proportions in the neoclassical manner. The square, including the façade wall, was subsequently built by the city of Paris on the request of the King. But no buildings were constructed at

Figure 15 Place Vendome, Paris (*Photo credit*: John Habraken)

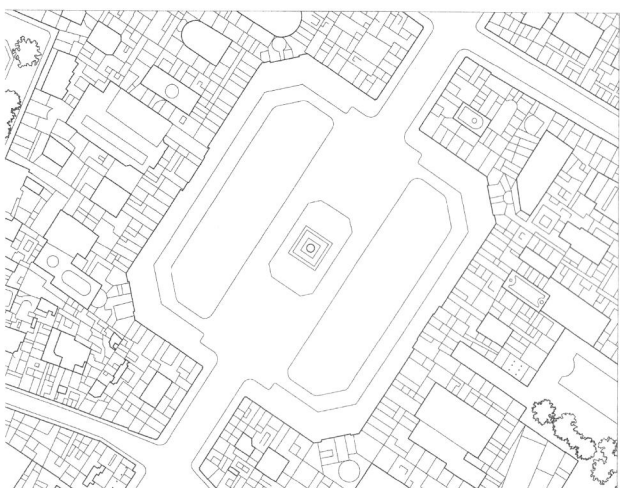

Figure 16 Plan of the Place Vendome, Paris. Behind the uniform façade are different houses (*Source*: Aurelli, 2016) (*Image credit*: Maria Sheherazade Guidici)

that time behind the façade. The land behind was for sale. In the next two decades, noblemen, bankers and other prominent and wealthy citizens who served the king in various administrative and financial functions built their houses there with their own architects. These buildings kept changing and adapting over time. But the façade as Mansart built it is still what we see today.

Mansart's scheme was a remarkable interpretation of what happens when one designer provides the spatial framework within which other designers subsequently can do their own thing. This is also an example of design task separation. A number of the built projects shown at the beginning of the book are contemporary examples of the use of levels as well.

In this and other historical examples, we can understand how large contemporary buildings built today will eventually establish their own hierarchy of changeable subsystems. The very size and permanence of such large built frameworks make their façades, for example, a relatively short-term garb. At the same time, interior flexibility is now responding to a large and varied population. By their sheer bulk, high-rise and other large projects de facto become three-dimensional extensions of urban fabric. Inside, public space becomes increasingly important as a permanent framework around which day-to-day use, either residential or commercial or administrative, or some mixture of uses, may settle in. Seen in this way, it's not hard to understand the exciting latent architectural potential of such new environments without historic precedent in project types such as educational, healthcare and multifamily projects.

Levels and Change

To better understand levels and the distinction between levels, we can study what happens when change occurs. Architects design buildings within the spatial and formal context set by the urban designer and local regulations. Their work requires them to respect, for instance, the layout of streets, the size of blocks, the division of lots in the block and architectural *themes* of various kinds (discussed earlier). But within that context and the regulatory environment, they are free to act. They can adjust the design of the building in many ways. Indeed, different architects can build buildings in different places in an urban tissue but will share the street network and other thematic qualities set by the urban designer. Although the urban design constrains their work, they are free within those constraints to do their own thing. While this oversimplifies an often-complex choreography, it remains a basic principle.

However, when the street network or the configuration of public spaces changes, the designs of the buildings have to adjust. The urban designer cannot act without affecting the designs of the architects. The relation between levels is, therefore, asymmetrical. Change on the level of the building does not (generally) affect the higher level of the urban design, but change in the urban design affects the lower level of the buildings.

It's clear that this distinction is independent of the identity of the parties involved. We can talk about architects designing buildings and urban designers designing street patterns, or we can talk about homeowners owning buildings and the municipality maintaining the public streets. In both cases, we make the same distinction in the physical world between those parts that belong to one level (the streets) and other parts belonging to a lower level (the buildings). This distinction is so natural that its implications are understood by everybody.

From this, it's clear that the built environment is organized in levels, and if we look further, we will find more of them. For instance, we talk about urban systems like highways and railroads and utility grids, and we understand them to be of a higher level than the streets of the neighborhood or the utilities buried under the neighborhood streets. Here again, the same relationship holds. When a major traffic artery has to be cut into an existing neighborhood network, the lower level of local streets must adjust. This kind of intervention, of course, has set off a great deal of conflict, as we know from history. But within the given structure of highways, we can change the pattern of local streets without affecting the higher-level traffic pattern, except where they intersect. Here again, the importance of the design of interfaces between levels is apparent.

Relating to a Higher Level
The Place Vendome, referred to earlier, was not a unique intervention. Earlier in the 17th century, King Henry IV initiated the building of the Place Royale (today known as Place des Vosges). Citizens could buy lots around it on the condition that the façades of their houses would be built according to a preconceived design, including a public arcade on the ground floor. The Place des Vosges is larger than the Place Vendome and makes a more domestic space with its trees and flower beds and its more home-grown architecture. But the square's façade wall is clearly the result of a common set of *themes* (see 'Thematic Design'), although in practice, it was built one lot at a time.

Although both squares have uniform or nearly uniform façades all around, the distribution of ownership is different. In the case of the Place Vendome, the façades were actually part of the urban infrastructure, like the pavement of the square or the statue in its center. But in Henry IV's Place des Vosges, the façades are owned and erected by the private citizens.

Taken as examples of designing on levels, the difference is significant, however. In the case of the Place Vendome, designers only decided what to do on their own level of control behind the already-erected façade. In the case of the Place des Vosges, the higher-level designer established rules or themes to constrain lower-level design. He basically told the lower-level designer: "Do whatever you want, but make sure you do the façade my way." (See also the NEXT21 case at the beginning of the book.)

The latter case is more complicated but also more flexible, because establishing rules or themes for lower-level design can be done in many different ways. The setback rule, for instance, telling architects to keep houses at a certain distance from the street, belongs to that mode of interaction. By the same token, an urban designer may impose a building height restriction or stipulate that all façades be done in a given material or that certain patterns (e.g., bay windows of a certain projection but of any detailed design) should be followed for the sake of a consistent and well-conceived public space.

This way of working makes the urban designer reach across the level distinction to constrain lower-level design. It introduces a certain coherence in the lower level where normally variety is the inevitable result of different designers each doing their own thing.

Mansart built what was to perform for a long time and to serve many. He thereby provided a context for what might change more frequently and serve individual clients. In general, such a distinction of levels of intervention separates what is relatively permanent from what is relatively changeable. But the way Mansart applied this principle challenged conventional notions. The façade of a building is normally seen as the expression of that particular building. Here, it became part of the more permanent urban design.

As a counterpoint to these many historic examples, we can see how large contemporary buildings tend to change their skins (Figure 17). This is, in many ways, the opposite of Mansart's Place Vendome. Here, the buildings, to prolong their lives, shed their skins when the urban environment changed and energy-efficiency standards increased. The curtain wall façade almost acquires autonomy; it may be part of the building, but it may also help shape urban fabric. We find examples of this all over the world and know that there are specialists in designing and constructing these now-autonomous façades. Regulatory instruments and financing have followed suit.

Relating to a Lower Level
As the examples show, relating 'vertically' across levels of intervention means looking two ways: upward to inhabit and respect the context shaped earlier and downward to frame and stimulate the work of other actors who come in later.

Figure 17 An office building in Seoul, Korea, 'shedding' its old skin and acquiring a new one, meeting new energy standards and giving an architectural expression in keeping with the time and place (*Photo credit*: Boris Feldblyum and Edward Stojakovic)

It is in looking 'downward' that we come to a crucial Open Building concept: *capacity*, discussed in more detail later. It's not really a difficult concept to understand. When we walk into an empty room, we may say, "This could be a bedroom, but it might also be a study or perhaps a playroom for the children." By saying this, we indicate the capacity of the room for holding lower-level designs. In the same way, an urban designer, who decides about building lots and street widths, will ask what kind of buildings could be built if the lots have certain dimensions. Or they may consider what ways there are to park cars in a given street width and how trees might be planted in it. In all those cases, the designer does not determine the lower-level design decisions but must have a fair idea as to the range of solutions possible within what is proposed. *Capacity analysis* is discussed later.

Relations on the Same Level

Those who work in a given location but on different 'sites' relate 'horizontally' with each other. In the levels model, they work on the same level of intervention. This is what different architects each designing a building in a given urban framework do or those designing different offices in an office Base Building do. In the latter case, different architects working at the same level will understand the importance of the 'demising wall' in an office building, separating one tenant space from another. They will also all share the Base Building's common facilities, utility lines and circulation systems (corridors, stairs and elevators) and, often, building design standards established by the Base Building architect/building owner. But within those constraints, they each do their own thing, keeping out of each other's territory and almost inevitably sharing design constraints and ways of building. Individual design teams will also understand 'contract limits' in a site where various designers are each designing a separate building, each respecting the property lines of their client. Both are examples of avoiding direct horizontal relations. Both have significant legal as well as technical ramifications.

Throughout history, monolithic 'shared party walls' have separated individual dwellings and constrained agents relating horizontally and controlling space on both sides. This situation is met in one of two ways. First, adjacent inhabitants agree informally to respect the interdependence of their territories and, when one seeks a change to their dwelling, they take care not to disturb their neighbor's part of the shared wall. Property lines in this case run down the middle of these walls.

The second way is that neighbors agree to the introduction of a third party who takes responsibility of the shared party wall (and, by extension, all such 'common' elements). The latter is what is called in the United States a 'common interest development' or 'condominium.' In the latter situation, it is only the paint on such walls or another layer of some kind that is individually and independently controlled. This way of managing control and territory is familiar in all building types and has to do with the imperative of avoiding what we call '*horizontal relations*' (relations at the same level in the environmental hierarchy).

Particularly since the advent of MEP systems (mechanical, electrical and plumbing), the 'territorial crossing' of parts of each of these systems has become extraordinarily complex and entangled. The complexity is evident during design, construction and later when change is involved. Drainage systems are a good example. From the shower and water closet in a multifamily dwelling or hospital patient room, the drainage pipes drop into the ceiling space of the space below and then run horizontally until they reach a common pipe shaft and, from there, run to

Figure 18 Drainage piping serving a dwelling unit 'upstairs' is visible in the ceiling of a yet-to-be-finished unit in a multistory residential condominium in the United States. This is a typical case of territorial entanglement (*Photo credit*: Stephen Kendall)

Figure 19 A part of van Eesteren's extension of Amsterdam (*Source*: Courtesy of KLM Aerocarto)

the sewage pipes under the street and from there to the sewage treatment facility serving a city district.

In the case that one party controls the entirety of the route, relatively little controversy ensues if part of the system needs to be replaced or repositioned – it's only inconvenient to disturb an occupant when the pipes serving the space upstairs leak or need replacing. However, if the route these pipes take crosses multiple territorial boundaries – either vertically in the environmental hierarchy or horizontally, as between neighboring territories – boundary frictions and legal disputes are bound to occur when one party decides to change (upgrade, relocate or remove) their part of the entire system. It is here that interface agreements (in space and dimension) that respect territory are critical to a well-performing system. The same is true of other such utility or installation services or systems (wiring, ductwork and so on).

An example of what happens when horizontal relations are not understood comes in the entanglement of drainage and other piping whose route from each plumbing fixture to the common sewage line in the building passes through another territory. This is evident in Figure 18 inside a building, but would rarely occur at the level of urban design unless specific easements are used.

The Disappearance of Levels

An example of the disappearance of levels will help explain what this means. Until his time, Berlage was the last to work with the level distinction in urban design in the Netherlands. In contrast, Cornelis van Eesteren's internationally renowned post-WWII extension of Amsterdam (Figure 19) was not structured by higher-level urban space. Following CIAM ideology, he arranged building volumes within free-flowing space. Urban space was no longer structuring lower-level design. As a result, urban designer and architect both used the same medium, and it was no longer clear where urban design stopped and architecture began. This confusion still plagues the profession.

The disappearance of levels of intervention was not restricted to the distinction between urban design and architecture. It also took place within buildings. Modernist architectural ideology claimed top-down design control. The masters of the avant-garde taught us by example that full vertical control, including even the design of furniture, was necessary to achieve good architecture. They lived in a time of fundamental change in which all design conventions and building habits were rendered obsolete. In such uncertainty, it is understandable that those responsible for large projects insisted on full vertical control.

However, the upheavals of modernity only reinforced an attitude that already prevailed in the time when architects only did special buildings like churches, palaces and grand houses. It goes back to Palladio, whose marvelous villas we tend to understand as firmly controlled by a single hand. In that sense, Le Corbusier's Unité d'Habitation, fully controlled too and conceived as standing in a park, is very Palladian.

We have been educated in a tradition that was ignorant of the uses of levels. Mass housing – government sponsored or built by private developers – in which dwelling units are integral to the design of the buildings they occupy – and are not independent – is part of that ignorance. The Open Building approach seeks a remedy to the rigidity and uniformity that comes from excessive vertical control and the loss of levels.

Levels and Our Modernist Legacy
Modernist ideology did not recognize architecture in relation to levels, either upward in urban design or downward in interior organization. Indeed, Modernist environment, for all its novelty, can be understood, to a large extent, as the reduction of complex urban fabric to a coarse single-level product. The result was its inability to make large things without imposing uniform, rigid repetition. In this respect, the 20th-century avant-garde movement was a regressive movement. It is truly ironic that our time, which calls itself dynamic and full of change and individuality, has produced an architecture more rigid in its articulation and less capable of dealing with the dimension of time than any period before in human history.

We still suffer the consequences of that tradition. We say that we have rejected the Modernist's dogma of 'form follows function,' yet we still expect each project we engage in to respond to a 'program,' listing in some detail expected functions to be accommodated. In contrast, a time-based architecture must assume functions to be largely unpredictable except in the most general terms. Where architecture cannot follow function anymore, it must adopt a new attitude to establish a context for change and variety by inhabitation and use. This will lead to an articulation of levels of form-making. But that also implies distribution of design task responsibility, and we have not yet abandoned the modernist opinion that such distribution is a dilution of the architect's role. The dilemma also renders academia clueless. Change and the

distribution of design tasks are not yet addressed in architectural theory, nor do they feature in schools' curricula. Our regulatory environment is equally at odds with reality, a problem demanding intense scrutiny and adjustment.

Later, we return to the roots of the Open Building approach and discuss how a residential Infill industry will change the culture of building. This new industry will bring a new level of intervention into full play in the design, financing, regulation, production and long-term usefulness of large residential projects.

Finally, perhaps the most important argument for encouraging an understanding of the use of levels is the recognition that it is the basis for environmental sustainability.

The lower levels in the built environment hierarchy represent the 'fine-grained' units of control to adjust quickly to rapidly evolving technologies and social trends, while the higher levels secure longevity and stability.

The Emergence of an Infill Level
The idea that the built environment is organized hierarchically, discussed earlier in terms of urban design and architecture, also extends downward. We find in many buildings how the inner non–load-bearing partitions can be changed without effecting the basic building structure or its shape, as noted before. Here, we can distinguish 'Infill elements' like partition walls but also kitchen and bathroom equipment – operating on a lower level in the built environment relative to the building. The same relationship as we found between buildings and local streets is found here. We can remodel a building and change the distribution of partitioning of spaces and related equipment without changing the larger architectural infrastructure or its external shape. But when we begin to change parts of the building and demolish load-bearing walls or extend a façade to get more room inside, we expect adjustments in the Infill.

As noted earlier, a matter of terminology comes up here. It can be argued that what we call a 'building' includes the Infill as much as the load-bearing structure, all of the mechanical systems, the façades and roof. Therefore, a new term must be coined for what

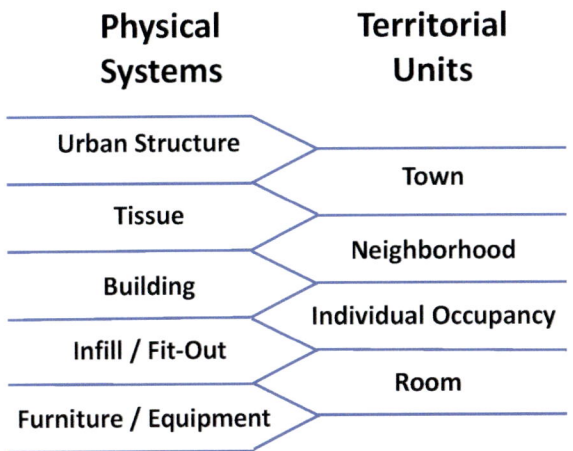

Figure 20 An Infill or fit-out level of intervention is only now emerging in multifamily housing and healthcare facilities, albeit with a great deal of resistance (*Source*: Habraken, 1998)

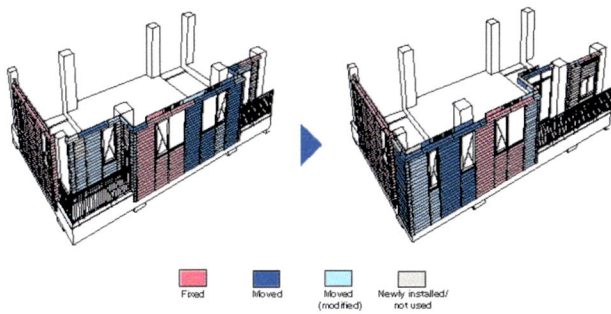

Figure 21 NEXT21: The façade system was developed by one team. It is designed to be used by the architect of each independent dwelling corresponding to changes in the dwelling unit designs. The skeleton remains fixed as a 100-year investment (*Credit*: Osaka Gas Company)

is left when the Infill is taken out. This is called 'Base Building' (or Support, core and shell, skeleton (in Japan), Primary System, etc.). In this way, we can say that a building is comprised of two levels: the 'Base Building' level and the 'Infill' level.

Once we see the concept of levels operating in the built environment, we discover the same hierarchical relation in many places. So far, we have been looking at environmental forms, but within their technical systems, we find the same subdivision in levels. Take, for instance, windows in a façade. We can replace them with other windows of a different make or design but use the same opening in the façade made for the original windows. In that case, we do not have to change the façade wall itself. When we decide to change the façade wall, however, and make different window openings, the window itself, obviously, must adjust. In this instance, the façade wall will operate at a higher level (Base Building level) and the window at the Infill level.

In all conduit systems (piping, wiring and mechanical ventilation ducts), we find similar hierarchical organizations. In the example of buildings and streets given earlier, the sewage system follows levels, too: there is the system in the house and there is the sewage main running in the public street. On a still higher level, there will be the collector and treatment system of the district or the city. This is why we can also say that the Open Building approach is equivalent to the design of complex adaptive infrastructure systems such as those mentioned here.

BALANCING PERMANENCE AND CHANGE

Addressing the uncertainty of change and the natural variety of use and client and user expectations was the problem that gave rise to the Open Building approach in the first place. Although the SAR's initial charge was focused on the Netherlands, the problem was general: it arises in any society, within any economic or political system, and is independent of technical solutions.

Can anyone seriously argue that the everyday built environment is ever finished? The transformations of its spaces and built forms are, after all, the basis for all our design commissions. We always change what was done before, in most cases by someone else. This means that the actions we take and what we hand off to the future matter a great deal and are fundamental responsibilities, even if we don't have a crystal ball to know what the future holds.

As many of the cases presented at the beginning of the book show, change is a reality during our designing, as we learn more about the project we're working on and rethink our own prior 'design moves.' We wouldn't have to engage in designing if we knew everything at the outset: designing is what we do to find out – to reach agreement on – what should be made by someone else for use by still others. Change is also a reality for clients, as their requirements and forces outside their control evolve, during the run-up to construction and over time. And we know through experience that changes (known as 'change orders' in the US building industry) are only too familiar during construction. In short, although we know too little about it, as noted later, change of function, façades, floor plan layouts, technical systems and so on is normal, albeit at different cycles, during multiple decades of use.

Balancing permanence and change is certainly in accordance with our everyday experience. People who own houses know they can change their houses, even tear them down to replace them with new buildings, without affecting neighbors or the street layout of their neighborhood. But when the street layout is changed and the municipality decides to cut-in a new street or to widen an existing one or to rearrange a street's location or install or change utilities or change zoning designations, inevitably, adjustments must be made on the lower (house) level.

FIVE CHARACTERISTICS OF EVERYDAY BUILT ENVIRONMENT THAT OPEN BUILDING DESIGNS FOR

Change and permanence, of course, go hand in hand. City blocks and streets are stable, lasting for centuries, while the buildings and spaces within their boundaries are frequently repurposed, demolished, enlarged and replaced, often at densities higher than when originally built. It takes more people to agree to change the city block than to move an interior partition; that's one reason the urban block is slowest to change. It operates at a 'higher level.' Buildings remain in place, while they may increase in volume, either vertically or horizontally. Old doors are filled in and new ones cut in; façades are altered to meet changing tastes as well as to improve building thermal performance. And inside, buildings undergo change all the time – the interior design profession and the massive interior remodeling industries in every country are a sign of this.

Yet we know of instances where streets and boulevards are cut through old tissue. Hausmann exerted top-down control to transform Paris between 1853 and 1870, albeit always accepting familiar architectural typology. Streets for cars become pedestrian zones when a broad consensus emerges to do so, as many cities around the world have experienced for a very long time.

While efforts at historic preservation may strive to freeze certain characteristics of built environment – whether individual buildings, 'classes' of buildings, parts of buildings or entire urban neighborhoods – environments that are truly alive sustain themselves and attain resilience through incremental change and adaptation. Much of this change happens inside buildings, invisible to the casual observer. In this sense, everyday built environment is not so much an artefact as it is an organism, continuously renewing itself and replacing individual parts, spaces and structures, giving it the capacity to persist.

The balance between what will change and what will remain long term becomes increasingly important – and controversial – when projects become larger and larger, involving more and more people with varying interests. A project of several hundred dwelling units or commercial shops or offices or a medical center cannot just stay rigid as time goes by. Such projects must adapt to life's variety. A skyscraper in which a few thousand people work is not a building but a vertical environment the size of a small town, always evolving, often containing a multitude of varied and changing functions. A suburban neighborhood of row houses that, for various reasons, must increase their footprints or experience an increase in density faces social (territorial) and physical design stresses that are well known.

Technical Strategies for Handling Change
The Open Building approach offers a two-pronged strategy to handle change.

From a technical perspective, Open Building seeks products, systems specifications and building methods where parts and subsystems can be replaced with a minimum of interface problems. This means that subsystems that are expected to have a long life are clearly separated from parts expected to wear out more quickly or need to be changed to obtain better performance or meet changing preferences. One example is the now-frequent replacement of entire façades with new skins as shown earlier, increasing thermal performance and giving a building a new appearance.

Another example of this, mentioned several times in this book, is competitive Infill companies that can fill in empty spaces in buildings to meet changing occupancy requirements. Every office building project is a good example. Some tenants may use one or the other of a variety of competitive 'systems furniture' services; others may simply have a contractor fill in their space according to their interior architect's specifications.

We call this capacity to substitute parts with those giving higher performance technical 'disentanglement.' That and the design of interfaces are a key to innovation in the building industry. The design of interfaces goes well beyond such common interfaces as those between electrical appliance plugs made by various companies and the terminations where they are inserted, also made by competitive companies.

This desired 'disentanglement,' however, meets the reality that in the long history of building, new systems have been introduced one after the other without a view to the consequences, producing a kind of creeping entanglement. Understanding the history of such technical entanglement, mirrored by those working with these systems in the field, can help us. Up to the third quarter of the 19th century, the major systems of interest to architects

Figures 22 MIT's main group, with the dome at the head of the complex of building wings and courtyards now embedded in the much larger campus (*Photo credit*: Dave MacKenzie)

and builders were structural systems – concrete, masonry, wood and then steel and cast iron. Beginning in the latter part of the 19th century and quickly accelerating since then, we have experienced an explosion of systems to make contemporary buildings habitable and to perform according to changing building standards (e.g., seismic, fire and net-zero energy) and changing social preferences and economic drivers. Now, multiple piping, wiring, ductwork systems are enmeshed – entangled – into every building, from their point of entry at service points to every outlet, plumbing fixture and appliance.

Open Building has something to say about how to handle these issues in practice. A number of the cases presented earlier show exemplary cases of handling entanglement in the process of designing and building and in the long-term life of the environment.

In a sociopolitical perspective, handling change requires the recognition of territory and territorial boundaries. Put most simply, this means distinguishing the parts, both physical and spatial, that are shared ('the commons') from the parts, both physical and spatial, that are under the control of individual agents (individual persons, social groups, companies, etc., depending on the 'level' of the environment we're discussing).

Change and Large Projects

Large projects are with us to stay. But to be sustainable, they must become increasingly fine-grained and planned for change. As noted before, commercial office buildings have, for many decades, offered tenants empty floor space to be fitted out by specialized fit-out companies according to a design done by a designer of the tenant's choice. In shopping malls and even airport concourses, retail space is left empty for the retailer to take care of. These are utterly conventional, if not always smoothly operating or of high quality. Major international corporations with large portfolios of such buildings steer a large array of other players to be sure that their assets remain agile and valuable, either to sell or to hold. We believe this is a phenomenon that is a harbinger of things to come across all kinds of 'everyday' buildings.

One of the most striking examples of a large building designed for higher education that exemplifies the principle of designing for change and that we can learn from is the very large main building complex of the Massachusetts Institute of Technology in Cambridge, Massachusetts. Designed by the engineer William Welles Bosworth and built in 1916, it borrowed from large industrial buildings in its highly repetitive concrete structural frame. Rooms and departments were intended to be formed using, in the words of the civil engineer designing the project (Bosworth), "curtain walls" of lightweight materials that could be built or removed to make classrooms or offices as needed (Jarzombeck, 2004). It has since undergone many large and small changes, including changes to the interior façades of corridors, relocation of academic units, filling in of previously open courtyards, upgrading of mechanical systems, etc.

Balancing permanence and change in the built environment is, therefore, one of the most important and difficult things society has to do, and we – design professionals – are part of that work. This regenerative capacity is leading us to recognize the critical importance of a circular economy, shifting from linear material consumption toward a circular economy within an industrialized construction industry. A circular economy, simply put, is "a systemic approach to economic development designed to benefit businesses, society, and the environment. In contrast to the 'take-make-waste' linear model, a circular economy is regenerative by design and aims to gradually decouple growth from the consumption of finite resources" (the Ellen MacArthur Foundation, https://ellenmacarthurfoundation.org/topics/circular-economy-introduction/overview).

The Importance of Studies of Change in the Built Environment

Finally, serious longitudinal studies of how a building stock or everyday built environment change are important but, unfortunately, quite rare. Five examples are worth citing. One focuses on multifamily residential buildings, another on educational facilities, the third on the healthcare environment. A fourth is work in the morphogenetic tradition in geography, and a fifth is a study on incremental development of self-built housing in Mexico City, typical of many urbanizing areas in the Global South.

Minami, Kazunobu. (2016). The Efforts to Develop Longer Life Housing with Adaptability in Japan, BE16 Tallinn and Helsinki Conference; Build Green and Renovate Deep, 5–7 October 2016.

This paper discusses efforts to develop longer-life housing with adaptability in Japan beginning in the late 1970s. The Japanese government, in cooperation with private-sector and academic entities, started research and development projects to design and build longer-life housing that is adaptable with time. Early examples include the Kodan Experimental Housing Project (KEP) and the Century Housing Project (CHS). Research has been conducted on the outcomes of those experimental projects to determine whether the attempted adaptability has worked or not over the 30-plus years that people have been living in them. The research found that the housing with adaptable Infill has been able to adjust to changes in family size and lifestyles in the KEP and CHS projects.

Lee, Joshua. (2019). Flexibility and Design: Learning from the School Construction Systems Development (SCSD) Project. New York, NY: Routledge

This book reports on a longitudinal analysis of a particularly robust midcentury modern experiment, involving a number of school buildings, called the School Construction Systems Development (SCSD) project. It draws conclusions for the challenges facing clients and design professionals in meeting the evolving demands of education.

Pilosof, N. P. (2020). Building for Change: Comparative Case Study of Hospital Architecture. HERD, 14(1), https://doi.org/10.1177/1937586720927026

This study assesses how architectural design strategies impact the flexibility of hospitals to change over time. Most hospitals are designed for highly specialized medical functions, which is often in conflict with the need to design the hospital facility to accommodate evolvement and change of functions over time.

Architectural design strategies provide different approaches to the need to design for a specific medical program while planning for its future change. The study compares two hospital buildings with very similar configurations and medical programs but with significantly different architectural design strategies: One was designed for an unknown future medical function, and the second was designed for a specific medical function. The study analyses the two hospital buildings by their design strategy, planning, design process and construction by phases and compares their change in practice over the 12 years before the paper was written.

The ISUF (International Seminar on Urban Form) was formed in 1994. The publication of its journal, *Urban Morphology*, began in 1997. The various 'schools' of urban morphology working both within and between academic disciplines and national intellectual traditions began to cross-fertilize. This is sometimes known as the morphogenetic tradition in geography. A key figure in introducing German scholarship to the latter was M. R. G. Conzen (2004). He developed terminology, techniques of analysis and concepts that other researchers have subsequently developed further. Interdisciplinary research has also led to new analytical techniques and a growing international body of research on the form of towns and their incremental transformation (www.sciencedirect.com/topics/earth-and-planetary-sciences/urban-morphology).

Andrade-Narváez, J. (2016). Viviendas en Proceso. Unidad Habitacional Cohuatlan, Ciudad de México 1973–78. Arquitectura Social. TAVI 30 años de Experiencias (editors Martin, A. and Andrade, J.). UAM-X, México.

Jorge Iván Andrade Narváez has studied housing growth through time. The purpose of his studies was to develop and apply a method that was developed to detect and measure the physical changes over time to self-produced dwelling units. The study was done on the information collected in Santa Ursula, a popular neighborhood located in the south of Mexico City. The method is based on the assumption that dwellings in a popular, informal neighborhood have an order in their way of growth and change; they do not appear randomly. Professor Andrade has designed and presented three examples of the application of this method. The first one in Santa Ursula, the second one in the Palo Alto house complex and the third one in the Xacalli house complex. All three are located in Mexico City.

There is also the book *How Buildings Learn* (Brand, 1994).

These are just a few examples. But we know far too little about how our building stock and built field change. We know too little about the forces acting at work, the agents involved, the technical systems at play, and the territorial boundaries that force us to recognize that the built world is not monolithic or subject to unitary, top-down control.

READINGS

Alexander, C., et al. (1977). *A Pattern Language, Towns, Buildings, Construction*. Oxford University Press, Oxford.

Andrade-Narváez, J. (2016). Viviendas en Proceso. Unidad Habitacional Cohuatlan, Ciudad de México 1973–78. *Arquitectura Social. TAVI 30 años de Experiencias* (editors Martin, A. and Andrade, J.). UAM-X, México.

Aurelli, P.V. (editor). (2016). *The City as a Project*. Ruby Press, Berlin.

Brand, S. (1994). *How Buildings Learn; What Happens after They're Built*. Viking, New York.

Conzen, M.P. (editor). (2004). *Thinking about Urban Form: Papers on Urban Morphology, 1932–1998/M.R.G. Conzen*. Peter Lang Publishing, Bern.

Ellen MacArthur Foundation. https://ellenmacarthurfoundation.org/topics/circular-economy-introduction/overview

Gideon, S. (1963). *Space Time and Architecture*. Harvard University Press, Cambridge, MA, pp. 374, 386.

Habraken, N.J. (1998). *The Structure of the Ordinary: Form and Control in the Built Environment*. MIT Press, Cambridge, MA.

Jarzombek, M. (2004). *Designing MIT*. Northeastern University Press, Boston.

Kendall, S. H. (editor). (2019). *Healthcare Architecture as Infrastructure: Open Building in Practice*. Routledge, London.

Lee, J. (2019). *Flexibility and Design: Learning from the School Construction Systems Development (SCSD) Project*. Routledge, New York, NY.

Military Standard. (1691). Section 2.5.2. www.wbdg.org/FFC/M1691/MIL-STD-1691_2016.pdf

Minami, K. (2016). *The Efforts to Develop Longer Life Housing with Adaptability in Japan*. BE16 Tallinn and Helsinki Conference. Build Green and Renovate Deep, 5–7 October 2016.

Newman, O. (1973). *Defensible Space: Crime Prevention through Urban Design*. MacMillan Publishing, New York

Pilosof, N.P. (2020). Building for change: Comparative case study of hospital architecture. *HERD*, 14(1), https://doi.org/10.1177/1937586720927026

Propst, R. (1968). *The Office: A Facility Based on Change*. The Business Press, Elmhurst, IL.

Sdoutz, F. (2011). *Broadacre City: FFLW and His Vision for the Urban Future*. www.mediaarchitecture.at/architekturtheorie/broadacre_city/2011_illustration_004_en.shtml)

Ventre, F. (1983). *NBSIR 83–2662: Documentation and Assessment of the GSA/PBS Building Systems Program – Background and Research Plan*.

Capacity Analysis – A Key Tool of the Open Building Approach

INTRODUCTION

One question always comes up when we discuss the Open Building approach in new construction: "If we don't have a detailed program of requirements (or brief), then how do we go about designing a building or an urban tissue?" Or, for that matter, "How does an investor know how to invest or a regulator know how to approve building plans without the details of unit mix, unit layouts, all mechanical systems drawings and so on?"

The other question that always comes up has to do with what has to be done to explore the accommodation capacity of existing buildings. Interior architects often get this request from clients: "Help us find a space in an existing building where we can relocate and that can accommodate not only our organization's current needs but our future needs when we expect to add staff."

Another question concerns how an investor can make a decision to convert an existing asset to a new use or mix of uses, or to reconfigure it in a significant way. As we noted before, at the time of writing, this question was facing building owners, financial institutions and city officials due to huge vacancy rates in city centers as well as suburban office buildings driven by changes in work patterns. Converting office buildings to housing became a very important topic. The question faced by the investors and city officials and financial institutions was: "Is this office building well suited for conversion to another use, particularly residential – and is that conversion economical now and in the long term?"

To address the second question, we go into some depth in the next part of the book in addressing the problem of an office-to-housing conversion and how capacity analysis can help.

In what follows in this part of the book, we give a broad overview of capacity analysis. We then discuss a formal operation using zones, margins and grids. A more complete discussion of these design aids can be found in *Variations: The Systematic Design of Supports* (Habraken et al., 1972). These are aids in the formulation of standards for the planning of units of occupancy within a designed or yet-to-be-designed Base Building or a building that needs to be converted to another use entirely.

Zones, margins and grids are also useful in the design of urban tissues, but that subject is touched upon only briefly. This use is discussed more fully in *SAR73, Deciding on Density* and *The Grunsfeld Variations* (see Appendix Two).

In this part of the book, we discuss the following:

- What is capacity analysis?
- Capacity analysis as part of a design process
- A methodological problem
- Evaluating possible uses
- How capacity links form to function
- The use of zones and margins
- Zones and margins as part of capacity analysis
- Zones and margins in urban design
- Using zones and margins: an example in housing design: sectors and basic variants
- Grids as design tools for buildings and urban tissues: kinds of grids; grids in urban design
- Summary of the use of grids in designing

WHAT IS CAPACITY ANALYSIS?

Visiting a house offered for sale, we will usually walk into an empty room and say, "This could be a guest room" or "here is where I could put my study." And we imagine how the furniture could be arranged and may even consider alternative furniture layouts. When we do this, we are assessing the *capacity* of the space to hold certain activities.

In a similar way, an urban designer may subdivide a city block into lots or parcels of certain sizes, because those sizes allow building types of a certain kind to be built. The lot sizes and resulting block size, street width and location and size of other public uses and spaces are set and together, they offer the desired *capacity* to hold lower-level interventions (i.e., discrete buildings).

On the building level, the architect of an office building is faced with a decision about the distance between columns and distance between the central core(s) and the façade. These factors, along with site constraints coming from the higher level (zoning and other site conditions) are the basis for first design moves. The design team will compare possible tenant layout alternatives by sketching how a structural bay allows subdivision into workstations or smaller rooms. They will also study how multiples of that bay may also produce a useful floor surface for expected sizes of occupancies. Variable sizes of tenant spaces can also be considered along with alternative layouts. Considerations are given for natural illumination and perhaps ventilation as well as access to mechanical systems (heating, air conditioning, mechanical ventilation, cabling and piping). Egress and fire safety are also considered.

Or a client may ask their design team to evaluate an existing nonresidential building for possible conversion to residential occupancy or other use. In this case, several things have to be considered, such as floor-to-floor height, the pattern of structural elements, façade-to-core (corridor) depth, how to handle the placement and size of new vertical pipe shafts, whether to use raised floors to handle horizontal distribution of drainage and other conduits (and with this, the needed adjustment of existing exit stairs and elevator stops) and so on.

Analysis of capacity assumes the distinction of levels, discussed earlier. For example, a room is the higher-level form; the furniture arrangement, by which we assess the rooms' capacity, makes another (lower) level. In building design, the bay size, as determined by party or shear walls or distance between columns, makes space on the (higher) building level, along with the fixed MEP (mechanical, electrical and plumbing) infrastructure. The partitioning used to subdivide that space operates on a lower or Infill level, along with the variable (Infill) parts of the MEP infrastructure. Some or all of the façade may be part of the higher level, and some may be part of the lower (Infill) level (as in street-level façades of mixed-use urban buildings).

CAPACITY ANALYSIS AS PART OF A DESIGN PROCESS

The design of a Base Building is a matter of evaluation and optimization, as discussed before when we outlined the Open Building approach. Here, we need to state a very important question and principle:

How can the greatest variety in use and functional idiosyncrasies (and changes over time) be accommodated using as few infill elements as possible? Generally speaking, the best and most economical solution will be one in which the only variable (Infill) elements are those that, at some time in the future, will require adaptation. If there are too few variable elements, the Base Building will not be able to accommodate changes and will become an anachronism and an economic burden for its owner. If too much is made variable, money and effort will be wasted in providing possibilities which will never be used.

The same is true for Infill elements. For the designer, it's important to know the factors that play a role in the optimization process in order to evaluate them properly. But it is also necessary to explore the changes that may be made in the future; what will have to last a long time, and what will be replaced or moved at certain intervals?

Yet, everyone knows that nobody can predict the future. Added to that fact is that despite a few studies mentioned before, we know far too little about the lifestyles of future generations or the impulses that lead people to change something in their homes or about future technology supporting evolving occupancy demands. There is no definitive answer to the question of when or for what reason buildings are altered or reconstructed. In any case, the design of alterations will, in almost all cases, be accomplished by design teams and their clients, which are different from those who designed the Base Building to begin with.

One of the reasons why we know so little about the factors that may lead to change and variation – in housing in particular but more generally – is that, except as pointed out before in office buildings, present-day design and development practices (both public and private investments) leave only the most superficial opportunities for change. People use the buildings as they come. In the case of housing, the perennial shortage of housing prevents the expression of preference through the natural workings of market choice. Further, technical entanglement of occupancy units one above the other in multistory buildings is a major deterrent to change. As discussed elsewhere, when drainage piping and other utilities of one unit are only accessible from the ceiling space of units below in multitenant buildings, rigidity is the result.

Of course, we can make some generalizations; there are certain trends. There are still people and organizations who own their own buildings and have the means to alter them at almost any cost, even if they were not originally built for adaptation.

CAPACITY ANALYSIS – A KEY TOOL OF THE OPEN BUILDING APPROACH

So the answer to the question of how much capacity for change and variety to build in is not easy to answer. Gradually accumulated experience is often the best rule. Longitudinal studies of how buildings change and the cost of change are therefore greatly needed, as noted. An exception is the work done in the Netherlands in the office and healthcare sectors by Dekker using a sample of facilities over a 20-year period (Kendall et al., 2012).

Four principles for the design of Base Buildings follow from observations of buildings that have undergone incremental changes.

- **First, each demised 'territory' in a Base Building must allow for a number of different layouts. A demised territory is a legally separated space (often fire separated as well) in a building.**
- **Second, it must be possible to change the total floor area, either by additional construction (vertical or horizontal) or to change the size of demised territories by shifting the boundaries of the units of occupancy.**
- **In the third place, Base Buildings or parts of a Base Building should optimally accommodate both residential and nonresidential functions within reason (thus the concept of 'beyond single use').**
- **Fourth, to the greatest extent possible, the parts filling in a Base Building, as well as the parts used to build it, should be capable of being recycled or put into a secondary marketplace. This is how the Open Building process can most clearly contribute to a circular construction industry and economy.**

Clearly, not every Base Building will have to satisfy all these criteria. The relevant criteria will have to be determined according to each situation. When all the basic layout variations that a Base Building can accommodate are documented, then we can study the relationship between the possible uses, their realization and their cost.

A METHODOLOGICAL PROBLEM

Everyone knows that in the design of new buildings, skilled designers never start their design process with an entirely blank slate. There are always constraints and assumptions, such as the size and shape and topography of the site; any natural or man-made features that should be recognized; the likely building typology; the local zoning and building regulations; a rough budget and with it a rough building area; a rough idea of what function or functions the building should be able to accommodate; a general idea of the construction methods; financing tools available and so on.

The Open Building approach addresses a recurrent and important methodological problem. When confronted with two alternative proposals, how can a client know which one serves a given target population or market best? This question is also valid in any 'vertical' design relation: that is, higher-level decisions are always based on assumptions of lower-level use. On the urban design level, plot size and setback rules are based on expected and desired types of buildings. On the residential building level, more than a century of housing design has yielded a range of familiar unit types that can help shape the design of a residential Base Building. But in each case, the designer of a Base Building must assess its capacity for a representative range of Infill variations. Casual 'back-of-the-envelope' studies won't suffice.

Design studies over the past few decades have provided formal methods that can help well-trained design teams analyze a building's capacity for Infill variations of a desired quality. This formal method is particularly relevant when the problems outlined above recur – that is, when they are repetitive. Instead of approaching the problems as if they only present themselves to an office once or twice, a method can save time, provide accountability and transparency and aid communication.

This part of the book introduces a formal way of assessing capacity. There are likely to be others. Some readers will certainly declare that formalization of an approach to addressing the above problems is overkill and is not needed. We also recognize that once a formal way of working is learned and repeated enough times within a firm or among team members who work together frequently, it can 'go into the background' or 'default mode.' Yet when team members change, having a more formal method can be a real time-saver.

We also think that, if for no other reason, the effort to formalize a way of working enables computational tools to be developed

to help us. In any case, we suggest that the concept of capacity should be taken seriously because this kind of assessment requires the ability to think about design constraints and to think in variations.

On each level of the environmental hierarchy (urban planning, urban design, architecture, etc.), we need to be able to generate a representative range of possible variants to assess what our design offers to those who will inhabit what we have created. The ability to think in variations is an empowering skill. We can't zero in on a single 'best' lower-level solution and repeat it to shape our higher-level form. Instead, we need to be able to consider thematic variations that we want to design for. As we outlined in the last part of the book, types, patterns and systems are venerable concepts – or themes – with which we develop variations that can be sketched out or notated quickly. Any formal method to assess capacity is only a tool to use this basic skill more efficiently.

EVALUATING POSSIBLE USES

As noted above, in optimizing the design of Base Buildings, and in doing so efficiently and cost-effectively, there are two technical problems that have to be approached systematically. First, there is the evaluation of possible uses. How can one be sure the design of the Base Building is best for a specific situation? By definition, a Base Building is an architectural infrastructure which allows choice and decision flexibility in the layout of fully independent occupancy units in it. To avoid mistakes and to facilitate communication, our evaluation process should be based on a method that checks what layout alternatives can be accommodated that satisfy the criteria and design constraints. This is a complicated process involving the comparison of a series of layouts. The evaluation is even more difficult when, rather than wait until the whole process has been completed, the designer wants to ascertain at the sketch design stage whether the Base Building will accommodate the preferred layout alternatives.

As we design, we may work in two directions, upward or downward in the 'levels' hierarchy. When we walk into a room and assess its uses by imagining the arrangement of furniture, we operate on the lower level (imagining what furniture can be accommodated) to evaluate the usefulness of the higher-level form. This is a familiar activity somewhat akin to site evaluation.

But when we operate on the higher level looking 'downward,' capacity analysis becomes a tool to justify the decisions we make relative to what is offered to the lower level. The urban designer will conduct a study of building types and their dimensions, street layouts and dimensions and the position of public functions in order to settle on lot sizes, block configurations, public spaces and so on. This is done without, of course, designing the buildings – a separate design task undertaken by someone else (see the urban design cases at the beginning of the book). At another level, an architect will conduct a study of typical arrangements of office furniture and partitioning to settle on the column spacing and other aspects of a Base Building for an office building. In this way, we conduct lower-level design explorations, not to determine what will be done there but to make sure that decisions made on the level we operate on provide the adequate context for lower-level interventions by others at a later stage.

Capacity analysis links designing on different levels. It offers a means to assure the hierarchical continuity of the urban design or building design we are working on without freezing it from top to bottom.

With the separation of Base Building from Infill, a new interface between designers is introduced. For instance, the designer of a Base Building cannot just show a few floor plans to justify their proposal. They must find out what **range** of possible plans – given certain requirements, constraints and values – might be possible in the proposed Base Building and at what cost.

This is where capacity analysis comes into play. In the Open Building approach, capacity analysis means that a design team will make a design and, during each of its various iterations during schematic design, will be able to demonstrate how it will accommodate a variety of Infill decisions without forcing the design to change. In simple terms, this means 'fixing' a form and studying what lower-level variants it can accommodate. After evaluating the results, what is 'fixed' can be revised and 'tested' again until everyone agrees that the design is good enough to meet all stakeholder requirements.

The design team might use two colors in their drawings – one for the Base Building elements and their configuration and another for the Infill elements and their layout. This is an iterative process. If there is a team of consultants, each will be asked to follow the same logic and ways of documenting this conversation, importantly including the MEP and structural engineering consultants.

It needs to be said that for a form – a building or an urban block – to have meaningful capacity at all, it should not be neutral. A well-articulated higher-level form suggests possible uses. It is an inspiration in the way the landscape – a water's edge, a stone outcropping or a beautiful row of trees – may enhance the capacity of a building site. Different parts of the site can have different qualities. This is a kind of dialogue between levels. To enter into a dialogue, someone must say something to get started. In our case, we must make a tentative design to get started. Here, we find an opportunity for architectural articulation not apparent in the case of top-down or unified design control.

HOW CAPACITY LINKS FORM TO FUNCTION

Assessing the capacity of a given space is such a common operation that we hardly pause to think about it. Yet it is worth attention as well as formalization. Capacity of a space links a given form to function. But it differs in two ways from the form-follows-function routine. To begin with, the form must be there first. We have to propose a form (e.g., a Base Building design), then evaluate it against a variety of layouts or functions. Then we adjust the form based on what we learned, test it again and so on until we get agreement. This can become quite involved, as already noted. Second, it relates the form not to one function but to a number of possible alternative functions or layouts. Our assessment of a room, for instance, concludes that it can be either a guest room or a study. The chosen lot size may hold a residential building as well as a shop or small office building.

We don't decide on function but evaluate the proposed form for what it can accommodate.

An architectural or urban design office might maintain a capacity database in its shared computer library. Building up such a reference from scratch is a good way to acquire a sense of spatial dimensions and dimensions of building elements of all kinds. New members of the firm can be encouraged to contribute to the database. Ultimately, all designers must end up knowing capacity of a human size by heart. After all, a skilled designer knows what can be done in, say, five feet: a corridor, a small bathroom, a sidewalk, three seats in an airplane, etc. From such basic knowledge, a talented designer can be expected to quickly come up with capacities for dimensions and room sizes in their designs. We want a relatively inexperienced architect or urban designer to understand exactly what is gained or lost when a street or block size, a structural bay or a room size is increased or reduced by 1 foot (or even 4 inches). Working on a single building, they may compare parking capacity in the basement with capacity for variable living spaces and healthcare or educational spaces on upper floors to find an optimum bay size.

It should be evident by now that capacity analysis itself is based on certain assumptions, conventions and rules or constraints. Defining and 'designing' these constraints is therefore an important part of capacity analysis. Studying and developing design constraints and rules before undertaking a specific design is akin to making and learning rules before playing a game or sport. For instance, in playing tennis, rules must be known such as serving rules, scoring rules, what is off-side or a violation, etc. After knowing all the rules, players can develop plays and many strategies without violating the rules. Similarly, studying and making design constraints equals making and learning rules in tennis, and capacity analysis equals strategy analysis.

Again, the concept may seem intuitively familiar to seasoned practitioners, but we suggest that its more systematic use in both new construction and conversion of buildings to other uses will greatly enhance any project's design process. This process will facilitate often-complex exchanges between client, design team and consultants and financial lenders, especially as projects become larger and more complex and fast-paced, and as office and design teams undertake work in cultures other than their home territories.

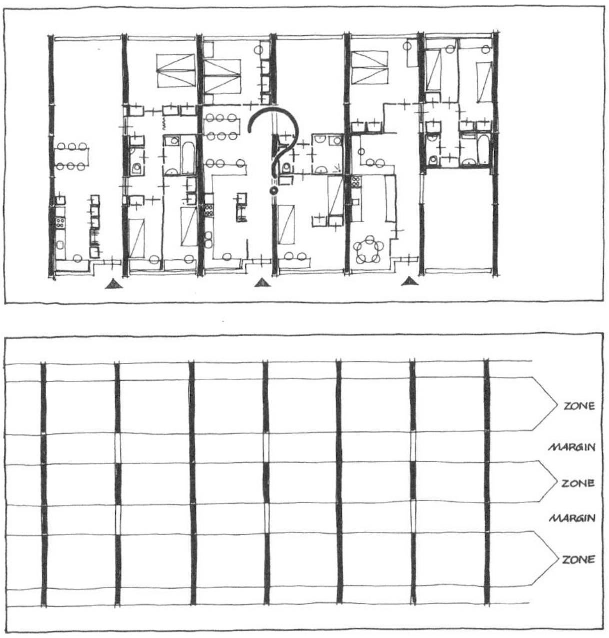

CAPACITY ANALYSIS – A KEY TOOL OF THE OPEN BUILDING APPROACH

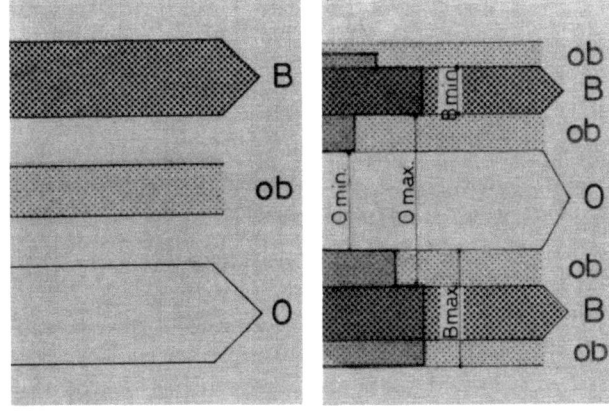

Figure 1 An example of zones and margins in a design study of a Base Building using parallel bearing walls with openings to allow separate bays to be combined into larger units (*Source*: Habraken et al., 1972)

THE USE OF ZONES AND MARGINS

At the SAR, in the mid-1960s, design methods were developed for architects to use in designing large residential projects using the principle of separating the tasks of designing a Base Building from the Infill (SAR65). At that time, the concept of zones and margins was developed. The tool is more generally useful, however. For example, the tool is helpful in the design of urban tissues, in healthcare, administrative, retail and educational buildings.

In what follows, we offer a discussion of the use of zones and margins as a possible way to conduct systematic capacity analysis (Habraken et al., 1972).

In the pair of drawings (Figure 1), examine the lower drawing first. It shows a simple structural layout of a residential Base Building, in which a number of extra (horizontal) lines have been drawn. These horizontal lines form a system of zones and margins which aid in the systematic development of variations in layout that satisfy one specific set of criteria. Zones and margins can be used as aids in the design of buildings within which independent occupancy units can be built that conform to such criteria. Zones and margins, then, are aids in the formulation of standards for the planning of units within a designed or yet-to-be-designed Base Building.

In the top drawing (Figure 1), the hypothetical Base Building with its variable Infill is shown, with a question mark. The examples show that the spaces are placed in the zone/margin system according to certain conventions. Certain rooms may overlap one or more zones but end in margins. Other areas can be completely within one zone or one margin. Note that the question of Infill access to MEP systems is not addressed yet.

The examples shown are of a building constructed with load-bearing walls with openings between bays, placed strategically to allow multiple bays to be combined into larger 'territories' or filled in to make a series of smaller demised spaces. Other structural systems are, of course, possible. The layout examples in the top drawing are not chosen at random; they are part of a larger group of layout alternatives, in which the arrangements of the rooms conform to specific rules which reflect the standards of the designer. Zones and margins are fixed bands (independent of the specific layouts) of certain dimensions within which spaces

Figure 2 In the development of an urban tissue, we can use zones for what is regularly built (B), another zone for what is regularly open (O) and a margin (ob). The drawing at the right shows how these can be used to show maximum and minimum B and O zones. Note: An ob margin can have a dimension of 0 (*Source*: SAR73) (*Source*: SAR73)

can be placed according to certain conventions. The design of a Base Building is based on a set of standards that are incorporated in a specific zone/margin system.

In the following discussion, we will explore the development of the method and the underlying concepts, rules and techniques which can be used as part of capacity analysis for the design and evaluation of Base Buildings.

CAPACITY ANALYSIS – A KEY TOOL OF THE OPEN BUILDING APPROACH

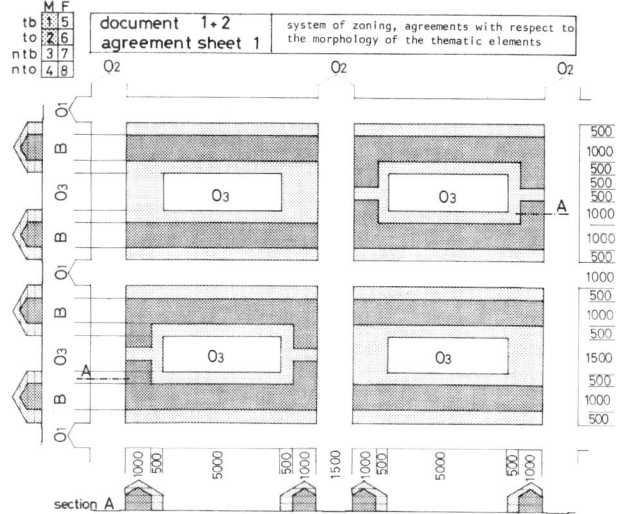

Figure 3 Here is a sample document showing in plan and section how a four-block part of an urban design can be represented using zones and margins (*Source*: SAR73). Note: This 'tissue model' can, of course, be transformed, bent or cut to fit the specific conditions of a site (*Source*: SAR73)

ZONES AND MARGINS AS PART OF CAPACITY ANALYSIS

With the design of Base Buildings of any kind, designers have to make decisions about the position and dimension of material without knowing the floor plans that eventually will be built in. This means that they cannot make decisions on the basis of floor plans. They have to work from possibilities of floor plans – that is, the capacity to accommodate variety and change of floor plans and functions. To be able to do so, they must be able to make general statements about the possible distribution of spaces in the Base Building and to compare alternative designs.

Zones are areas with specific architectural significance but with only general spatial qualities. The principle of zones can be used on all levels of the built environment, but on each level, we will define different kinds of zones.

By the arrangement of zones, the designer determines the most general organization of spaces. For instance, offices in office buildings each have their own specific combinations of zones, depending on the concept of office involved. The same goes for residential buildings, healthcare facilities and schools. The distribution and 'shape' of zones is a first general ordering of space, to be specified in later stages of the design process. That is, zones do not have to be 'straight' but can curve, for example.

It should be obvious that if any function can go anywhere, the use of zones loses its purpose.

With the help of such zones and assumptions for possible positioning of functions, it is possible to quickly generate a series of candidate 'basic variants' that give a good idea of the capacity of the Base Building to hold a variety of occupancies within the assumed values. With zones mediating between the two levels of intervention (Base Building at the higher level, Infill at the lower level), it is possible to efficiently evaluate the relation between floor plan values and Base Building capacity and to tinker with either the values or the Base Building design to arrive at a desired solution.

The use of zones thus helps a design team to formulate rules and agreements between the parties involved. In a design project, more specific agreements can be attached to the zones: designers can propose what kinds of spaces and what kinds of elements are allowed in a given zone. They make rules about the way the zones can be used. These agreements may serve to coordinate the work of different designers, including structural and mechanical engineers, cooperating in complex projects.

ZONES AND MARGINS IN URBAN DESIGN

Before going into more depth on the use of Zones and Margins in building design, we can briefly discuss this notation method in urban design. In that case, the zones indicate areas to be built or to be left open and are used to show the capacity of an urban design to hold certain architectural solutions that can be studied by varying either the urban design or the assumed building typology (Figures 2 and 3).

USING ZONES AND MARGINS IN HOUSING DESIGN

When separating design tasks is actually put to work, the party designing the Infill will be offered a space within a Base Building which has certain characteristics. They will value certain parts of the space more than others. These differences can be important when the building designer makes decisions about the location of different kinds of spaces or functions. Every building will have differing arrangements of components (for example, bearing walls or columns) and will offer its own characteristics and potential. (See drawing on the left in Figure 4 as an example of a structure using uniformly spaced bearing walls.)

It is up to the designer of the Infill to choose where certain types of spaces are located. A typical question that the designer might ask is this: Is it necessary for a bedroom to be on an external wall? Within a Base Building, two areas can be distinguished: one on the perimeter and one totally internal. Each of these is suitable to a different purpose. (Note: In some jurisdictions, bedrooms are not permitted without windows; in other places, in spaces with

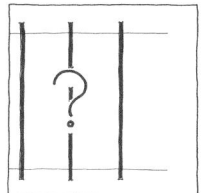 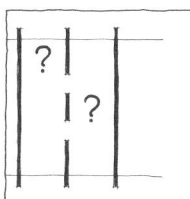 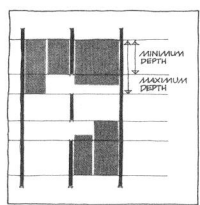

Figure 4 In a hypothetical Base Building, we ask what it can accommodate. To assist, we add the idea of minimum and maximum depth of spaces – the basis for zones and margins (drawing on the right) (*Source:* Habraken et al., 1972)

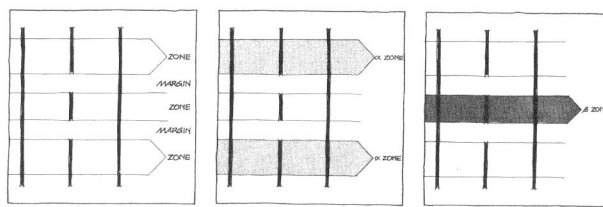

Figure 5 Alpha and beta zones and margins in between them (*Source:* Habraken et al., 1972)

very high ceilings, bedrooms on elevated platforms and with low walls can be placed internally.) (See middle drawing in Figure 4; openings have been made in one bearing wall, explained later.)

In general, what rooms should be located on an external wall? To answer this question, we could study a large number of plans drawn up by residents themselves. Observations would show, for instance, that bedrooms are (almost) always placed on an outside wall. Two lines can be superimposed on the plan of the Base Building indicating the minimum and maximum depth of such rooms. These lines define an area within which a certain kind of room can be located (see drawing on the right in Figure 4).

Conversely, before the space is divided up, two lines can be drawn parallel to the façade (see drawing to the right in Figure 4). The following convention will apply concerning the location of rooms within the area bounded by these lines: A room behind the façade will never be shorter than the width of the first band and never longer than the width of both bands together. Later, we will show that such a convention is especially useful when applied to certain kinds of rooms.

The areas described by these lines are called zones and margins. These are areas within a Base Building in which certain kinds of spaces are located according to specific rules. Which kinds of spaces relate to which zones will be discussed later, when the relationship between the size of a zone and the size of spaces is examined (see drawing on the left in Figure 5).

The zone adjacent to the façade is called the alpha zone. In the illustration (middle drawing in Figure 5), there are two alpha zones because there are two façades. There are three basic characteristics to an alpha zone: It is an area within a dwelling unit; it is an internal space; and it is an area which is adjacent to an external wall. The location of the alpha zone within a dwelling unit means that it is part of a larger private area, that is the whole of the dwelling unit, and is distinguishable from the public area in which the unit is located. The definition of an alpha zone is this: *an alpha zone is an internal area, intended for private use and is adjacent to an external wall*.

Based on this definition, alpha zones can be identified in any space that is used for housing. The second area that can be identified in the illustration (drawing on the right of Figure 5) is that area with no direct relationship to the outside. This area is called the beta zone. The beta zone is also suitable for the location of certain yet-to-be-defined kinds of spaces. In accordance with the definition of an alpha zone, we can now define a beta zone: *a beta zone is an internal area, intended for private use, and is not adjacent to an external wall*.

In Figure 5, there are two alpha zones and one beta zone. The example also shows that the two zones do not touch. Between two zones, there is always an area called a *margin*, which is defined as follows: *a margin is an area between two zones, with the characteristics of both these zones and taking its name from them*.

Because a margin has the characteristics of the two adjacent zones, we name it after these zones: between an alpha and a beta zone, there is an alpha/beta margin (see left-hand drawing in Figure 5).

Within a Base Building, the area that is used for the planning of the dwelling can always be divided into alpha and beta zones. But there are, in addition, other spaces that are outside the dwelling itself, which can also be classified into zones. The building that has been chosen as an example could have spaces for balconies or porches, outside spaces that are really part of the dwelling unit and are intended for private use. These are called delta zones. *A delta zone is an external area intended for private use*.

According to this definition, a garden, for example, will be located in the delta zone. Between the alpha zone and the delta zone is the alpha/delta margin (see middle drawing in Figure 6).

The separation between inside and outside occurs in the alpha/delta margin; in other words, the façade is in that margin. So, when a designer indicates the alpha/delta margin, they indicate the area in which the façade must be located. When this margin is wide, it means that the façade does not have to be in a uniform plane from dwelling to dwelling or bay to bay.

In the illustration on the right side of Figure 6, the area on the other side of the dwelling unit provides public access to the dwelling. This zone is the gamma zone, thus: *A gamma zone can be internal or external but is intended for public use*.

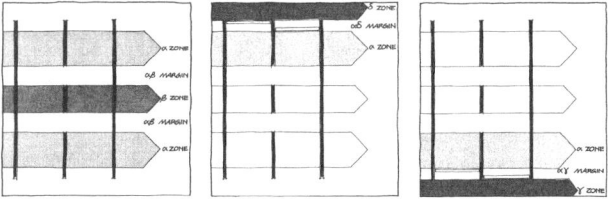

Figure 6 Alpha, beta, delta, gamma zones and their adjacent margins (*Source*: Habraken et al., 1972)

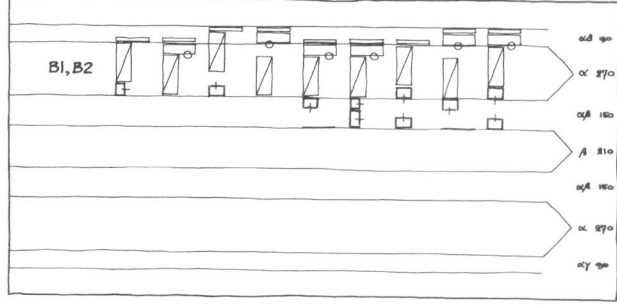

Figure 7 A diagram of a zone and its adjacent margins and possible use that can be accommodated in various ways (e.g., bedroom) (*Source*: Habraken et al., 1972)

An alpha/gamma margin occurs between the alpha and gamma zones. From top to bottom, we can identify the delta, alpha, beta, alpha and gamma zones with margins between them. This zone distribution represents either a row house or gallery access apartment, with a street or open access gallery on one side and a private balcony, porch or yard on the other.

It should be clear that other types of housing (e.g., double-loaded corridor type) can also be characterized by indicating their own zone/margin distribution.

The designer of a Base Building uses an arrangement of these zones as a base to draw conclusions in the design process. The zones also enable a design team to find the best location for ducts, openings in floors and walls, places to connect wiring and piping from the Base Building to those in the Infill, and so on.

At the same time, the zones allow the designers to judge the implications of these decisions on the possible arrangements of remaining spaces. One might say that each decision that adds elements to the Base Building will limit the number of variations possible in the building's design.

Each decision in the design of a Base Building must therefore be judged on its impact on the possibilities it gives and the possibilities it eliminates. In other words: the zones are a tool that enables the designer to relate each technical decision to possibilities of use and, vice versa, to relate each general requirement of use to its technical implications.

The general rule formulated in what has been explained so far – that specific living/working spaces should end in two succeeding margins – leaves so much open that experienced designers will feel the need to add other rules in the course of the design process. Such additional rules can be a great help in further organization of a Base Building framework and give the parties involved in the design process the means to translate more specific requirements into the same language.

Examples of such additional rules could be:

- Sanitary cells will be found only in β zones
- Or sanitary cells will be found either in β zones or α β margins
- Bedrooms (in housing or healthcare facilities) will be found only in α zones
- Load-bearing elements will not be found in α zones
- Vertical MEP shafts will be found only in α β margins

It is precisely this possibility to add specific rules as the design process proceeds that makes good communication possible. Each general decision can thus be formulated, and its implications can be studied by the parties involved.

Sectors

A sector is a certain free length of a set of zones with their adjacent margins. For example, the space between two load-bearing walls or between other structural columns in a Base Building can be called a Sector. Zones give only one dimension; sectors give two. A Sector can be analyzed on its possibilities of use for different combinations of functions. Base Buildings may have material (e.g., columns or bearing walls or partial bearing walls) that intersect the zones. Therefore, the analysis of the resulting sectors is an important exercise in the evaluation process.

The sectors are the built spaces given to the occupant (household, medical department, classroom grouping, etc.) for further partitioning or combination into a specific functional unit (e.g., a dwelling, an office suite, a classroom cluster, a medical department, etc.). We can say that, for example, a dwelling in a Base Building is a Sector group. In that case, in principle, each group of adjacent sectors can be a functional unit.

Basic Variants

If a given sector group can be seen as an area for a functional unit, then a great many possible floor plans can be expected in a

CAPACITY ANALYSIS – A KEY TOOL OF THE OPEN BUILDING APPROACH

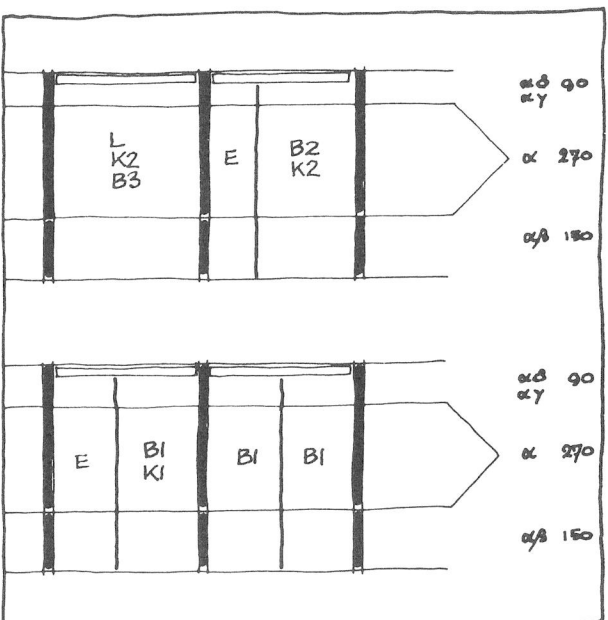

Figure 8 A diagram of several sector groups with indications of possible uses shown, such as L for living, K for kitchen, B1/B2 for different sizes of bedrooms, etc. (*Source*: Habraken et al., 1972)

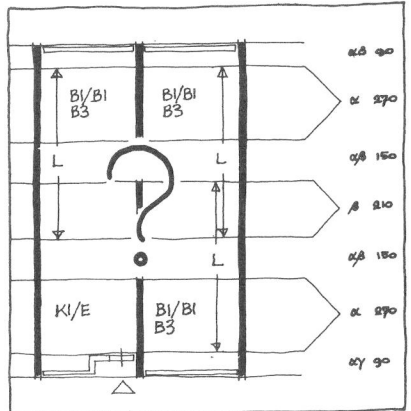 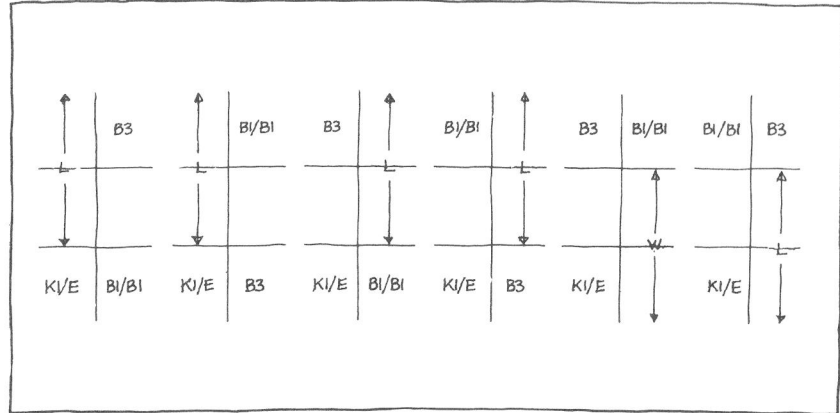

Figure 9 Diagrams of basic variants in one dwelling (sector group) (*Source*: Habraken et al., 1972)

building composed of many sectors. Even if we only consider the floor plans according to the rules on which the building is designed, in most cases the number of possible variations is very great.

To get an idea of the number of variations in a given sector group, the concept of basic variations is important. *A basic variant is a notation of the position of functions for specific living/working spaces and general living/working spaces.*

As shown in Figure 9, the different functions attached to the spaces can be coded (e.g., LR, BR, ER (exam room), etc.). In the drawings of sectors, the codes for the space functions are noted. This notation does not give the dimension of the space required. It only states that the function stated can be located in that place. Such a notation in the area of one functional unit (sector group) gives a basic variant.

In any given area, the series of possible basic variants can be written out. They give a considerable amount of information on the different living/working patterns possible in the given area. Each basic variant gives a great many possible subvariants: that is, specific floor plans that all have the same functional pattern.

An analysis of the basic variants gives valuable information on the properties of a given design.

GRIDS AS DESIGN TOOLS FOR BUILDINGS AND URBAN TISSUES

The purpose of grids is to help position objects in space. Dimension follows from where things are. In using grids as design tools, it's good to remember that position comes first, followed by dimension. Positioning of parts relative to grid lines can be subjected to rules. For instance, we can stipulate that an element is on the center line of a grid line or between two lines. Each system may have its own positioning rules, determining how the relations of parts will be decided. Knowing position rules of two systems, we know how these systems may relate. With the help of grids, traffic of parts in space can be organized in three dimensions. (See the NEXT21 case for example)

Kinds of Grids
Some regard Lucien Kroll as an anarchist architect. He is known for his renovations of massive housing blocks first built in the 1960s and 1970s in Europe. He partially erodes these monolithic blocks to then graft onto them domestic elements like bay windows, gables, dormers, French balconies and windows like strange weeds growing from rocks. He first gained fame for his design of the student union building in Louvain – La Neuve University. The façade of the building is a collage of varied elements, each designed by another member of his team. Some of the masonry work is the result of free improvisation by masons encouraged by the architect to exercise their creativity. Inside, students designed dormitories by themselves, producing spaces no architect ever dreamed of.

Few know that this idiosyncratic complexity is governed by well-ordered modular principles with which the architect was thoroughly conversant. Kroll understood early on that freedom thrives on the systemic – that indeed, systems spawn complexity and variety. Not surprisingly, he used the computer long before most of his colleagues did.

Unfortunately, grids have become confused with architectural shapes, giving both architecture and grids of all kinds a bad name. But the purpose of modular grids is not to make grid-like forms.

As Kroll and others such as Frank Lloyd Wright demonstrate, the modular grid is a tool for positioning building parts and communicating their position in an efficient manner. With this understanding, grids as such do not dominate the forms they serve. After all, we do not expect the coordinates used to map the earth to be visible in the waves of the ocean, nor would we expect coastlines, mountain ridges, rivers and ships to follow those grid lines on any consistent basis. Of course, there are exceptions. For instance, the surveyors involved in the settlement of the American West used the rectangular coordinates of longitude and latitude to lay out vast areas for settlement. We can still see the evidence of this flying over the mid-western United States. Yet we can determine without error where all objects are located on the earth's surface and what distance they are from one another. Today, discrete global grid systems (DGGS) are used to index data on the spherical earth as a basis for GIS (geographic information systems).

In the past, spatial coherence among parts in the composition of buildings was related to the size of common elements. Northwestern European architecture was measured by the size of the bricks. All dimensions of windows, doors, walls and buttresses were expressed in 'headers' derived from the short side of the brick. In Japan, of course, the tatami is the unit of design in traditional architecture, albeit with two predominant sizes, one prevalent in the Tokyo region, another in the Osaka/Kyoto region. In North American balloon or platform frame building, the distance between studs served as a module: three of them to fit in 4 feet, the latter being the size of drywall and plywood or other kinds of sheet material.

We know that dimensions of building parts were never exact multiples of either bricks or tatami or center-to-center distances between studs or posts. Bricks have mortar joints, and therefore, a header is a brick width plus a joint, and physical sizes derived from the header are plus or minus joints. Likewise, rooms b a s e d o n tatami mats are separated by walls and wall thickness is to be either added to or subtracted from the multiple of tatami to arrive at a true size of a space or a wall.

The point is that traditional building practice used sophisticated systems of dimensioning, understood by all parties involved, from producers to users. Their value was not in standardization of parts – tatami may vary in exact dimension from region to region, and bricks of all sizes are available – but in efficiency of communication among parties. When carpenters were told what size of brick was to be used and how many

CAPACITY ANALYSIS – A KEY TOOL OF THE OPEN BUILDING APPROACH

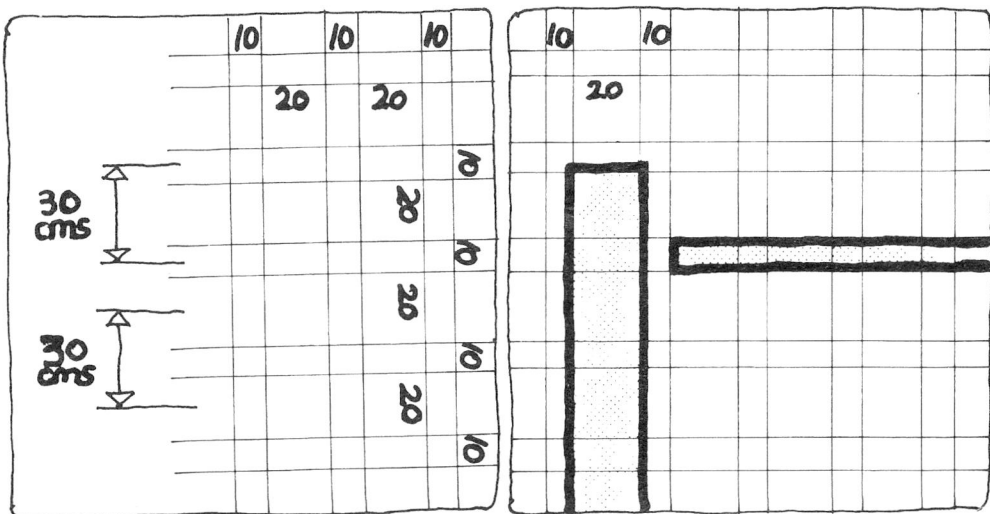

Figure 10, 11: A band grid with 30 cm (12") center-to-center spacing and a diagram showing that rules can be set for positioning material elements. E.g., Base Building walls can be placed in or end in a 20-cm band, while Infill walls can be placed in or end in the 10-cm band (*Source*: Habraken et al., 1972)

Figure 12 Multiple related grids used in planning NEXT21 (*Source*: Shu-Ko-Sha Architecture and Urban Design Studio)

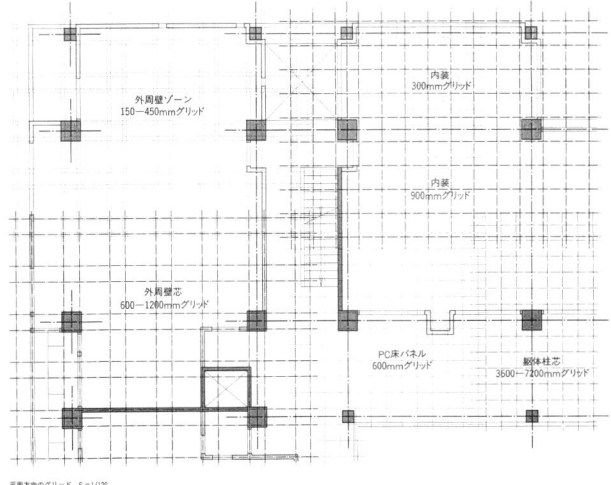

headers the window size was to be, they could make a window that would fit. Vernacular dimensional language was a device to coordinate work by the trades.

Today's pluriform environment doesn't allow a single product like a brick to support all communication in the field anymore. The building is now a composition of systems, each with its own modular principles. Different buildings may contain different systems and materials. We therefore would benefit from new means to keep track of the distribution of parts in space and of their dimensional interdependence. Grids help us do this. They serve to locate parts in space and to determine how shifting of one part may affect the size of another.

In the early work at the SAR, when work was underway to develop methods for architects to design Base Buildings when floor plans were not known, the problem of coordination was quickly identified as a crucial issue. At the same time, studies in modular coordination were underway in Europe. SAR proposed the use of a *band grid* such as in the two figures below, based on the international standard of a 4" (10-cm) planning module.

In fact, for a single large project, more than one grid may be used (again, refer to NEXT21 at the beginning of the book). Starting from a basic grid, other grids, serving their own systems, may have modules derived from the base grid module by multiplication or subdivision.

Interrelated grids may operate on different levels of intervention as well. A building's structure, for instance, may be based on a module of 5 feet, while a single foot or even 4 inches may be best for the deployment of partitioning and other fit-out subsystems.

Grids in Urban Design

In urban design, on the other hand, modules of 10 or 20 feet may be in order. Such modules can be coordinated with building-level grids of finer grain. In no case, however, are grids meant to 'give form' or in other ways define the architectural or urban qualities. Grids are meant to position elements in space relative to other elements. Grids can be useful in establishing the parameters of building design done by other parties, as the following diagrams show (Habraken et al., 1981). (These are just 6 diagrams from a series of 12 from this study.)

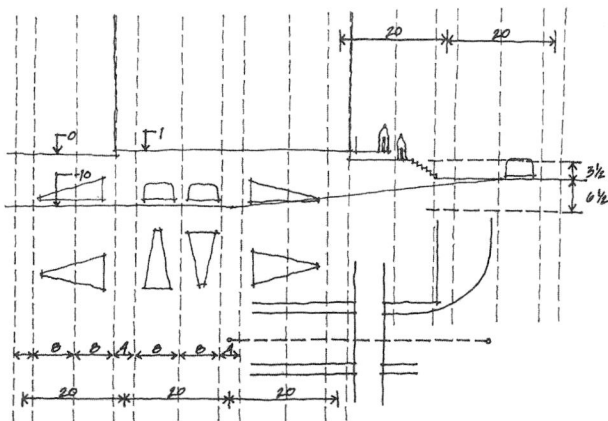

Figure 13 This diagram gives a cross section through a building and half of a street (*Source*: Habraken et al., 1981)

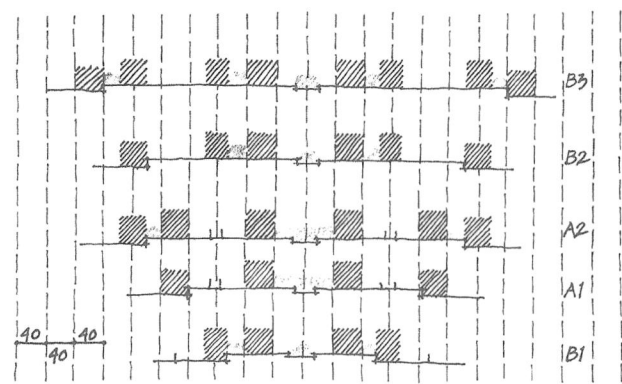

Figure 14 Alternative cross sections of a superblock (*Source*: Habraken et al., 1981)

This particular street is raised 6½" above the normal street level. A sidewalk is again 3½" higher. This creates a garage level under the building that can be reached from the street. The street itself, however, stays in close relation with the first floor of the building proper. The whole cross section is laid out on a band grid of 4" × 8" intervals in a rhythm of 4", 8", 8", 4", 8", 8", 4", etc. In the other direction, there is a straight rhythm of 8" intervals not shown here. This rhythm creates a larger interval of 20". from the center of one 4" band to the center of the next 4" band.

An important principle of the method followed here is that each element within the agreements of the urban design theme must follow clearly defined position rules. In this case, for instance, one rule implies that a building's façade will always be placed within a 4" band and that, unless explicitly stated otherwise, all columns will be placed in the 4" bands. It follows from this that there is a certain margin of variation for the façade but that it is a narrow one. The face of the façades – as we will see later on – can, within that margin, step back and forth a few feet. Had the rule been chosen that the façade would be in the 8" band, the freedom to stagger the façade would obviously have been much greater.

Although within these position rules it is not yet known exactly where a façade wall will be, it is known 'nominally.' In the discussion of the rules, we will work within the nominal dimensions. For instance, the building here is nominally two 20" modules deep. With the rule adopted here, that the face of the façade must lie in the 4" band, the actual distance between the two outer faces of the front and back can vary 2" × 4". In the same manner, we see that the street is 8" × 20" wide nominally.

With the profile from Figure 13 as a given, we can develop a series of alternative cross sections of a superblock of which the raised residential road is the spine (Figure 14). Cross section A1 is perhaps the most 'normal' one. Behind the buildings along the residential spine, we see backyards over the garage. Another building faces the outside of the block. From there, A2 follows by adding a pedestrian street with another building.

There is, however, another alternative in which the pedestrian street is placed immediately behind the first buildings along the spine B1. From there, B2 and B3 follow. Obviously, in these alternatives, the backyard spaces of the buildings along the spine will be on the side of the raised residential street that forms the spine. In these instances, backyards will take the position of the sidewalks in A1 and A2. Note that the grid lines given in this sketch are 40" apart (see also Figure 13). The pedestrian streets are therefore nominally 20" wide.

The cross sections of Figure 14 are minimal cross sections. They give a backyard space – including the fire lane – from building to building of 80" nominally with four large modules. Other larger dimensions could have been chosen. Each dimension includes from four to seven large modules and gives its own possible arrangement of cars and lanes in the below-grade parking space.

On the left-hand side of Figure 16, we again have the building along the raised residential street. If the ground floor is for commercial use, it should be at sidewalk level. The right-hand sections give the same building but this time with a raised floor along the sidewalk. This should be adopted if dwellings are to be on the ground floor. The distribution of other floor levels is devised in such a way that dwellings can have two floors – always with at least one room of greater height that connects both floors. Vertical dotted lines are 20" modules.

This sketch illustrates the possible interplay of urban spaces and buildings. The sketch is done on the 40" module. It also illustrates how the 'thematic' position of the elements (the buildings

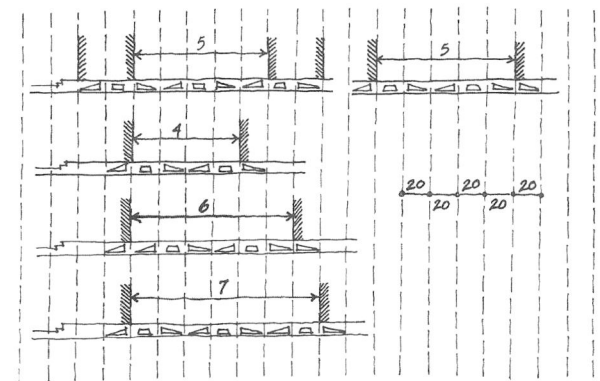

Figure 15 Cross sections of Figure 14 (*Source*: Habraken et al., 1981)

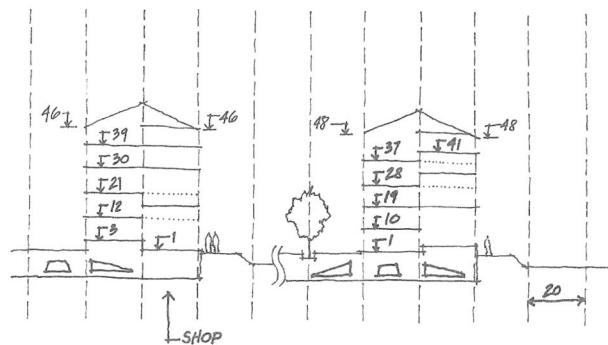

Figure 16 Rules on vertical dimensions shown in a cross section diagram (*Source*: Habraken et al., 1981)

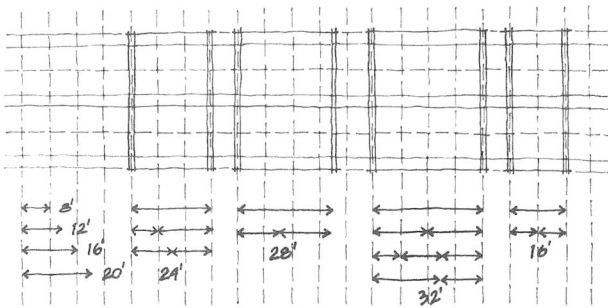

Figure 17 This diagram gives possible positions of party walls at grid lines 8" apart. Building widths will be increments of 8" (*Source*: Habraken et al., 1981)

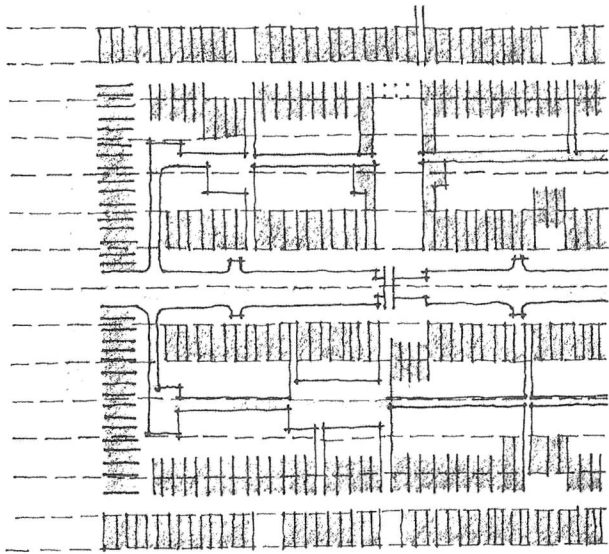

Figure 18 Sketch of the A2-type tissue (*Source*: Habraken et al., 1981)

in this example) can be interrupted to create a recognizable and site-specific tissue.

Summary of the Use of Grids in Designing

In summary, grids are tools for positioning elements in space – buildings, streets, partitions, mechanical systems and so on. They are not meant to dictate built form or dimensions. Even on a single level (e.g., urban design, building design, Infill, etc.), we always find ourselves coordinating a variety of sub-systems. We know that each may have its own positioning rules for deployment. Using position rules for building parts in space is not unlike using a beat in music. It gives a base for modulation. The grid may be rigid and repetitive like a single beat, but positioning rules may allow for a variety of placements of the same part, and we are always free to ignore rules or to deviate from them for the sake of the overall composition. Even a deviation is a known position in the grid, as longitude and latitude are used to position us on the earth's surface. In this way, the grid becomes a design tool; not a form but a means for making form.

It's worth noting that when *SAR65* was developed, computers as design aids did not exist. Now, with powerful computational tools at our disposal, it remains to be seen what can be done with the use of grids as tools.

READINGS

Habraken, N.J., et al. (1972). *Variations: The Systematic Design of Supports*. MIT Press, Cambridge, MA.

Habraken, N.J., Aldrete-Hass, J., Chow, R., Hille, t., Krugmeier, P., Lampkin, M., Mallows, A., Mignucci, A., Takase, Y., Weller, K., Yokouchi, T. *The Grunsfeld Variations: A Report on the Thematic Development of an Urban Tissue*. MIT Press, Cambridge, MA.

Kendall, S.H., Kurmel, T.D., and Dekker, K.D. (2012). Healthcare facilities design for flexibility. Final report. *Cost Modeling Workshop: Analysis of Initial Capital Asset Investment and Future Costs of Adaptation*. Prepared by the National Institute of Building Sciences, Washington, DC, pp 153–174.

A Detailed Study of Capacity Analysis in Adaptive Reuse – Office to Residential

In what follows, we present a study of how the Open Building approach can be used in the conversion of an obsolete office building to residential use. We should note that the *Capacity Analysis* process discussed in what follows is *not* what actually happened.

- The Challenge of Conversion of Office Buildings to Residential Use
- Getting the Design Constraints Right
- Studying MEP Constraints is a First Step for Capacity Analysis
- DWV Systems in an Open Building Design Strategy
- Description of Fixtures
- Organizing Piping Traffic Inside Infill Partitions
- Capacity Analysis Study of the Kales Building
- An Open Building Alternative to Conversion
- Vertical MEP Pipe Shaft Positioning Study
- A Design Process for Conversion Using Capacity Analysis
- Organizing Drainage Piping in a Bathroom in Three Variants
- Conclusions

THE CHALLENGE OF CONVERSION OF OFFICE BUILDINGS TO RESIDENTIAL USE

In 2023, at the time of writing this book, a great deal of attention was being paid to the huge stock of downtown office buildings around the United States – and much of the world – that have become underutilized due to a widespread shift to working from home and other fundamental changes in the nature of work. This current reality presents a problem for building owners who have to carry real estate portfolios at a substantial financial loss. It also means that the economic and social life of downtowns face new pressures to adapt to the new realities. Some writings cast this as a tipping point in the way we invest in real estate: from design for single use to design beyond single use – or design for change more generally.

This is not an entirely new problem, having been recognized decades ago, leading to a number of research projects and conferences in many countries. However, the magnitude might be new, at least in some locales. In any case, the rapid upsurge of office building vacancy rates has forced think tanks, city planners, building owners, financial institutions and others to ask the question if these buildings could be quickly and cost-effectively reconfigured or converted to other uses. Conversion to residential use is now the prime but not the only targeted new use. Urban designers, architects and engineers are taking this seriously, along with investors, developers, affordable housing advocates as well as construction companies and manufacturers of building elements.

But because most buildings have *not* been designed for change and are largely designed and financed for single uses, the wholesale conversion of office buildings to other uses remains confused and expensive. Conversion is often complicated by excessively 'deep' floor plates, obsolete regulations, design practices and construction methods. This fact is belied of course in the case of such buildings as the former John Hancock tower in Chicago and many other very large buildings, which have, over time, seen many uses occupying them. But, as we noted before, we know next to nothing about this because there are so few longitudinal studies examining what takes place when such changes occur.

One thing we can be sure of: the issue of territory – discussed earlier in the book as the needed territorial autonomy of occupancies in multi-occupant buildings – is always present as a challenge but is rarely addressed.

GETTING THE DESIGN CONSTRAINTS RIGHT

Before embarking on a full *capacity analysis*, a few words are necessary about getting the *design constraints* right. There are hundreds of design constraints guiding us when we are designing. There are two basic kinds of constraints in all design processes: implicit and explicit.

Firstly, there are always, in a design situation, a large number of implicit constraints that are so obvious to us that we do not bother to formulate them. No one would propose to place the bed in front of the door. This indicates that we always operate in an implicit solution space that is already much smaller than the one bounded by the explicit constraints . . .

Secondly . . . there are additional constraints that must be made explicit . . . constraints can only come from the consideration of possible – desirable or undesirable – alternatives. **Without** *such alternatives there is nothing to approve of or to reject, and we cannot learn about our values and preferences. (Habraken, 2019)*

STUDYING MEP CONSTRAINTS IS A FIRST STEP FOR CAPACITY ANALYSIS

Of the hundreds of constraints involved in any design process, of both kinds noted, we think that there is little doubt that constraints having to do with mechanical, electrical/data and plumbing (MEP) systems and pathways have become increasingly complex in all kinds of buildings as well as at the level of urban planning and design. These elements of infrastructure wend their way inside buildings and under streets, connecting daily life to both supply and disposal systems that have come to dominate our infrastructure planning at all levels. They cross territorial boundaries and levels of interventions, from furnishings to Infill walls and ceilings to Base Building parts of these systems, to power generation plants and waste treatment facilities at the city or regional level.

In the design of projects in which each unit of occupancy is fully independent (a basic Open Building principle), the design of the pathways for these elements of infrastructure plays a dominant role. Unfortunately, they are too often left to be solved after floor plans are decided or are decided in detail on the site by the subcontractor who gets there first. When we implement a project using the Open Building approach – either a new project or a conversion such as the study discussed here – we can't afford to be casual about these pathways and their interfaces.

In the case study of the capacity analysis that follows, therefore, figuring out the MEP pathways constraints is a central focus.

Experience is showing that a raised floor of varying thickness in tenant spaces (for horizontal pathways of drainage and other piping, wiring and ducts) is often very helpful to achieve full floor plan autonomy in multistory buildings, including allowing the position of bathrooms and kitchens to part of Infill. If the placement of bathrooms is fixed, then such raised floors are not such a necessity. (See the TILA case at the beginning of the book.) Use of a raised floor or a hollow floor allows floor plan layout decisions on one floor to be made without entangling the spaces below. (See PlusHome, TOPUP and NEXT21 at the beginning of the book.)

In new construction, we now see a trend toward 'depressing' the floor elevation of tenant spaces some distance below the floor elevation of public spaces/corridors. This provides pathway space under raised floors in tenant spaces (usually classified as Infill elements) for horizontal MEP systems (see TOPUP).

However, the use of such raised floors, no matter how thin, is not possible in an adaptive reuse or conversion project unless one of several design strategies is implemented:

1. Installation of a raised floor throughout the entire floor plate on each floor. This may require installation of new fire stairs to align with the new 'raised floor' elevation of the public corridors and, at the same time, adjustment of the elevator stops to align with the new elevation of the public corridors.
2. Maintain the fire stairs and elevator stops at their existing elevations along with the public corridors. Once inside the front door of each occupant space, enter a 'foyer' whose floor is at the same elevation as the public corridor. Then, one or two steps (depending on the thickness of the new raised floor) or a ramp leads up onto the new raised floor of the unit of occupancy, under which unit-specific (Infill) horizontal piping and other mechanical systems are installed. This is problematic because ramps consume space but may be needed when handicapped accessibility is required.
3. Adopt a 'thick-wall' strategy for horizontal routing of drainage and other piping inside tenant spaces, thus avoiding any change in the floor elevations of either public space or occupancy spaces but necessitating the placement of a number of strategically positioned vertical 'pipe' shafts in the floor plate.

The latter strategy (#3) is a design constraint used in the conversion study that follows. It presents certain very specific issues that are explained.

In conventional residential high-rise buildings, drainage pipes of an individual sanitary fixture, bathtub or shower penetrate vertically through the floor at or near each fixture (see Figure 1). During conventional design processes, such penetrations are determined after the layout plan is fixed. There are few or almost no horizontal connections between fixtures inside the same dwelling unit. Horizontal drain lines serving fixtures in one dwelling are

Figure 1 Floor penetrations for each plumbing fixture are indicated in red in an actual multifloor building in the United States (*Source*: Li, 2004)

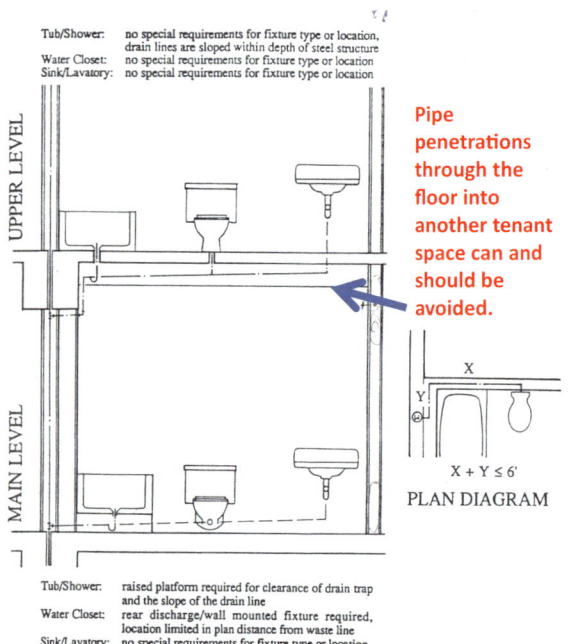

Figure 2 Two ways of handling drainage piping in stacked occupancy territories: The top (upper level) is problematic because drainage pipes penetrate the floor slab, causing significant limitations on future fixture relocations and causing potential legal disputes during maintenance, or when changes are made in that unit, implicating the dwelling unit below. The preferred solution is shown in the "Main Level" in which all horizontal drain lines remain within the unit's territorial boundaries before attaching to the Base Building's common vertical shaft (*Source*: Li, 2004)

conventionally hidden in the ceiling of the dwelling unit immediately below (see Figure 2).

As a result, there are usually the same number of penetrations in the floor as there are plumbing (bathroom or kitchen) fixtures.

That is, when there are 20 sanitary fixtures, tubs and showers in one floor, it might require 20 penetrations of the floor slab. It's no wonder that there are always many dozens of penetrations in a residential high-rise building. The challenges are many: each penetration must be fire-stopped; the exact position of the penetration is critical to align with fixtures and partitions; errors are very expensive to correct and may come into conflict with structural elements.

After a building is designed and built in a conventional way, plumbing pipes are fixed to and through the floors. This results in a kind of dependency and rigidity among stacked vertical dwelling units, making dwelling unit layouts heavily dependent on other floors above and below. Once a typical floor is designed, there is very little freedom to obtain a significantly different unit layout for other floors – or to change layouts at any time – because of the drainage piping entanglement.

The entanglement between piping and the building construction causes trouble in at least four ways – from preconstruction to postconstruction use and future changes.

1. First of all, for architects, this entanglement causes multiple redesigns before construction begins and results in the likelihood of change orders later, often without fee compensation unless this is understood when writing the agreement for professional services. The problem is that layout decisions are interdependent among floors. Once a floor layout is determined (or changed), especially in regard to drainage plumbing, the other floor layouts have to correspond. Without confirming the architectural plan, other consultants such as mechanical and electrical and even structural engineering can't work independently or efficiently. The excessive interdependency causes design delay and conflicts. Decision flexibility is severely reduced.

2. Second, these plumbing entanglement problems produce high-rise residential building designs that can offer only a very few unit plans or mix variations from floor to floor. Therefore, conventional multifloor residential buildings cannot offer variation corresponding to real variation found in the market. Again, decision flexibility is severely reduced, both in rental projects and in for-sale projects.
3. Third, the entanglement of pipes causes boundary conflicts and legal disputes between dwelling units. In the US, condominiums are well known to be the most legally troubled building type, perhaps due in part to this problem. For example, when a drainage pipe serving the upper floor is leaking, it causes inconvenience for the lower-floor unit and violates territorial autonomy. Individual fixture penetrations on the floor can increase the potential of floor leaking issues.
4. Finally, these entanglements cause difficulties for future adaptations. Once a conventional building is built, it is almost impossible to have a bathroom on a given floor move to another location or even to be enlarged in the same location with additional or upgraded fixtures and layouts.

In the Open Building approach, dividing a building into two design tasks also means dividing the design of drainage system (and other MEP systems). Drainage pipes and other MEP infrastructure parts positioned inside an MEP shaft (including the floor penetration) should be regarded as a part of the Base Building, because these elements serve multiple occupancy units and require replacement only at 30- to 50-year intervals – lasting longer than the Infill portions of these same systems. All drainage pipes inside a unit of occupancy's territory belong to the Infill. The largest of these are pipes requiring a slope, carrying black wastewater to their corresponding drainage pipes located inside MEP shafts.

This is quite different from conventional projects where the distinction between 'common' and 'individual' drainage piping is confused, as the above shows.

DWV SYSTEMS IN AN OPEN BUILDING DESIGN STRATEGY

Drainage piping (DWV or drain, waste, vent) is more difficult than other MEP system in housing compared to ventilation, cabling or water supply systems. In residential DWV systems, waste is carried via water by means of gravity, but in ventilation, electrical or domestic water systems, gravity obviously does not apply.

In Open Building projects, there are several design restrictions in designing residential DWV systems. Dividing the plumbing system into two decision levels requires knowledge of design constraints to guide design.

To accomplish this goal, initially, some fundamental rules or constraints are set as part of an Open Building strategy, a number of building codes are applied and some conventional practices are assumed as evaluation criteria. Accordingly, this study uses the following criteria:

1. Horizontal drainage pipes slope @ 1/8" per foot (a standard US code requirement)
2. All sanitary fixtures are above floor (rear-discharge) rough-in (OB principle)
3. All horizontal drainage pipes go into fit-out partition walls (but cannot cross doors) (OB principle)
4. All wastewater discharges into vertical MEP stacks inside the territorial unit (OB principle)
5. There are no floor penetrations except Base Building MEP shaft openings (OB principle)
6. The use of code-approved 'air-admittance valves' is assumed for all plumbing fixtures (except toilets)
7. HEPvO waterless waste valves (or their equivalent) are used for gray water drainage lines (replacing conventional 'P' traps)
8. We assume a separation of black- and gray-water drainage piping.
9. All products must be available in the US market.

DESCRIPTION OF FIXTURES

NOTE: In the following, the discussion of the alternative Open Building strategy, and all illustrations, are taken from a study by Li, Jing Qiang. 2004. *Designing Constraints for Capacity Analysis of Residential Floor Areas*; MARCH thesis under the supervision of Stephen Kendall, Ball State University.

There are typically seven fixture types in a residential dwelling unit. These fixtures are HVAC units, water heaters, washing machines, sinks, toilets, bathtubs and showers. In what follows, individual fixtures are briefly described and analyzed for the purpose of developing design constraints.

Toilets

There are two kinds of flush systems in toilets. One is a pressure-assisted flush system and the other is a gravity-flush system. The former is usually used in transportation vehicles (e.g., boats) or facilities with a lack of water, in installations where water conservation is important for reasons of economy or water scarcity or in installations where effluent must be pumped to a higher elevation. Increasing numbers of toilets in commercial establishments use pressure-assisted toilets. The second – gravity-flush – is the most conventional.

The second distinction in toilets is the direction of the outlet or discharge. The conventional type in residential and many other applications is the downward outlet. This kind of fixture is floor mounted. The other type is rear discharge. This is available in wall-hung (e.g., Geberit) and floor-mounted versions. The wall-mounted rear discharge type is familiar in institutions, public facilities and other situations were maintenance personnel like the absence of obstructions to cleaning the floors. Finally, we have the floor-mounted rear discharge type (see Figure 3).

Downward-discharge toilets cannot be applied in an Open Building installation because their waste outlet passes through the floor. It does not meet one of the criteria set earlier. The exception to this rule is the use of a raised Infill floor of sufficient height, under which horizontal drainage piping with required slope can be installed. This study does not utilize this approach. Further studies are needed using the raised-floor strategy.

In the floor-mounted rear-discharge type (Figure 3), the center-line of the outlet is 4" above the floor. This is an important dimension, because it presents constraints in deciding the distance from the toilet to a MEP shaft and also the interrelations within partition walls, as the following sections show.
Similarly, water in bathtubs and showers is drained out by means of gravity. This causes difficulties in installing bathtubs or showers in an Open Building way because there is no space for a horizontal pipe under the tub or shower, set at conventional elevations, to have enough slope to the main vertical drainage pipe in the

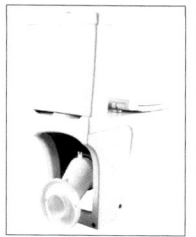

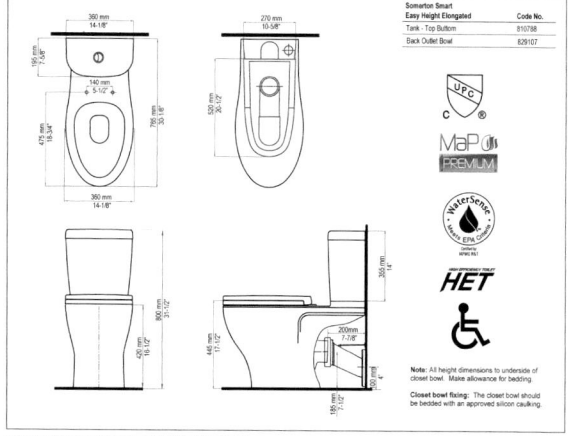

Figure 3 Toilet product with the center-line of its rear outlet 4" above floor rough-in. This kind is available from several companies distributing their products in the US market such as Caroma, Inc.

MEP shaft. The only way to solve the problem is to raise the tub or shower base to get a reasonable height to slope the drainage pipe above the floor.

According to research of products on the market conducted for this study, there are basically two kinds of drain installations for bathtubs. One is the conventional way for bath drain installation, in which a pipe penetrates the floor at the fixture, with a 'P' trap in the ceiling of the space below, therefore violating a key Open Building requirement. The second is called a 'back-outlet'

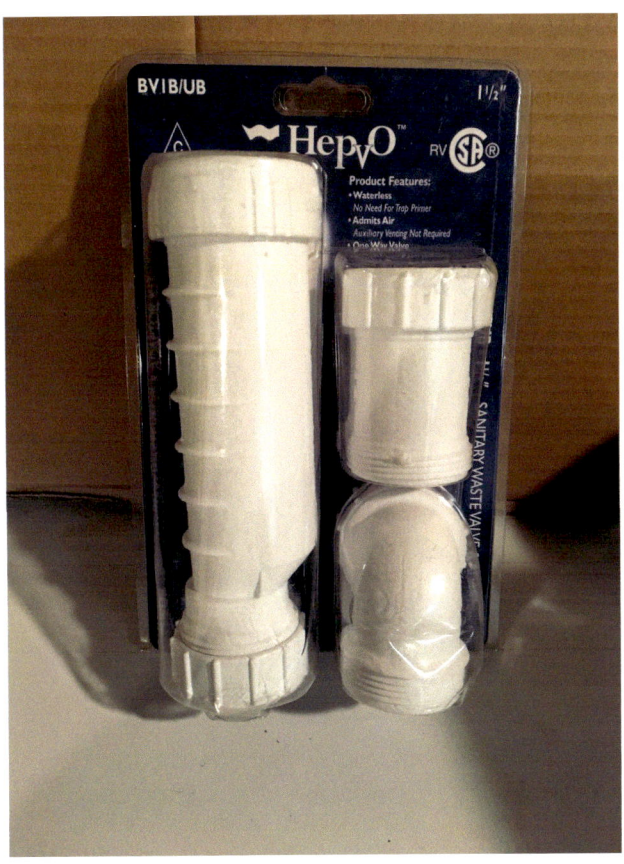

Figure 4 A waterless waste valve eliminates the need for a conventional 'P trap.' (www.wavin.com/en-gb/catalog/waste-water/waterless-traps/wavin-osma-hepvo-waste-valve)

type, for bath drain installation. It drains water horizontally without a floor slab penetration at the fixture.

The rear-outlet drain installation of the bathtub and shower is selected for use in this study. To eliminate the problem of the 'P trap' for a tub or shower, the study uses a waterless waste-valve Figure 4).

ORGANIZING PIPING 'TRAFFIC' INSIDE INFILL PARTITIONS

In this study, all wastewater from each sanitary fixture goes through horizontal drainpipes placed inside Infill walls to vertical drainpipes located in a Base Building MEP shaft. (*Note:* The actual enclosure of Base Building MEP shafts is part of the Infill.) For reasons of appearance, horizontal drainpipes in the Infill are placed inside partition walls (rather than surface mounted). In addition, electrical wiring, low-voltage wiring, and other wires go inside partitions and above dropped ceilings. Partitions in residential units are typically very full of piping, wiring and ducts. In an Open Building installation, it is critical that these MEP lines be very carefully organized and not left to on-site decisions by plumbing subcontractors.

The following partition wall study was done as part of the study (Figures 5a, b, c). The goal is to design an Infill partition wall system that applies in Open Buildings Infill installations, that is

a. Capable of carrying piping and wiring;
b. Can contribute to off-site kiting and on-site installation (not part of this study) but also
c. Makes future reconfigurations less costly and wasteful than today's methods.

Infill partition walls with MEP carrying capability are interior nonbearing, light-gauge steel stud walls. They are also 'wall-liners' against demising walls between dwellings which do not include MEP systems.

Normally, in conventional partition walls, there are several openings in the studs for horizontal channel bracing. Wiring and piping run somewhat randomly through these openings. These openings are pre-punched; several models are available on the market. Some manufacturers offer customized punching for customers' special needs. Since there is already a service available in the market, a clear method regarding the position and dimension of these openings is needed.

In this study, wiring, drainage pipes and water supply piping all go into the Infill partition walls (and some above dropped ceilings). Therefore, it is important to have well-located and -dimensioned openings in studs to carefully organize the 'traffic' consisting of drainage-pipes, water supply lines and wiring. All fixtures producing wastewater can be categorized in two partition zones based on their outlet height (Figure 6), large enough for drainage pipes to pass through and high enough to get the necessary slope inside the wall to reach the MEP stack. As known, 5½" studs with acoustical isolation material, are widely used as framing for Infill partition walls. Including ½" gypsum board in both sides, the partition wall is 6½" thick. 3½" studs are also used to accommodate smaller pipes and cabling.

Usually, toilet discharge pipes are 3" in diameter and other drainage pipes are 1½" or 2". Toilet drainage pipes (and drains from bath and shower tubs) are positioned in the lower drain zone (LDZ – see Figure 6). The higher drain zone (HDZ – Figure 6) is for lavatory and sink drain lines. Another ceiling zone is not shown.

After determining the openings in studs, a full description is possible regarding the organization of drainpipes inside the

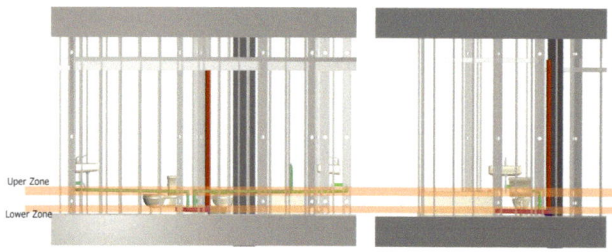

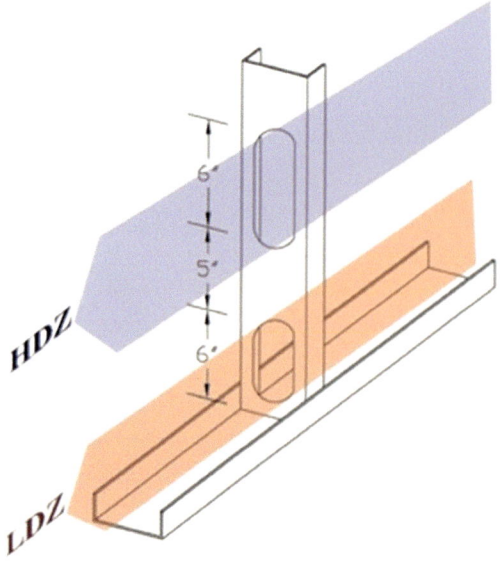

Figure 6 The ideal stud design to accommodate both the LDZ and HDZ drain lines

One of the difficulties is solving piping connections in the lower drain zone (LDZ). For high drain zone (HDZ) and ceiling drain zone (CDZ, not shown), drainage pipes from fixtures can simply drop down to connect with the horizontal pipe below at an appropriate angle (Figure 6).

However, situations in the LDZ are different, because LDZ fixtures are only 1" to 2" higher than the LDZ horizontal discharge pipe. Therefore, angles from an LDZ fixture to a horizontal drainage pipe vary depending on the fixture's location. The various angles and elevations are only predictable within a range. To give order to these conditions, an Open Building approach's constraint is set for LDZ piping as follows: In LDZ, there will be an extra wall layer when drainage pipes from two LDZ fixtures discharge into the same partition wall.

CAPACITY ANALYSIS STUDY OF THE KALES BUILDING

Following an explicit determination of constraints (so far, the focus has been on the MEP systems; but many other constraints would ordinarily have to be established), a capacity analysis can be undertaken. The study that follows attempts to demonstrate the importance of 'designing constraints' when doing capacity analysis. It used the Kales Building, an historic 20-story office building in Detroit, Michigan, which was planned for conversion to residential occupancy (Figure 7).

The narrative that follows explains what actually happened, then follows with what an Open Building approach could have offered. We need to be clear that what is presented here was not implemented but was intended to show an alternative to conventional practice.

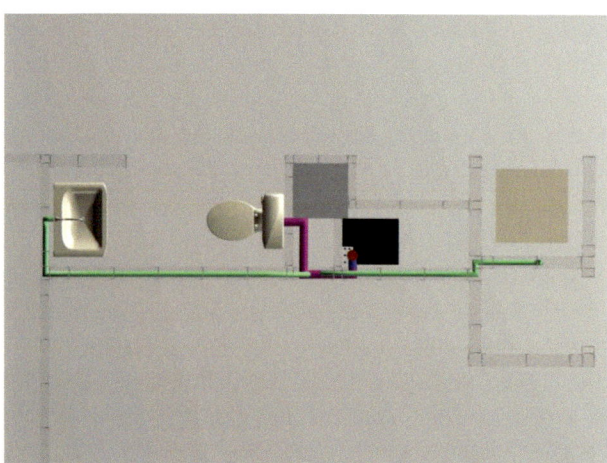

Figure 5a, b, c These diagrams use a digital model to help design the partition wall. In these diagrams, openings on studs are specified. Green pipes represent 1½"- or 2"-diameter drainage pipes serving fixtures with 'high' outlets (e.g., kitchen sinks, lavatory bowls, etc.) They run through the higher opening (Figure 6). Purple pipes represent 3"-diameter drainage pipes which serve toilets and accept waste from green pipes. Dark-brown pipes are vertical 5"-diameter drainage pipes that belong to the Base Building, gathering waste from all dwelling units and transporting the waste to the city drainage system. Figure 5b gives a 3-dimensional detail

partition walls in different circumstances. This can help in designing better bathroom and kitchen layouts in which fixtures are given appropriate locations.

During the development of these design constraints in this study, difficulties and problems always occurred in the LDZ zone.

Figure 7 The Kales Building in downtown Detroit, Michigan (*Photo credit*: Stephen Kendall)

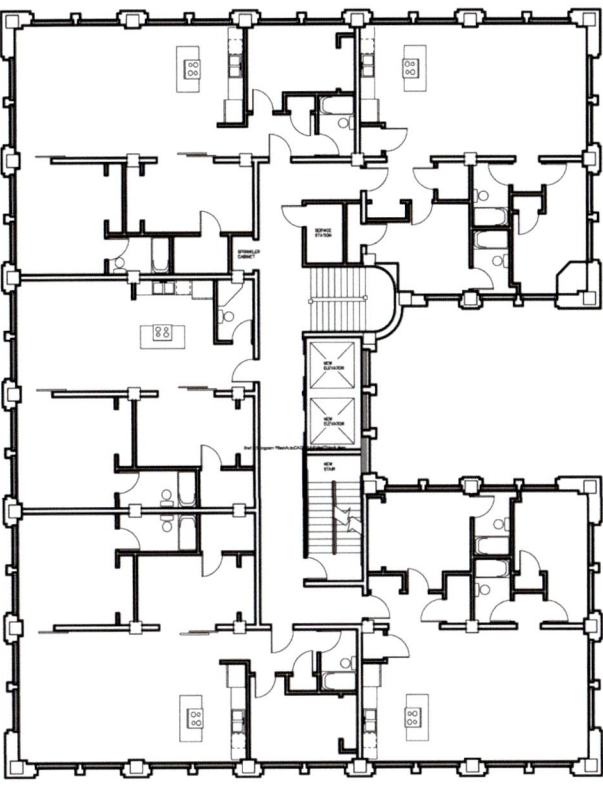

Figure 8 This drawing shows the first schematic design of one typical lower floor with seven apartments (*Source*: BVH Architecture, Inc. Detroit, MI.)

A real estate development company began the process of purchasing the property in question (an abandoned historic 20-story office building in Detroit) and obtained the approvals and financing to proceed with its conversion to 80 apartment units for the rental market. The development company began organizing the financing, including a mix of state and national historic tax credits and bank loans. In the beginning of the project, it conducted a market analysis to make a unit count decision, unit mix and unit layouts, as well as the rents. The first conversion design was based on those projections. Cost estimates were determined based on the roughly sketched architectural scheme and engineering designs (Figure 8).

However, the financing scheme had some difficulties, and other conditions in the market changed in terms of interest rates and competition in the local market. These uncontrollable changes caused the marketing plan for the building to change. The architect completely revised the unit mix and floor plans (Figure 9), with the same effect to the mechanical, electrical and plumbing designs and cost estimates. This happened three times (Figure 10) with no additional design fees. At a certain point, a decision was made to 'freeze' the design to enable building permits to be granted, construction bids to be obtained and construction undertaken.

AN OPEN BUILDING ALTERNATIVE TO CONVERSION

What follows is a methodical process, based in large part on the MEP constraints discussed earlier, in which a typical floor plate is analyzed to determine an optimum variety of unit sizes, given a 'reasonable' target suited to the market. This involves a series of design studies in which two things are assessed.

- First, alternative placements of demising walls separating units are studied.
- Second, vertical MEP shafts are positioned.

Given an initial or trial layout of demising walls and shafts, the capacity of the floor plate to accommodate a range of unit sizes and the capacity of each demised space to accommodate a range of layouts is evaluated. Then MEP stacks are re-positioned, and the same capacity analysis is repeated. These studies are done using

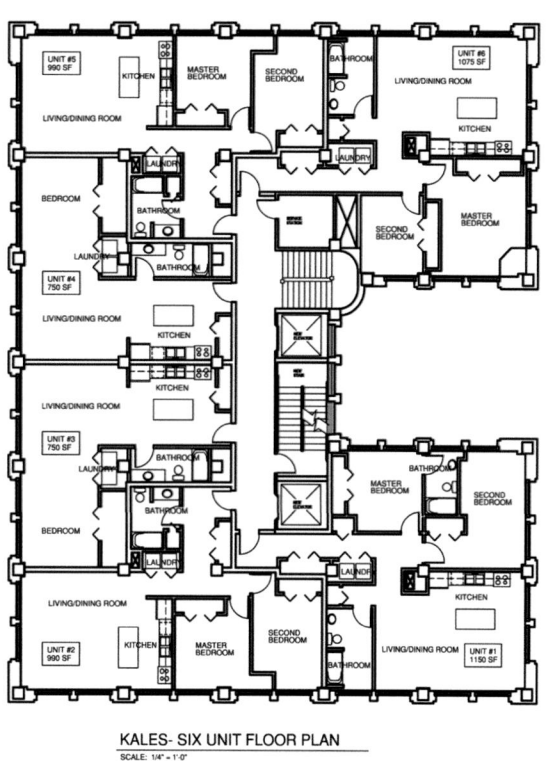

Figure 9 This drawing shows the second design round with six apartments (*Source*: BVH Architecture, Inc. Detroit, MI.)

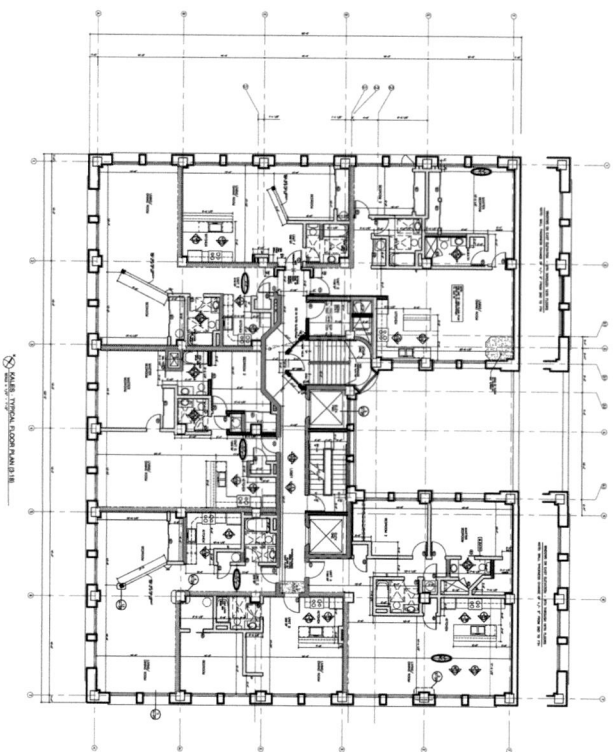

Figure 10 Shows the third redo of the design due to the developer's new market analysis. Now there are again seven units in a typical floor from the 3rd to the 15th floor (*Source*: BVH Architecture, Inc. Detroit, MI.)

a test-fit process, in which accommodation capacity is evaluated given certain clearly defined technical and market constraints.

Before and during the test-fit process, some technical constraints need to be set up as criteria that can be used in evaluating the interim designs. As discussed, the focus in this study was on the development of design constraints in the plumbing system and, more specifically, in the DWV (drain, waste and vent) elements, with specific reference to the vertical MEP shafts and the 'traffic management' of DWV lines within individual units. We chose this focus because it is the most difficult of all of the utility systems.

In the test-fit process, many layouts were developed, using constraints derived from conventions in the industry and from a variety of technical studies based on Open Building principles. In this test-fit process, some layouts were inevitably found to be unacceptable (comparing them to conventional layouts and the layouts proposed by the project architect), while some others were satisfactory. Then, based on lessons learned, the MEP stacks are repositioned and the test-fit process repeated. This design process continues until an agreement is reached about optimum unit mix layout variety.

This design process is a trial-and-error process that eventually can become intuitive and may, in time, be supported by advanced computer-aided design once the problems and constraints are clearly formulated.

VERTICAL MEP PIPE SHAFT POSITIONING STUDY

In conventional building design processes, as noted, plumbing pipes penetrate floors in 'sleeves' depending on each fixture's locations and the structural system design. This is because the plumbing design is done after the layout plan design is fixed and the practice of routing drain lines through dwelling unit territories below (hidden in ceilings) has been accepted.

However, as already noted, in the Open Building strategy chosen for this study, potential layout plans are studied in advance by means of capacity analysis, including the Base Building MEP shaft locations. In this process, all reasonable and potential layout plans that a MEP shaft can accommodate are explored. However, it is difficult to position MEP stacks at the beginning of the design process, especially for those new to the Open Building approach.

To study the positioning of MEP shafts, a number of conditions must be defined, including the organization of the (proposed – in the case of a new building) floor plate of the building into zones adjacent to the façade(s), zones with no natural illumination and so on, oriented parallel to each other in one direction on a building floor plate. In addition, sectors can be defined. Sectors are basically sections of the zones of a certain size, making up potential dwelling units (dwellings can consist of one or more sectors) or partial sectors. A given zoning can be divided into a variety of sectors. Within a given sector, the idea is that a number of functional area distributions (living room, kitchen, etc.) can be made.

Note: The basic strategy for zones, margins and sector analysis and related methods is given in the previous section of the book.

Once this basic zoning is done, more detailed issues such as MEP stack locations can be examined, as follows. Of the many constraints or conditions requiring consideration in this decision process, two are mentioned and one is discussed in more detail.

- **First, it is assumed that no drain piping serving an individual unit will penetrate the unit's floor into the lower unit's 'territory' or ceiling space.**
- **Second, it is assumed that no horizontal pipes within the unit will cross a doorway, as mentioned previously.**
- **Third, it is assumed that the location of MEP stacks is directly related to the structural system.**

To demonstrate one condition in which the latter consideration is accounted for, we use the idea of a 'space cell' in a building using a column-and-beam structural system. This is the structural system found in the Kales Building. This assumes either a steel beam and column or concrete two-way slab with reinforcing primarily between columns (Figure 11).

In Figure 11, five different zones are defined based on their spatial and structural system relations. Black stands for the Column Zone. Gray is added to zones between each column where beams or the main slab reinforcing are positioned, known as Beam Zones. There are always two light-gray zones on both sides of a Beam Zone: Along Beam Zones. Also, there are usually four orange zones located diagonally around a column, Around Column Zones. The rest of the space is the Center Bay Zone, which is shown in pale yellow.

When an architect subdivides such a space cell, Figure 12a is one normal way to make a smaller space. In Figure 12b, c, alternate placements of the same subdivided space are regarded as unusual or less acceptable, especially in residential projects, because both create spaces around the space cell that may cause spatial inefficiencies.

In order to explore general constraints for positioning MEP stacks, Figure 11 is merged with Figure 12 to make Figure 13, in which an MEP stack is located in different zones to explore spatial capacity given alternative stack positions (shown with an X).

In Figure 13a, an MEP stack is located in the Center Bay Zone. In this circumstance, there are two locations that optimize access for bathroom placement: two good access locations and two unacceptable access locations.

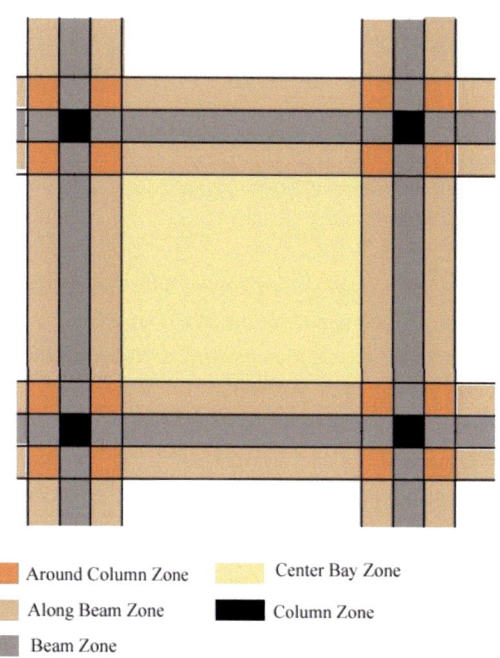

Figure 11 Diagram of structural constraints for positioning vertical MEP shafts

A DETAILED STUDY OF CAPACITY ANALYSIS IN ADAPTIVE REUSE – OFFICE TO RESIDENTIAL

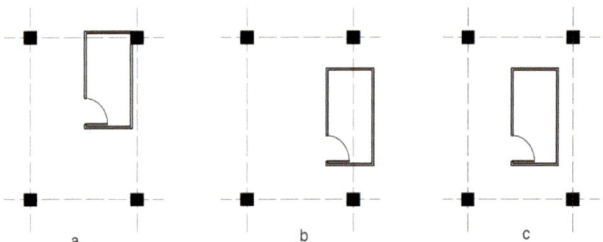

Figures 12 a, b, c: Alternative positions of a given space cell

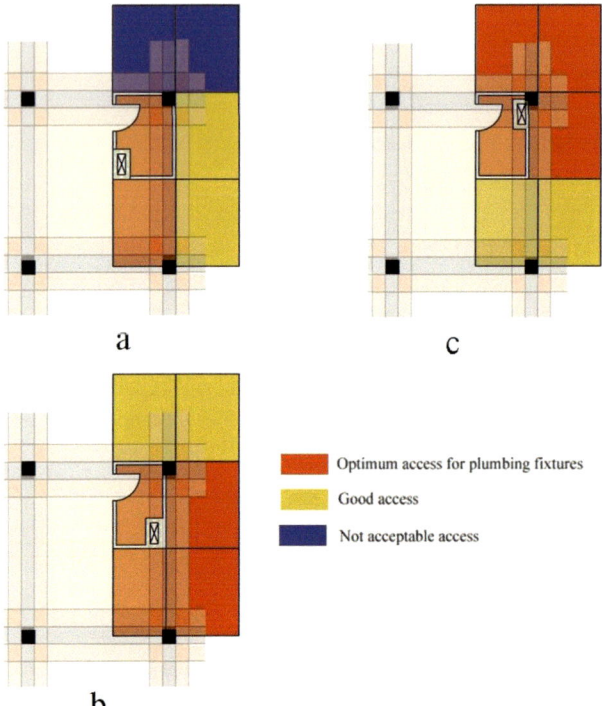

Figure 13 Positioning a space cell with plumbing fixtures vis-à-vis the column/beam diagram

In Figure 13b, an MEP stack is located in the Along Beam Zone. In Figure 13c, an MEP stack is located in the Around Column Zone. In both of these latter circumstances, there are four optimum access locations for the bathroom and two good access locations.

From the capacity analysis in this example, it is clear that Around Column Zone and Along Beam Zone are appropriate places for locating MEP stacks, and the Center Bay Zone is not as favorable. But in Figure 13a, after partition walls are removed and the MEP stack remains, it causes an awkward situation in which the space cannot be designed as a living room because the stack is standing in the middle of the space cell defined by the building's columns. This greatly reduces the capacity of the space to accommodate a range of functional layouts. Similarly, in Figure 13b, the MEP stack's position eliminates the possibility of combining two adjacent construction bays as one big open space such as a living room or combining two smaller dwelling units into one.

In other words, MEP stacks located in the Center Bay Zone or the Along Beam Zone eliminate important layout variations. The study concluded that Around Column Zones – but diagonally around the column – are always the priority locations for positioning MEP stacks. This principle appears to be generally applicable. However, in some specific circumstances, Along Beam Zones are also suitable for placing MEP stacks. Only in a few circumstances can Center Bay Zones be considered as suitable for placing MEP stacks.

Note: This kind of analysis will produce different results in, for example, wood- or steel-framed floors with one-way joists and beams, post-tensioned concrete slab floors or floors made of precast concrete elements or mass-timber panels.

A DESIGN PROCESS FOR CONVERSION USING CAPACITY ANALYSIS

The following is a step-by-step demonstration of how to design a floor plate in a high-rise building being converted to residential uses. In retrospect, the design process initially involved a great deal of trial and error. The following is an attempt to revisit the design process and therefore to clarify how capacity analysis is done for others who may get into the field and who may be asked to provide decision and design flexibility. However, residential design work is complex, requiring a certain level of professional training and knowledge beyond what is explained here. This chapter does not try to explain every step. Many principles of common sense to professionals are assumed as conventional knowledge, for example, the arrangement of sanitary fixtures, normal room sizes and arrangements and so on. Many standards exist in handbooks and references, such as the proportion and layout of different-size rooms.

Step 1 – Initial Floor Plan Study Process

The developer was attempting to have the 20-story building listed as a historic building to obtain more lenient financing terms for its conversion to residential occupancy. An architectural firm (BVH

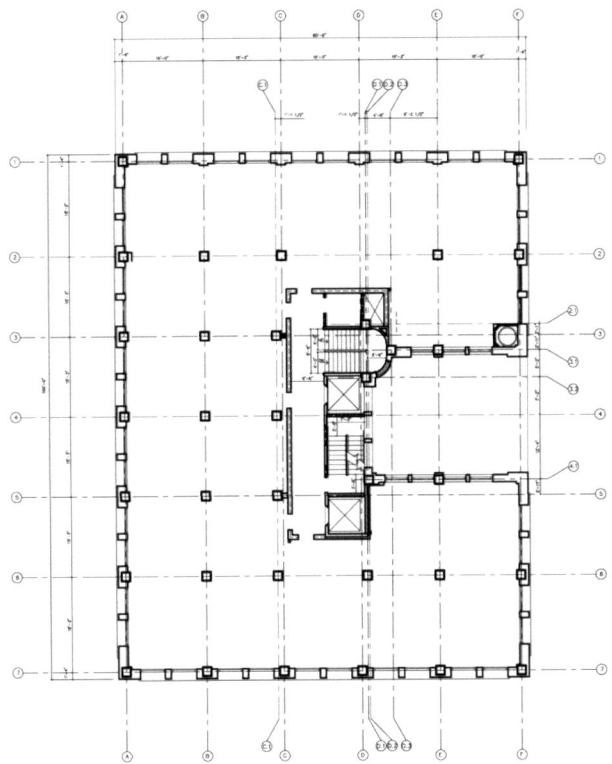
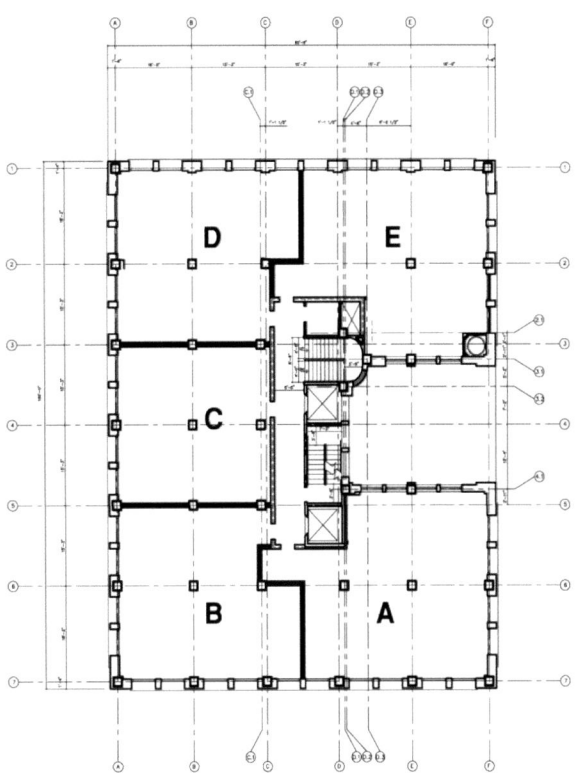

Figure 14 The Base Building after partition walls and fixtures are removed: the 'shell' of the building remains and is ready for capacity analysis studies and MEP stack location decisions

Figure 15 Five basic units are defined by using demising walls

Architecture Inc., Detroit, Michigan) had already developed a series of floor plate layouts and unit designs, as the Figures 8, 9 and 10 show. It is probably a good idea to avoid studying the original plan drawings too closely except to understand the basic unit sizes and types. However, it is recommended that conventional plans be reviewed after some variations are explored. They can provide baseline rationale as to "Why didn't I use these unit plans?" "Are these plans better for the market?" and so on.

All interior non–load-bearing partitions and fixtures should be deleted from the original plan drawings, leaving the skeleton of the building (columns, floors, exterior walls) and the public circulation (stairs, elevators, public corridors and walls and building risers and equipment rooms) (Figure 14).

Step 2 – Placing Demising Walls to Create Basic Unit Sizes and Margins

Using demising walls (walls separating different occupant spaces or legal 'territories'), the floor plan can be divided into a number of average-size units. In this example, the average unit size is between 800 and 1,000 ft^2 (75–93 m^2), resulting in five basic units (Figure 15). Margins or 'swing spaces' can be placed between each unit based on the column arrangement and the openings in the exterior walls (Figure 16). Other demising wall distributions and margins in the same Base Building are possible based on different assumptions about unit sizes. It should be noted also that in the proposed unit distribution that follows, other variations of unit sizes are possible, such as very large units on the same floor as well as even smaller units.

Step 3 – Developing an Individual Dwelling Unit

Once a tentative distribution of unit 'territories' is made (Step 2), it is possible to explore the capacity of each territorial unit in terms of the floor plans it can accommodate. In this demonstration, Unit A is selected. Three dwelling unit sizes are found to be possible by placing the demising wall in three locations that share the same entry door to the unit (fixed as part of the Base Building decision).

Note: The decision to make the entry door to each dwelling unit part of the Base Building decision – therefore 'fixed' – is not always necessary but is a design constraint used in this demonstration.

It is highly recommended to choose the medium-sized unit to develop variations at the beginning. After developing the medium-sized unit variations (most of these variations on layout ideas

A DETAILED STUDY OF CAPACITY ANALYSIS IN ADAPTIVE REUSE – OFFICE TO RESIDENTIAL

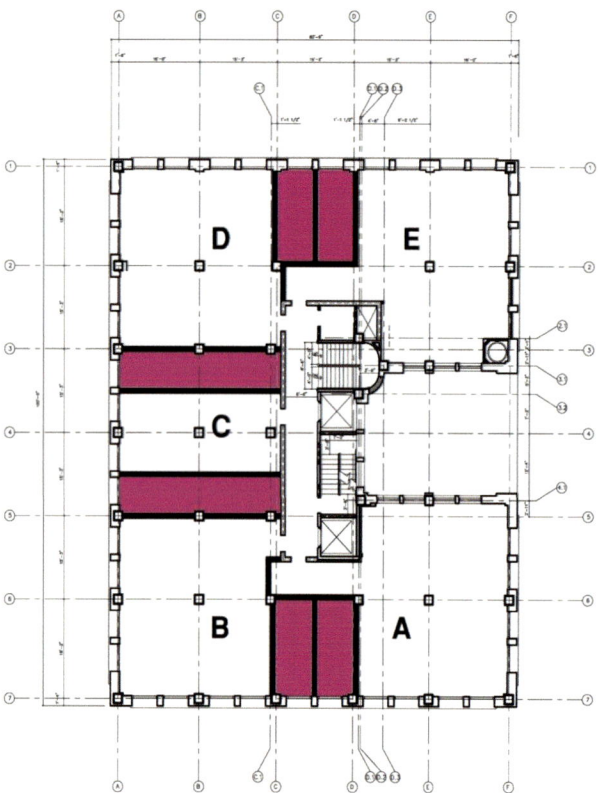

Figure 16 Margins or 'swing spaces' are created by shifting demising walls, giving a variety of unit sizes on a floor

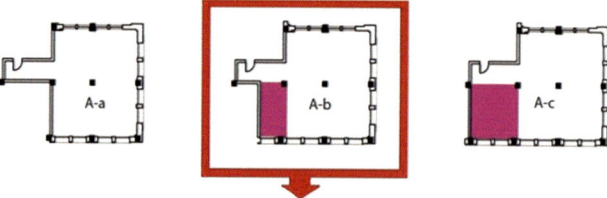

Figure 17 Among three sizes, the medium-sized unit (A-b) is chosen for further study and development

TABLE 1
Relationship of spaces to exterior openings

Required to have exterior opening(s)	Prefer to have exterior opening(s)	Not necessary to have exterior opening(s)	Require no exterior opening(s)
Living Room	Dining Room	Bathroom	Laundry Room
Bedroom	Kitchen		Utility Room

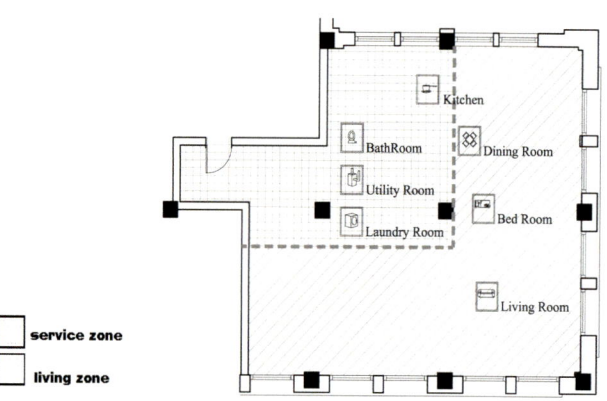

Figure 18 Different rooms are placed in two zones inside a unit

are similar), they can be simply modified by enlarging or eliminating rooms.

Step 4 – Placing Rooms Inside the Unit

a. Rooms & unit shape study

Before starting this step, it's necessary to study the relations between different functional areas (rooms) and the unit shape and size. In a typical residential unit, there are basically seven different kinds of spaces: living rooms, bedrooms, kitchen, bathroom(s), dining room, utility room and storage rooms or closets. Among these rooms, some (by code or convention) need to be next to an exterior wall; these are living room and bedroom (in some jurisdictions, for some buildings such as conversions, bedrooms need not be adjacent to the façade in cases in which high ceilings allow light and ventilation in bedrooms with partial-height walls or bedrooms built on a raised platform with lower walls). Some rooms are preferred to have exterior openings, such as the dining room and kitchen. Bathrooms and kitchen do not necessarily have exterior openings; utility room, laundry room and storage room require no exterior openings (Table 1).

b. Study the capacity of the space

In order to understand the unit space and locate MEP stacks in suitable places serving a range of floor plans, the unit space is studied and analyzed in different ways. In Figure 18, the functional division of the space is analyzed. Based on the shape of the unit and also the depth and width, two zones are defined. One is the service zone and the other is a living zone. Living rooms and bedrooms are placed in the living zone, in which they can have exterior openings. Utility room, laundry room and storage rooms are placed in the service zone. Kitchen and dining room are placed between zones because they can be placed in either zone depending on the design circumstance.

c. Study the relation between rooms and MEP stacks

The second move is to categorize rooms by their relations with MEP stacks, yet to be positioned. Basically, there are three kinds of rooms. (1) Rooms that need to be directly next to an MEP stack. These are 'public' bathrooms and master

TABLE 2
Spaces in relation to adjacency to the MEP stack

Rooms needing to be directly adjacent to an MEP stack	Rooms needing to have a continuous wall connected to an MEP stack without door openings	Rooms with no need to connect to an MEP stack
Bathroom	Laundry Room	Living Room
Master bedroom	Utility Room	Bedroom
	Kitchen	Storage

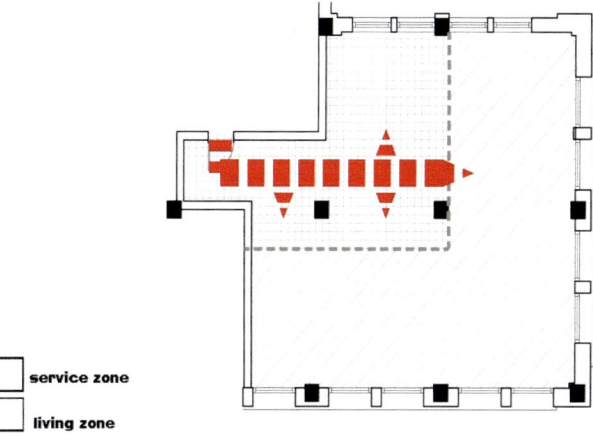

Figure 19 A circulation zone passes through the service zone to each room inside the unit

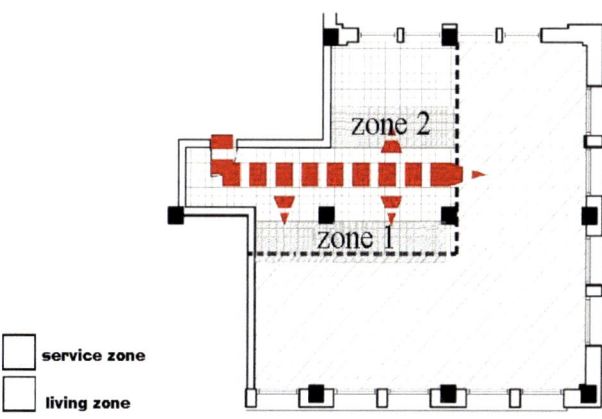

Figure 20 Two zones that are suitable for placing MEP stacks are shown

bathrooms. (2) Rooms that need to have at least one continuous wall without door openings connecting to a MEP stack; these are utility room, laundry room and kitchen. The distance from these rooms to the MEP stack can be further (up to 50') based on constraints introduced earlier. Rooms that need no wall and connections with MEP stacks include living rooms, bedrooms, dining room and storage room (Table 2).

d. Study the circulation flow inside the unit

The circulation of the layout plan also affects the locations of MEP stacks. Normally, in high-rise residential buildings, public spaces that are part of the Base Building – such as fire stairs, elevators and public corridors – are located in the core of the building. The result is that the entrance of the dwelling units is always located on the side of the dwelling unit's service zone. Typically, there is always a circulation flow across the service zone distributing to each room (see Figure 19).

Step 5 – Locate the MEP Stacks

Note: In some countries or jurisdictions, MEP stacks must be placed adjacent to public corridors for easy access for purposes of maintenance and upgrading. This limitation was not followed in this study.

a. Deciding on the number of MEP stacks in a unit

Theoretically, one MEP stack can serve one dwelling unit and a variety of layouts in it. However, there are two constraints in that case. (1) There are not many variations to be offered when there is only one MEP stack in one unit. (2) As shown in Figure 20, there is always a corridor crossing the service zone and dividing it into two parts. This crossing 'cuts' the service zone into two parts in which one MEP stack cannot connect to the other side of the corridor. Therefore, we decided that there should be two MEP stacks, located on both sides of the corridor. Subsequent drawings demonstrate these points more fully.

b. Define suitable zone for MEP stacks

In this step, comprehensive knowledge is required as well as the sense of different room sizes. During this part of the design process, the layouts of different-sized rooms have been studied Knowledge of technical rules and design constraints proved to be useful in making MEP stack location decisions.

After studying various circumstances in terms of shape of the unit, circulation paths and so on, two zones suitable for placing MEP stacks are defined (Figure 20).

However, only defining suitable MEP zones is not enough to find the exact spots to locate MEP stacks. After the positioning zone diagram is overlaid on the appropriate construction bay diagram, 11 positions are defined. Those located at the intersections of the two diagrams can be defined as the more optimum MEP positions. In Figure 21, A, B, C, F, are located at the intersections of two overlapping diagrams. L, H, J, K are therefore not so suitable for placing MEP stacks.

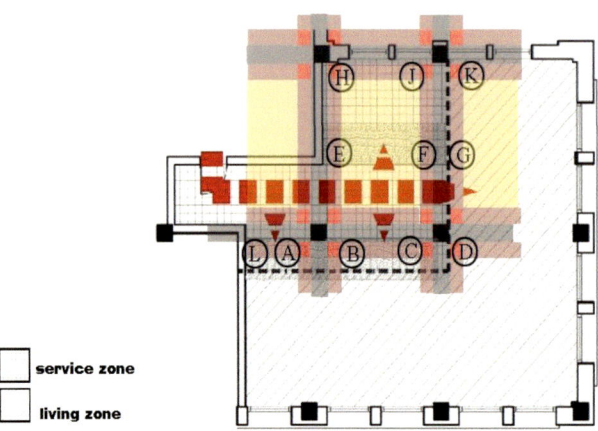

Figure 21 Two diagrams are overlapped to define optimum locations for placing MEP stacks

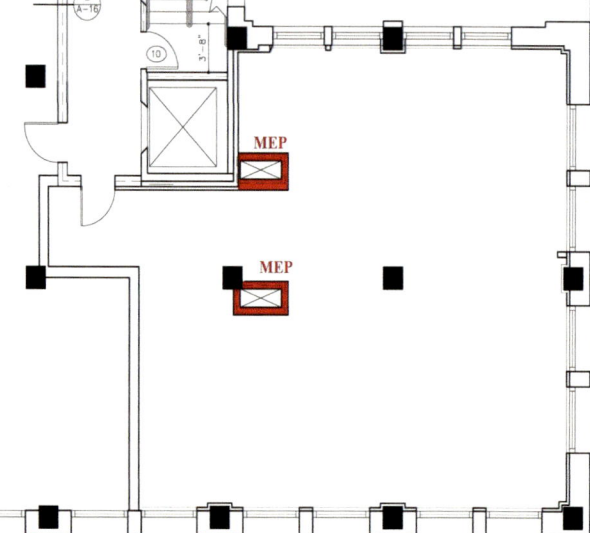

Figure 22 After studying alternative locations of MEP stacks, the positions are fixed. Note: This study did not examine the precise dimension of the MEP stacks, which may vary in size from top to bottom in a tall building

(Trial-and-error processes are already applied in those locations, demonstrating that they are not suitable for placing MEP stacks.)

Thus, A, B and C are defined as suitable locations for the MEP 'below' the circulation flow. Two (E and F) are suitable positions for the MEP stack on the other side of the circulation flow (Figure 21). These optional positions are suggested also in light of the earlier discussion of MEP stacks in relation to building structure.

c. Eliminating unsuitable MEP locations

In this step, optimal MEP locations can be selected by eliminating others based on the kind of 'dialogue' as follows. In Figure 21, A can be eliminated because it narrows the space of potential circulation flow; it creates a 'not too big, not too small' space in which a bathroom and a door entrance cannot fit; and it is too large only for an entrance doorway. When locating MEP stacks, it is recommended to think about or foresee (if not explicitly sketch) potential rooms around the MEP stack. Theoretically, an MEP stack should be surrounded by rooms that need to connect to it. Therefore, potential living room, dining room, storage rooms are better when they avoid MEP stacks.

A C position can also be eliminated because this is located on the 'right' side of the service zone, making the stack inaccessible to possible 'plumbing-dependent' spaces to the left side of the service zone in the diagram. Nevertheless, there are two potential circulation flows between the left side and C. In conclusion, they are not suitable locations for placing a MEP stack.

Similar to the situation of C and D, F can be eliminated.

Therefore, B and E are defined as suitable MEP locations to develop unit layout variations in this instance. Moreover, the orientation and size of a MEP stack should be determined during the process of developing more detailed variations. Sizing the MEP stack is another design process not discussed here (Figure 22).

A DETAILED STUDY OF CAPACITY ANALYSIS IN ADAPTIVE REUSE – OFFICE TO RESIDENTIAL

USING THE CONSTRAINTS

The following discussion demonstrates the use of these constraints in the Kales Building.

Note: It appears that these constraints are general and systematic enough for application in other high-rise residential floor plan capacity analysis. They are thus proposed as useful tools for practitioners who want to design Open Building projects under similar circumstances.

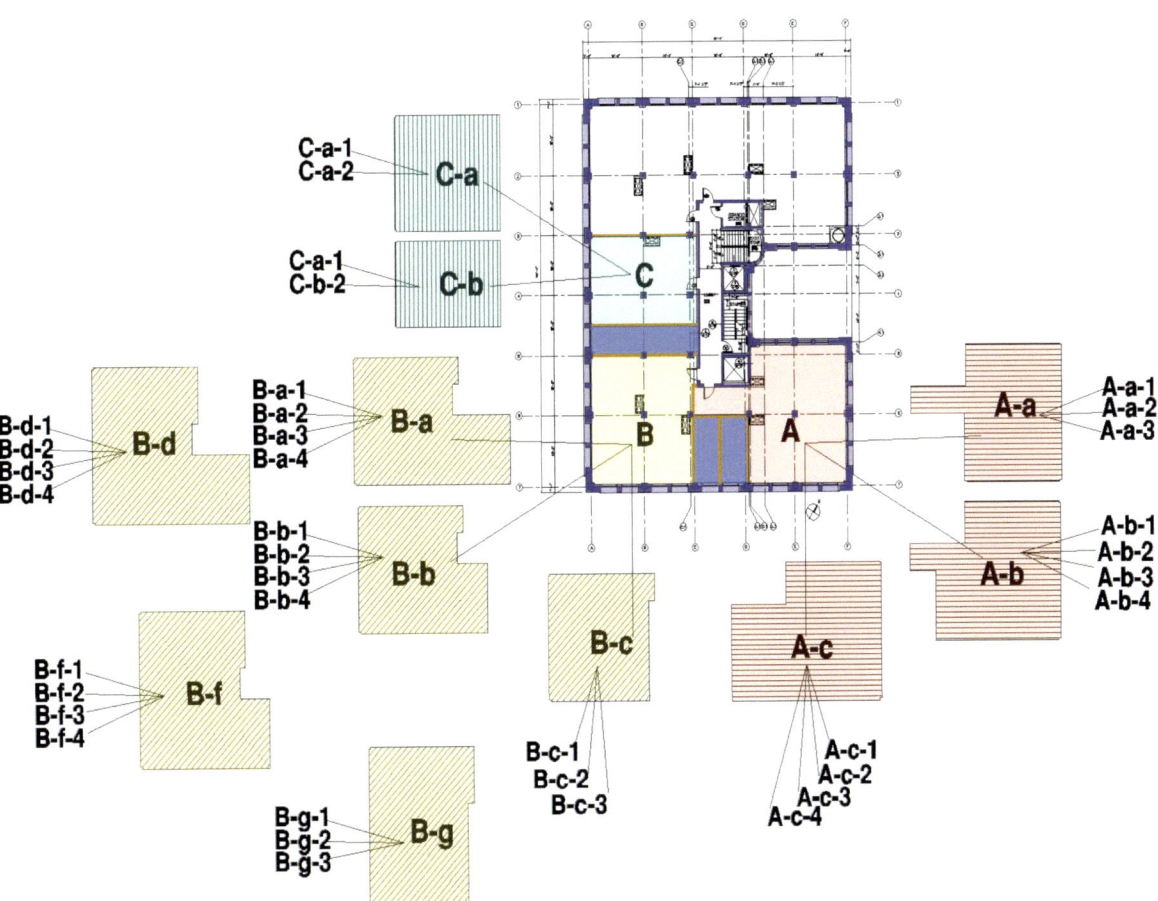

Figure 23 A diagram shows possible layout variations that the Kales Base Building can offer. For each dwelling size, a number of floor plans are possible

A DETAILED STUDY OF CAPACITY ANALYSIS IN ADAPTIVE REUSE – OFFICE TO RESIDENTIAL

In Figure 23, MEP stacks are located as a part of the Base Building. As noted, demising walls can be positioned to create margins between units and result in units of various sizes (size variations), for instance, A-a, A-b, . . . B-a, . . . For each size variation, various layout plans (unit layout variations) can be developed, for instance, A-a-1, A-a-2, . . . Therefore, there are approximately 60 variations. Thirty variations have been developed for all three of the unit types (A, B and C).

In order to fully demonstrate the approach, four variations are selected out of a total of 30 to present more technical details. In these diagrams, the dark- and light-blue color stands for the Base Building; red zones are where MEP stacks can be located. (Actually, MEP stacks belong to the Base Building, but are shown in red in order to emphasize them and make them easily visible). Walls in green are Infill walls; magenta walls are demising walls which separate unit territories. The color cyan indicates areas that do not need MEP stacks. Orange areas indicate they have pipes going to the MEP stacks.

Note: In all cases, a heating and cooling unit is situated above a dropped ceiling in the entryway to the dwelling unit, supplied by piping in the Base Building but thermostatically controlled by each occupant.

a. Variation example: A-b-1

Figure 24 This is variation A-b-1 layout floor plan

A DETAILED STUDY OF CAPACITY ANALYSIS IN ADAPTIVE REUSE – OFFICE TO RESIDENTIAL

The layout floor in Figure 24 shows no differences to conventional designs. However, the significant difference is that all drainage pipes have no entanglements with the building floors (or the Base Building). To approach these criteria, sanitary fixtures must follow the constraints developed earlier and use the technical methods for installation. The flowing diagrams show more details of the piping system for this unit.

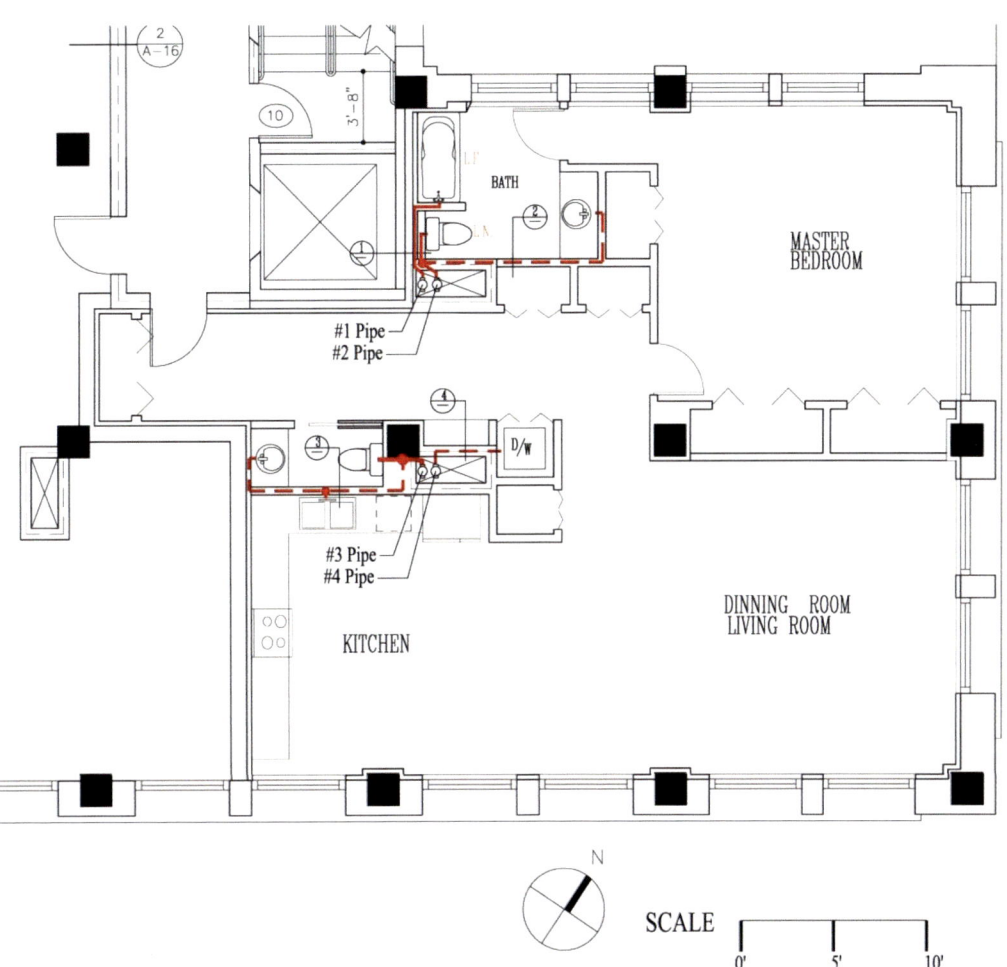

Figure 25 Piping diagram A-b-1 layout floor plan

A DETAILED STUDY OF CAPACITY ANALYSIS IN ADAPTIVE REUSE – OFFICE TO RESIDENTIAL

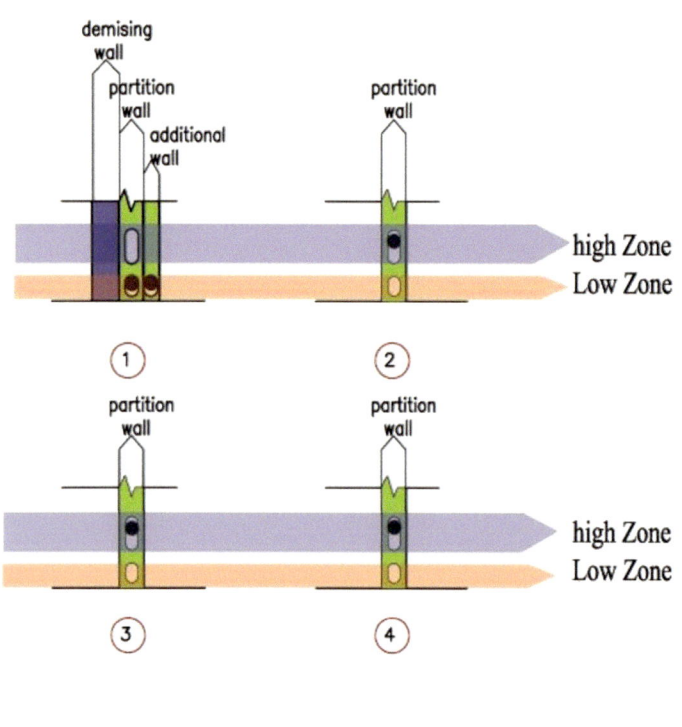

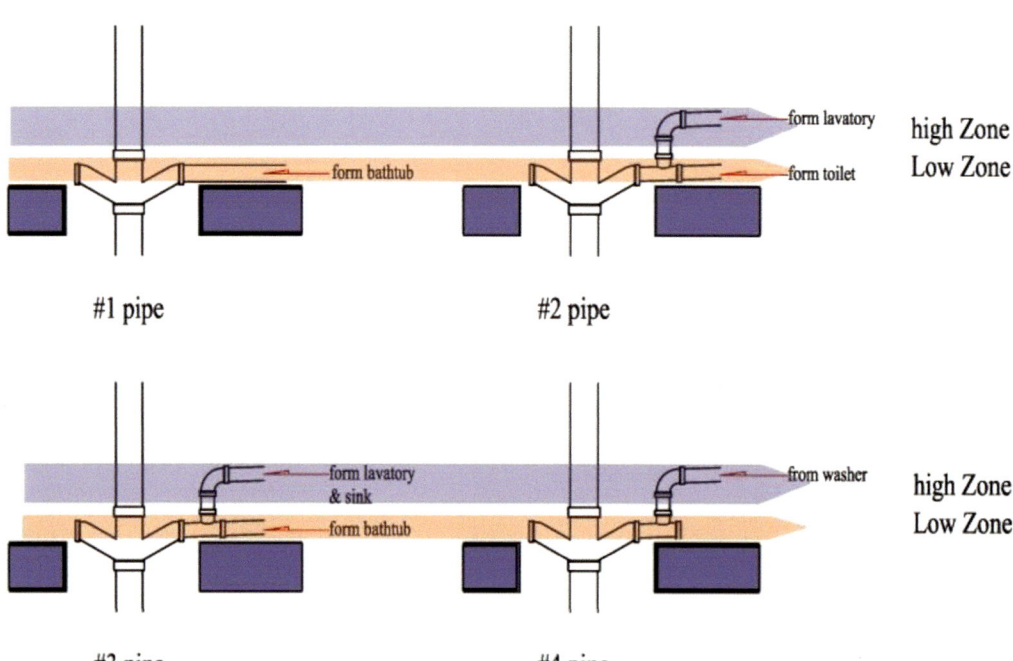

Figure 26 Horizontal pipe routing zones in A-b-1 layout floor plan

b. Variations example A-b-2

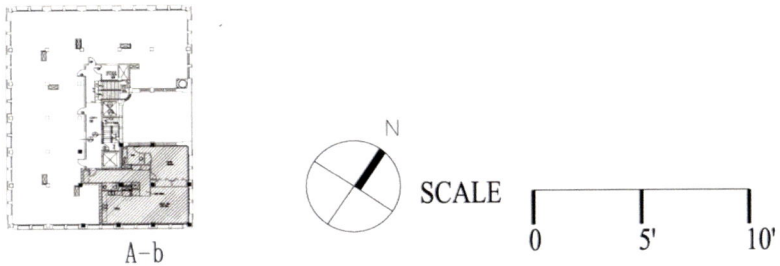

Figure 27 A layout variation for the A-b-2 size unit

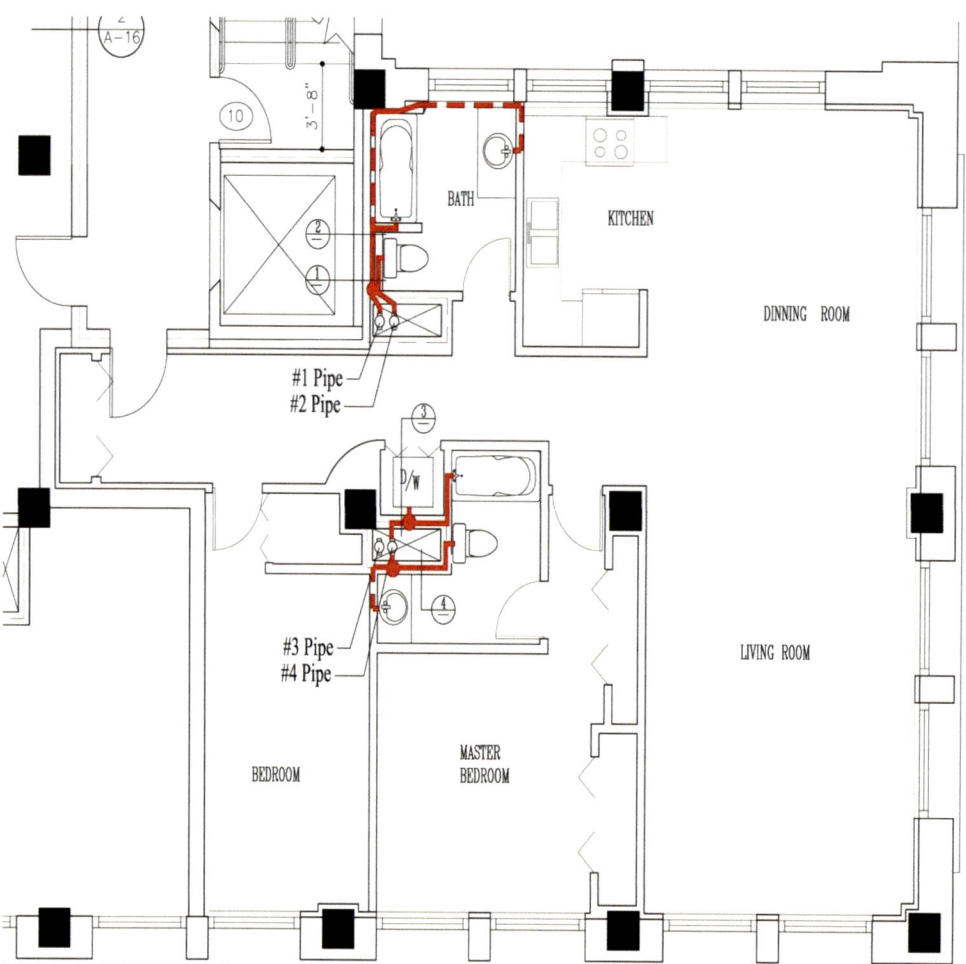

Figure 28 Piping diagram A-b-2 layout floor plan

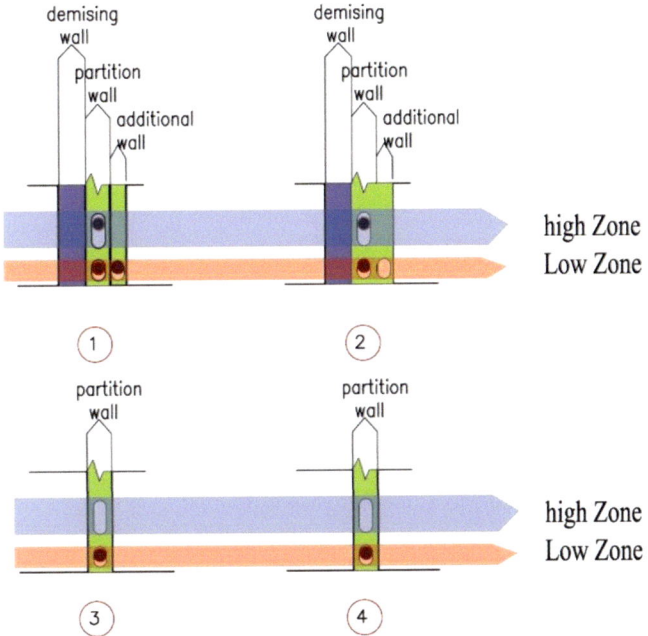

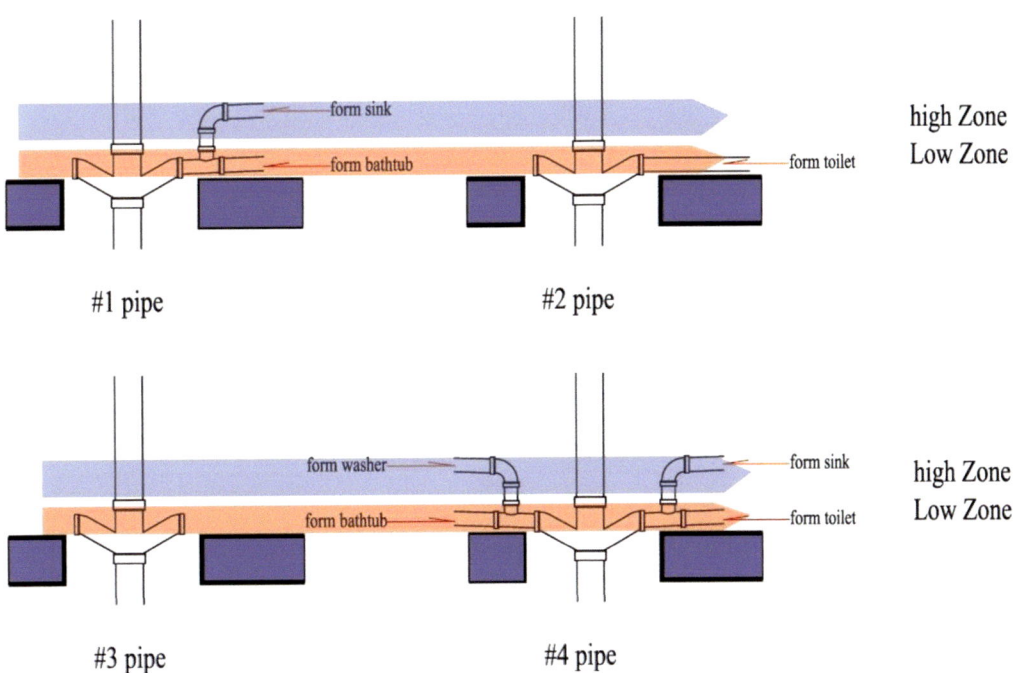

Figure 29 Horizontal pipe routing zones in A-b-2 layout floor plan

A DETAILED STUDY OF CAPACITY ANALYSIS IN ADAPTIVE REUSE – OFFICE TO RESIDENTIAL

c. Layout variation for unit B-b-1

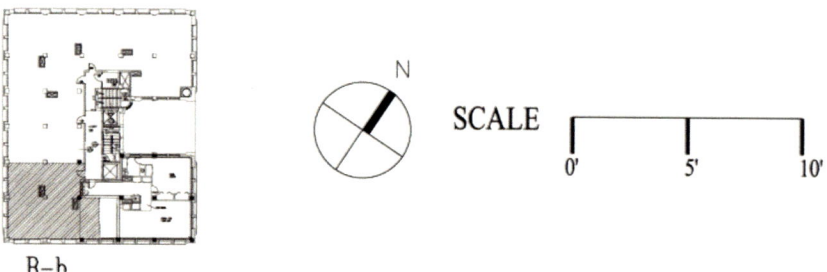

Figure 30 Variation B-b-1

A DETAILED STUDY OF CAPACITY ANALYSIS IN ADAPTIVE REUSE – OFFICE TO RESIDENTIAL

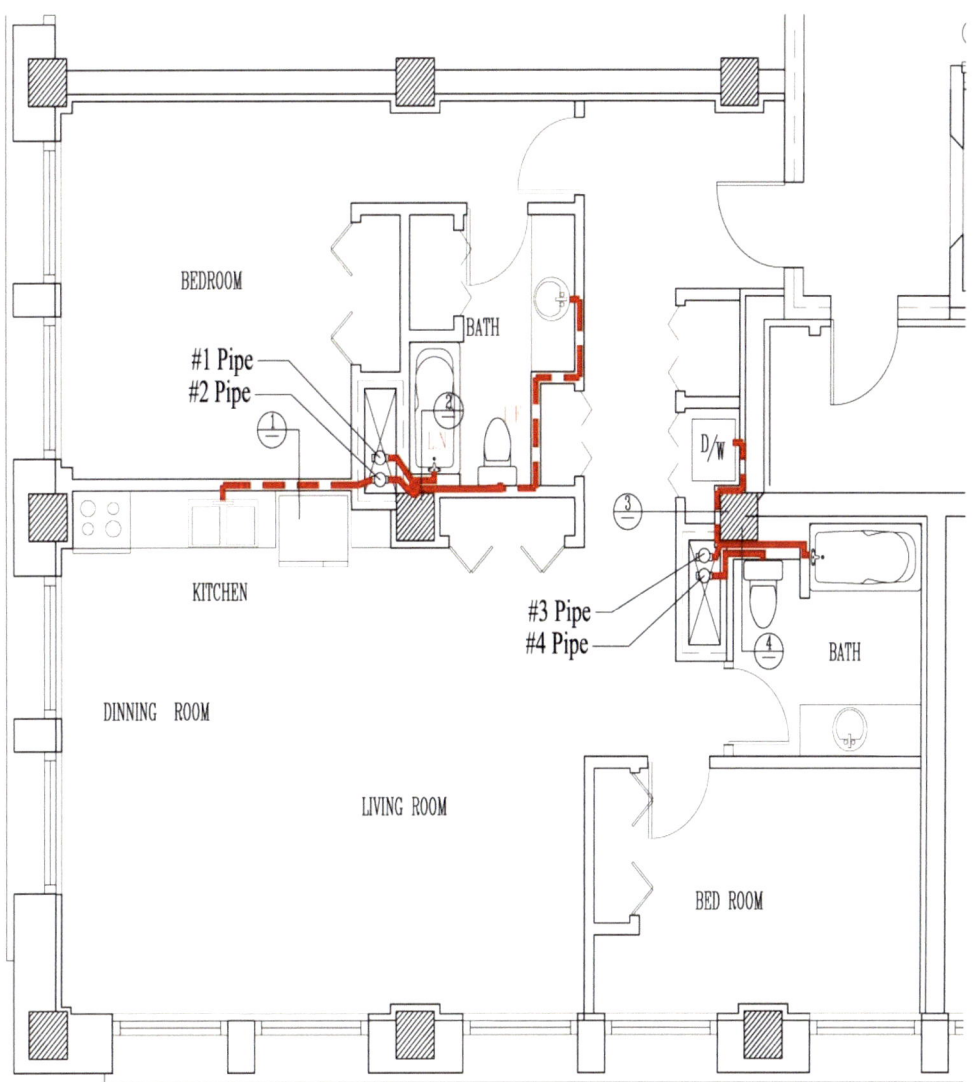

Figure 31 Piping diagram for Variation B-b-1

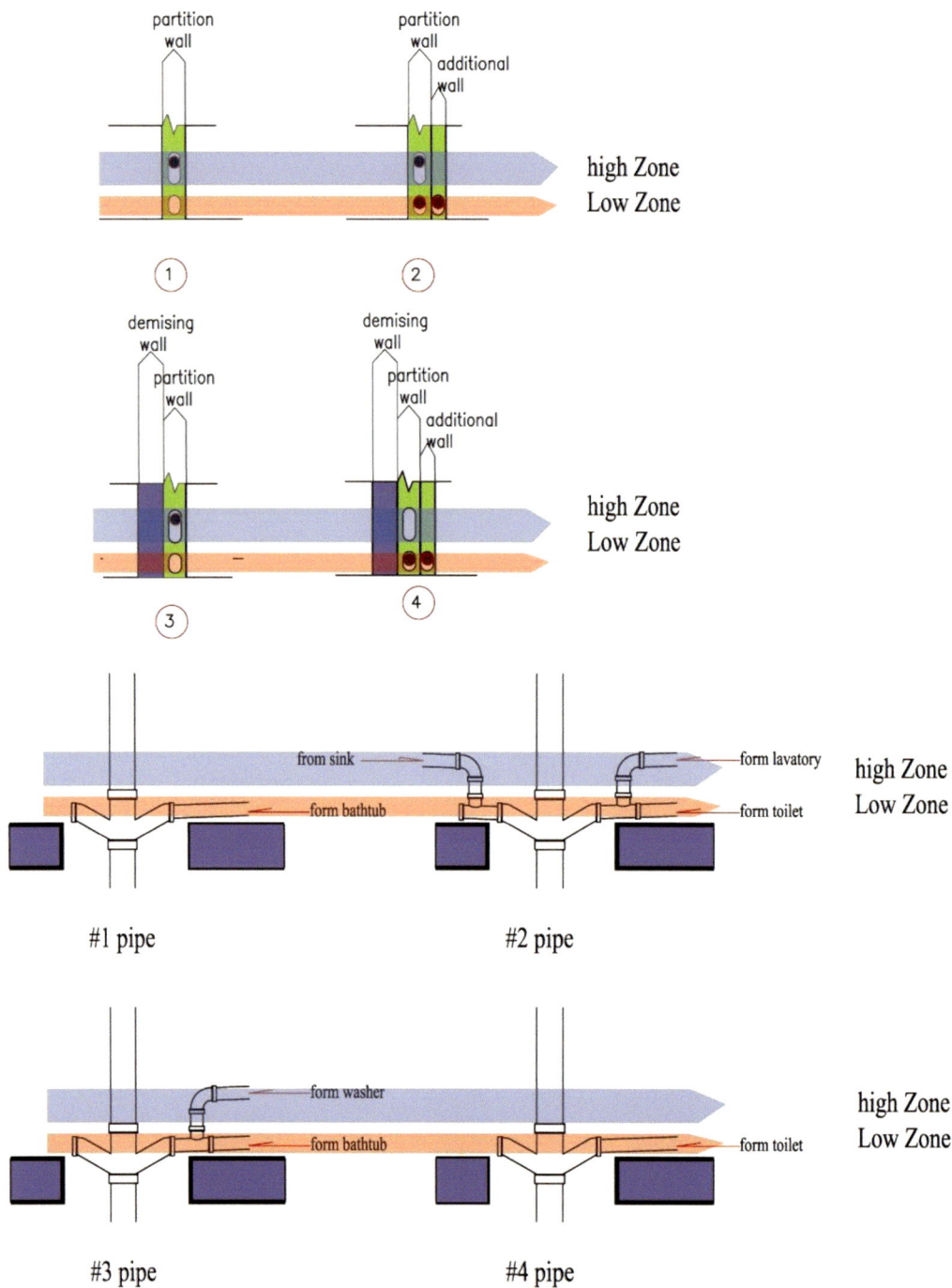

Figure 32 Horizontal pipe routing zones in B-b-1 layout floor plan

A DETAILED STUDY OF CAPACITY ANALYSIS IN ADAPTIVE REUSE – OFFICE TO RESIDENTIAL

d. Variation B-c-1

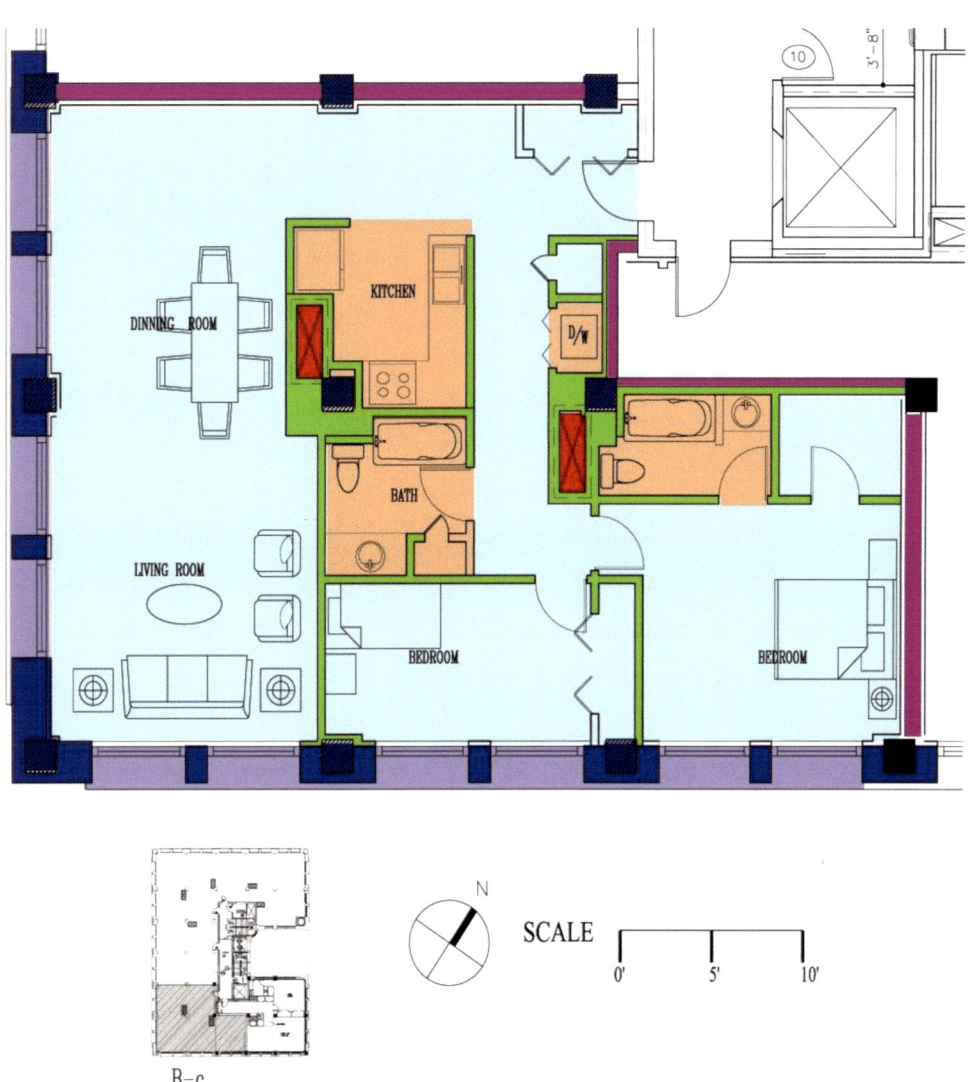

Figure 33 Variation B-c-1

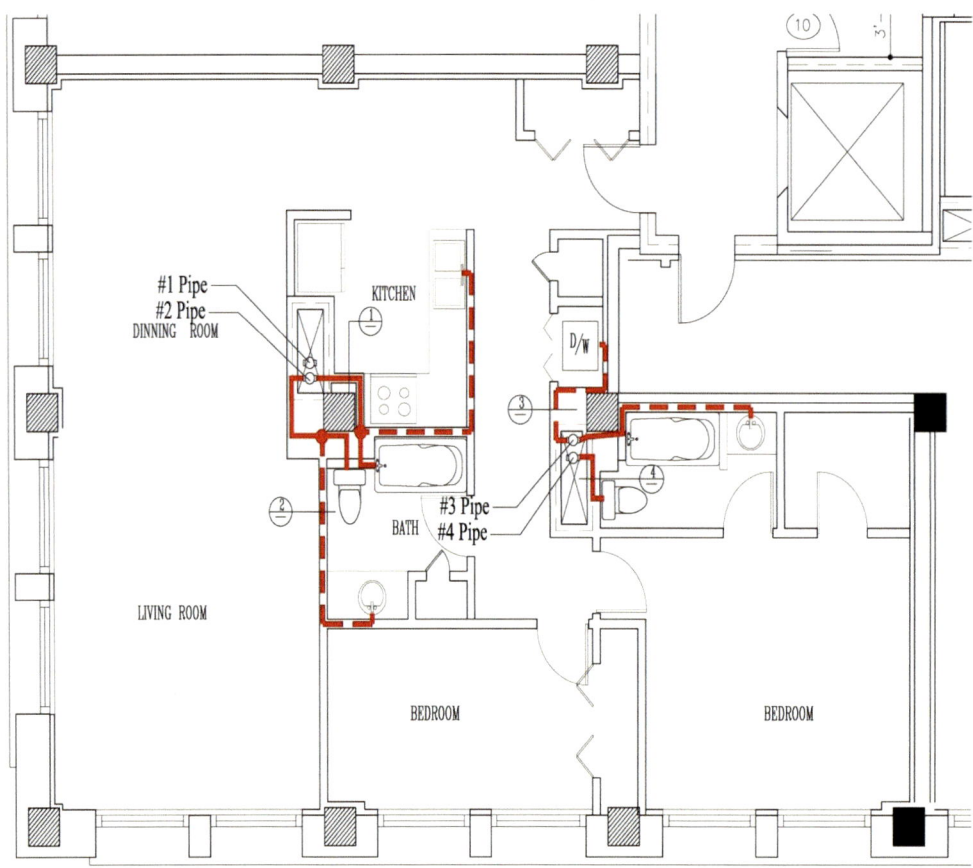

Figure 34 Piping diagram for Variation B-c-1

A DETAILED STUDY OF CAPACITY ANALYSIS IN ADAPTIVE REUSE – OFFICE TO RESIDENTIAL

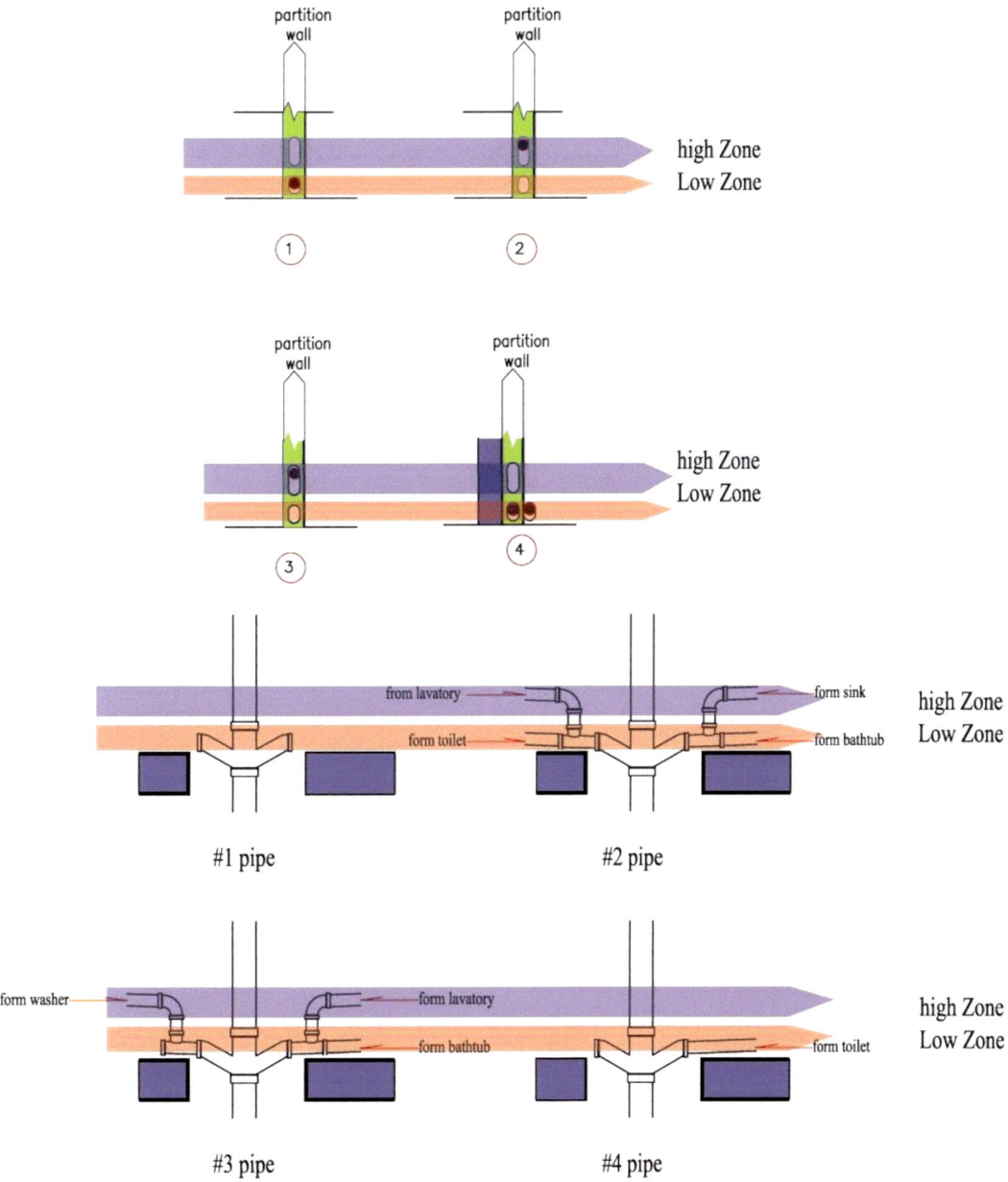

Figure 35 Horizontal pipe routing for Variation B-c-1

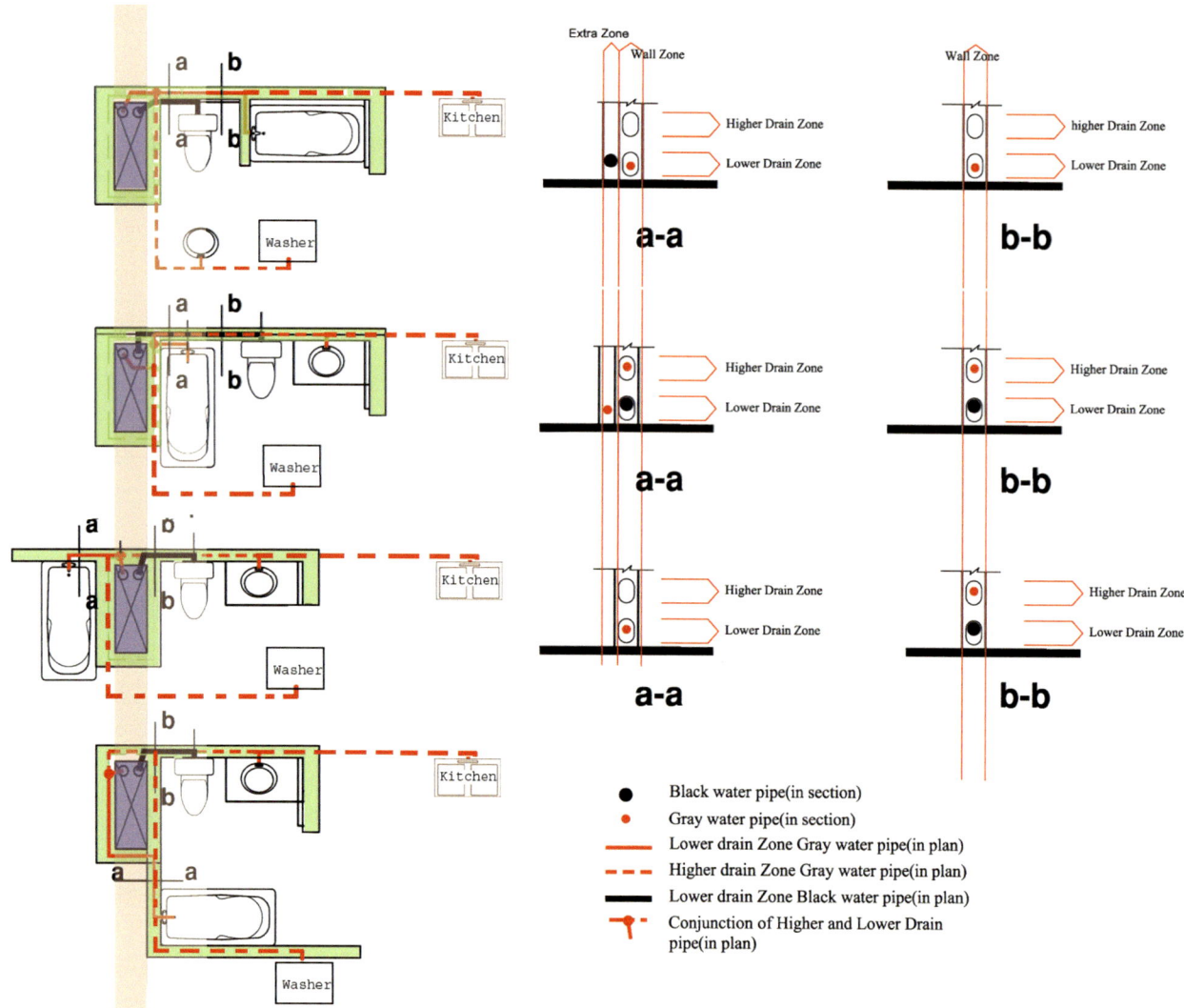

Figure 36 These four situations are taken from the case study

ORGANIZING DRAINAGE PIPING IN A BATHROOM IN THREE VARIANTS

The following composite Figure 36 gives the relations between bathroom fixtures and a MEP shaft in the previous demonstration layouts. Four typical bathroom layouts are given (top to bottom in Figure 36) in order to describe a series of technical rules in organizing the 'traffic' inside partition walls to satisfy the criteria. It is important to note that the study here focuses on fixture distances to a MEP shaft and fixture arrangements in a bathroom.

In the top diagram, a toilet and a bathtub discharge into the same partition wall, and the toilet is closer to the MEP shaft. Because toilet and bathtub belong to the LDZ, both of their drainpipes go through the LDZ opening in the stud. Moreover, they need to be separated in two drainpipes, because the toilet drains black water and the bathtub drains gray water. Therefore, an additional Infill wall is needed, to allow each drainpipe its own route to the MEP stack without interruption or collision.

The question of how to decide which pipe goes through which partition wall needs to be answered. In order to get more useful floor space, additional wall thickness should be minimized. To approach this goal, another constraint is set: when toilet and other LDZ fixtures share one partition wall to route the drainpipes to the same MEP shaft, the discharge pipe of the fixture closer to the MEP shaft drains goes through the additional wall. As shown in the top diagram, toilet and bathtub share the same partition wall in draining, while the toilet is closer to the MEP stack. According to the draining rule, one additional wall is attached to the partition wall between the toilet and the MEP shaft. Similarly, one additional wall is attached but for the bathtub to drain because the bathtub is closer to the MEP shaft than the toilet. However, in the third diagram, the toilet and bathtub are using different partition walls to drain. The 'extra wall' constraint does not apply to this circumstance.

CONCLUSIONS
Four findings emerged from studying the problems encountered in the conventional design process used for the Kales Building conversion:

1. The problem of unnecessary and uncompensated work for architects and engineers when the developer's requirements are uncertain or changing
2. The problem of the insufficient decision flexibility for the developer
3. The problem of the severe limitation of dwelling unit variations to offer to a shifting market, and
4. The problem of lack of provision for long-term adaptability.

The Open Building approach was studied as an alternative, giving answers to these four problems. The unit variations were developed by using the methods and following the technical constraints outlined earlier. From the architectural layout drawings, there appear to be no significant differences to conventional high-rise residential unit layouts; however, these unit layouts are developed based on the Open Building approach.

We believe that the Open Building approach, demonstrated here, has some significant advantages. It offers:

- **Decision deferment or decision flexibility for the developer.**
- **Various unit options for future occupants (in a for-sale market) or the building owner (in the case of a rental property).**
- **Reduced territorial entanglements between units of occupancy.**
- **Clarity in how Infill can be effectively delivered as a unified service per unit of occupancy, suggesting what is discussed at the end of the book as a residential Infill industry with a sizable market.**
- **A way toward a systematic approach to MEP systems that can be very effective in delivering variety, no matter who is deciding on the variants.**

Conventional design processes can never achieve these results. More such studies are needed, of course, under additional real-world constraints.

READINGS
Habraken, N.J. (2019). *The Appearance of the Form*. Routledge Revivals. Routledge, London.

Li, J. (2004). *Designing Constraints for Capacity Analysis of Residential Floor Areas*. March thesis under the supervision of Stephen Kendall, Ball State University.

How a Residential Infill Industry Will Change the Culture of Building

INTRODUCTION

We've noted earlier in the book the emergence of an Infill level as a general trend first appearing in contemporary times in the office building sector. This level has many names: tenant work; fit-out; fit-up; Secondary System; Infill and so on. Accompanying this trend has been the growth of the interior design profession and many players in the product manufacturing sector whose products can 'count' as 'equipment,' as well as specialized divisions of large construction companies. Until now, this new level has had no generally accepted name but has become a de facto convention in many sectors: office buildings, shopping centers and airport concourses have evolved with a clear separation between the long-lasting part of these real property assets and the more mutable parts. It's worth noting that some industry standards such as the LEED certification system of the US Green Building Council make a separation between 'core and shell' and 'tenant fit-out work':

Building Design and Construction: Core and Shell: This rating system is designed for projects where the developer controls the design and construction of the entire mechanical, electrical, plumbing and fire-protection system – called the core and shell – but not the design and construction of the tenant fit-out. Recognizing that the division between owner and tenant responsibility for certain elements of the building varies, LEED BD+C: Core and Shell is designed to complement both the LEED ID+C and LEED O+M rating systems. (US Green Building Council)

Educational and healthcare facilities as well as housing, however, remain outliers in this more general trend. In those sectors, no such separation exists except in a very limited number of cases, discussed elsewhere.

While this separation has become conventional in some real property sectors, no Infill industry in the sense we mean it has emerged. For this reason, we believe it is appropriate to conclude the book where the Open Building approach began: a residential Infill industry as a key basis for a regenerative residential building stock. This is not intended to ignore the importance of a movement toward a mature Infill industry in serving all real property sectors.

Everyone knows that housing is 'different.' Our residential building stock constitutes the largest proportion of the totality of everyday built environment. It has the largest social and economic impacts and, to a large extent, 'makes a culture.' Non-residential buildings become residential, and vice-versa. Yet, when this part of our everyday environment becomes rigid and unresponsive to life's changing dynamics, the ripple effects are felt everywhere: in our daily lives, in the ways we organize our investments and building activities and on the ability of people at all income levels to be well housed.

Living in a responsive (residential) building stock is too important in too many ways to be left to chance. Because of these reasons, we address the following topics in what follows:

- An outdated residential industry culture
- One developer's perspective
- How residential Infill companies would work
- A question of business structure and culture more than technology
- Open Building and government
- Developments toward a residential Infill industry in PR China
- What we have learned
- A shift in emphasis
- What we should be arguing for

AN OUTDATED RESIDENTIAL INDUSTRY CULTURE

A little history helps put our present situation in perspective. From the early to mid-1900s onward, residential construction projects on an unprecedented scale became an important subject for professional design practice. Often, these took the form of large multifamily housing blocks, often called 'mass housing,' in the extensive extensions to and redevelopment of urban centers, funded by central governments. This happened in many countries in the post-WWII decades, independent of political economy: in Western and Eastern Europe, Russia, South America, Japan, Korea and PR China, among other places.

Such extensive single-use, high-density developments occurred to a very limited extent in the United States, largely funded by various levels of government as 'public housing' in what was ironically called 'urban renewal.' Privately developed low-density suburban sprawl – supported by favorable governmental incentives, cheap gasoline and investments in highway infrastructure – was the dominant form of urbanization, with the home building and banking industries (and all levels of government) in full support.

Administrators of government subsidy and pension funds as well as private-sector developers expected architects and engineers to tell them how to build large numbers of housing projects at once as a secure investment. This meant that for the first time in the history of human settlement, everyday environment, both urban and suburban, became a dominantly professional product. This professionalization of housing is now considered the proper formal way to make urban environment. Everything else, the improvised products of a millennia-old way of incremental urban growth, is still alive in a productive way around most megacities today and is known as 'informal settlements' or 'DIY culture.' In a building, regulatory and financing culture dominated by professionals (architects included), it is considered an anomaly and often scorned despite its ubiquity and economic (and environmental and resource consumption) implications.

Since the early years of the 20th century, this formal way of delivering single-family attached and multifamily housing has become a complex network dominated by technical and design professionals including government administrators, lending institutions, regulators, product manufacturers, builders and politicians. But despite this, it has failed to 'solve the housing crisis.' Perhaps one reason is that it has also failed to successfully harness the full power of industrial production, logistics, data management software, despite the continual enlargement of the technical repertoire of hardware and software, off-site prefabrication and other improvements.

Most telling, from an Open Building perspective, has been its refusal – or inability – to accept – as general matter – a direct and instrumental role for inhabitants in the process. These dual failures are related: this was the insight that led to the concept out of which the Open Building approach emerged in the early 1960s. The result of the widespread inability of the professional class to grasp the relationship between these dual failures is that while everything else today can be made in large quantities for less and less money and at increasing levels of quality, serving a sophisticated market at all income levels, dwellings in large residential projects and in the single-family market – for that same society are more expensive every year – and too often of lesser quality.

In other words, contemporary housing remains the result of an outdated professional culture that has little incentive to change its ways. This is not difficult to understand, because it is always a risk to change your way of working, and there is no reason to do so as long as you make money. But we believe the change in attitudes and ways of working is crucial if our goal is – as it must be – a truly living, affordable and resilient built environment.

ONE DEVELOPER'S PERSPECTIVE
Frank Bijdendijk, one of the most astute and experienced housing developers in the Netherlands (and founder of the National Renovation Platform in Europe) is an advocate of the Open Building approach. He has clear things to say regarding the challenges in the policy arena to the widespread adoption of Open Building (Bijdendijk, 2022).

1. *"First, we have to look at ownership rights in the real estate sector. This is based on the principle that everything above and below a piece of land and that associated with it is the property of the landowner; within the real estate sector, this also applies to everything attached to it. So, at first glance it might seem that it is difficult to reconcile full ownership over the INFILL to the inhabitant. We could determine juridical constructions that solve this problem in part. But for an adequate and universally usable legal separation of ownership of BASE BUILDING and INFILL, many legislative changes are necessary."*

2. *"Secondly, we have to consider environmental law (or regional planning). This gives local Government the ability to determine the use of land. An exhaustive list of permitted uses can therefore stand in the way of allowing a much-needed use for the land in question. It would be better to have a list of things which are **not** possible so that there is unlimited space for everything else. That is much wiser in a dynamic society,*

in which no one knows what will happen or what the requirements are in the market."
3. "Thirdly we have to consider the building codes and regulations. One of the most pressing questions that may arise from the application of the regulations is what is the standard that applies to renovations? Are they the same standards as in current new construction or are they the same standards that prevailed in the initial development of the real estate? The latter seems more reasonable than the first, because existing buildings undergoing renovation or transformation and having to adapt to new build standards are often unenforceable."
4. "A fourth category of regulations that we have to consider are shaped by the legislation that covers gas, water, electricity as well as the connection requirements of utility companies. The legislation and connection requirements give the utility companies a kind of monopoly position. And there might be, in terms of user control, significant complications making it very costly."

"The degree to which all of these regulations work prohibitively is not only an objective truth as a direct result of the content of the rules themselves, but also depends to a large extent on the smoothness with which they are applied. And that is a subjective matter, because with good will, it is also evident that within current legislation, regulations and local ordinances a lot is still possible. But if this good will is lacking, there are countless opportunities to greatly reduce user-control. Even on that point there is still a lot to do. On the one hand we need to work on raising awareness on the enforcement of regulations, on the other hand we have to work hard to be convincing and put forward convincing arguments."

"Furthermore, flexible use of existing real estate does not always fit within the traditional financial parameters. This is especially the case in change of use, which costs not only additional investment resources but also often just leads to a new acceptable return when the first existing value is written off. That problem is often apparent with vacant offices, shops and industrial buildings. Investors have long been reluctant to implement these write-offs in the hope of an improvement in the market. And curiously enough, the commonly used valuation methods on write-offs also stood in the way, because these methods often came out from the fictional assumption that the real estate within a certain time (e.g., two years) will be entirely rented. In such a case the methods were not appreciated by the reality, so writing-off was unnecessary. Large write-offs suddenly also raised questions. And therefore, most investors opted for gradual change despite the fact that the real and current market value was now much lower than that of the book value."

"This can create barriers to redevelopment. This was especially true in the early years of the economic crisis (2008–2010). But meanwhile investors have accepted the new reality. In completely vacant office areas, for example, residual values of around €200 ($242)/$m^2$ floor space are already taken into account. Some talk of offices as having m^2-price equal to that of the floor covering!"

"If the write-off is accepted, the problem is whether as a result there is additional investing that has an appreciation that is higher than the investment. The appreciation depends of course on the rental possibilities, the rental price level and the expected rent price development after transformation. The problem is then to finance that investment if the necessary equity is missing. Here we can come up against the ingrained approaches of the banks. They are used to finance only after rental. They finance then on the basis of guaranteed cash flow. This can be quite difficult at the present time because the traditional markets fail, and buildings need to be specifically made suitable for variable and changing use. The demand for such capacity is a feature of the market of today and tomorrow. That means a new vision is needed for the financier who was accustomed to single-tenant contracts for five to ten years. For it is precisely small-scale rental to changing users and rental contracts with short terms that have a future. It seems controversial, but in this market, it is wise to offer leases for workspaces that can be cancelled on a monthly basis, the same as with living spaces. That is totally against tradition, but by opening the back door like this we may stop the resistance at the front door. This new way of thinking in the world of real estate financing must be accepted."

"If the financier goes into this, then they finance no guaranteed cash flow but a market-conforming building. Guaranteed cash flow and market conforming buildings have two entirely different magnitudes. In the latter case, other criteria are taken into account, such as location, capacity for variety and change, and the appearance of the building. Unlike the signed leases of reputable parties, they are far more difficult to put across to the back office. But there are clear signs of a change in forward thinking financiers and where they are going to take this."

HOW INFILL COMPANIES WOULD WORK

In time, we see a residential Infill industry consisting of competitive, government-certified companies, operating in a particular market. These companies will deliver everything that can be decided independently per dwelling as a single-source service under a unified design-production-installation contract. Their service will be competitive based on cost, service, brand and quality. These companies will draw upon the worldwide availability of always-improving products and subsystems, and some may develop and patent their own products to distinguish their 'brand.'

These companies will be competitive with the more 'traditional,' disjointed mode of operation in both new construction and repositioning existing non-residential buildings for residential use or in upgrading existing multifamily residential projects one-unit-at-a-time.

To be sure, this business practice won't displace the ongoing piecemeal work of upgrading existing buildings when only a new set of kitchen cabinets is being installed, a dwelling's floor finishes are being replaced, upgraded electrical service is required or a new toilet is to be installed. Such 'granular' improvement of an existing housing stock should and will continue, introducing new products and methods incrementally as is now the case internationally.

At a certain point, however – decided both technically and in terms of cost – as any remodeling contractor will tell us, it makes more sense to fully 'gut' (clean-out) a dwelling unit rather than to remodel in a piecemeal way.

The service of Infill companies involves organizing all work and products per dwelling unit, accounted for per dwelling, under one contract. In new construction, this service engages a project's critical path when decisions are to be made about the specifications of each dwelling, whether by the developer or by the future occupant, but after the Base Building has been designed. In the reactivation or conversion of existing buildings – either upgrading residential properties or converting buildings to residential use – the service offered is to fill in fully 'gutted' spaces one at a time, on-time and on budget. In reactivating existing buildings, all 'common' infrastructure elements, including the mechanical, electrical and plumbing (MEP) parts of the Base Building, will have been upgraded and reconfigured as needed for long-term capacity (not just a one-off renovation), ready for each unit's Infill to be installed and connected to Base Building infrastructure.

Infill companies prepare well-organized 'packages' or 'kits' of parts off-site. The parts and small assemblies are delivered in the correct number, sequence and dimension, using the latest in laser tools for accurate site measurements. These packages, along with the coordinated delivery of other parts straight from manufacturers or suppliers, are bar-coded and delivered to the site and brought into the empty space through a balcony window by a boom truck or, on tall buildings, using a boom lift (also used for window washing) or via the service elevator and through the unit's front door. Once inside, they are installed by a multiskilled team of workers who stay with the job until it is finished. Only minimal cutting of parts is required, thus producing very little on-site waste, debris and noise. Such companies will compete on their ability to use the latest enterprise management software and the latest consumer-oriented products from the market and their ability to deliver on-time and on-budget. They deliver at various price points and hand over a user's manual and multiyear maintenance agreement.

Working this way means an end to choreographing separate subcontractors, with all the familiar scheduling, blame-shifting and quality-control problems. This new mode of operation means implementing true teamwork into residential construction. Infill company product/service solutions are truly systematic, which does not mean uniform solutions but quite the opposite, because good systems enable rather than block variety.

A complete Infill package will include everything making that space habitable – the thousands of discrete parts including parts for making walls, doors, door frames and hardware, all wiring, piping and plumbing fixtures, lighting, cabinets, appropriate heating, air conditioning, ventilation equipment and so on. The space may be rented and the Infill purchased. The Infill may even include the front door as well as part of the building's façade directly related to each independent dwellings' floor plan. (see NEXT21 at the beginning of the book)

As already noted, social structure and conventions and the local market will dictate which parts of a multifamily residential building will be 'fixed' or common and which will be 'movable' or decided per dwelling unit.

It's quite reasonable to question how such businesses can operate when a building stock is highly varied. In many countries and regions, building technology (wood-frame vs. concrete vs. heavy timber vs. steel structure, etc.) varies considerably, as do access types and dimensions (e.g., floor-to-floor; column spacing; façade-to-elevator core, etc.). Given these variables, Infill companies will have developed systemic solutions, with variations. Experience world-wide shows that the routing of piping (drainage and domestic water supply), cabling and ventilation ducts within demised spaces requires special attention and offers the best opportunity for systemic product solutions.

A QUESTION OF BUSINESS STRUCTURE AND CULTURE

As we've already noted, the residential building industry today is, after more than 100 years of delivering large projects, still dependent on having floor plans decided first. Everything else follows – financing, construction documents, zoning and building approvals, construction and certificates of occupancy.

Construction today depends on organizing ad-hoc contracts among many subcontractors, each delivering labor and products to complete the specified work. This is the mode of operation whether the project is an entire building, a building complex or a single unit of occupancy. Both the conversion of existing buildings to new uses and new construction are organized in a similar way. As more subsystems have come into residential construction over time, conforming with technical innovation, market demand and to successively increased performance standards, each with its own specialized trade, this mode of operation has become the Achilles' heel of construction and its management. Partly as a result, most large general contractors have become project managers with no workforce of their own, allowing them to apply downward pressure on subcontractors to lower project costs. While this may be a prudent business model for general contractors and subcontractors in an industry that is notorious for its up-and-down swings directly related to swings in the general economy – hiring when the market is hot and laying off workers when business is slow – it is not reliable. This is particularly problematic when the labor pool of skilled workers is shrinking. It is unable to deliver affordable housing, nor does it deliver acceptable quality on any regular basis.

Because the existing building industry has been unable to break out of its obsolete habits and mode of operation, an Infill industry of many competitive, certified companies is likely to come into being by outside actors entering the stage because they see untapped opportunities with fresh eyes.

There is precedent for this in other industries. IBM, for example, developed a culture and a clear set of corporate rules well suited for handling the demands of clients of its mainframe computers. But when the personal computer came into existence and individuals rather than corporations became the customer base, IBM was awkward and slow to adapt. Its rules and processes did not match the new realities. Dell and then Apple were born with business models targeted to the individual consumer. Henry Ford is another example, having had the insight that a market existed for something better than horse-drawn carriages. The automobile industry with its supply chains was born. At first, he offered only black cars, utterly uniform in design. But as this new mode of transport became familiar and showed its advantages, he was able to introduce variety while maintaining quality and holding down costs. Many competitive companies joined the market. A ubiquitous infrastructure of roads, highways, expressways and all the ancillary land-use functions associated with transportation followed, coming into being to support the automobiles and other vehicles being produced. Elon Musk introduced the Tesla, coming out of nowhere, and, at the time of writing, leads the way in the movement toward the electric vehicle, with most large automobile companies playing catch-up.

Sometimes, established companies recognize the disjuncture between their origins and the market and move internally to activate something like this innovation process. They create subsidiaries or divisions, sometimes known as 'skunkworks,' to try out new models of business operation to meet new challenges and opportunities. This happened in the commercial construction sector, when large construction companies spawned new divisions specializing in tenant fit-out for the office and shopping-center markets. The same thing happens in architecture firms when market opportunities are recognized by either the acquisition of niche companies or hiring new people to spearhead a new corporate posture.

In the same way, we think that some 'design-build' companies may well develop successful residential Infill services, which will stimulate competition and innovation and which, in turn, will lower costs. This, in turn, will put residential Base Buildings, as a new kind of architectural infrastructure, in demand as the pragmatic basis for a regenerative building stock. Of course, the headwinds are very very strong.

DEVELOPMENTS TOWARD AN INFILL INDUSTRY IN PR CHINA
Governmental Initiatives

In 2010, at the China-Japan Long-Life Sustainable Housing International Summit Forum, the China Real Estate Association launched the Initiative to Build Long-life Sustainable Housing for the whole society and industry. On May 18, 2012, the China Real Estate Association and the Japan-China Association for Building and Housing Industry jointly signed the Letter of Intent for Cooperation in the Construction of China-Japan Housing Demonstration Projects. Both sides reached an agreement to support China and Japan to further deepen exchanges and cooperation in the development of demonstration projects.

Japan had for years been studying and building prototypes of what they call S/I housing (S/I meaning skeleton/Infill). This development has been extensively discussed elsewhere (see Appendix Two). In fact, a Long-Life housing law had been passed by the Japanese parliament in 2009, providing incentives to developers to build such residential projects. Millions of single-family detached houses have been built using this law and its technical provisions, but very few multifamily projects have been realized.

This agreement for cooperation, signed in 2012 between China and Japan, proposed to build a new type of Chinese Long-life Sustainable Housing featuring long life, high quality and low energy consumption. The means to achieve this goal was to harness the power of industrial production in the support of new methods of construction. The China Institute of Building Standard Design & Research of China Construction Technology Consulting (CCTC) was entrusted to conduct organizational and management research, technology research and development, and to design and implement demonstration projects. A number of contracts were agreed to, to carry out the first series of demonstration projects.

In 2014, the first long-life sustainable housing demonstration project, Greenland · Nanxiang William Mansion, was completed. It attracted wide interest from the building and housing industry and society. The second series of demonstration projects in 2015 and the third in 2017 were completed one after another. By the end of 2019, the total construction area of the national demonstration projects has reached over 1 million m^2 (10.8 million ft^2). Long-life sustainable housing has led the transformation and upgrading of China's contemporary new housing construction methods with new concepts, new models, new standards and new systems. At the time of writing, despite a serious downturn in the Chinese real estate sector, these advances appear to be helping to solve the bottleneck of China's urban and rural living environment construction. They may help realize the future-oriented green and sustainable development construction by breaking through the barriers of China's long-standing traditional production and construction methods.

Guided by S/I (Japanese term for skeleton/Infill) and Open Building methods, the coordination of the design and construction of the Primary structure, exterior building envelope, installation pathways and interior decoration (Infill) is being realized. This is also reflected in the coordination of architectural, structural, MEP and interior fit-out specialists, as well as the whole process of overall planning, design, production, construction, operation and maintenance.

One outcome of these developments is that a growing number of Chinese companies began to enter the Infill business, called 'industrialized interior decoration' in China. This was stimulated by the release in 2018 of the Design and Assessment Standard for Long-Life Sustainable Housing. This standard was developed and is being promoted by the China Institute of Building Standard Design and Research (CBS), a national government agency (Liu and Wu, 2022).

Heneng
An early leader in industrialized interior decoration was Henenghome (Heneng). The president of Heneng started in business investing in, developing and selling software to manage hotel reservations (reportedly used in 75% of Chinese hotels in 2016) and manufacturing a pharmaceutical for children (now used by most hospitals). He later got into real estate development. Around 2008, seeing a market in the interior decoration business, he started Heneng, a company that supplied thousands of complete Infill packages to public rental housing projects in several large cities in China, and began supplying the single-family luxury market and the for-sale condominium market, healthcare and educational facilities.

Their logistics strategy involved delivering as much as possible from their own factories. Their goal was to deliver exactly the right quantity of each subsystem, with each delivery bar coded as to which building, which floor and into which dwelling unit a given bundle of parts was to be delivered.

By mid-2020, after just five years in full operation, the company had completed over 100,000 apartment units, 4,000 hotel rooms and over 60,000 m^2 (646,000 ft^2) of public buildings including hospitals, schools, commercial chain stores, offices and renovation of existing buildings. Some clients are government controlled, such as public housing projects. Projects like residential condominiums, schools, hotels, gyms and hair salons were all privately owned. By 2020, about 90% of their work was in new construction, about 10% in improving existing buildings. They recognized that improving existing buildings is a bigger market, so their leadership intended to expand in that market.

Heneng developed their own manufacturing facilities in several parts of China to make everything: metal studs of various sizes, all finish panel materials for walls and floors, doors and steel door frames, door hardware, etc. Their 'quick-connect' water piping system did not require licensed plumbers. At the height of their success, they could complete a mid-sized apartment in seven days – from a raw space to installed furnishing – with a trained multiskilled installation team of four workers. In 2020, they had five factories in China, each with the production capacity of 50,000 apartment units per year, with a supply radius of 300 km (185 miles). This supply ability allowed them to be competitive in renovating existing buildings, and beginning in 2020, they intended to face customers directly in showrooms.

They use technologies such as big data, cloud computing and AI to connect their BIM+ERP+MES system – what they call their Heneng digital fabrication platform. They developed their own design software (based on BIM – building information system), which allowed designers to freely design (they have over 2,000+ wall surface patterns and finishes to choose from: wood, fabric, marble, etc.) and avoid worrying about drawing details of their Infill system (the software does that itself). When designs are finished, they automatically generate orders to their ERP (enterprise resource planning) system and send the orders directly to their production line (MES or manufacturing execution system) without human interference. This means all data comes from the same origin; the same model is used from design to manufacture to installation and maintenance; and every project has a digital twin. This combination of the digital and industrial worlds maximizes efficiency and connects the whole industrial supply chain.

In 2023, the company reported that it had 102 patents and a 100% factory production rate. For large-scale projects, they reportedly saved 50% time; on small-scale projects, they save 75% time. Also, they saved 65% on material waste, and the repair rate was lowered 95% compared to traditional construction methods. They continued to upgrade their software and logistics systems. The developers they worked with saved money and time using their services.

An Example of a Heneng Installation

The following figures show some of the technical solutions offered by Heneng followed by a sequence of images of their typical seven-day process of filling in an empty dwelling unit.

Figure 1 An example of a Base Building built by the Beijing city government and filled in by Heneng (*Source & image credits*: Heneng)

Figure 2 A mock-up of the Heneng wall and floor system for bathrooms (*Source & image credits*: Heneng)

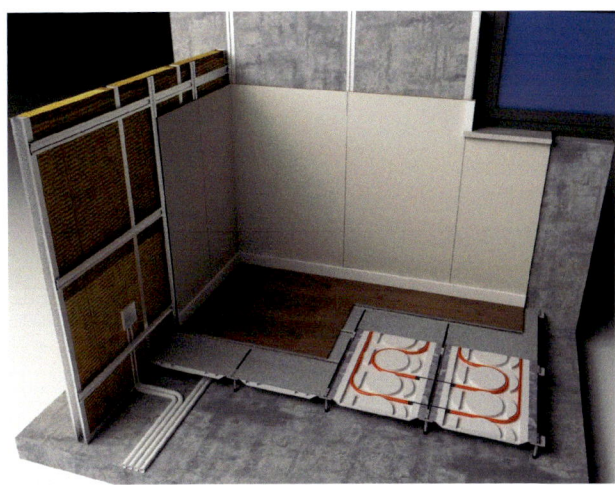

Figure 3 A mock-up of the Heneng wall and floor system showing an early version of hydronic (hot water) raised floor system (*Source & image credits*: Heneng Inc.)

Figure 4 An example of a space ready for fit-out installation (*Source & image credits*: Heneng Inc.)

Figure 5 Day 1 (*Source & image credits*: Heneng Inc.)

Figure 6 Day 2 (*Source & image credits*: Heneng Inc.)

Figure 9 Day 5 Overhead piping and ducts. (*Source & image credits*: Heneng Inc.)

Figure 7 Day 3 Installing warm floor pipes (*Source & image credits*: Heneng Inc.)

Figure 10 Day 6 (*Source & image credits*: Heneng Inc.)

Figure 8 Day 4 (*Source & image credits*: Heneng Inc.)

Figure 11 Day 7 (*Source & image credits*: Heneng Inc.)

Figure 12 Day 7 Installing furniture (*Source & image credits*: Heneng Inc.)

The executive director of Heneng, in private correspondence with the author in 2021, said,

"Some traditional construction companies are trying to do what we do, but it is hard for a construction company to transform their whole system from construction management to production. These are two different fields, and it takes time to shift to a new mode. The market is huge; we hope there are more companies to join us so we can make the industry better together."

Problems with Heneng and Recent Developments
In the first decades of the 21st century, the Beijing city government initiated massive urban extensions to the east and south of the city. They were meant in part to house city government employees who work in government offices being relocated there, and they were being offered for-sale dwellings in multi-family high-rise projects.

As mentioned, Heneng had already, by that time, launched its Infill system and had been improving it step by step. By the time the Beijing city government started to implement the new urban extensions in 2020, Heneng, which had largely served governmental 'social housing' (rental) housing projects (in Beijing and other cities), began offering an updated product/service to developers of these for-sale projects. But residents began refusing to buy them due to quality-control problems caused by problems of leaking pipes in its patented water supply piping system and acoustical problems with the hollow raised floors and hollow walls.

As a consequence, and needing a suitable Infill system, the R&D section of the Beijing Housing Industrialization Group Co. Ltd. (BHIG), one of Heneng's former clients, was ordered by the Beijing city government to initiate research to produce a new Infill system in 2020. The goal was to fix the problems of Heneng's Infill system. Three parties invested in BHIG. The Beijing Government Social Housing Center (Beijing Urban Housing Corporation's proper name) was the biggest and main party among the three investors.

In what follows, 'Infill V1/V2/V3' is a definition from the Beijing Housing Industrialization Group (BHIG), not from Heneng or from a common industry standard. Earlier Infill systems, largely copied from the Japanese industry with high raised floors, which had no hydronic floor heating, was known as V1. Heneng's Infill system, with its hollow (raised) floor with hydronic floor heating, was regarded as V2 according to this definition by BHIG.

In a role reversal, BHIG expected to complete the work of revising Heneng's Infill system and to have a satisfactory V3 system (see note above) by the middle of 2022 that corrected the problems of Heneng's Infill system. The new V3 was the result of cooperation among several private companies including Zhong-Zhu Jian-Ke (Infill company name). However, Heneng did not participate because it was so busy in the market selling its own Infill system.

Wang Qiang, CEO of Zhong-Zhu Jian-Ke, was CEO of Heneng before 2019, when he left to start his own company. Wang Qiang became co-owner of the new V3 wall and floor systems as well as the improved water supply and quick-connect electrical wiring systems. Other cooperating companies included producers of kitchens and bathroom units. Because the proprietary parts are not very complex, they are not difficult to copy. Therefore, Wang Qiang reported that he must keep improving, updating and developing the elements to keep ahead of competitors.

It is important to note that once development is complete, V3 will be available immediately to any company to include in their own competitive Infill product/service, including such companies as Zhong-Zhu Jian-Ke, Inc. and Qing-Zhou Hong-Mei Decoration Company, Heneng and others. However, BHIG will wait for several years to put V3 into its for-sale projects, in both the developments to the East and South of Beijing, after several demonstration projects are evaluated and proven to be acceptable to residents.

V3 System Development
The principle underlying V3 is shown in the following diagram and photos of the showroom.

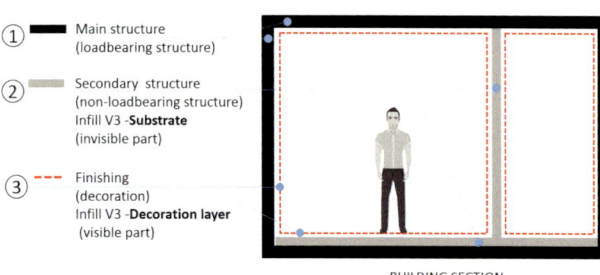

Figure 13 Diagram by Liu Peng, *First Grade Architect, Studio Leader, Beijing Institute of Architectural Design*

Note: The two element groups – 2 and 3 – in Figure 13 are identified as such because they represent two parts of Infill in the Chinese market. (1) Main structure corresponds to the Base Building; (2) and (3) correspond to Infill components.

TABLE 1

Summary of improvements undertaken in V3 (1st column) to correct problems in Heneng's V2 Infill system (2nd column) (*Credit:* Liu Peng)

	Improvement of Infill V3.0	Purpose (The problems of Infill V2.0 solved)
1	Separate the manufacture of decoration layer and the base substrate (the invisible part), which means connecting the decoration layer onto the substrate is no longer done in the factory but on site.	• Provide much more choices to the occupants, designers, contractors and all related parties. • Except for Infill factories, more manufacturers like various decoration layer manufacturers could be involved, so that both the speed and quality could be improved.
2	Make the substrate more modularized	To improve the speed and quality.
3	Make the substrate more solid by changing some materials, including supporting and filling materials	• To reduce the deformation of the substrate. In Infill V2.0, ceramic floor tiles could not be used or could easily crack due to the deformation of the floor substrate • 2. To improve the user experience. In Infill V2.0, occupants complain that the floor and partition wall sound hollow when walking or knocking on them, which is regard as low quality, influenced by traditional experience, habit or culture.
4	Change the floor system of washroom from one waterproof layer into two spaced layers	To solve the leaking problem
5	Make wiring cable integrated and modularized with easy quick-connect joints	

Photographs of the V3 Industrialized Infill System

Figure 14 V3 Infill floor base module: Concrete, factory-produced floor-heating module, replacing the earlier version used by Heneng. The user feedback was that the V2 floor sounded 'hollow' to residents, indicating 'cheap' construction. The floor heating pipes are visible, snapped into place in the floor module (*Source and Photo credit of the following figures* (Figures 14–21): Liu Peng, Senior Architect; First Grade. Beijing Institute of Architectural Design)

Figure 15 V3 Infill washroom floor module on adjustable legs: bathroom/washroom floor now has two layers of waterproofing

HOW A RESIDENTIAL INFILL INDUSTRY WILL CHANGE THE CULTURE OF BUILDING

Figure 16 V3 Infill wall base module: Here, the inside construction of the base Infill wall module is shown. The finished module is solid, filled by casting foam concrete among the studs. This was a response to criticism by users, who thought that the hollow stud walls of previous versions sounded 'cheap.' The surface of the finished module is cement board, ready for any finish surface.

Figure 17 V3 Infill quick-connect cabling system: This photo shows the position of electric wiring along the ceiling and entering the wall base module from the top

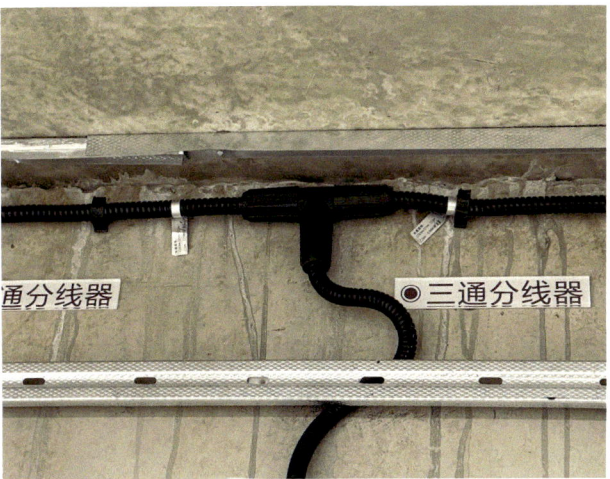

Figure 18 V3 Infill quick-connect cabling system: This photo is a detail of one connection of the quick-connect electrical wiring system

Figure 19 V3 Infill quick-connect cabling system: This is a photograph of the electrical switch panel inside the wall base module at about 2.5 m above the floor. Electrical wiring is fed through the white plastic conduits, which are eventually buried in the foam concrete inside the stud walls

Figure 20 V3 Infill quick-connect cabling system: This is a photograph of the electrical wall panel inside every wall base module

Figure 21 V3 Infill quick-connect cabling system: This photo shows the quick-connect cabling system at the 'breaker panel' (top), the washer/dryer connection (lower left) as well as at the control of the hydronic floor heating system (bottom right)

Redefining Base Building and Infill Contents

In March 2023, BHIG (Beijing Housing Industrialization Group) announced that it had launched a new development. The goal was to increase the speed of industrialized housing in general as well as Infill installation. This was to be accomplished by doing more work in the factory, with less on-site assembly work.

Of particular note were two decisions:

1. **The first is to stop using the modular raised-floor heating elements (Figure 7). Instead, the floor heating pipe pathways would be incorporated as grooves in factory-produced pre-cast concrete floor elements, installed as part of the Base Building construction.**

2. **The second development is that the vertical pipe shafts have become Base Building elements, with 'smart' connections for Infill piping connecting to the Base Building pipes in the shaft.**

What this means in essence is that in this new development, the principle of separating Base Building and Infill remains a central strategy, while more of the total building has moved into the Base Building category of decision-making. There are several goals:

1. To reduce on-site work,
2. To reduce reliance on human labor,
3. To increase quality control, and
4. To reduce costs

There is no decrease in dwelling unit layout variety and capacity to change layouts over time. Further, V3, with its concrete modular raised floor elements, will continue to be used in renovation projects. Other technical innovations are expected.

Industrialization in the building industry in PR China is being driven by the dramatic increase in demand for housing, the decrease in availability of human resources in the building industry and the need to meet the demand for a building stock with 100-year life spans. The S/I (Open Building) model appears to have demonstrated its ability to deliver housing that is not only less expensive, faster and of higher quality to deliver initially but also adaptable – one unit at a time – to changing household and demographic requirements over time. Reports from PR China indicate that the Open Building model also contributes to reducing the massive demolition of tens of thousands of apartment buildings that generates waste, pollution and the disruption of urban life and creates a drain on the national economy.

As of late 2023, as the real estate market in China was in a period of serious decline, contacts informed the authors that the impact on Infill was hard to predict. On one hand, as the market was in a downturn, the investments and improvements in this industry could very well be reduced. On the other hand, the shortage of skilled manpower is a national problem, because of the sharply reduced birthrate and the disinterest on the part of young, educated people to enter the construction sector, despite high levels of unemployment. At the same time, higher building quality is required due to the depressed but competitive market, so continued innovation in the direction of 'industrialization' in the construction sector and investments in an Infill industry will be especially important in such a context. That may well push the development of Infill. High quality and low cost are the opportunity in any downturn. If the further development of Infill could be successful in pushing the building process to have both high quality and low cost, it would have a big future China.

WHAT WE HAVE LEARNED

In the European context, post-WWII mass housing became possible when governments decided to make money available to subsidize not-for-profit residential construction. The Netherlands was ahead of its time and was one of the first to do this, even in 1902. Before that date, workers sometimes started to collectively save money to build houses that were made available to participants by lottery. Churches and socialist parties made money available as well, but all that effort did not match the rapid growth of cities. To make sure that government money was well spent, bureaucrats, being asked to distribute the subsidy money, wanted professionals to be responsible for its use. Inhabitants were not invited into the process, and this shaped a well-established professional housing culture. The housing industry is now a purely professional culture in which, a full century later, government negotiates with architects, bankers, sociologists, politicians and other professionals but not the inhabitants.

Something very much like this happens presently in most countries around the world, even when the role of government is minimal and the role of private developers is dominant. The inhabitants are not part of the decision-making process except in the luxury market. Even there, it is rare to invite inhabitants to take control and take responsibility, because the habits of the industry continue to ignore the value of full independence of individual dwelling units in large projects.

From its beginnings, Open Building proposed reintroducing inhabitants in that culture. This would happen by shifting responsibility to occupants for the design of their individual dwelling interiors with everything needed to make dwellings habitable. This never happened except in a few hundred instances that are now well publicized.

Open Building has always focused on reestablishing the role of inhabitants. This came from a reading of history that showed that complex living environmental fields always were bottom-up technical results. Small-scale initiatives could become rich and beautiful environments that could live and renew themselves for centuries. Uniformity was rare, but when it happened, it was always the result of top-down visions and belonged, for the most part, to special monumental projects.

Today, both top-down unified control and contemporary technology produce rigidity and uniformity. We believe that this is a temporary problem that the Open Building approach can deal with. The fact that everyday uniformity is only happening in the world's richest and technically most advanced cultures (and not in informal settlements) tells us again that the thrust of the original Open Building approach was not basically a technical but a political one.

Introducing the Open Building approach as a technical innovation aimed at making the building stock sustainable, as in the case of PR China, without getting the inhabitant involved, was an important shift in emphasis. It was also a brilliant thing to do. This has allowed a new industry to demonstrate how it deals with each dwelling unit, even when the design is repeated many times, as an independent job in which all parts are defined, produced, packaged, shipped on time, delivered and installed on-site by a multiskilled team per dwelling or other occupancy. At the same time, it does not demand any change in the larger project design or execution, operating like any other subsystem company hired by the familiar project management.

We have learned that Open Building Infill companies have two agendas they can choose to deal with:

- **The first agenda is to make dwelling users independent actors in an entirely new market**
- **The second agenda is to develop and establish an industrial Infill technology**

We now see that Infill companies (called 'industrialized interior decoration' companies in PR China) are entering the market, making the second agenda demonstrate its power. These companies, encouraged and incentivized by various methods of governmental 'pushing' and normal efforts to seek competitive advantage, are serving both rental social housing and the market of condominium home buyers. They are also serving other sectors, such as healthcare, schools and commercial real estate. They deliver everything to make an empty space habitable, in one integrated process, from factory to multiskilled installation teams. These companies save their clients' money, reduce waste, deliver a completed unit in 7 days or less and offer a multiyear warrantee. They are now beginning to meet the market of individual buyers in their showrooms for both new construction and the reactivation of existing buildings.

Given this information, we believe that in time, the first agenda is inevitable.

Based on what we now see at the time of writing, for Infill companies to get into business, it is not important for them to consider the social and political management of a market of autonomous inhabitants. **It is not important to talk about user control.** Inhabitants still remain outside the professional network. The power to change that reality is simply missing.

In time, however, with the separation of design tasks (one to design Base Buildings and another to design and deliver the Infill), inhabitants will be able to take care of their own units of occupancy. They will be able to change their dwellings with the help of the INFILL company that installed the unit they currently live in, or they can replace what they have by an entirely new design, possibly by another competing Infill company.

OPEN BUILDING AND GOVERNMENT

Governments at several levels (national, regional, state, local) have key roles to play if an Infill industry is to emerge and become established. We think their key role is to establish certification criteria for Infill companies and regulatory instruments for buildings constructed by separating the long-lasting parts from those that change more regularly and frequently. There is also a role for private-party/third-party certification systems, such as LEED, BREEAM or other energy-related systems now in wide use. This is a larger subject that deserves its own careful study, related to each country where the Open Building approach has potential.

Over time, the century-old professional network will find reason to adapt and will be able to serve a true Open Building environment. All this suggests a straightforward government policy:

Encourage the development of industrial Infill systems.

These will be product/service system companies that do not need to argue for user control. Instead, they can compete with ongoing housing companies for fitting out of new or existing housing projects, or convert obsolete buildings to new uses, with economically competitive services.

If they become available, the market for autonomous Infill units will develop by itself, as we see it happening in PR China.

WHAT WE SHOULD BE ARGUING FOR

The many hundreds of successful residential Open Building projects that are already on record show that the Open Building approach applied to residential architecture does not depend for success on advanced Infill systems. The variety of examples shown earlier and in other published books and reports shows that there are many reasons to adopt the Open Building approach and that they take various architectural, social/organizational and technical forms. But progress is slow and resistance to change remains strong.

It's a familiar fact that productivity in the building industry has declined over the past half century. The current infatuation with the century-old idea of building fully fitted-out boxes in factories and trucking them to a site to be stacked up with cranes is only producing rigid buildings with a marginal first-cost savings. The proposition made here is that to successfully turn around the outdated professional housing culture and to improve productivity, commercially successful Infill systems and competitive companies delivering them are needed. And, in the long run, keeping a national housing stock up to date, affordable and sustainable – and efficiently converting buildings to new uses – requires the availability of many certified Infill companies.

The proposal to separate Infill design from Base Building design and to make each dwelling unit fully independent was usually considered to be too expensive compared to the traditional mode of tying the design of the Base Building to the initial Infill design, uniform or not. Despite evidence to the contrary (the yearly expenditures on remodeling residential buildings or converting nonresidential to residential often equals or exceeds investments in new construction), no one believed that change or variety at the level of the individual dwelling was important to consider. This was the case even though no one argued against the idea that being able to decide on your own dwelling design was a good idea.

So it is not surprising that it is only in the last decade or so that pioneering companies have appeared, in several countries, to offer the service of delivering and installing each residential unit as an integrated, single-source and separate task. An early initiative (MATURA – reported on elsewhere) in the Netherlands in the late 1980s and early 1990s finally closed down due to lack of sustained investment. A few companies have struggled in Japan against strong headwinds of the major construction companies that dominate the building industry. These fledgling companies have based their business models not on the fragmented construction industry model of organizing labor and materials per project but on an industrial systems model.

An Infill industry based on an industrial model – the basis of the success in the automotive and other complex consumer products industries – is rooted in the understanding that a robust system is not a limitation on variety but enables variety and does so efficiently. Marketing directly to consumers ultimately makes sense.

There is no doubt that systematically organized Infill systems far exceed other existing 'building systems' in number of discrete parts and in the complexity of accurately fitting into a building that is already in place. But the contemporary tool kits in the design and building and product manufacturing industries now have what is needed for this job.

The same imbalance of forces identified in *Supports: An Alternative to Mass Housing*, first published in English in 1962 and reissued in 2021, is still present today. As was true then, assuring a clean separation of tasks between what is common in large residential projects and what is decided per unit of occupancy was identified to be not a technical problem but a problem in the political and policy arenas.

The absence of user control of the entirety of their own dwellings in large projects produces its own culture and policy environment. This stands in sharp contrast to, for example, the automotive industry, consumer electronics and even the proliferation of individual products used in constructing housing. In the present culture, deep innovation in building processes is retarded, reaching a circular economy is more difficult and large building companies are less likely to figure out less expensive ways of building. As long as society excludes the household unit from a direct – disintermediated – economic role in the production of large housing developments, Open Building would be unable to expand more broadly.

We refer again to the imbalance of control. Companies leasing space in offices have economic power, while users in large, multifamily housing projects are, even in market economies, largely passive recipients and have no direct voice. Whereas in office buildings, users (i.e., companies signing office-space leases) control Infill, in housing, there is no Infill to begin with – no Infill level and no separation of design tasks.

But even though we believe it to be crucial, we – architects and other design professionals – should be careful about putting too much weight on declaring that inhabitants and users must be able to choose. That makes it a political discussion for which we – in our roles as design professionals – are not, in general, well equipped, nor do we carry much credibility in that arena. That is why we need allies in the financing, political and policy arenas.

It is probably futile to attempt to reorganize existing development and building companies. We won't succeed. They are not motivated to change, even when their profits shrink in economic downturns, and certainly not when their businesses are booming in good times. The professional class – worldwide – sees no advantage in a residential Infill industry at present. In most cases, the existing players in the building industry make money now and do not see advantage and only assume greater risk trying a new way.

Existing development and construction companies in the housing sector – as noted by many observers, including the executive director of Henning in China, discussed earlier – do not understand the full power of industrial production as a complementary mode of productive activity in the residential building stock, a misunderstanding that inhibits innovation and cost reduction.

It is time to shift priorities: rather than arguing for user control as the driver, we should show that an Infill industry can and does deliver higher quality at lower cost compared to the traditional way of building. It is a better path toward a circular economy.

One important lesson can be learned from the last 50 years of attempts to introduce Infill as a concept in residential projects. Initially, the argument was that users must have control of their personal environments. This was, in essence, a political position impacting distribution of decision-making control and only indirectly subject to design decisions. The argument was that once a new pattern of decision-making would be in place, design decision-making would need to adjust accordingly. This has not happened.

What we should be arguing for, therefore, is the clear separation of design tasks: this separation is the key, not the identity of the parties' making decisions.

In conclusion, we should say only one thing:

User control need not be the primary driver. Open Building makes the act of building more economical: you get more for your money, not just initially but over time, because property assets gain value, even if occupants do not initially have a say. We should instead show that an Infill industry can deliver higher quality at lower costs and that this will, in time, produce an Open Building environment. In such an environment and industry restructuring, user control can follow naturally.

READINGS
www.usgbc.org/discoverleed/certification/bd-c-core-and-shell/

Bijdendijk, F. (2022). The Future of Open Building Resides in the Existing Stock. *Residential Architecture as Infrastructure: Open Building in Practice* (editor Kendall, S.). Routledge, London.

Liu, D., and Wu, Z. (2022). Research, Development and Implementation of Long-life Sustainable Housing in China. *Residential Architecture as Infrastructure: Open Building in Practice* (editor Kendall, S.). Routledge, London.

Postscript 1
Toward a New Research Agenda

Donald Schön has argued that each profession – medical doctors, as much as engineers, lawyers and architects – must go beyond their knowledge base and exhibit a certain artistry to be good professionals. Architects don't need to be reminded of that. Nevertheless, if creativity is an essential ingredient for all professional expertise, it is, by itself, not enough to define a profession's expertise. A profession needs to have a specific domain of knowledge by which to be identified. It also must have the specific skills needed to intervene successfully in that domain.

For contemporary architects, we believe that domain is everyday environment in its full complexity. In this way of thinking, there are two large areas of inquiry that relate exactly to these two conditions for true professionalism. One has to do with our knowledge of environmental form. The other has to do with design methodology – or ways of working. The knowledge of environment as an autonomous and living organism, following its own laws, can provide us the basis on which our design acts will inevitably rest. The study of methods pertains to the design skills we need in order to do our part in a larger field of interventions. The two together suggest a domain of knowledge and skills particular to the architectural design profession.

We hope readers will agree that research along the lines of the Open Building approach and the five interconnected characteristics discussed in this book is relevant for the architectural profession at large today. With the appropriate skills and knowledge, our profession will be better equipped for the realities that large projects present and for the increasingly complex distribution of design control in contemporary practice. Equally important, it can contribute to the creation of urban fabric of a fine-grained quality compatible with large projects of all kinds. Such fine-grained large undertakings will make them more resilient to change, more sustainable in the face of the existential threat of climate change and more responsive to human life in all of its rich diversity.

Perhaps more than answers, our research should be able to frame the pertinent questions in a compelling way. The Open Building approach has some answers but certainly not all, and ultimately, what is needed are changed attitudes, incentives and practices – both in the public sector and the private sector, both on the demand side and on the supply side. Inventive architects, planners, engineers and others will be able to find new strategies, but unless we ask the right questions and take a long view, we can't make the needed progress.

Postscript 2
Tools of The Trade

Figure 1 From a study for an urban tissue by Christina Gryboyanni, M.S. Arch. St. program, Massachusetts Institute of Technology

We close the book with the introduction and conclusion to a set of 10 short essays that one of us (John Habraken) wrote summarizing a lecture he gave at the Department of Architecture at the Massachusetts Institute of Architecture in 1996 called 'Tools of the Trade.' The 10 essays addressed a number of concepts and tools that will be familiar to readers of this book and is a kind of summing up:

1. Managing Parts
2. Against Program
3. Systems – Collective Properties
4. Patterns – Engaging the Client
5. Types – Sharing Wholes
6. Transformations
7. Levels of Intervention
8. Capacity vs. Function
9. Geometry and Abstraction
10. Positioning
11. Teaching Thematics

These essays were addressed to John Habraken's colleagues and students at MIT. We conclude the book with these words addressed to colleagues in the academy where both of us spent many years.

THE QUALITY OF THE COMMONS

"On various occasions, most recently in a lecture for the Department of Architecture at MIT, I have argued that our profession's avant-gardist attitude is at odds with our claim that everything to be built is a legitimate subject for architecture. That claim was first put forward in the heroic days of Modernism and is now generally accepted. Our profession is fully immersed in the everyday environment. This fact implies a new task for architecture, radically different from its historic mission. We have failed, so far, to take the measure of it.

The everyday environment is something continuous, both in time and space. It is also something we have in common: convention is its guide and consensus its mode of operation. These are issues of little value to a profession preoccupied with what is exceptional and new. Hence the new task demands a shift of attitude that does not come easily. The difficulty is not a matter of quality. The conventional can be of very high quality as many extant environments demonstrate. This quality of the common, in fact, is the benchmark against which individual interventions are measured. The merely exceptional and the merely new may fall short of it. The outstanding, of course, must surpass it.

The way we see ourselves as architects determines the knowledge we seek, the methods we apply, and the skills we possess. In what follows I will point out specific instances of method, skill, and knowledge of general value in the making of architecture that nevertheless are not part of our discourse today, nor taught with consistency, because they have to do with the quality of the common.

Less encumbered by real world constraints, our teaching, more so than our practice, reveals our hopes and dreams. It sanctifies and magnifies them. Today's teaching does not see the common as a source of architectural skills, methods, and knowledge, and pays little attention to cooperation and coordination among designers. Hence today's architecture students, who will be designing places of work, office buildings, schools, hospitals, shopping malls, airports, apartments and suburban houses, come out less well equipped than they could be.

A rift between our practice and our teaching is often perceived by parties from both sides, who seem to be equally perplexed and irritated by it. Because neither those practicing nor those teaching are in the habit of discussing the quality of the common, the latter will not figure in their dispute. Yet, this negligence may well be the cause of the rift, its symmetry keeping the dialogue off target.

Those among us eager to improve it, too often find that the everyday environment, driven by everyday practice, refuses what we want to contribute. Our expectations are not met, our hopes disappointed, our good intentions not honored. We may be jilted suitors because we do not know the object of our devotion for what it truly is. As long as we ignore how conventions and common values make the everyday environment work, it may elude us, regardless of the sincerity of our attempts and the nobility of our motivations.

In more than a century of upheavals, innovations, and transformations, the wholeness of the built environment has often been declared at risk, a concern easy to sympathize with. Yet this does not justify thinking ourselves designated saviors. The problem is comprehensive. We may well be part of it. Moreover, what is perceived as incoherent may be only unfamiliar. The built environment may be more structured than we think. In any case the everyday world will, eventually, impose its ways on us, rather than the other way around.

Hence our motivation can be selfish. The everyday world may or may not need us, but we need the everyday world, being already dependent on it for the bulk of our efforts. In our single-minded pursuit of the special we have forgotten that excellence grows from what is shared and that quality has its roots in common soil. What feeds on its own must eventually atrophy for want of substance. Architecture, no matter how one may define it, cannot afford to ignore where it comes from.

To facilitate saying what I have to say, I use two words in a special way. They must be explained.

I speak of 'a field' to evoke the wholeness of a certain built environment in all its variety and richness of form. A field is both the physical context for, and the subject of our designing. A field is built form as a continuity, known not by its outer boundaries, but by its inner properties.

Properties found in any field may be put in two categories. Some are peculiar and related to a single intervention only. Others are common to the field at large and expressive of the conventions and agreements governing it. Those held in common I will call the 'thematic' properties of the field. I call them thematic because they are sustained by actors accepting them as a 'theme,' making their own variations with them. Any intervention we make reveals qualities derived from both categories. It can be safely said that there is no such thing as a wholly thematic intervention nor a wholly un-thematic one. The most exceptional building will share some thematic aspects with the field it is located in. The most thematic building will have some unique features setting it apart.

I discuss ten ways in which the thematic is manifest in the field and connects to our designing. These do not, by any means, exhaust the thematic. Nor are they necessarily the best selection from it. I point them out because they come from my own experience, but I trust most of them, if not all, are familiar to my colleagues. All are a mixture of concepts (ways of seeing the built environment) and methods (ways of designing). The two, of course, are mutually dependent. Some of them have already been part of workshops done, at one time or another, by faculty of the MIT Department of Architecture. Others are less familiar. Several were the subject of a course in Thematic Designing I taught in the years before my retirement from MIT. Some I learned about from colleague architects, others from personal experience in research and practice.

On first sight the ten issues may seem disparate. Yet they all belong to the realm of the thematic, a territory largely uncharted,

POSTSCRIPT 2

but not necessarily unknown. I offer no map of it but argue it habitable and nourishing and therefore worthy of further exploration. All its features have to do with cooperation and coordination among designers and other decision makers in the field.

My exposition of the ten ways must necessarily remain brief and general. It would be easy to expand on each, but that would defeat the main purpose of this report, which is to argue a link between our neglect of thematics and the weakness of our methods and skills in teaching and practice. I should make it clear, too, that I report on my own experiences and insights and not based on any objective survey. It is hazardous to generalize about the built environment. While I am foolhardy enough to do so nevertheless, I try to reveal the prejudices and experiences my generalizations come from.

I draw lessons from historic environments where fine-grained fields of great beauty and richness still can be observed. But I try to pay particular attention to design tasks typical for our times: The large building – institutional, commercial, or residential – and the large project, where urban design and architecture merge. There the everyday environment assumes shapes never seen before, and the need for thematic knowledge and skills is most urgent. Large-scale interventions are here to stay and may only become larger in the future. We must accept them as the true challenge they are, but should be capable to make them, inside their large volumes, fine grained and resilient like our historic references.

Nobody builds alone. The very act of building is one of cooperation. Making a design is to communicate what is to be put together by others, for others. There is a limit to innovation. The world cannot be re-invented with every project. When designing, we must deal with what we consider peculiar to the job at hand. All else must necessarily remain in the realm of convention.

Indeed, there is only a profession to the extent that we can formalize a common base of knowledge, method, and skills. We know as much, but do not speak of it. It somehow does not fit in the way we explain ourselves. We must hence explain ourselves anew. We need theories that throw light on the thematic roots of architecture, and a historiography that traces them.

The study of thematic form will liberate us from self-imposed limitations that have become counterproductive. Knowledge, for instance, is by definition shared. When individual expression is the dominant concern, it will not accrue. Skills must first be appreciated as applied by others. When we are reluctant to borrow, the effort of acquiring them seems excessive. Skills come from methods and methods also are thematic by nature. When we only wish to do our own thing, they easily seem unnecessary constraints.

Likewise, forms like patterns and types, as I will discuss in chapters Four and Five, are vehicles for the coordination of our designing. When we do not seek common ground, we do not need them. Levels of intervention, as discussed in chapter Seven, hierarchically relate design responsibilities (for urban design, architectural design, and interior design, for instance). If the project is seen as a top to bottom job in the hands of a single party, the articulation of levels is easily ignored; the distinction becomes blurred and the product monolithic. Systems, discussed in chapter Three, are pre-determined sets of parts the spatial relations among which are rule based. We will only honor systemic constraints when we are prepared to accept rules and selections already used by others.

Thematic properties are valuable when designing is seen as a cooperative effort. Without such a view they remain unattractive. They demand dedication and exercise to be mastered properly, while no such discipline seems necessary when designing is primarily seen as a form of self-expression. Moreover, they lack glamour. But their application will make fields prosper.

What is shared needs to be taught – it is the very substance of curriculum. We expect the individual teacher to contribute something unique – rightly so. Nevertheless, an education must first of all be an initiation in common skills and their architectural application. The quality and scope brought to that task are what should distinguish a good school from a poor one. A gifted teacher, of course, will also be able to teach a gifted student how to transcend the thematic, not only rendering the field healthy, but making it bloom.

In the last chapter I expand a little on aspects of teaching thematics and how it relates to teaching studio. I draw from my experience with the Thematic Design course already mentioned earlier. This was not a course about designing, but a design course. Students were given assignments requiring them to make form. The emphasis, however, was on skill and method, not on meaning and expression. As thematics is the source of complexity and richness in the field, my hope was to make students feel at ease with complex form and the transformation of it. This, to my mind, constitutes the essence of our design abilities.

Finally, these being the days of the computer, a word should be added about the use of this instrument. Experience has convinced me that the professional pursuit of thematic qualities needs the computer. This is not surprising. The problem of thematics is a problem of our time. The tools of our time should be in sympathy with it. Thematics is based on principles of transformation. The computer can transform easily. Thematics produces complex forms. The computer helps to render complexity transparent and to make it manageable. Thematics implies the sharing among designers of data on form. Computers are good in making data accessible. In short, the computer is highly compatible with thematic designing.

•••••••••

I have spoken of thematic qualities in the field and of tools derived from them. Accepting my specific suggestions requires a shift of perspective. The way we see architecture, and hence ourselves, is involved. My report, first of all, wants to be a contribution to that re-examination.

Architecture, when all is said and done, pursues the beauty and autonomy of built form. We must consider how that worthy quest is to be conducted. Beauty in the built environment needs to be cultivated. Thematics is where cultivation of architectural form begins. It does not guarantee good architecture but provides a fertile soil for it.

Autonomy arises where architecture is no longer expressing its maker but touches universals. It belongs first of all to the field, which is too large, and too complex, to be the invention of a single party or the product of a single moment. The autonomy of the field governs the autonomy of architecture by lending it thematic order. Architecture's autonomy, to be sure, should not be confused with the autonomy of the architect, which does not exist. We are beholden to the field. Our work may be guided, it is hoped, by a desire for personal integrity. But we cannot demand acceptance of it for that reason only. Our task is to contribute to the field.

Those imbued with (post)modern values may find it difficult to take seriously the idea that the fate of architecture depends on the contemplation of the ordinary and the cultivation of the common. Moreover, the academic mind, trained to ask questions and mistrust convictions, may be reluctant to accept a proposed direction. Yet the latter may appreciate that, to see the way I suggest, some hard questions must be dealt with first. The former may remember how, not long ago, the avant-garde took pride in pursuing what many thought was beyond the pale.

Appendix One
A Brief Overview of the International Open Building Movement

THE ORIGINS IN THE NETHERLANDS

In 1964, 10 well-known architecture firms in the Netherlands, all fully involved in designing housing projects, decided to set up and finance a research office to study what the implementation of the Support/Infill idea would involve for architects. They worried that the national debate about housing focused on costs and production (prefab concrete panels, etc.), not about social and architectural issues. They felt increasingly marginalized. They hoped a research program in architecture for housing might make politicians and technocrats listen to them. Known as SAR (Stichting Architecten Research or Foundation for Architects Research), this was, as far as we know, the first broadly supported and focused research entity in the history of the architecture profession.

The initial research at the SAR focused on design tools (*SAR65*) to help architects design 'Supports' with the capacity to accommodate a variety of independent dwelling units initially and over time. The underlying concept was that control over the design of personal environments should rest with occupants. This meant separating design tasks, one task being focused on the architectural infrastructure all occupants share, the other task being the design of individual, independent dwelling units. Additional research on technical, regulatory and building economics issues through the 1970s and 1980s helped pave the way for continued developments toward Open Building implementation. That work also included extension of the ideas to urban design (e.g., *SAR73*; *Deciding on Density*, etc.).

A few pioneering architects were learning to design, and a few general contacting companies were willing to construct Support projects in the Netherlands in the early 1980s that did not cost more than the traditional way, although there was heavy resistance. Economic studies demonstrated that supports could in fact cost less (Dekker, 1982). This in itself was a breakthrough, because builders were generally reluctant to change their habits and give up what they saw as their way of assuring unified control and profit – the completion of an entire project from foundation to setting the tile and the fixtures and cabinets in the bathrooms. When given a set of drawings with the Infill taken out, they had the tendency to make cost proposals for construction that did not fairly represent the true value of a building without its Infill.

Several experimental projects during those decades were built as 'tests of concept.' Now, years later, many hundreds of multiunit housing projects based on separated design tasks are on record in various parts of the world, the results of clients wanting them for pragmatic reasons. More come to light every year, many undertaken by parties with no idea that there is a theoretical foundation and no idea of precedents. In a predictable fashion familiar to the field, a number of projects have been realized by architects who do not want to be seen as doing something like someone else has done before. A few exemplary residential Open Building projects, among many others, were discussed earlier in the book, and in two books: *Residential Open Building* (Spon, 2000) and *Residential Architecture as Infrastructure: Open Building in Practice* (Routledge, 2022). Many other published reports, academic studies and many professional journal articles in many languages have been published as well (see Appendix Two).

A number of formal organizations were launched in the Netherlands starting in the 1980s to carry the work of the SAR forward and to advocate for wider implementation. These included the Open Building Foundation (Stichting Open Bouwen or SOB) and OBOM (Open Building Development Model), the latter being a research group at the Technical University Delft launched by Professor Age van Randen in the mid-1980s. The OBOM research group undertook systematic technical studies in close collaboration with building industry partners and building regulators. Their work focused on questions of MEP systems deployment at both the support and the Infill levels, and their interfaces. In the 1990s, SAR-International Network was launched to lend structure to the informal, worldwide network of those who advocated the SAR ideas. These are chronicled in *Housing for the Millions* (Boosma et al., 2000).

But after a period of time, these organizations receded from an active role and were disbanded. Only now, at the time this is being written (2023), a new generation of academics and practitioners in the Netherlands is showing interest in these developments (www.openbuilding.co) (Kruit, 2022).

JAPAN

Between the 1970s to around 2000, a number of major research efforts were also launched in Japan, led by Professor Kazuo Tatsumi and his colleagues at Kyoto University and Professor Yositika Utida and his colleagues at the University of Tokyo. This work was undertaken with broad participation of government, academic and corporate entities. This led to a number of experimental projects (called S/I housing, standing for 'Skeleton/Infill'), the most notable being NEXT21 in Osaka, in 1994, shown earlier in the book. Many hundreds of projects are on record by private developers and public agencies.

In 2009, the Long-Life Housing Law was issued by the Japanese government based on the initiative of a now retired minister. It created a new certification system for residential buildings classified as excellent long-term housing.

The law assumed that a building is a combination of technical subsystems each of which has its own use-life, depending on wear-and-tear or user preferences. The most adaptable building is one in which each subsystem can be changed or replaced with minimum disturbance of other subsystems, based on the separation of what in the Japanese industry are called *skeleton* and *infill*.

The law offered technical solutions on the basis of which certification would be based. An easy-to-remember example is the requirement that vertical drainpipes must be renewed after about 50 years, while the building is expected to live more than a century. To meet the requirement, the law suggests that an empty space next to the functioning drain is made available during initial construction in which to install the replacement pipe. When a building meets all such conditions, the owner gets a predetermined tax break.

As it happened, many single-family homeowners took advantage of the law, but so far few if any of the large developers building large multifamily condominium projects have done so. The law is considered unsuccessful at least for the latter market. The Ministry of Land, Infrastructure, Transport and Tourism (MLIT), which administers the certification process, is, at the time of writing this book, frustrated with the so-called excellent long-term housing system, as only 2% of the 800,000 condominiums for sale between January 2010 and December 2020 have been certified.

Although the tax break, in theory, enables the producer to ask more money from the owner, there is no appreciation or incentive among the professionals to change their ways of working. Japan was the first where several Infill companies were founded, but to judge from what we know, while it promoted change, the 2018 law did not encourage innovation. Instead, it told the professions what solutions to implement (Minami, 2022).

FINLAND

The principles of Open Building were first studied in Finland in the 1990s. However, the concept did not spread widely within Finnish housing design practice for a number of years. Architect Ulpu Tiuri was among the first to study Open Building implementation in the Finnish context. In 1993, the city of Helsinki and the National Technology Agency TEKES organized an Open Building Technology competition to find new solutions towards citizen-oriented homes with the capacity to change over time. Esko Kahri (Kahri & Co. Architects at the time) submitted one of the winning proposals and built a block of rental dwellings together with VVO as the developer. Kahri was among the first architects in Finland to adopt the Open Building approach in his practice. In 2001, Helsinki City and the Finnish Technology Agency arranged a second Open Building competition in Helsinki. For their winning competition entry, Ark Open (formerly Kahri & Co.) architects, in cooperation with SATO (a developer), Tocoman (a data management company) and TEKES (the National Technology Agency), developed an online project management system called PlusHome for dwelling unit sales, customer service, and material quantities. This system allowed the smooth communication of every party's interests and needs. The main features of the PlusHome project were the use of Open Building methods (i.e., separation of design tasks), a variety of layouts and apartment sizes and a selection of surface materials, fixtures and appliances from which the future residents could choose, with immediate feedback on costs. As the project was successfully implemented and finished in 2005, SATO started shifting their own housing developments toward Open Building.

APPENDIX ONE: A BRIEF OVERVIEW OF THE INTERNATIONAL OPEN BUILDING MOVEMENT

Between the years 2005 and 2013, SATO realized, together with architect Esko Kahri, seven projects with over 700 dwelling units using the PlusHome concept.

The TILA (2007–09) and Harko (2019) projects were realized in Helsinki by SATO developers and designed by architect Pia Ilonen. The core idea of her approach provided residents with a 5-m- (16.4") high 'raw-space' unit of either 50 m² (538 ft²) or 102 m² (1,100 ft²). The small units could be merged or larger units separated in the future, according to the inhabitants' demands (from a legal perspective, this is not difficult). (See two Finnish projects presented earlier in the book.) (Franke, 2022).

KOREA

For decades, the Korean government has pursued a mass housing policy in its multifamily housing supply, accounting for almost 75% of all housing units, in order to solve the problems of a housing shortage. As a result, although the general building technology has developed over the years, the current housing process has generated a number of problems. These problems include lack of diversity to meet resident's diverse needs, absence of any concept of resource conservation to meet urgent global environmental issues and methods of construction that do not consider maintenance or change. As a result, the housing stock is rapidly aging. Demolition and rebuilding are required in only 30–40 years following initial construction. A new paradigm for housing design and construction is needed.

Given this background, Korea's national government research unit has been conducting research for more than 20 years on new design methods and building technology for apartment buildings and long-life housing. Based on these studies, the government implemented a housing performance indicator system in 2006. Despite this, the performance measures such as durability, variability and ease of maintenance did not improve. At that time, 100-year housing research and mock-up housing were constructed, and the results were provided to the private sector. However, the construction costs were 10–20% higher than the conventional approach. In order to solve this problem, a long-life housing (100-year) certification system was implemented in 2014, and research was conducted to reduce construction costs and to verify the technology and the delivery system. At the same time, a pilot project was built based on the results of the research, with completion expected in 2019. This work continues in the mission of 100-year housing in Korea (Kim and Yang, 2022).

PR CHINA

In PR China, a large but still informal network of architects, government agencies and researchers continues to write, produce design guidelines, and build projects in the long search for 100-year sustainable housing, planned for incremental change. This work started in the 1980s, led by Bao Jaisheng, at that time a professor at Nanjing University School of Architecture. He designed the Hui Feng Xin-Cun in Wuxi in 1987. Numerous postoccupancy studies have been published on this project. There were early contacts with Dutch and Japanese proponents of the Open Building approach. Architects Ma Yunyue and Zhang Qinnan led an early experimental project to encourage Infill companies to come into the market in Beijing. These were singular initiatives that had little influence at the time.

The most recent major governmental effort, led by Dr. Liu Dongwei, chief architect of the China Institute of Building Standard Design and Research, was launched in 2018, called Long-Life High-Quality Housing. This followed several years of intensive cooperation and professional exchanges with colleagues in Japan. (See Chapter 9, *Residential Architecture as Infrastructure: Open Building in Practice*.) This, in turn, has stimulated a rapid increase in so-called 'industrialized interior decoration' companies, which is the Chinese name for Infill systems companies. At the time of writing this book, several competitive companies were delivering tens of thousands of Infill packages per year. These developments are outlined earlier in the book when we discuss developments toward an Infill industry (Liu and Wu, 2022).

THE EMERGENCE OF INTERNATIONAL AND NATIONAL COUNCILS

In the belief that these ideas, practices and research supporting them needed a more formal international platform, an international Open Building Implementation network was formed in 1996, meeting in Japan, under the umbrella of CIB. CIB stands for

APPENDIX ONE: A BRIEF OVERVIEW OF THE INTERNATIONAL OPEN BUILDING MOVEMENT

the International Council for Research and Innovation in Building and Construction (https://cibworld.org). By 2022, this largely academic Open Building network (CIB W104) had more than 300 people in its contact list from more than 20 countries and had accumulated a substantial record of published, academic peer-reviewed papers, presented at yearly conferences in many countries around the world since its founding. Unfortunately, this body of work is not easily accessible at this time.

In 2017, the Council on Open Building (www.councilonopenbuilding.org) was launched in the US, with the goal of expanding the sustainability agenda to include the proposition that buildings and neighborhoods must be planned for incremental change, based on separating design tasks and cooperation among designers. In 2019, the Council held an international conference in Los Angeles – *Open Building for Resilient Cities* – with peer-reviewed papers from many countries and moderated panels including US and international practitioners in urban design, housing, healthcare and educational facilities design. The council organizes professional conferences, webinars, interdisciplinary design exercises and case studies demonstrating that the principle of separation of design tasks as a basis for planning for change is already conventional in some project types (e.g., urban design, commercial and retail real estate) but needs to become a general practice in all large, complex real property investments.

As of this writing (2023), a number of large architectural and engineering firms and clients are members of the council, which has a board of directors of 16, representing prominent architectural, engineering, and urban design firms as well as clients and academic researchers. A series of design workshops and webinars was ongoing in 2021–2023, organized in four 'strands': urban design, healthcare, educational facilities and housing. A second international conference under the theme *Beyond Single Use* was held for Boston, Massachusetts, in 2023.

At about the same time (2018), a group of architects in the Netherlands already designing large residential and mixed-use projects in an Open Building way organized themselves into a cooperative network (www.openbuilding.co), organizing research, teaching and other promotion activities around the theme of Open Cities, Open Architecture and Open Systems. The TU Delft and other Dutch architecture schools had faculty and students involved. The members of this group actively pursue this approach in practice, primarily in urban design, housing, mixed-use and adaptive-reuse projects, sometimes combining the roles of architect and developer.

Another network of architects and governmental agencies in PR China continues its advocacy of long-life housing. And a network of researchers in what is called the Global South continues its work to find breakthroughs and to collaborate with government agencies and practitioners in working toward Open Building Implementation under circumstances very much different from the initiatives in the so-called developed world (Osman, 2022).

READINGS

Boosma, K., van Hoogstraten, D., and Vos, Martijn. (2000). *Housing for the Millions: John Habraken and the SAR (1960–2000)*. NAI Publishers, Rotterdam.

Dekker, K. (1982). *Supports Can Be Less Costly*. Dutch Architect's Yearbook, Amsterdam.

Franke, C. (2022). Open Building in Finland. *Residential Architecture as Infrastructure: Open Building in Practice* (editor Kendall, S.). Routledge, London.

Kim, S., and Yang, H. (2022). Plan for 100-Year Housing in Korea. *Residential Architecture as Infrastructure: Open Building in Practice* (editor Kendall, S.). Routledge, London.

Kruit, C. (2022). Open Building's Recent Developments in the Netherlands. *Residential Architecture as Infrastructure: Open Building in Practice* (editor Kendall, S.). Routledge, London.

Liu, D., and Wu, Z. (2022). Research, Development and Implementation of Long-life Sustainable Housing in China. *Residential Architecture as Infrastructure: Open Building in Practice* (editor Kendall, S.). Routledge, London.

Minami, K. (2022). Japan's Act Concerning the Promotion of Long-Life Quality Housing. *Residential Architecture as Infrastructure: Open Building in Practice* (editor Kendall, S.). Routledge, London.

Osman, A. (2022). Open Building in the Global South. *Residential Architecture as Infrastructure: Open Building in Practice* (editor Kendall, S.). Routledge, London.

Appendix Two

Sources of Information of the Open Building Approach, Thematic Design and a Glossary of Terms

Related books and publications in English (listed chronologically by publication date)

Habraken, H.J. (1962). *Supports: An Alternative to Mass Housing*. Published in Dutch under the title: *De Dragers en de Mensen*. Scheltema en Holkema, Amsterdam.

Habraken, N.J., and van Olphen, Hans. (1965). *SAR 65, Brief Outline of the SAR Principles and Methodology (SAR65)*. First Publication of the Basic Principles of SAR Method for Support Design. SAR, Eindhoven (Available in *The Short Works of John Habraken*. Routledge, London, 2023).

Habraken, N.J., and van Olphen, Hans. (1965). *SAR65: Rules for Design: A Summary*. One of the Two Fundamental Reports on the Work of the SAR, Eindhoven.

Propst, Robert. (1968). *The Office: A Facility Based on Change*. Business Press International, Elmhurst, IL.

Habraken, N.J. (1970). *Three R's for Housing*. Scheltema & Holkema, Amsterdam, originally published in *Forum*, vol. XX, no. 1, 1966.

Habraken, N.J. (1972). *Supports: An Alternative to Mass Housing*. English edition, Praeger, New York (1999) Reissue (editor Teicher, J.). Urban International Press, UK (2021) Reissued Under the Routledge Revivals Open Building Series (2019) (editor Kendall, S.).

Habraken, N.J., Reyenga, Henk, and van der Werf, Frans. (1973). *SAR 73, the Methodical Formulation of Agreements in the Design of Urban Tissues*. First Publication on Basic Principles of SAR Method on Urban Tissue Design, SAR, Eindhoven.

Habraken, N.J., Boekhold, J.T., Thijssen, A.P., and Dinjens, P.J.M. (1976). *Variations: The Systematic Design of Supports*. MIT Press, Cambridge, MA.

Dluhosch, E. (editor). (1976). *The Cultivation of the Ordinary*. IF (Industrialization Forum), Université de Montréal, Montreal, Canada.

Habraken, N.J., Kapteyns, Joop, and Carp, John. (1977). *Deciding on Density: An Investigation into High Density, Low Rise, Allotment for the Waldeck Area, the Hague*. SAR, Eindhoven.

Utida, Y. (1977). *Open Systems in Building Production*. Shokoky-Sha Publishers, Tokyo.

Van der Werf, F. (1980). Molenvliet-Wilgendonk: Experimental Housing Project, Papendrecht, the Netherlands. *Beyond the Modern Movement: The Harvard Architecture Review*. MIT Press, Cambridge, MA, vol. 1, pp. 160–169, Spring.

Habraken, N.J., Aldrete-Haas, J.A., Chow, R., Hille, T., Krugmeier, P., Lampkin, M., Mallows, A., Mignucci, A., Takase, Y., Weller, K., and Yokouchi, Y. (1981). *The Grunsfeld Variations: A Demonstration Project on the Coordination of a Design Team in Urban Design*. MIT Laboratory for Architecture and Planning, Cambridge.

Dekker, K. (1982). *Supports Can Be Less Costly*. Dutch Architect's Yearbook, Amsterdam, The Netherlands.

Hatch, C. Richard. (1984). *The Scope of Social Architecture*. Van Nostrand Reinhold, New York, part 1, chapters 2–6, pp. 22–77.

Carp, J.C. (1985). *Keyenburg: A Pilot Project*. Stichting Architecten Research, Eindhoven, The Netherlands.

Habraken, N.J. (1985). *The Appearance of the Form: Four Essays on the Position Designing Takes Between People and Things*. Awater Press, Cambridge (Reprinted as Part of the Routledge Open Building Series – Revivals, 2019).

Habraken, N.J. (1988). *Transformations of the Site*. Awater Press, Cambridge (The Precursor of *The Structure of the Ordinary*. MIT Press, Cambridge, 1998).

Templemans P.H. (1990). *Towards a Flexible Stock of Buildings: The Problem of Cost Calculations for Buildings in the Long Run*. Proceedings, CIB World Congress, New Zealand.

Prins, M., Bax, C., and Plat, T. (1990). *A Decision Support System for Building Flexibility and Costs: Design and Decision Support Systems in Architecture*. Kluwer Academic Publishers, Amsterdam, The Netherlands.

Hamdi, N. (1991). *Housing Without Houses: Participation, Flexibility, Enablement*. Van Nostrand Reinhold, New York.

Van Randen, A. (1992). *Entangled Building . . .?* Werkgroep OBOM, Delft, The Netherlands.

Fassbinder, H., and Proveniers, A. (1992). *New Wave in Building: A Flexible Way of Design, Construction and Real Estate Management*. Eindhoven University of Technology, Eindhoven, The Netherlands.

Iselin, D., and Lemer, A. (editors). (1993). *The Fourth Dimension in Building: Strategies for Minimizing Obsolescence*. Building Research Board, National Research Council, National Academy Press, Washington, DC.

Van der Werf, F. (1993). *Open Ontwerpen* (in Dutch). 010 Publishers, Rotterdam.

Reijenga, Postma Haag. (1993). *Renovation by Open Building System, Princes Beatrixlaan, Voorburg* (editor Yagi, Koji). Process Architecture, Tokyo, vol. 112, pp. 44–46.

Hasegawa, A (editor). (1994). *SD 25: Collective Housing of the Near Future: NEXT21 – Experiments in Symbiotic Living with Nature*. Kajima Institute Publishing Company, Tokyo.

Dekker, K. (1998). *Consumer Oriented Renovation of Apartments: Voorburg, The Netherlands*. CIB Best Practices Papers. CIB Web Site. www.cibworld.nl.

Beisi, J. (1998). *Adaptable Housing Design*. Southeast University Press, PRC, Nanjing.

Lahdenperä, P. (1998). *The Inevitable Change: Why and How to Modify the Operational Modes of the Construction Industry for the Common Good*. The Finnish Building Center, Helsinki.

Tiuri, U., and Kendall, S. (1998). *Characteristics of Open Building in Experimental Housing: Proceedings of the Open Building Workshop and Symposium*. CIB Report Publication 221, Rotterdam.

Tiuri, U., and Hedman, M. (1998). *Developments Towards Open Building in Finland*. Teknillisen korkeakoulun arkkitehtiosaston julkaisuja 50, Helsinki.

Habraken, N.J. (1998). *The Structure of the Ordinary: Form and Control in the Built Environment* (editor Teicher, J.). MIT Press, Cambridge, MA.

Gann, D. (1999). *Flexibility and Choice in Housing*. The Policy Press, University of Bristol, UK.

Kendall, S., and Teicher, J. (2000). *Residential Open Building*. Spon, London.

Boosma, K., van Hoogstraten, D., and Vos, Martijn. (2000). *Housing for the Millions: John Habraken and the SAR (1960–2000)*. NAI Publishers, Rotterdam.

Kendall, S. (editor). (2001). Infill/Fit-Out Systems: Toward a Residential Infill Industry. *Open House International*. Urban International Press, Gateshead, UK, vol. 26, no. 3.

Kahri, E., Anttonen, S., Esko Enkovaara, E., Illonen, P., Juha Kämäräinen, J., and Viita, P. (editors). (2001). *Resident View to Urban Living*. Rakennustieto Oy, Helsinki.

Tarpio, J., and Tiuri, U. (2001). *Infill Systems for Residential Open Building; Comparison and Status Report of Developments in Four Countries*. Helsinki University of Technology, Department of Architecture 75, Helsinki.

Goldhoorn, Bart. (2001). *The Free Plan. Russia's Shell and Core Apartment Buildings*. Project Russia 20. A-Fond Publishers, Moscow and Amsterdam.

Friedman, A. (2001). *The Grow House*. McGill-Queen's University Press, Montreal & Kingston.

Friedman, A. (2002). *The Adaptable House: Designing Homes for Change*. McGraw Hill, New York.

Leupen, B., Heijne, R., and van Zwol, J. (editors). (2005). *Time Based Architecture*. 010 Publishers, Rotterdam.

Habraken, N.J. (2005). *Palladio's Children: Seven Essays on Everyday Environment and the Architect* (editor Teicher, J.). Taylor and Francis, London.

NEXT21 Editorial Committee. (2005). *NEXT21: All About NEXT21*. Osaka Gas Co., Ltd., Osaka, Japan.

Kendall, S., and Office of Properties and Buildings (editors). (2006). *Systems Separation-Open Building at the Inselspital Bern, INO Project; A Symposium Focused on the INO Hospital Project New Center for Intensive Care, Emergency and Surgery*. Stampfli Verlag AG, Bern, Switzerland.

Ellingham, Ian, and Fawcett, William. (2006) *New Generation Whole-Life Costing: Property and Construction Decision-Making Under Uncertainty*. Taylor & Francis, New York.

Kendall, S. (2006). *A New American Townhouse*. Trafford Publishing, Victoria, Canada.

Till, J., and Schneider, T. (2007). *Flexible Housing*. The Architectural Press. Oxford, UK.

Adaptability and Innovation in Healthcare Facilities: Lessons from the Past for Future Developments. (2008). *The Howard Goodman Fellowship Report*. The Health and Care Infrastructure Research and Innovation Centre (HaCIRIC), London, UK.

Friedman, A. (2011). *Decision Making for Flexibility in Housing*. Urban International Press, Gateshead, UK.

Ilonen, Pia, et al. (2011). TILA Housing, Helsinki. *Arkkitehti (Finnish Architectural Review)*. Finnish Association of Architects, Helsinki, vol. 4, pp. 28–39.

Jia, Beisi (editor). (2011). Architecture Beyond Space: Time, People and Architecture. *New Architecture 6/2011*. New Architecture Magazine Publishers, PRC, Shenzhen, pp. 6–88.

Kendall, S.H., Kurmel, T.D., and Dekker, K.D. (2012). *Healthcare Facilities Design for Flexibility. Final Report*. Cost Modeling Workshop: Analysis of Initial Capital Asset Investment and Future Costs of Adaptation. Prepared by the National Institute of Building Sciences, Washington, DC, pp. 153–174.

Kahri, E., Illonen, P., Juha Kämäräinen, J., and Viita, P. (2014). *Helsinki Seaside Sustainable Quarter*. Proceedings, UIA Architect Conference, Durban, SA.

Habraken, N.J., Mignucci, A., and Teicher, J. (2014). *Conversations with Form: A Workbook for Students of Architecture*. Routledge, London.

Kahri, E., et al. (editors). (2016). *Construction in Residential Design, General Criteria*. Rakennustieto Oy © Building Information Foundation, Helsinki.

Kahri, E. (editor). (2016). *Guide RT 93–11232 Transformation in Housing Design: Status and Main Design*. Rakennustieto Oy © Building Information Foundation, Helsinki.

Lifschutz, A. (editor). (2017). *Loose-Fit Architecture-Designing Buildings for Change*. John Wiley and Sons, Oxford, UK, AD 05, vol. 87.

Kendall, S. (editor). (2019). *Healthcare Architecture as Infrastructure: Open Building in Practice*. Routledge, London.

APPENDIX TWO: SOURCES OF INFORMATION OF THE OPEN BUILDING APPROACH AND A GLOSSARY OF TERMS

Matsumura, S. (2020). *Open Architecture for the People: Housing Development in Post-War Japan*. Routledge, Oxford and New York.

Kendall, S. (editor). (2022) *Residential Architecture as Infrastructure: Open Building in Practice*. Routledge, London.

Akbar, Jamel. (2021) *Crisis in the Built Environment: The Case of the Muslim City*. Insan Publications, Istanbul, Turkey.

Kendall, S., and Dale, J. (editors). (2023) *Short Works of John Habraken*. Routledge, London.

Kendall, S., and Habraken, N.J. (Forthcoming, 2024). *Open Building for Architects: Professional Knowledge for an Architecture of Everyday Environment*. Open Building Series, Routledge.

A FEW KEY WEBSITES

www.thematicdesign.org
www.habraken.com
www.drstephenkendall.com
www.councilonopenbuilding.org
www.openbuilding.co
www.top-up.amsterdam/gebouw-top-up/
https://marckoehler.com
https://mei-arch.eu/en//

Glossary of Key Terms

Open Building: The international movement committed to making the Open Building approach normative. Open Building design seeks to deal with the proper separation of design tasks, recognizing the hierarchical organization of built environment already well understood in the distinction of the professions of urban planner, urban designer, architect, interior architect, furniture and equipment designers, etc. This is the essence of the built environment as a living organism. Separation of design tasks is an essential aspect of built environments that are alive and sustained and yet continue to evolve and retain coherence. For example, in designing a large office building project, the task of designing independent units of occupancy is separated from the task of designing what all the units of occupancy share. The same principle can be applied to many other kinds of projects, including laboratories, shopping centers, medical and educational facilities, large residential projects, campuses and neighborhoods. One of the reasons to separate design tasks is to reduce costs and distribute risk and to provide decision flexibility; another is to enable work at various levels to proceed simultaneously; another is to enable independent units of occupancy to change without disturbing other units of occupancy or the shared infrastructure. This requires that each unit of control (e.g., a dwelling unit in a building or a building in an urban tissue) is in fact fully independent, technically and legally.

Thematic design: Everyday environments always have been highly thematic. We immediately recognize a Venetian Gothic palace, an Amsterdam canal house, a Georgian London terraced house, or a Pompeiian courtyard house as members of particular form families, inseparable parts of the urban fabrics that were shaped with them. Other built fabrics, on first sight, may seem chaotic and difficult to read, but on closer scrutiny, we always find thematic aspects. Every culture has its own conventions, habits and ways of working and using. In the past, biased Western observers thought traditional Middle Eastern urban environments disorganized while, in fact, they have a highly structured thematic complexity. The architectural themes have different names like pattern, type, style or system. As in music, we recognize a theme by what is constant in the variations that we hear or, in this case, see. Form themes are what designers operating in a given location share, while the individual variations are their own. The balance between theme and variations is the most fascinating aspect of any built fabric.

Cultivation of everyday environment implies designing with themes. This demands particular skills and ways of working. How to find a good balance between theme and variation, between what we share and what we do individually? How do themes come about? How to decide, for instance, on the consistent adoption of a building type or entryway pattern or familiar issues like setback rules and height restrictions? Is it by top-down rules, collective ad-hoc agreements or implicit common understandings among designers? Often, a single higher-level design offers a shared context for many lower-level designs and, by so doing, sets thematic constraints for them that are considered reasonable and representative. Urban design, for instance, makes a shared context for individual architectural designs, assuming they will follow certain architectural types or patterns. In a similar way, a Base Building design makes a shared context for individual residential units of a certain kind. How do we know if a higher-level design offers the right context for lower-level design preferences? How do we inspire lower-level variety?

Levels: The concept of levels is directly related to the design of Infrastructure systems. For example, urban designers 'operate on another level' than the architect. In this case, the built environment is divided into two groups of things: those that are decided about by the urban designer and those that are the concern of the architect. This distinction is evident in explaining what happens when things change on one level or another. The architect designs a building within the context established and documented by the urban designer. She must respect, for instance, the layout of streets and rights-of-way and the division of lots in the block and, for example, certain patterns, themes and typologies. But within that context, she is free to act and make her own variations. She can change the design of the building in many ways. Indeed, different architects can build different buildings in different places in an urban tissue but will share the street network and the types

GLOSSARY OF KEY TERMS

and patterns that are meant to yield coherent variety, explicitly notated in the urban designers' plan. Although the urban design constrains their work, they are free within those constraints to do their own thing. However, when the street network must be changed for whatever reason, the buildings may have to adjust. The urban designer cannot act without affecting the designs of the architect. The relation, therefore, is asymmetrical and hierarchical. Change on the level of the building does not affect the higher level of the urban design, but change in the urban design affects the lower level of the buildings.

Those who work in a given location relate 'horizontally' on the same level of intervention. Those who relate 'vertically' do so from different levels of intervention: looking upward to inhabit and honor the context shaped earlier, or downward to frame and stimulate the actions of those who come in later. These relations are relations of forms; forms sharing certain aspects, forms interpreting a given context, forms setting context for others: All designing is intervention, and each intervention triggers response. Change of form is the language we share. This is the meaning of a hierarchical structure of the built environment.

Capacity: Capacity means that something can accommodate something else, often an unknown something. This is a familiar concept; for example, when we walk into a room in an apartment we are considering buying, we think to ourselves, "I could use this room as a home office or perhaps a bedroom" or "We're thinking of our future family needs, so I'm wondering if I can add a second bathroom and divide this big room into two bedrooms" or "I wonder if I could buy the apartment next door when my elderly parents come back to live with us, since we don't want to move." We are doing an informal capacity analysis or exploration when we think this way. Beyond this informal way, more formal and precise methods are available and needed to assure clients of the proposed design. In architectural terms, a building that offers capacity will have a 'higher-level' configuration of spaces and physical forms that can accommodate a variety of configurations on a 'lower level.' That means that the configuration on the lower level (e.g., walls and piping) can change without forcing change on the higher level (the system of physical elements belonging to the Base Building decisions), but a change on the higher level will force an adjustment to the lower level. In the context of the separation of Base Building and fit-out, capacity refers to a range of variations in floor plan and use within the constraints of a given Base Building.

Sharing thematic qualities: When design tasks are separated (a basic principle of the Open Building approach), and yet a fully alive coherence is desired from the work of multiple players over time, shared values are essential. We might call these conventions. For example, in urban design, it makes sense that certain patterns, themes and typologies are agreed upon to be shared – to harmonize various interventions, each of which can make its own variation on these shared architectural values. We might call this thematic design. Historic fabrics that have sustained themselves for centuries are good examples (think of Boston's Back Bay, Amsterdam's canal environment, Bologna's arcaded streets, Kyoto's historic Machia neighborhoods, etc.), contemporary urban tissues less so because we have developed an unfortunate tendency to emphasize how each intervention can be as different as possible from the next; the only thing bringing about coherence then is coercive regulations.

Design methods for Open Building: The built environment as an autonomous and complex living entity that we want to cultivate (it will be there whatever we professionals do) raises questions of the skills we need to do so successfully. Once we recognize that we must cooperate and interrelate among designers working on a common task, **design methodology** – the study of *how* we design and the development of new and more effective **ways of designing** – becomes an urgent and necessary subject. For instance, the straightforward and reasonable question of how we can find out whether an empty Base Building can allow the kind of unit designs that we (and our client) value triggers various methodological responses (e.g., capacity analysis). How we can best reach and **notate agreements about shared form** (e.g., themes and types and dimensional constraints) in a given urban fabric is a methodological question as well. A few methodological design tools are already available, such as capacity analysis, the use of zones, sectors, basic variants and band grids and the principle of sharing values and reaching agreements about such elements of architecture as typology, patterns, systems, variants and structure.

Infrastructure: Infrastructure is the general term for the basic physical systems of a business, region or nation. Examples of infrastructure include transportation systems, communication networks and sewage, water and electric systems. In respect to the Open Building approach, infrastructure is the hierarchical organization of basic elements of a complex system in which higher levels of the system dominate lower levels, but lower levels are free to change or be replaced by more up-to-date parts performing the same function. For example, electrical service constitutes an infrastructure system in itself. From the power generation facility to the laptop or electrical appliance, there are many 'levels,' each deployed, owned, leased and managed by a different party, crossing many territorial boundaries and each capable of being replaced with higher-performing parts while maintaining the entire system's functionality. The same can be said for a public water supply or a public sewage/wastewater system, all dependent on good interfaces between levels of intervention. In Open Building, the urban design dominates the buildings, and the buildings dominate the interior fit-out, each a level of decision-making that can be separated to good effect, when good interfaces are used.

Base building (sometimes called Support, Primary System or skeleton): A Base Building is a complete architectural infrastructure (not a structural skeleton), with capacity for variable size and layout of units of occupancy, ready for independent fit-out. It consists of all spaces and building elements that are common to all units of occupancy. These common elements generally include the building's structure, enclosure (or most of it), elevators, fire egress stairs (and perhaps corridors) and all common or shared MEP systems serving independent units of habitation. Walls or parts of walls separating units of occupancy (called demising walls in the US) are considered to be part of the Base Building once fixed but are generally able to be changed (with obvious implications to adjoining territories) without disturbing the permanent Base Building.

Infill (sometimes called fit-out or Secondary System): Refers to a what is decided independently for each unit of occupancy. An Infill system is the integrated bundle of products and services used to fill-in a 'serviced' space in a building, to make it ready for use or habitation. Infill includes everything installed within the legal (and fire) boundaries of a single unit of occupancy, that is, within the walls or floors separating that unit of occupancy from other such units. The Infill bundle includes the MEP (mechanical, electrical and plumbing) systems specific to and within the occupied space, as well as walls, doors, cabinets, plumbing fixtures, lighting fixtures and most if not all surface finishes. The Infill might include some of the façade (e.g., windows) if legally defined to be part of the unit of habitation. Whether part of a building's façade is Infill or Base Building is a technical as well as a cultural question; whether the Infill includes the bathroom is another question to be resolved in each case.

Infill business: An Infill company offers the service of designing and fitting out a legally defined space in a Base Building, under a unified contract with all the installers and products required (i.e., not the use of independent subcontractors). This unified contract assures a good product/service, delivered on time for the agreed-upon price. Certified Infill companies meet recognized performance standards governing all similar companies in a given governmental jurisdiction.

Index

Note: **Boldface** page references indicate tables. *Italic* references indicate figures.

access system *33*, 34
adaptive reuse study (office to residential): alternative to conversion 161–162; capacity analysis in 154; challenge of 154; design constraints 154, 160; drainage piping in bathroom 182–183, *182*; DWV systems 157; fixtures 157–159, *158*; Kales Building 160–161, *161*, *162*; MEP constraints 155–157, *156*; overview 154; piping traffic inside walls 159–161, *160*; problems encountered in 183; toilets 158–159, *158*; vertical MEP pipe shaft positioning study 162–164, *163*, *164*; waste piping 157–159, *159*; see also design process for building conversion using capacity analysis
Alexander, Christopher 123–124
alpha zone 147–148, *147*, *148*
Amsterdam canal houses (the Netherlands) 122, *122*
Amsterdam extension (the Netherlands) 133, *133*
Arkitema Architects (building architects) 14, 16

Back Bay (Boston, Massachusetts, USA) 122, *122*, *123*
Base Building: capacity and 112; concept 19, 111; definition 111; designing 114, 142, 145–148, *145*; Infill separation and 111–112, 116; lifestyles and, designing to 129; Oregon Health Center 91–92, *92*; Plus-Home 53; principles for designing 142; production process 113; redefinition 196–197; Santa Monica High School Discovery Building 105; separation of design tasks and 116; Shenzhen University Engineering School 99, *100*; space allocation in 147; TILA 57, *58*; see also Support
bathroom drainage piping 182–183, *183*
Beijing Government Social Housing Center 193
Beijing Housing Industrialization Group Co. Ltd (BHIG) 193
beta zone 147–148, *147*, *148*
Beyond Single Use conference (2023) 209
Bijdendijk, Frank 185–187
Bosworth, William Welles 137
bottle-crate image 71–72, *71*
Broadacre City development concept 117
built projects *see specific name*

capacity: Base Building and 112; concept of 132; for dwelling variation 54; linking form to function 144; question about 140
capacity analysis: in adaptive reuse study 154; definition 140–141; design process and 141–142; evaluation and 112, 143–144; grids and 149–153, *151*, *152*, *153*; of Kales Building 160–161, *161*, *162*; margins and 145–149, *145*, *146*, *147*, *148*, *149*; MEP constraints and, studying 155–157, *156*; methodological problem of 142–143; overview 6, 140; zones and 145–149, *145*, *146*, *147*, *148*, *149*; see also design process for building conversion using capacity analysis
change: balancing permanence with 115, 135–139; in everyday built environment, importance of studying 137–139; large projects and 137; levels and 130–131; longitudinal studies of 137–139; technical strategies for handling 136–137
Chicago School 120
Chikazumi, Shinichi 44, 50
China *see* Infill industry in PR China; PR China; *specific built project name*
China Construction Technology Consulting (CCTC) 189
China-Japan Long-Life Sustainable Housing International Summit Forum (2010) 189
China Real Estate Association 189
'commons, the' 6, 202–205
control of space 127–128, *128*
Conzen, M. R. G. 138
cooperation and separation of design tasks and 2–3
Council on Open Building 209
COVID-10 pandemic 120
crop rotation 32–33

Dale, John R. (architect) 76, 103
defensible space 128
delta zone 147–148, *148*
Design and Assessment Standard for Long-Life Sustainable Housing (2018) 190
design constraints 154
design process for building conversion using capacity analysis: advantages of 183; demising walls placement for basic unit sizes/margins 165, *165*, *166*; floor plan study 164–165, *165*; individual dwelling unit development 165–166, *166*; MEP stacks location 167–171, *167*, *168*, *169*, *170*, *171*, *172*, *173*, *174*, *175*, *176*, *177*, *178*, *179*, *180*, *181*; overview 164; room placement inside unit 166–167, *166*, **166**, *167*, **167**
disentanglement 33, 72, 115, 136
'dough,' kneading 30–33
downward relations 131–132
drainage piping 133, *133*, 182–183, *182*
Dutch Foundation for Architects Research (SAR) 110, 113–114, 206
DWV (drain, waste, vent) systems 157

education built projects: longitudinal study of 138; Santa Monica High School Discovery Building 102–108; Shenzhen University Engineering School 96–101; *see also specific name*; urban/campus built projects
Engineering School (PR China) *see* Shenzhen University Engineering School
everyday built environment: balancing permanence and change 115, 135–139; change in, importance of studying 137–139; characteristics, overview 9, 115; definition 3; longitudinal studies of change in 137–139; note about characteristics 115–116; Open Building approach designs and 115, 125–126; separating design tasks 115–120; territory, importance of/understanding 115, 126–128; thematic design 115, 121–126; *see also* hierarchy, inherent in everyday built environment; *specific characteristic*

façades: glass 128; Molenvliet 41–42; NEXT21 46, *47*, 124–125, *135*; Place des Vosges 131; Shenzhen University Engineering School 98; Sydhavnen/Sluseholmen 16–17
Finland 207–208; *see also specific built project names*
fixtures 157–159, *158*
floor plans/systems: INO Intensive Care Facility 72–73, *72*; Molenvliet *41*; NEXT21 *45*, *47*; Oregon Health Center *93*, *94*; Plus-Home *55*; Sammy Ofer Heart Building *81*, *82*; Shenzhen University Engineering School 98–99, *98*, *99*; TOPUP *65*, *66*
form-based codes, adoption of 121
Frantzen, Tom 64
Fukao, Seiichi 44

Garnier, Tony 117
Gaudi, Antonio 122–123
government and the Open Building approach 198–199
green spaces 26, 33, *33*, 42, 46, *46*
grids *45*, 149–153, *151*, *152*, *153*
Grönig Arkitekter 16

Habraken, John 202
Hassan Fathy's mud-brick vaulting systems 125
healthcare built projects: COVID-19 pandemic and 120; INO Intensive Care Facility 69–77; longitudinal study of 138; Oregon Health Center 84–95; Sammy Ofer Heart Building 78–83; separation of design tasks in 119–120; *see also specific name*
HED (building architects) 106
Heneng (Heneng-home) 190–191, *191*, *192*, *193*
HENN Architects 30, 35

hierarchy, inherent in everyday built environment: change and levels 130–131; concept of levels and 128–129, *129*; disappearance of levels 133–134; higher level, relating to 131; historical examples of use of levels 129–130, *130*; Infill level 134–135, *135*, 184; levels of intervention and 9, 115; lower level, relating to 131–132; modernist legacy and levels 134; process selection and 129, *129*; same level, relating to 132–133
historic preservation movement 121
Holabird and Roche Marquette Building (Chicago, Illinois, USA) *119*
horizontal relations 132–133
Hutong gate (Beijing, PR China) *126*

Infill: Base Building design from 145; Base Building separation and 111–112, 116; definition 111; Heneng Infill system 190–191, *191*, *192*, *193*; layouts 67; level 134–135, *135*, 184; production process 113; Santa Monica High School Discovery Building 105; V3 system 194–195, *194*, *195*, *196*; *see also* residential Infill industry
Infill industry in PR China: Base Building redefinition 196–197; government initiatives 189–190; Heneng and 190–191, *191*, *192*, *193*, *193*; V3 system development 193–194, *194*, **194**, *195*, *196*
information/data management system 54, *54*
Initiative to Build Long-life Sustainable Housing 189
INO Intensive Care Facility (Inselspital, Bern, Switzerland): aerial view *77*; background information 71–72; bottle-crate comparison 71–72, *71*; changes to Secondary System 73–74, *74*; corridor spaces 76; exam room 76; floor system 72–73, *72*; light wells 76; partitioning building systems 73; Phase One 69, 77; Phase Two 76, 77; Primary System 72, *73*, *74*, 76; project data 70; Secondary System 72, *74*; spatial organization *74*; surgery suite layout 73–74, *75*; System Separation and 71–74, 76; technical system organization *74*; Tertiary System 72, *74*
Inselspital Hospital Campus Master Plan (Bern, Switzerland): aerial view *30*; background information 30; 'dough,' kneading 30–33; ideas, key 32–33; implementation sequence *36*; model *29*; objectives 31–32; overview 31; project data 29–30; requirements, implementation 33–34, *33*, *36*; rulebook 31–32; sustainability and 35–36; topography 30; urban quarters 30, *31*, *32*; zoning plan *35*
interior design profession 118–119
International Council for Research and Innovation in Building and Construction (CIB) 208–209
International Seminar on Urban Form (ISUF) 138

INDEX

Japan 207; *see also specific built project names*
Japan-China Association for Building and Housing Industry 189

Kahri, Esko 53, 207–208
Kales Building (Detroit, Michigan, USA) 160–161, *161*, *162*
Katwikjk Inner Harbor Project (Katwikj, the Netherlands): aerial view *25*; background information 26; collaborators 26, 28; colonnade *28*; concept drawing *28*; project data 25; separation of design tasks and 28; street view *27*; Van Olphen's comments 26–28
Korea 208
Kroll, Lucien 150

La Pedrera apartment buildings 122–123, *123*
large housing projects 4; *see also residential built projects; specific name*
Le Corbusier 46, 117, 127
LEED certification system 184
Lee, Joshua 138
levels: change and 130–131; connection *33*, 34; Infill 134–135, *135*, 184; of intervention 9, 115; Oregon Health Center *93*, *94*; *see also* hierarchy, inherent in everyday built environment
Liu, Dr. Dongwei 208
longitudinal studies of change in everyday built environment 137–139
Long-Life High-Quality Housing 208
Long-Life Housing Law 207
Loos, Adolf 16

Macchi, Giorgio 71
Machiya dwellings (Kyoto, Japan) 122, *123*
Mansart, Jules Hardouin 129–131
margins 145–149, *145*, *146*, *147*, *148*, *149*
Massachusetts Institute of Technology (MIT) complex 137, *137*
MEP (mechanical, electrical/data and plumbing): constraints 155–157, *156*; in Oregon Health Center 91; organization 91; stacks location 167–171, *167*, *168*, *169*, *170*, *171*, *172*, *173*, *174*, *175*, *176*, *177*, *178*, *179*, *180*, *181*
Minami, Kazunobu 138
Molenvliet (Papendrecht, the Netherlands): aerial view *37*, *40*; background information 38; courtyard entry *41*; entry courtyard *41*; façade 41–42; garden, rooftop *42*; ground-floor layout *41*; interior view *127*; personalization over time 42, *42*; project data 37; Support 38, 40, *40*; urban tissue and 38, *38*, *39*

Narváez, Jorge Iván Andrade 138
Netherlands, the 206; *see also specific built project names*
Newman, Oscar 128
NEXT21 (Osaka, Japan): background information 44; Chikazumi's comments 50; cooperation on two levels 41; coordination grids, dimensional/positional 44, *45*; as experimental project 207; façade 46, *47*, 124–125, *135*; floor plans *45*, *47*; future context for 49–50; gardens, private 46, *46*; interiors of units 47, *47*, *48*, *49*; levels/'tables' 50; as open building research laboratory 48–50; present context for 49–50; project data 43; urban context *43*

office building design 118–119, *118*, *119*, 131, *132*
Open Building approach: applications of 4–5; argument for 199–200; communication 113–114; contribution of, most important 6; coordination, problem of 112–113; councils, emergence of international and national 208–209; definition of 9; evaluation 112–114; everyday built environment designs and 115, 125–126; examples of 9; in Finland 207–208; fundamental principle of 109; government and 198–199; in Japan 207; in Korea 208; large housing projects and 4; movement 4, 206–209; in the Netherlands 206; operations 113–114; origins of 109; overview of 6–7; practice and, focus/improvement 1, 5; in PR China 198, 208; purpose of 1–2; research agenda, new 201; separation of design tasks and 1–2, 109, 116; sources of information on 4, 210–212; sustainability and 1; terminology 111–112, 213–215; 'Tools of the Trade' and 202–205; urban problem and, prototypical 109–111; *see also specific built project example*
Open Building Development Model (OBOM) 206
Open Building Foundation (Stichting Open Bouwen or SOB) 206
Open Building Implementation network 208–209
Open Building for Resilient Cities conference (2019) 209
Open Building Technology competition 207
open space 32, 35, 38, 164
Oregon Health Center (Portland, Oregon, USA): background information 86; Base Building 91–92, *92*; concept planning 88; design process 86, *87*, 88; final design 92; floors/levels *93*, *94*; main entry *84*; MEP system organization 91; northern view *95*; Open Building concepts 88; post-completion 92; project data 85; space planning 88, *89*, 90–91, *90*
Osaka Gas 44, 48
Oussoren, Claus 64

PATCH22 residential housing *62*, 64
permanence, balancing with change 115, 135–139

INDEX

Pilosof, N. P. 138
piping: bathroom 182–183, *183*; drainage 133, *133*, 182–183, *182*; DWV systems 157; traffic 159–161, *160*; vertical MEP pip shaft positioning study 162–164, *163*, *164*; waste 157–158, *159*
Place des Vosges 131
Place Vendome (Paris) 122, 129–131, *130*
plots 32–36, *33*
Plus-Home (Arabianranta, Helsinki, Finland): background information 53; Base Building 53; capacity for dwelling variation 54, *55*; floor system *55*; garden side *51*; information/data management system 54, *54*; interior views *55*; privacy screens, sliding *53*; project data 52
PR China 198, 208; *see also* Infill industry in PR China; *specific built project name*
public space, shrinking 13

quality of the commons 202–205

RABO Vastgoed 26
Reijenga, Henk 20
residential built projects: longitudinal study of 138; margins in 146–149, *147*, *148*, *149*; Molenvliet 37–42; NEXT21 43–50; PlusHome 51–55; separation of design tasks in 120; TILA 56–61; TOPUP 62–68; zones in 146–149, *147*, *148*, *149*; *see also* large housing projects; *specific name*
residential Infill industry: argument for 199–200; Bijdendijk's perspective 185–187; business structure/culture and 188–189; companies' roles in 187–188; culture of building and 134; lessons from 197–198; outdated residential industry culture and 184–185; overview 184; in PR China 189–197; *see also* Infill industry in PR China
resilience 106–107

Sammy Ofer Heart Building (Tel Aviv, Israel): background information 79; design process 79–80, *80*; evolution of building 81–83; floor plans with medical programs 81, *82*; phases of building 81–83, *81*; project data 78; urban context 78
Santa Monica High School Discovery Building (Los Angeles, California, USA): background information 104; Base Building 105; benefits, unanticipated 107–108; bleacher stairway *108*; cafeteria *107*, *108*; commons area *108*; courtyard entrance *102*; Infill system 105; lab space *108*; new building concept 104–105, *105*; Open Building principles and 105, *106*, *107*; project data 103; resilience and 106–107; rooftop outdoor classroom *108*; separation of design tasks and 106; sustainability and 106–107
SATO (private developer) 53, 208
Schön, Donald 3, 201
School Construction Systems Development (SCD) project 138
sectors 148, *149*
separation of design tasks: Base Building and 116; cooperation and 2–3; in government facilities design 119; in healthcare built projects 119–120; ignoring, results of 117; importance of 115; Infill and 116; ion shopping center design 118–119; Katwikjk Inner Harbor Project and 28; large housing projects and 4; life cycles of parts of sustainable parts and, mirroring 117; in office building design 118–119, *118*, *119*; Open Building approach and 1–2, 109, 116; opportunities for working out new interfaces and 2; relations and 2–3; in residential built projects 120; Santa Monica High School Discovery Building and 106; social structure and 116; Sydhavnen/Slusholmen and 14, 16–17; urban/campus built projects and 117–118
Shenzhen University Engineering School (Shenzhen, PR China): background information 98; Base Building 99, *100*; campus setting view *96*; departmental groupings 98–99, *99*; façade 98; floor plans 98–99, *98*, *99*; interior design 99, *100*, *101*; overview *101*; project data 97
shopping center design 118–119
Slusholmen *see* Sydhavnen/Slusholmen
Soeters, Sjoerd 12
space: control of 127–128, *128*; defensible 128; empty 'raw' 57; green 26, 33, *33*, *42*, 46, *46*; open 32, 35, 38, 164; public, shrinking 13
Steelcase (furniture company) 119
Support: concept 109; definition of 109, 111, *112*; Molenvliet 38, 40, *40*; SAR and 110; *see also* Base Building
sustainability: Inselspital Hospital Campus Master Plan and 35–36; Open Building approach and 1; Santa Monica High School Discovery Building and 106–107
Sydhavnen/Slusholmen (Copenhagen Harbor, Copenhagen, Denmark): aerial view of *12*, *14*; awards 18; background information 12; canal view *10*, *15*, *17*; façades 16–17; guidelines, architectural 17–18; housing program 12–13; master plan 13, *13*; project data 11; public space and, shrinking 13–14; separation of design tasks and 14, 16–17; site 12, *12*; Slusholmen 12, 14, *15*, 17–18; urban blocks 14, *15*, 16–17, *16*, *17*
System Separation (SYS) 71–74, 76
systems furniture market 118

INDEX

technical infrastructure 33, 34–35
technical strategies for handling change 136–137
territorial boundaries, clarifying 112
territory, importance of/understanding 115, 126–128
thematic design 115, 121–126; coherence with variety, enabling 121–122, 122; designing with themes 125–126; importance of 115; as natural phenomenon 122–123; patterns 123–124; systems 124–125
TILA (Helsinki, Finland): background information 57; Base Building 57, 58; bathrooms 57, 60; development/occupancy process 57, 59; empty 'raw' space 57; individualization 60, 61; interior views 61; project data 56; recognition received 208; regulatory review process 60; southern view 56
Tocoman data-cost office 53
toilets 158–159, 158
'Tools of the Trade' 202–205
TOPUP (the Netherlands): background information 64; building core 65; capacity for unit layouts 64–65, 64, 66; floor systems 65, 66; infill layouts 67; interior views 64, 65, 68; legal/regulatory constraints 64; as open building 65–66; project data 63; rating chart 68; sketching unit 66; technical approach 64; urban context 62

unified control 127
University of Oregon Medical School (OHSU) 86, 88, 90–91
upward relations 131
urban/campus built projects: grids in 151–153, 152, 153; Inselspital Campus Master Plan 29–36; Katwijk Inner Harbor 25–28; margins and 145, 146, 146; separation of design tasks and 117–118; Sydhavnen/Sluseholmen 10–18; Westpolder Bolwerk 19–24; zones and 145, 146, 146; see also specific name
urban fabric 1, 20–21, 30–32, 44, 114–115, 120–121, 123, 127, 130–131, 134, 201
urban problem, prototypical 109–111
urban quarters 30, 31, 32
urban tissue 38, 38, 39, 111, 145
US Green Building Council 184
Utida, Yositika 44

V3 system development (PR China) 193–194, 194, **194**, 195, 196
van Eesteren, Cornelis 133
Van Olphen, Hans 26–28
variants, basic 148–149, 149
vertical MEP pipe shaft positioning study 162–164, 163, 164

Wang Qiang 193
waste piping 157–159, 159
Westpolder Bolwerk (Berkel en Rodenrijs, the Netherlands): architects 20; background information 20; Berkel Street/The Golden Neighborhoods 20–22, 20, 22; development area 20–21, 20, 21, 24; Planka Street 20–21, 21; project data 19; residential program 23–24, 24; street view 19
Workstage development project 119
Wright, Frank Lloyd 117, 127

zones 145–149, 145, 146, 147, 148, 149